UNHEALTHY HOUSING

Research, remedies and reform

Edited by
ROGER BURRIDGE and DAVID ORMANDY
The Legal Research Institute
School of Law
University of Warwick
UK

E & FN SPON
An Imprint of Chapman & Hall

London · Glasgow · New York · Tokyo · Melbourne · Madras

**Published by E & FN Spon, an imprint of
Chapman & Hall, 2–6 Boundary Row, London SE1 8HN**

Chapman & Hall, 2–6 Boundary Row, London SE1 8HN, UK

Blackie Academic & Professional, Wester Cleddens Road,
Bishopbriggs, Glasgow G64 2NZ, UK

Chapman & Hall Inc., 29 West 35th Street, New York NY10001, USA

Chapman & Hall Japan, Thomson Publishing Japan, Hirakawacho
Nemoto Building, 6F, 1–7–11 Hirakawa-cho, Chiyoda-ku, Tokyo
102, Japan

Chapman & Hall Australia, Thomas Nelson Australia, 103 Dodds
Street, South Melbourne, Victoria 3205, Australia

Chapman & Hall India, R. Seshadri, 32 Second Main Road, CIT East,
Madras 600 035, India

First edition 1993

© 1993   Roger Burridge and David Ormandy

Phototypeset in 10/12.5pt Trump Medieval by Intype, London
Printed in Great Britain by St Edmundsbury Press, Bury St Edmunds,
Suffolk

ISBN 0 419 15410 8

A catalogue record for this book is available from the British Library

Library of Congress Cataloging-in-Publication data
Unhealthy housing : research, remedies, and reform / edited by Roger
   Burridge and David Ormandy. – 1st ed.
      p.   cm.
   Includes bibliographical references and index.
   ISBN 0–419–15410–8 (acid-free paper)
   1. Housing and health.   2. Housing and health–Great Britain.
3. Housing policy.   4. Housing policy–Great Britain.   I. Burridge,
Roger.   II. Ormandy, David.
   RA770.U55   1993
   362.1'969'8–dc20   92–21146
                                                              CIP

♾ Printed on permanent acid-free text paper, manufactured in
accordance with the proposed ANSI/NISO Z 39.48–199X and ANSI
Z 39.48–1984

CONTENTS

CONTRIBUTORS

Brenda Boardman is a Senior Research Fellow sponsored by Power-Gen at St Hilda's College, Oxford. She works at the Environmental Change Unit at the University of Oxford, researching into affordable warmth and fuel poverty in British homes. She is the author of *Fuel Poverty*.

Roger Burridge is a barrister and lecturer in the School of Law at the University of Warwick. He has conducted research into the regulation of dilapidated housing and he is co-author with David Ormandy of *Environmental Health Standards in Housing*.

David Byrne is a Senior Lecturer in the department of Sociology and Social Policy at the University of Durham. He is co-author with Jane Keithley and others of *Housing and Health: The relationship between housing conditions and the health of council tenants*.

Ken Collins is Honorary Senior Clinical Lecturer at University College and Middlesex School of Medicine, London University. He is a Member of Staff of the Medical Research Council and editor of *Annals of Human Biology* and *Journal de Physiologie*. He is the author of a number of books including *Hypothermia: The facts*.

Jean Conway is Lecturer in Housing at Sheffield Hallam University. She has worked at the London Housing Aid Centre as a researcher.

Jonathan Gabe is a Senior Lecturer in Legal, Political and Social Sciences at South Bank University, London.

Hugh Freeman is Honorary Professor at the University of Salford, editor of the *British Journal of Psychiatry*, Vice-Chairman of Mind and consultant to the World Health Organisation. He is the author of *Mental Health and the Environment*, *Mental Health Services in Europe: Ten years on*, and *Community Psychiatry*.

Geoff Green is the Healthy Cities 2000 Coordinator for the City of Liverpool. He was formerly Principal Strategy Officer for Sheffield

City Council and Director of Birmingham Community Development Project. He is co-author with David Blunkett of *Building from the Bottom*.

Michael Howard is a Senior Environmental Health Officer with Great Yarmouth Borough Council specializing in health and safety. He was formerly a lecturer in environmental health at the University of Salford.

Sonja Hunt is a partner in Galen Research, Manchester, carrying out research into health measurement and quality of life assessment. She was formerly organizer of a programme evaluating health systems at the Fairleigh Dickinson University, USA and then Senior Research Fellow at the University of Edinburgh.

Jane Keithley is the Director of the Institute of Health Studies at the University of Durham. She is co-author with David Byrne and others of *Housing and Health: The relationship between housing conditions and the health of council tenants*.

John Kellett is a consultant psychiatrist and Senior Lecturer in Geriatric Medicine at St George's Hospital Medical School, University of London.

Roderick Lawrence is an architect and Lecturer at the School of Architecture at the University of Geneva. He is currently appointed to the Centre for Human Ecology and Environmental Science at the University of Geneva. He is a consultant to the Committee for Housing, Building, and Planning of the Economic Commission for Europe and author of *Le Seuil franchi: logement populaire et quotidienne en Suisse romande, 1860–1960* and *Housing, Dwellings and Homes: Design theory, research and practice*.

David Mant is a Clinical Lecturer and honorary consultant in Public Health Medicine at the Department of Public Health Medicine and Primary Care at the University of Oxford. He is also a principal in general practice at the South Oxford Health Centre. He runs the General Practice Research Group at Oxford University which has a special interest in research into the prevention of disease and the application of clinical trials and epidemiological methodology to practical problems of public health and primary care.

Thomas Markus is Emeritus Professor of Building Science at the University of Strathclyde, Glasgow and has taught and written widely about the relation of housing and health, building environment, energy, climate, design methods, building economics and building performance. He is currently Jubilee Professor at the Chalmers University of Technology, Gothenberg.

Eric Mood is a Professor in the Department of Epidemiology and Public Health at the School of Medicine, Yale University, Connecticut. He is Chairman of the Committee on Housing and Health of the American Public Health Association and has supervised revision for the model housing codes adopted by many cities and states in the USA. He frequently participates in activities organized by the World Health Organisation.

David Ormandy is an environmental health consultant and Associate Research Fellow at the Legal Research Institute, the University of Warwick. He is editor of *Housing Law Update* and co-author with Roger Burridge of *Environmental Health Standards in Housing*.

Josephine Prior is the Project Manager for *BREEAM* at the Department of the Environment's Building Research Establishment – *BREEAM* being the BRE Environmental Assessment Method.

Ray Ranson is a Senior Environmental Health Officer with the London Borough of Lambeth and a World Health Organisation housing hygiene consultant. He is the author of *Healthy Housing*.

Gary Raw is Head of the Human Factors and Health Section of the Department of the Environment's Building Research Establishment, researching health, comfort and human behaviour. He has published and been involved in research in sick building syndrome, health and housing conditions, subjective response to traffic noise exposure and the design of small homes.

David Strachan is Senior Lecturer in Epidemiology in the Department of Epidemiology and Public Health Studies at St George's Hospital Medical School, University of London. He has worked in general practice prior to pursuing his research interests in respiratory disease and indoor environments.

Colin Thunhurst is Senior Lecturer at the Nuffield Institute for Health Studies at the University of Leeds. He is currently a Health Planning Advisor for the British Council in Islamabad.

PREFACE

This collection of studies is directed towards the growing recognition that the buildings we inhabit for shelter, warmth, and safety can cause harm, harbour pests, and encourage sickness. It is more than a record of the major hazards that poor housing can present, and reflects the efforts of the research community in recent years to understand the character and extent of housing defects as contributors to human illness and injury. Whilst the majority of the studies concentrate upon the quest for explaining the nexus between inadequate housing and the ill health of its occupiers, the early chapters address the practical, methodological and conceptual obstacles confronting investigators. Subsequent chapters indicate some of the responses that would be appropriate to obviate the hazards revealed.

The contributors to this book are from a wide range of disciplines and backgrounds. They include practising doctors, medical scientists, epidemiologists, academics, architects, lawyers, housing administrators, environmental health officers and statisticians. The variety of approaches to housing and health is indicative of the multidisciplinary enterprise that is required to alleviate housing-related illnesses, and encourage the provision of healthier housing. By combining their insights, and by sharing both the obstacles and the opportunities which they encounter, the contributors hope that they will engage even wider interests and disciplines. Whilst the studies which follow illustrate a broad array of research expertise, and describe the intricacies of medical diagnosis, the book sets out to be of practical value to those with a layperson's interests in housing and health. It recognises the contribution that local studies can make, and acknowledges the futility of scientific inquiry which remains obscured from non-professional gaze.

The commitment of intellectual inquiry to practical reform is echoed in the dedication by the various contributors of the proceeds of their work to Shelter, a charity campaigning and providing housing on behalf of the homeless of Britain.

The contributors all wish to acknowledge the efforts of colleagues, friends and families in the preparation of this book. It has taken well over two years to materialize – a delay for which the editors pay tribute to the patience of the prompt responders, and apologize for their own defaults. Those involved in all the contributions are too numerous to mention, and the specific acknowledgements which follow are representative of a much wider circle.

A general acknowledgement by the editors should first be made of the illusory impression that claims to the authorship of ideas can create. The commodification of knowledge, legitimized and fulfilled in the invocation of copyright, suggests an individual achievement that belies the collective adventure. This book is a compendium of thought, analysis, and imagination on the subject of unhealthy (and healthy) housing which is most accurately represented in the bibliographies and references at the end of each chapter. Whilst the contributors are all leading experts in their field, whose opinions and observations deserve sensible consideration, they all acknowledge in their sources and references their debt to the efforts of others. Behind the chapters, tables and statistics are the research respondents about whom we all write, and who are rarely acknowledged. We do.

More specific tributes include thanks to the Baywood Publishing Co. for their agreement to reprint Chapter 9 by Jonathan Gabe and Paul Williams, most of which appeared previously in *International Health Services* Journal (1987), Volume 17, Number 4; thanks to Plenum Publications Corp. of New York for permission to reprint the Tables in Chapter 10; Rentokil plc for their permission to use the photographs in Chapter 12; and thanks to Bellhaven Press for their agreement to the use of Table 1 and Figures 5 and 6 in Chapter 17, the copyright of which remains with Brenda Boardman.

Some contributors have acknowledged the support, criticism or comment of others in their individual chapters. Michael Howard wishes to dedicate Chapter 12 to his daughter, Olivia Judith Howard. The families and friends of all the contributors have been acknowledged *en masse*. The editors also acknowledge the resilience and forbearance of their collaborating authors, and especially thank Carol Chapman, Ken Foster, John McEldowney, and Ann Stewart from the School of Law at Warwick University for their help and advice; Steve Battersby, Jim Connolly and Richard Moore for sharing thoughts; all at Chapman & Hall but especially Martin Hyndman, and Lorraine Schembri for keeping the faith; Mandy Gentle for spending her Christmas proof reading; and Jan Price, Sue Glassfield, and Ben and Joe Burridge for being there, and not shouting when we were not.

Roger Burridge and David Ormandy
Legal Research Institute
University of Warwick

INTRODUCTION

There are two objectives in presenting this collection of studies of the relationship between housing conditions and the health of occupiers. The first is to provide a comprehensive account of recent investigations of a subject which has in the past decade attracted renewed interest and writing (Byrne *et al.*, 1986; Smith, 1991, Ranson, 1991). A secondary objective is to present the research in a form which explains the uncertain progress from empirical investigation to policy implementation. Researchers into the relationship between the housing environment and the human condition have whetted the appetites of housing managers, health administrators, general practitioners, and tenants groups for accounts of their investigations. Frequently, however, reports are restricted to pages of medical journals and assume a background knowledge only commanded by their own professional elite. This presentation places the research into specific housing hazards within a context which first explains the parameters of scientific investigation in this field. It subsequently explores some of the potential for reform and remedial action.

Until recently, the potential threats that the home environment can carry for the health of those within had faded even from the pages of medical, housing and social scientific journals. In the 1980s concern had again emerged, prompted by an awareness that housing policy was focusing exclusively upon issues of tenure and allocation, while some traditional hazards and many modern ones were receiving scant attention. The studies here, in returning to a 19th century concern for healthy housing, suggest that a 21st century response should again firmly base housing policy upon the protection of public health.

The primacy of shelter as an essential requirement of human existence renders it liable to inquiry into its sufficiency for the preservation of life. Since the primary function of housing is to provide protection from the hazards and exigencies of the outdoor environment, it is pertinent to scrutinize its effectiveness in performing the task and to ensure that it does not replace the external dangers with fresh internal threats. As our knowledge of pathology has broadened and the technology of building advanced, so expectations of an acceptable standard of housing have risen. Advanced societies, such as those in western Europe and North America might be expected to develop a range of standards which aspire to more than the bare necessities of healthy occupation. That indeed is the case; in the US the *Principles of Healthful Housing* were drafted (American Public Health Association, 1939), in England and Wales there has been the *Manual of Unfit Housing* (Ministry of Health 1919, Ormandy and Burridge, 1987) and in western Europe the *Guidelines for Healthful Housing* (WHO, 1988), and more recently, *Healthy Housing*, (Ranson 1991). Even without such documentation, few would deny that the fundamental requirement of domestic shelter should be that habitation is possible without danger to health.

Victorian society, alarmed by the contagions of cholera and typhoid and concerned at the debilitating effects of illness and injury to the nascent industrial economy, responded with a succession of punitive and preventive legislation to protect occupational and domestic health. The catalysts for sanitary reform were a mixture of middle class philanthropy and self-preservation overlying labour needs and the spectre of civil unrest. The legislative interventions prompted by Chadwick and Simon were justified by a firm, scientific base for their reforming activities (Finer, 1952). The historical association between research and reform of public health is epitomized in the collaboration between Alexander Stewart (physician) and Edward Jenkins (barrister) in their presentation of joint papers, *The Medical and Legal Aspects of Sanitary Reform*, to the Social Science Congress at Manchester in October 1866 (Flinn, 1967).

The present collection provides both an authoritative source book of the most significant hazards present in English housing, and an introductory primer for remedial activity and reform. It is a contribution to the request by the Department of Health and Social Security in 1980,

The Working Group found that epidemiological, sociological and medical research had not progressed so far as to allow different material and social elements in the conditions or experiences of individual members of the population to be distinguished and exactly quantified. Indeed, this shortcoming in the capacity to analyse the reasons for the unequal distribution of health in populations represented, and unhappily still represents, a major challenge for all the sciences concerned with health. A concerted research strategy, aimed at cutting unnecessary premature deaths and rapidly promoting good health, as was recommended, continues to be very urgently required. (DHSS, 1980).

The structure of the book

This book is organized into three parts which replicate the process of design, empirical investigation and implementation that underlies the research enterprise.

Part One considers the conceptual and methodological challenges facing an inquiry into the health hazards of housing. It provides a foundation for understanding and evaluating the studies of specific hazards which form the core of the book. Since the revelations of systematic research are cogent justifications for policy implementation and reform, the concepts and methods of investigation utilized in any project frequently become the target for critique by those unhappy with the conclusions. The force of any findings or the conservatism of any conclusions is best appreciated by familiarization with the research process itself.

David Mant in Chapter 1 outlines alternative research methods, and explains the difficulties and doubts attaching to each. He provides a layperson's guide to health and housing research and a framework for understanding the studies which follow. His assessment of the value of different methodologies, which might not be shared by other contributors, is directed towards exposing the discrete world of research expertise to the untrained but understanding eye of the non-professional. He presents the research amateur with checklists for evaluating the professional empirical investigator. Colin Thunhurst in Chapter 2 also acknowledges the obstacles facing the natural scientist. He affirms the advantages of a social scientific approach, utilizing existing data to chart housing conditions and health profiles, thereby emphasizing the potential of local studies as a foundation for local health and housing policy. John Kellet's study of 'Crowding and mortality in London boroughs' (Chapter 10) and Jonathan Gabe's and Paul Williams's study of

'Women, housing and mental health' (Chapter 11) exemplify the local secondary data study espoused by Thunhurst.

The significance of spatial allocation of housing circumstances and health status is reasserted in the final chapter in Part One by David Byrne and Jane Keithley (Chapter 3). They challenge the merit of a research enterprise which seeks to attribute individual ill-health to 'bad housing' because of its emphasis upon individual pathology. Their perspective sites housing conditions as an environmental concern, differentially experienced within communities, classes and other social fractions fixed in space. They present a compelling and authoritative argument for the monitoring of community health, collectively based and spatially ordered.

Part Two is a compilation of key studies identifying and evaluating particular health hazards associated with housing. The contributions include examples of the alternative research approaches discussed in Part One. Most modern housing circumstances associated with ill-health are covered, namely coldness, dampness, mould growth, crowding, high-rise buildings, dangerous design and infestations. The studies reflect a Eurocentric bias and emphasize problems prevalent in the weather conditions affecting western Europe. There are inevitably some significant omissions; some important issues, like water purity, were outwith the present collection, largely because we viewed them as broader environmental concerns. Other hazards, such as radon, are emerging and deserving of inclusion but the identification and evaluation of the threats at present seems ill-defined.

In addition to the studies of specific hazards, Eric Mood in Chapter 14 sets out an overview of the preventive characteristics of healthful housing. He outlines the implications of a contaminated water supply, defective drainage, dangerous design features, and other common health hazards in the house.

An aggregation of the research effort points more confidently to the existence of the health threat, even if in Thunhurst's phrase (p. 28) it remains 'circumstantial'. Part Two as a whole presents the more confident stance adopted by Professor Susan Smith: 'Plausible biomedical explanations can be invoked to account for the adverse physiological effects of many environmental variables, especially cold, damp and mould' (Smith, 1989).

The effects of dampness, mould growth, and temperature on the health of occupiers are the subject of the first four chapters in Part Two. Sonja Hunt in Chapter 4 and David Strachan in Chapter 5 present different approaches and conclusions in their studies of broadly similar conditions. The distance between their positions emerges as a clear example of the significance of the research method employed, which is raised by Mant, Thunhurst, Byrne and Keithley in Part One. Both authors position their work within an analysis of the potential of epidemiological research. In a study of asthma among schoolchildren in Edinburgh, Strachan retreats from an initial conclusion of an established relationship between domestic mould growth and wheeze in children, which he considers ultimately unproven. Hunt, in contrast, reviews recent findings and comes to much firmer conclusions on the nexus between damp and mouldy housing and ill health. A major distinction between the two lies in the significance that each places upon the reporting of illness by occupiers. Hunt presents an alternative to the tendency to reduce the research to specimens on a laboratory bench, pinned out, observed and discarded to rematerialize in the columns of a report. In doing so she reflects a long-standing debate concerning the reliability of self assessment as a research method. Hunt and Strachan present contrasting perspectives in the design and interpretation of housing research.

Ken Collins in Chapter 6 analyses the health implications of both excessive cold and heat in the home. While hypothermia is regarded as a serious threat, especially to the elderly during cold winters, Collins raises other indoor climate related clinical conditions, including Sudden Infant Death Syndrome. A local study of the implications of cold homes is the focus for Thomas Markus's study in Chapter 7. He presents a detailed examination of the effects of cold, condensation, climate and poverty on the health of the population of Glasgow. Markus first specifies the material components of a dwelling which provide protection from external conditions. Having outlined the health risks attributable to inadequate protection, he then assesses the implications for the occupiers of Glasgow's housing.

In Chapter 8 Hugh Freeman presents a comprehensive assessment of the work on the relationship between high rise housing and its effects on mental health. Crowding and its effects on health are discussed next. Jonathan Gabe and Paul Williams in Chapter 9 approach a different aspect of crowding; they consider the effects of space on a group within society which is more exposed to effects of crowding than most others. Women are more ti ᵓd to the house and its immediate neighbourhood in our society, and Gabe and

Williams's study is an illustration of the specific effects that health threats in the home can have on collectivities. John Kellett in Chapter 10 investigates mortality in London boroughs, and reveals a strong sense of the urban organization of populations and the fractions within them.

In Chapter 11 Ray Ranson provides a detailed review of the lack of adequate home safety design and control and the resulting physical injuries and deaths. He also provides a checklist for home safety appraisal. Various animal invaders of human homes are described and illustrated by Michael Howard in Chapter 12 together with the associated threats to the health of their human hosts. Howard also discusses the means available to control and limit, if not prevent, the pests.

The use of temporary accommodation for homeless households has, over recent years, become an established form of housing. Finally in Part Two the health needs of hostel residents and the effects of the living conditions on their health is examined by Jean Conway in Chapter 13.

Part Three considers the uses to which the evidence gathered in existing research can be put. Suggestions are proposed for the positive application of the results for the construction of housing which not only avoids threats to health but which can be seen as a positive contributor to the well-being of the occupiers. Healthful housing is the objective of Eric Mood who carefully analyses enteric diseases, airborne infections, accidents, psychological and physical disorders and identifies the housing requirements necessary for their avoidance in Chapter 14. He exemplifies the application of research to the design of housing standards and a prescription for the healthy home.

The theme is taken up from the perspective of the architect by Roderick Lawrence who discusses in Chapter 15 the various models and principles to be taken into account in formulating housing and health policies in housing design. He considers the internal conditions of a dwelling and its relationship with the external environment. He develops a range of housing and health indicators from an ecological perspective, eschewing the narrow constraining influences of a prescriptive approach to housing design and construction in favour of proscriptive principles. His approach is developed in a checklist of housing indicators, which illustrate the limitations of many of the conventional approaches to housing and health.

The prospects for a healthier future are envisaged by Gary Raw and Josephine Prior in Chapter 16. They reflect upon the impact of housing on the environment and identify the contribution that construction methods and materials can make towards reducing pollution and improving the environment. They describe a scheme developed by the Building Research Establishment for the assessment of new houses, which accredits pullution-reducing and safety-enhancing features of house construction. They provide another example of the potential for developing practical guidelines and evaluation criteria directed towards the reduction of specific health hazards in the home environment.

Many of the studies in Part Two reveal the need to provide adequate warmth in the home. The plight of the elderly in particular has resulted in considerable attention being paid to fuel poverty. Brenda Boardman, who was responsible for the concept of 'affordable warmth', examines in Chapter 17 the implications of attaining adequate levels of heating and insulation. She describes the methodology for quantifying the amount of heat required in the home and analyses the costs of energy efficiency. Her study reveals the possibility of achieving affordable warmth and the avoidance of the climatic hazards outlined in Chapter 6, but her analysis also assesses the inadequacy of government programmes for the attainment of such a target.

Objectives, attainment targets and assessment criteria presuppose a process of evaluation and organized progress. In the background of such recommendations is a concept of reform based upon some form of legal intervention or administrative manipulation. The legal framework affecting housing conditions is described by Burridge and Ormandy in Chapter 18. They outline the development of the existing legislation available to control housing conditions. The modern state has an array of regulatory devices for intervention in the housing market, which have been developed alongside a complicated bundle of personal rights of redress against those who cause injury in the home. The relative advantages and disadvantages of these are reviewed in Chapter 18, and their effectiveness in dealing with unhealthy housing is considered. Burridge and Ormandy identify a trend away from the policing of public health towards a reliance upon private action and selective subsidy.

Finally, the prospects for the implementation of healthful housing policies in the cities are reviewed by Geoff Green, the Healthy City Coordinator for Liverpool. In a personal account of the frustrations of life and work in a Cities 2000 project, he reveals the gaps between the promise of attainment targets and the realities of a beleaguered local government. His cryptic account of urban intervention in housing supply echoes many of the themes developed in the earlier chapters. He sketches the forces and obstacles that confront the administrator, and is explicit in the reminder that the underlying influences are political and economic. The various calls that are made in these pages and elsewhere for an ordered and systematic approach to health and housing research require administrations willing to listen and respond with suitably coordinated policies. It is probably fitting that the local government administrator has the final words.

The housing context

Housing quantity and housing quality

Earlier (p. xi) the justification for investigating the extent and effect of housing failure was presented as a moral imperative that dwellings should be able to protect those indoors from the hazards outside, while avoiding fresh internal dangers. Eric Mood summarizes these hazards in Chapter 14 (p. 304). The identification of the attributes of healthy housing will also influence the social perception of the unhoused.

In addition, there is a direct relationship between deficiencies in the quantity of housing provision, homelessness, and inadequacies in the quality of provision. At first thought, homelessness might appear a more urgent humanitarian matter. An absence of shelter, particularly in lands with a hostile climate, ranks high with starvation, torture, arbitrary imprisonment or rampant disease as indices of inhumanity. Just as shelter may appear secondary in the order of a world that cannot feed itself, so in a land that cannot house its inhabitants, the health of those who have inadequate homes may seem of less immediate concern.

At its most extreme the argument could be refuted by the observation that there is little difference between a death suffered by starvation and one from hypothermia, and that the latter occurs both among those who have homes and those who do not. At a less emotive level, however, the concept of homelessness only has meaning in the context of some broadly accepted definition of adequate shelter. Is a cardboard box a home? Is a shed, or a bed in a hostel for eight hours? Thus the condition of occupied accommodation may be determinative of the occupier's status as homeless or housed. The social problem of those without shelter can only be addressed in the context of defined criteria as to what amounts to acceptable shelter. In the UK and US such criteria have been set by reference to the need to protect public health (Chapter 18).

There has been considerable difficulty in deciding what circumstances of occupation will be regarded as so inadequate as to amount to homelessness, as the courts and local authorities in England (Niner, 1989) have discovered. The House of Lords were confident that Diogenes's barrel would not amount to accommodation suitable for occupation, but they were also clear that a person was not homeless just because they occupied a house that was overcrowded or unfit for human habitation (Hoath, 1989, p. 62). As a result two legal concepts determine living conditions. The adequacy or otherwise of shelter for the purposes of any assistance as homeless is decided with reference to whether or not it is 'reasonable for their continued occupation' (Housing Act 1985, s. 58). The decision whether any dwelling is in such a condition as to warrant intervention to safeguard the health of the occupiers is determined by reference to its 'fitness for human habitation' (Housing Act 1985, s. 604). The existence of the two standards does not detract from the underlying acknowledgement that issues of homelessness anywhere will be closely implicated with questions surrounding the adequacy of any provision for the housed.

The need to control housing conditions by reference to a penal standard of unfitness for human habitation, has resulted in the formulation of criteria that can be employed in the national evaluation of housing stock. They provide the opportunity for periodically assessing the housing state of the nation. No such comparable norm prevails in other European countries although the United States shares a common history of public health control of housing conditions (Burridge and Ormandy, 1990).

One of the implications of the linkage between the quality and the quantity of housing provision is that the existence of a significant level of homelessness will influence those enduring inadequate or sub-standard housing. In much the same way as high levels of unemployment may dissuade those in employment from complaining about their circumstances or seeking increased payment for their work, so those suffering bad housing conditions may be encouraged to endure them in preference to wandering the streets.

For those who remain in slum conditions there is the ever present threat to orderly government of urban unrest. The spectre of cholera that prompted much concern in the 19th century is replicated in present day alarm that ascribes some responsibility for riots in the cities to the housing conditions of the citizens (Scarman, 1982, paras. 2.6–2.9).

Housing standards and housing economics

The quest for international improvement of housing is led by those concerned for the health implications of housing deprivation. The consequent articulation of health criteria has required a response from housing administrators which is capable of transcending the parochial preoccupation with national budgetary constraints and expenditure. Comparative studies of housing markets are emerging, especially in Europe. Tenure distinctions, age of housing stock, lack of comparably collated data and the complexity of alternative fiscal intervention via subsidy or taxation impede but do not prevent comparison.

The compilation of national statistics and the publication of international comparison can be as effective in the promotion of universal health as were the collation of mortality rates by early Medical Officers of Health (Chapter 19). The potential that such comparisons contain for complacency among the higher achievers, or even for the attainment of mediocrity, a massaged decline towards a mean already surpassed by better performers, is illustrated in recent attempts to evaluate international performance in housing supply by the Organization for Economic Co-operation and Development (OECD, 1990 Chapters 1 and 2). Their economic analysis pays scant attention to the costs of ill-health, and makes no mention of health concerns as a factor in the formulation of housing policy. The OECD further concluded that traditional concern over an adequate supply of dwellings has largely dissipated as most countries have achieved a balance or aggregate net surplus of dwellings over households (OECD). In its place are 'questions concerning housing prices, affordability, social segregation, maintenance and modernization, and neighborhood quality.' (OECD, 1990, p. 8)

This perspective can be met at two levels. The first is that such assessments are ill-judged or erroneous. The OECD suggestion that the quantity of housing provision is sufficient in England is belied by recent studies of homelessness (AMA, 1989), which indicate that the housing shortage extends beyond the problem of empty housing being available in inappropriate locations. Furthermore, on a global scale in 1987 it was estimated that 1000 million people lived in grossly inadequate shelter and that 100 million had no shelter whatsoever (Goldstein, Novick and Schaefer, 1990).

There is an alternative approach to the suggestion, such as that by the OECD, that housing policy is now restricted to the economic arena and concentrated upon issues of distribution and quality – where comfort, cost and life-style are the primary considerations. It is that such analyses stop short of revealing the health implications of substandard housing. The OECD study identifies a shift from quantity to quality concern and identifies common causes of housing decay, which confirms the urgency that should be accorded to healthy housing policies, such as those advocated by the contributors to this volume. The account of deterioration in the older inner city housing stock and in social housing constructed since 1960 is treated by the OECD as a concern of housing finance. Few would deny that private cost and government expenditure are major factors in the maintenance of the housing stock. Many would consider to be deficient a housing policy which overlooked the contribution that the home makes to the health of the community.

It is nonetheless important to recognize the financial implications of housing renovation. Existent housing and not future construction is the focus for a healthy housing policy in the UK and, to a lesser extent, other industrialized societies. In the UK activity until recently has been levelled at eradicating the deficiencies of the pre-1919 housing stock, but recent claims that the post-war public sector housing stock contains the latter-day slums (Byrne *et al.*, 1986) have prompted fresh initiatives.

Housing obsolescence and decay involves costly reinvestment in the housing stock, and enforced improvement or repair interferes with the rights of owners, placing on owner-occupier and landlord alike substantial financial responsibility (Grigsby, 1967). The older house tends to be more expensive to repair than the modern one because the rate of depreciation increases exponentially with the age of the dwelling (OECD, 1988, p. 84). In England, where there is a high proportion of older housing, the mean estimated cost of repair for dwellings built before 1919 was approximately ten times that for dwellings built after 1964 (DoE, 1988, para. 4.17). The total cost of repair was £12.6 billion. This latter figure may, however, disguise the disproportionately high cost of refurbishment of tower blocks in the public sector.

The tendency recently has been to evaluate the condition of a building on the basis of the cost of its repair. 'The expenditure required to carry out specified works provides a convenient measure of disrepair and allows different characteristics to be summed on a common base' (DoE, 1988, Appendix F). There may be an undeniable convenience underlying the common basis for summing the costs of disrepair, but an economic analysis is only meaningful if it follows an evaluation of the health hazards presented. The justification for interfering in landlord and tenant relationships in the 19th century was that public health was threatened. The same arguments today require the setting of standards which housing should fulfil to avoid known health hazards. Health-based criteria should precede analysis of the cost of any remedy, or a time-scale within which it should be achieved.

Thus it should not be assumed that a cost evaluation is the only available one; nor that an economic analysis is determinative of appropriate activity. An accountant's estimation, uninformed by the health risks, might counsel the inappropriate improvement of safe but unsightly conditions; or caution against an expensive remedy, critical to the health of the occupiers.

Controlling conditions and compensating loss

The absence of universally applicable criteria for efficient measurement and comparison is an obstacle to effective control. As Eric Mood cogently demonstrates in Chapter 14, the international community has recently made considerable progress towards the articulation of principles of healthful housing. The framework for establishing enforceable regulations for the control of unhealthy housing conditions which he advocates, illustrates the possibility of the coordinated improvement of international housing conditions, based upon the best available scientific knowledge. The model of regulation adopted in the USA has been the encapsulation of strict performance criteria which a building must fulfil in state-wide housing codes (see Chapter 14 and Burridge and Ormandy, 1990). These are enforced against landlords by the threat of prosecution for code violation.

The form of regulation in Britain tempers punitive sanctions with protective subsidy and is described in Chapter 18. Local practical initiatives to ameliorate substandard housing are dependent upon central government support paid out by local authorities to individuals in the form of repairs or improvement grants. Such remedies as local authorities can achieve are increasingly dependent upon the poverty of individual occupiers, and their eligibility for grant aid. The significance of health and housing research lies in the potential for redressing such a trend by elevating concern for the hazards of housing into the arena of public health rather than private penury.

The professional entrusted with the diagnosis of unhealthy houses in Britain is the Environmental Health Officer. The role is susceptible to similar discrepancies in diagnosis of the building as the doctor experiences in diagnosis of the patient – an aspect considered in detail by Sonja Hunt in Chapter 4. Underlying the Environmental Health Officers' approach is the protection of the occupier's health. The efforts of the Institution of Environmental Health Officers and others to promote an understanding of the adverse health effects of substandard housing maintain the public health ideal, but individual enforcement may still be confounded by the restrictions of the medical model practised by the local doctor. In such circumstances, housing conditions only become a health concern when the general practitioner can diagnose cause and effect. Those who turn to the courts are greeted with demands that they must establish blame for their illness upon a specific housing hazard. The legal notion of quantum of proof posits facts as apple-like objects, the accumulation of a sufficient quantity of which will tip the scales of justice either beyond the balance of probabilities or reasonable doubt. The legal concept has itself been the subject of considerable philosophical debate (Eggleston, 1983). It is a construct peculiar to legal discourse and is to be distinguished from notions of scientific proof and empirical verification employed by most of the authors in this book. In Chapter 18 we argue that the public protective and proactive powers of the local authority are increasingly replaced by the individual reactive remedy of the private law suit.

The tension between the collective and the public in contrast to the individual and the private is replicated in the contrasting models of social democracy and the free market. It is a theme expanded by Clapham, Kemp and Smith (1990, p. 224), who explore housing policy in the broader context of welfare provision. Their analysis of market failure, whilst not specific to the relationship between defective housing and the health of the population, can be drawn upon in support of an expanded welfare provision for achieving healthier housing.

In the past the impetus for reform has often depended upon private philanthropy and a moral case for the alleviation of poverty and the pursuit of social equality. In the 1990s the investigation of unhealthy housing conditions has a strong claim for urgent consideration as an issue of housing policy. It has already achieved some recognition as an appropriate objective of health policy.

The health dimension

Diagnostic difficulties

The acknowledgement that positive objective benefits have accrued since the deadly slums and insanitary sewers of Chadwick, Snow and Simon's day can obscure the significance of modern housing hazards. The busy killers of the 1840s – cholera, typhus, and diphtheria – have been largely contained and it is the prospect of incurable illnesses at large that nowadays alarms. Some of the studies in this book are a reminder that traditional home threats of hypothermia, respiratory illness and polluted water are still prevalent. Other conditions, such as condensation dampness and chemical pollutants, are modern phenomena. The health dimension of poor housing incorporates the investigation of housing related illnesses, their prevention and treatment, and the distribution of health services within differing sections of housing consumption.

The pathology of housing-related illness, which is the subject of the greater proportion of the studies in this book, exposes the relationship between poor housing, poverty and ill health. In searching for a causal nexus between the house environment and the human condition they avoid the assumption that the provision of healthy housing for all would eradicate illness, although they reveal the potential threats that housing can harbour and the preventive possibilities that would accompany a broader recognition of the problems.

Public health and private illness

Nineteenth-century reforms were directed towards sanitation, water supply, space and fresh air. They were based upon the notion that the miasma in the home, signified by foul stenches, carried the contagions afflicting urban society. In the twentieth century both miasma theory and the establishment of Sanitary Inspectors to control offending houses seem quaint. The progress of curative medicine, the provision of municipal housing and the improvement in popular wealth have rendered the approaches of that early legislation inappropriate, if not obsolete. The modern response to housing inadequacies has emphasized private initiative. Health and housing, however, are susceptible to the competing philosophies of private endeavour or public welfare which go beyond either the form of law or the method by which a service may be delivered. A more fundamental contrast emerges from the studies represented in this book, in which public health versus private illness is a recurrent theme.

The 19th century phrase 'safe as houses' summed up the investment potential of property and was never intended as an endorsement of the healthy conditions of dwellings. On the contrary the stability of the property market was built upon the rapid expansion of towns which harboured the diseases and epidemics for which the Victorian era is also notorious. Parallels between the 1860s, the beginning of Victorian concern for the iniquities of the rookeries and tenements, and the 1990s, can be drawn. Both periods witnessed a housing crisis most extreme at the centres of urban development; in both ages arguments over social reform focused upon the competing claims of unrestrained market and interfering state; and on each occasion housing reformers pointed to the effects that unhealthy housing was having on the health of occupiers as a justification for change.

Such similarities give credence to the notion that a New Public Health is emerging, borne of 20th century slums and freshly discovered diseases, but mindful of the social and psychological as well as physical aspects of the environment (Ashton and Seymour, 1988). The home has been identified as a site for the practice of the New Public Health. The renewed interest in the effects of housing on the health of occupiers has arisen from a convergence of housing circumstance, health policy and research endeavour. Preventive medicine and health promotion have been the watchwords of health reformers (Ashton and Seymour, 1988). The home as a source of ill-health has been identified in new investigations of housing hazards, some of it reflecting occupational concern over illness-inducing, sick buildings. Environmental impact has been felt on housing estates as keenly as in the countryside. There has been a slow acceptance that the purging of the city centres of back-to-back houses has made way for concrete flats where condensation is endemic. New allegations of housing market failure in the public and private sectors have prompted fresh calls for healthy inter-vention. It is against this background that the initiatives of the World Health Organization's call for national and local improve-ment targets has resonated.

The public health approach, as Byrne and Keithley argue in Chap-ter 3, accepts that combinations of individuals are identifiable, whether as a community, class or other collectivity by reference to common concerns or interests. It also suggests that health risks endangering a community can be more effectively addressed by remedial action directed towards the source of the hazard than can be achieved by the curative treatment of isolated individuals.

In the health and housing field the dissociation of communities into individuals occurs when an occupier consults a doctor because of a housing-related illness or complains to an Environmental Health Department about unhealthy conditions in their home. In each case the problem is invariably perceived as one that affects the individual and within the confines of the discipline of the profession contacted, an individual remedy will be regarded as the first priority.

Furthermore, as the first part of this book explains, in the investi-gation of the source of the illness which is placing the community at risk, the medical model predominates. This predicates the illness suffered as personal to the patient and tends to do so to the exclusion of conditions suffered by a community. The doctor is master of the volume of knowledge and experience defining specific illnesses. From observations of the patient's plight accompanied by scientific analysis of body temperature, blood, urine or other sample, the doctor proclaims the symptoms of the illness, and hence promotes a cure. The investigation may include inquiries about the individual's home circumstances, but the facts upon which the medical opinion is based are derived almost exclusively from the body of the patient. On the occasions when the doctor is also informed by a visit to the patient's home, it may be difficult to distinguish the poverty of the occupiers from the inadequacy of the building. Even when unsatisfactory conditions are blatant, the professional response is inevitably to attend to those problems which are within one's own expertise – doctors treat people, other experts cure buildings. Escape from the hazards of the home lies in the power of a local medical officer, to whom a general practitioner will refer a patient who is perceived as suffering health problems attributable to housing conditions. Medical officers, however, are severely constrained in the allocation of housing on the grounds of medical need. An applicant will invariably be required to establish that they have special needs which are related to some disability aggravated by their housing conditions. In Birmingham, for example, bad housing alone is not considered a sufficient ground for rehousing on medical grounds (Bakhshi, 1986). Local authority medical officers, not to be confused with the defunct office of Medical Officer of Health, who previously presided over the Environmental Health Department. The modern medical officers are appointed as health officials to intervene in housing. Their reliance upon the medical model and the condition of the individual occupier downplays the condition of the dwelling. Indeed even if an applicant is successful and of high enough medical priority to be offered fresh accommodation, the vacant house will be allocated to other tenants. The health divide distancing rich and poor is thus accentuated by a professional divide between general practitioner, community physician and Environmental Health Officer.

Economies of health

The curative response also militates against a preventive solution because of the fiscal tensions within health services. In a single financial year, cure may be cheaper than prevention. The curative approach assigns treatment of housing-related illnesses in Britain to the columns of the budget of the Department of Health rather than Environment. In so doing it relegates the cures to the rank-ordering of a health authority's priorities, rather than the preventive subsidies of local government's housing departments.

The escalating costs of treatments, the rising patient rolls and the ensuing pressures on local health services encourage the accountant's caution concerning matters publicly expendable. Argument concentrates upon the relative efficiency of public and private sector provision (Culyer and Jonsson, 1986). In the confines of the health authority, dispersed amongst doctors' consulting rooms, the economic influences on the identification and treatment of patients sickened by their houses continue to operate. Home visits are costly, and, as we have noted, the medical model dissuades investigation outside the consulting room or clinic. Emphasis upon the health effects of inadequate housing and the consequent transfer of responsibility to the health professions raises important questions concerning relativity of the risks revealed.

The establishment of a causal nexus between a house condition and a specific illness only serves to place the problem within the recent trend in health services for actuarial risk assessment. Reliance upon treating the medical symptoms rather than remedying the housing cause gives rise to uncomfortable questions of the apportionment of health resources and reduces the urgency of response by reference to other pressing health needs. These questions are reflected in the British Medical Association's handbook, *Living with Risk*. The train of inquiry develops away from the structure of housing in the direction of the plight of the patient compared to other sufferers.

The potential that housing holds for health promotion is the subject of a growing number of studies on the health needs of particular sectors of society. These recognize the disproportionate effects of housing circumstances on specific sectors, and the unequal provision of health services across differing housing tenures and localities. The elderly, the disabled, the young, women and ethnic minorities are more exposed to housing disadvantage than others, and such deprivation has significant implications for health needs (Smith, 1991).

The diagnosis of the plight of the occupier has parallels with the identification of the condition of the building. What is 'poor' housing? Damp may be uncomfortable or leave unsightly stains, but is it dangerous? And if it may be dangerous, how much risk is there that occupiers will become ill as a result? And even if they may become ill, how does that risk of illness compare with other modern hazards, like excess cholesterol, smoking or sunlight? And how ill will they become? Will they catch a cold occasionally or will they contract pneumonia and die? Even if they may die, what is the chance of their dying relative to the chance of their being run over? There may be a serious risk of significant ill-health, but is it a risk that can be avoided within the available social resources? Does the proportion of those at risk justify the expenditure necessary to mitigate the danger? And if it does, how does it compare with the hazards faced by those without a home? Perhaps more people become ill and die because they have no home at all than those who suffer but survive longer in an inadequate one. Over-enthusiasm for the economic model may be deterred by the inescapable, but hopefully unacceptable, acknowledgement that it is cheaper to condone death than to expend resources upon preserving life.

The economic approach inherent in these questions reflects current arguments over the cost of health services delivery. The potential for reducing the demands on such services by the amelioration of the conditions that give rise to illnesses is obscured. The climate that enabled housing policy to ignore the potential of the dwelling to cause injury to health is now changing. In a similar way to challenges that are being levelled at transport policy upon an appreciation of the environmental dangers of the car and its potential for causing injury to occupants and others, housing policy is now vulnerable to demands for greater environmental control. It is a process within which research plays a significant role.

Health and housing research has developed rapidly in recent years, encouraged by a wider emphasis upon the unequal distribution of health (DHSS, 1980; Townsend, Phillimore and Beattie, 1988). More recently, the need for a co-ordinated cross-disciplinary research programme has been urged (Smith, 1989). The dissemination of research and the assembly of different research approaches were the objectives of a series of conferences held at Warwick University on the subject of Unhealthy Housing. The conferences, at which the contributors to this book all presented papers, provided a timely platform for the work of a growing number of researchers, and illustrated the international character of the inquiry. Moreover, the recent studies illustrate the value of the comfortably funded epidemiological survey, as well as the potential for the more modest local study of secondary data.

The research endeavours recorded below are motivated by intrigue and the quest for explanation and elucidation. Their assembly in this book seeks to sustain the arguments that housing conditions contribute to the ill-health and premature death of some occupiers, particularly those on low incomes; that housing is a subject for concern and control as much as smoking, unbelted car driving, or cruelty to animals; and that past efforts to safeguard the health of many occupiers have been frustrated by successive refusals to acknowledge the conclusions of the research community, or to insist upon higher standards of proof than are acceptable elsewhere.

Bibliography

American Public Health Association (1939) *Principles of Healthful Housing*, APHA.

Ashton, J. and Seymour, H. (1988) *The New Public Health*, Open University Press, Milton Keynes.

Bakhshi, S. S. (1986) 'Medical Recommendations for Rehousing in Birmingham'. Paper presented at the *Unhealthy Housing – a Diagnosis* Conference, University of Warwick, 1986.

Burridge, R. and Ormandy D. (1990) 'The Role of Regulation in the Control of Housing Conditions', *Journal of Sociology and Social Welfare*, Vol XVII No. 1, March 1990, pp. 127–142.

Byrne, D., Keithley, J., Harrison, S. and McCarthy, J. (1986) *Housing and Health: the Relationship between Housing Conditions and the Health of Tenants*, Gower, Aldershot.

Clapham, D., Kemp, P. and Smith, S. J. (1990) *Housing and Social Policy*, Macmillan, London.

Culyer, A. J. and Jonsson, B. (1986) *Public and Private Health Services*, Blackwell, Oxford.

DHSS (1980) *Inequalities in Health*, Report of a Research Working Group chaired by Sir Douglas Black (the Black Report), HMSO, London.

EHCS (1988) *The English House Condition Survey 1986*, HMSO, London.

Eggleston, R. (1983) *Evidence, Proof and Probability* (2nd edn), London.

Flinn, M. W. (1967) 'Introduction to Alexander Stewart and Edward Jenkins', *The Medical and Legal Aspects of Sanitary Reform*, Robert Hardwicke, London (1867); reprinted, Leicester University Press.

Goldstein, G., Novick, R. and Schaefer, M. (1990) 'Housing, Health and Well Being: An International Perspective', *Journal of Sociology and Social Welfare*, Vol XVII No 1., March 1990 pp. 161–181.

Grigsby, W. G. (1967) 'Home Finance and Housing Quality in Ageing Neighbourhoods' in Nevitt, A. A. (ed.) *The Economic Problems of Housing*, Macmillan, London.

Heath, D. (1989) *Public Houses Law*, Sweet & Maxwell, London.

Hunt, S. M., Martin, C. J. and Platt, S. P. (1988) *Damp Housing Mould Growth and Health Status Part I*. Report to the Funding Bodies, Glasgow and Edinburgh District Councils.

Ministry of Health (1919) *Manual of Unfit Housing*, HMSO, London.

Niner, P. (1989) *Homelessness in Nine Local Authorities*, HMSO, London.

Ormandy, D. and Burridge, R. (1987) *Environmental Health Standards in Housing*, Sweet and Maxwell, London.

OECD (1988) *Urban Housing Finance*, OECD.

Ransom R. (1991) Healthy Housing, E. & F. N. Spon, London.

Scarman, Lord (1982) *The Brixton Disorders*, Penguin, Harmondsworth.

Smith, S. J. (1989) *Housing and Health: A Review and Research Agenda*, Centre for Housing Research, University of Glasgow.

Smith, S. J. ed. (1991) *Housing for Health*, Longman, London.

Townsend, P., Phillimore, P., and Beattie, A. (1988) *Health and Deprivation. Inequality and the North*, Routledge, London.

Whitehead, M. (1987) *The Health Divide: Inequalities in Health in the 1990s*, Health Education Council, London.

World Health Organization (1988) *Guidelines for Healthful Housing*, WHO, Geneva.

Part One

The Parameters of Health and Housing Research

1

UNDERSTANDING THE PROBLEMS OF HEALTH AND HOUSING RESEARCH

DAVID MANT

1.1

Introduction

Research into the relationship between housing and health is not easy. This may seem surprising because the relationship between poor housing and poor health is essentially self-evident. So why is the relationship so difficult to prove? The main problem is that inadequacy of housing is invariably associated with other hardships, such as poor nutrition, poor sanitation and curtailment of personal freedom, all of which prejudice health in its widest sense. In most cases, it is neither necessary nor desirable to try to untangle these threads of disadvantage. However, this is not an excuse for failure to describe and document the extent of the housing problem in Britain, nor the ill health with which it is associated. We have a social duty to try to identify those specific aspects of the housing environment which cause physical and mental illness, so that preventive measures can be taken. Research must be done and therefore the problems which will be met in undertaking this research must be understood.

1.2

Spot the method

The purpose of this brief chapter is to provide a layman's guide to the problems which beset the researcher in this field. It may act as a starting-point for the aspiring research worker, but it is intended primarily to help anyone interested in housing policy to read research literature critically. Research findings must be seen in the context of research methodology in order to understand the limitations of the evidence and to act wisely in formulating policy on the basis of research.

The process of understanding and interpreting research in the medical field is often called 'critical appraisal'. The first step in this appraisal is the identification of the question the research is trying to address and the method used to answer it. Identification of the latter not only prompts the asking of key questions which determine the validity of the research, but also sets limitations on its interpretation.

The research method used in housing-health studies can usually be assigned to one of the following categories:

1. *Descriptive*: describes, and sometimes correlates, housing conditions and health at one point in time.
2. *Case-control*: starts with ill people and compares their housing situation to that of healthy people.
3. *Longitudinal*: follows people in different housing conditions over time.
4. *Intervention*: records what happens when something is changed, for example, in a controlled experiment.
5. *Extrapolative*: measures directly a presumed health hazard but bases risk estimate on previous studies (often in a different setting).

The ability to recognize these five methodological approaches is the key to understanding and critically appraising housing-health research. The algorithm shown in Figure 1.1 may help in deciding which study falls into which category. A brief description of each type of study is given, followed by some practical examples.

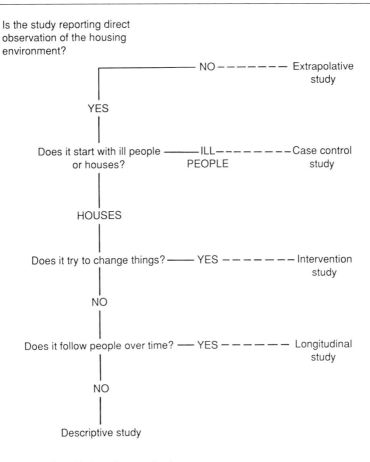

Is the study reporting direct
observation of the housing
environment?

Figure 1.1 Identifying the method.

1.3

Methods and their problems: descriptive studies

Identification

In a descriptive study the researcher simply tries to document
events. In the great majority of cases, the study unit is geographical
(e.g. an area or a collection of substandard dwellings) and the
research consists of a description of the state of the housing stock
and of the health of the occupants. There is no attempt at intervention, nor at following individuals over a period of time, hence

5

these studies are often termed 'cross-sectional' in methodological textbooks. The observations made can be quantitative (e.g. the relative humidity of rooms) or qualitative (e.g. expressed feelings of well-being or symptoms of illness), or a combination of both.

Problems

Social complexity

The health of a child in a poorly constructed tenement building will reflect a myriad of influences including the capability of its parents, the food it eats, the number of siblings it has, the smoking habits of others in the household, the standard of hygiene and its genetic make-up, as well as the physical characteristics of the house itself. Moreover, many of these factors will interact with each other. In this situation, it is extremely important to try to identify as many of these different influences as possible, and to collect information on those factors thought to be most important.

It must be recognized that, in some cases, the interrelation of factors is so strong that any attempt to separate their effect can be misleading. Many social indices (including social class itself) are very imperfect measures of social situations. Many important social variables which impinge upon health are difficult to characterize and may act within traditional social stratifications. In other words, there is a limit to the extent to which disentanglement is possible and common sense must be applied before complex statistics.

Subjectivity and bias

The observations in a descriptive study must be made by someone, and it is difficult to ensure that this someone provides an objective and unbiased description. This is achieved best if the researcher has no knowledge of events which might influence the factor being investigated, for example, the investigator documenting ill-health should be unaware of the housing situation of those being interviewed.

Achieving an unbiased answer from those occupying poor housing, either about their housing conditions or their health status, is even more difficult as they are invariably aware that their answer may influence what happens to them. Studies based predominantly on self-reported housing defects or health problems should therefore be avoided where at all possible.

Correlation and causality

A classic example of this problem is the very strong correlation between sunburn and ice-cream consumption – this correlation does not imply that one causes the other, but reflects the existence of a third factor which causes both. A similarly strong correlation may be demonstrated between poor housing and bad health and it can be equally misleading to infer causality. Descriptive studies are useful in forming hypotheses about causality but poor at proving them.

One particular problem of which to be aware is the 'trawling' of descriptive data for 'statistically significant' associations. It must be obvious that if a 95% confidence level is taken as the indicator of statistical significance, then the researcher will identify a spurious positive association by chance in 5% (one in 20) dips into the data. Trawls are frequently done and are usually to be deplored.

If causality is suggested in a descriptive study, it is important to look for two conditions:

(a) a clear consistent dose–response relationship between the environmental hazard and the extent of ill-health;
(b) A biologically plausible relationship between the environmental hazard and the illness in question.

If these two conditions are absent, a causal effect is unlikely.

Appraisal checklist

Three basic questions to ask about a descriptive study are as follows:

1. Has social complexity been taken into account? Have the relevant social variables been measured adequately?
2. Are the observations objective? Were the investigators likely to be biased? Were the subjects likely to have been truthful?
3. Are the investigators claiming causality? Is the relationship biologically plausible? Has a dose–response relationship been shown?

1.4

Case control studies

Identification

Case control studies begin with the disease (or state of ill-health) rather than the housing environment. They are an extension of the medical case series but are taken further by selection of a 'control' group. A case control study of the relationship between housing and asthma would recruit subjects with asthma, and a group of very similar people without asthma, and would compare the housing environments of the two groups. The advantage of the case control study over both a case series and a purely descriptive study is that, although it is a little more expensive, it is potentially much more convincing.

Problems

1. *Cases*: It might be thought that in medicine a case is a case: either someone has asthma or they do not. Unfortunately, this is far from true. Not only has a comparable definition to be constructed, perhaps taking into account levels of severity, but the method by which these cases will be ascertained must be carefully considered as controls (i.e. non-cases) need to be ascertained from the same source.

2. *Controls*: Problems over case definition and ascertainment are minor compared with the problem of selecting controls. The essential task is to choose someone. A balance must be struck between 'undermatching' and 'overmatching'. If you match a 90-year-old man to a 15-year-old girl, then their housing situation is likely to differ by virtue of factors other than the illness. If you try to match too closely, then there is no scope for identifying factors which may have contributed to the illness.

Housing studies raise some particularly thorny problems for the selection of controls. While it is common to match for area of residence in non-housing studies, this may be inappropriate as adverse housing characteristics relating to health may be geographically based. For most housing studies, general practice controls will be ideal, but for studies where the environmental hazard is spread over a wide but geographically discrete area (e.g. radon), the use of general practice controls will result in overmatching and a wider selection base (e.g. the electoral roll) is appropriate. Hospital controls have major disadvantages and should only be used after careful consideration.

3. *Recall*: In all research studies concerned with environmental problems the measurement of exposure to a particular hazard can be problematic. Case control studies are no exception, and as they often involve retrospective recall of events some time ago, they are particularly liable to systematic failures of memory (the so-called 'recall bias'). Not surprisingly, cases often remember key exposure events better than controls.

4. *Confounding*: The main difficulty which must be addressed in case control studies is that of 'confounding'. In some ways, this is a further example of the problem of social complexity, discussed previously in the context of descriptive studies. A 'confounder' is a factor which influences both exposure to a particular hazard and (independently) the likelihood of an adverse health event. For example, the method of heating may well act as a confounder in studies examining the relationship between dampness and respiratory disease: the method of heating clearly has a major effect on the relative humidity of the dwelling, while at the same time combustion products such as sulphur dioxide and nitrogen dioxide may well exert an independent effect on respiratory function. This problem of confounding is not terminal, and might be adequately dealt with by matching and by appropriate analysis. But it can only be dealt with if the potential confounding factors are identified and adequately measured during the study.

Appraisal checklist

Three basic questions to ask about a case control study are as follows:

1. Are the controls appropriate?
   Are they under- or overmatched
   Is the source of controls appropriate?
2. How is data on exposure collected?
   Are subjects likely to have adequate recall of events?
   Are cases likely to recall better than controls?
3. Have potential confounding factors been sought and measured?

1.5

Longitudinal studies

Identification

A longitudinal study seeks to follow a cohort of people, some of which will have been exposed to environmental hazards, over a period of time. The occurrence of ill-health can then be compared in exposed and non-exposed groups. Ideally this sort of study is done prospectively (i.e. exposure and outcome is documentated 'as it happens'), but retrospective studies are also possible if exposure and outcome can be easily documented from past records. Longitudinal studies are very reliable but are expensive and time-consuming.

Problems

1. *The right cohort*: The choice of an appropriate cohort of people to follow up is not easy and a balance must often be struck between representativeness and feasibility. Some of the best cohort studies have been done on unrepresentative groups of individuals (e.g. nurses and doctors) simply because of the likelihood of good compliance and ease of identification. The extent to which the experience of these special groups will reflect that of the rest of the population must be considered.

2. *Loss to follow-up*: The main logistic problem in cohort studies is maintaining contact with all participants, so that loss to follow up is minimized. In the best cohort studies this loss is less than 1% per year but often performance falls below this ideal. Good cohort studies also attempt to document changes of exposure as well as health outcomes as the study progresses. This requires regular contact with each member of the cohort.

3. *Good exposure data*: In prospective studies, where exposure is measured from the beginning before the outcome of exposure is known, then data should be good. In retrospective studies it is possible that records may be better for those who have developed disease – a similar problem to the recall bias in case control studies.

Appraisal checklist

Three basic questions to ask about a cohort study are as follows:

1. Is the cohort representative?
   Are the subjects in the study so unusual that generalization is difficult?
2. How many subjects have been lost to follow up?
   If loss is high (20% +), underestimation of hazard is possible.
3. Is exposure and outcome well documented?
   Exposure is more likely to be a problem in retrospective studies. More serious outcomes (e.g. death) are more reliable.

1.6
Intervention studies

Identification

Intervention studies are easy to identify because they report what happens when someone tries to change something – usually, in this context, they report a change in health in response to a change in the housing environment. They are called 'intervention' studies because, in general, they report deliberate attempts at manipulating the environment. The easiest study of this type to interpret is the 'randomized controlled trial' in which people are allocated (at random) to an intervention or to a control group and the effect on their health measured. Such trials are rare (but do exist) in the housing field. They are ethical if genuine uncertainty exists about the benefit of the intervention. Such a study is cited in the examples section of this chapter.

A more complicated type of intervention study is the so-called 'pseudo-randomized trial' which reports the results of non-deliberate interventions. This type of study is much more difficult to interpret as it depends on an assertion of 'natural randomization' which has to be proven rather than assumed, but it allows comparison with a control population when a deliberately constructed trial is unacceptable.

Problems

1. *Time changes*: The most unsatisfactory intervention study is the simple 'before–after' comparison. This is almost useless: invariably it is impossible to dissociate benefit due to the intervention from benefit due to the passage of time, however self-evident the benefit of the intervention may seem. (If it is that self-evident, a study is not needed!) A 'control' group is essential to an intervention study.

2. *Selection bias*: If people receive an intervention in an unrandomized way, there is always a reason for their selection – they are more deserving, more sick, more complaining, etc. These (often implicit) selection criteria obviously effect outcome.

3. *Subjectivity*: This problem has already been mentioned in the context of descriptive studies. If subjectivity is likely to be important, assessment should be done 'blind' – i.e. without the assessor knowing whether the subject is in the intervention or control group. A 'double blind' trial, where neither the subject nor the assessor knows who is in which group, is obviously unlikely in the housing context.

4. *Size problems*: Most trials are too small. They do not have the 'power' to be likely to detect with statistical significance an important difference in outcome between the trial groups. Important small effects are often missed. This is difficult for the non-specialist to detect, but a good study reporting a nil result will state what is the maximum beneficial effect which could have been missed because of the study size.

Appraisal checklist

Four basic questions to ask about trials are as follows:

1. Is there a control group?
   If not, the study is probably useless.
2. Were subjects randomly allocated to the intervention and control groups?
   Much better if 'yes'.
3. Was the assessment 'blind'?
   Again, much better if 'yes'.
4. Was the trial small and negative? Was the power of the study to detect a benefit stated?

1.7

Extrapolative studies

Identification

In clinical medicine new pharmaceutical products are tested on animals before they are given to humans. Expert committees have to extrapolate from the animal experience to the likely risk to people. In housing research 'extrapolative' decisions on policy have to be made on the basis of evidence provided by animal research and by high-level exposure of people to similar hazards in other environments. 'Extrapolative studies' attempt Àindirectlyà to estimate risk on the basis of research in other settings.

Problems

1. *Animal studies*: Perhaps the two best examples of extrapolation from animal studies involve formaldehyde and nitrogen dioxide. In both cases, it has been proven that exposure of laboratory rodents to high concentrations of these substances leads to adverse health effects – nasal cancer in the case of formaldehyde and bacterial infection of the lungs in the case of nitrogen dioxide. On the basis of these experiments, and in the light of the known concentrations of nitrogen dioxide (many produced by cooking) and formaldehyde (from cavity wall insulation and furniture) in a significant number of dwellings, quite high risk to humans was predicted. However, in direct studies of human populations no evidence at all for human carcinogenicity has been seen after long-term exposure to formaldehyde and the direct evidence of increased respiratory infection related to nitrogen dioxide exposure is at best inconclusive. The important point is that there is an inductive gap between animal studies and human experience which must be appreciated.

2. *High dose–low dose*: The second area of extrapolative difficulty arises from the need to estimate domestic risk from exposure to proven human carcinogens, such as asbestos, tobacco smoke and radon, which exist in far lower concentrations in most dwellings than those at which the carcinogenic potential of the substance was initially demonstrated. In the cases of radon and asbestos, carcinogenicity was demonstrated in production workers exposed

to very high concentrations in an industrial setting. With tobacco smoke, the concentration of smoke inhaled by the active smoker is in the region of 30–50 times greater than that inhaled by the passive smoker, but the situation is again complicated by the different chemical composition of inhaled and 'sidestream' smoke.

So there are two major problems:

(a) It is often difficult to measure the exposure accurately and therefore the dose–response function is poorly defined, even at high doses.
(b) An 'inductive leap' has to be made in extending the dose-response curve backwards towards the origin.

These problems have been widely discussed in the scientific journals, particularly in relation to the establishment of safe exposure limits for workers. The important point, once again, is to recognize that statements such as 'there is no safe limit' are based on extrapolation rather than direct observation, and that the confidence intervals on many of the estimates of risk from low-level hazards may be very wide indeed.

Appraisal checklist

Three basic questions to ask about extrapolative studies are as follows:

1. Is the extrapolation from animal or high-dose human exposure? If animal, is there any supportive evidence from human exposure?
2. How secure is the dose–response relationship in the initial (usually high-dose) setting?
3. What model is being used for 'backward induction'? Is the line constrained to pass through the origin? What alternative models have been considered?

1.8

Practising appraisal

In order to help the reader to understand how to apply the appraisal checklists, it is necessary to look at some practical examples. If possible, the papers cited should be obtained and read before proceeding further.

Example 1

Damp housing, mould growth and symptomatic health state (Platt *et al.*, 1989).
Identification: descriptive study.

Checklist point 1: Is social complexity understood?

Yes. The authors made every possible attempt to identify and measure the important social variables, particularly smoking, which were likely to influence outcome. They also acknowledged that it is impossible to achieve this aim completely.

Checklist point 2: Are the observations objective?

Yes and no. There is little question of researcher-induced bias because measurements of damp and recordings of illness were made independently. However, the health outcomes were based solely on the reports of occupants. No attempt was made to examine clinical records (e.g. prescriptions or health service contacts) or to take physiological measurements (e.g. of respiratory function).

Checklist point 3: Are the investigators claiming causality?

Yes. The biologically most plausible health outcome of damp, mouldy housing is persistent cough and wheeze. There was no significant difference in the proportion of adults in damp or mouldy households reporting these symptoms, but there was a significant difference (of about 12%) in children. There was also a significant dose–response relationship between these symptoms and dampness and air spore count in both adults and children. Causal relationship with other symptoms (the demonstration of which involves many significance tests and approaches trawling status) is less secure.

Conclusion

A very good descriptive study. The main weakness is the lack of objective measurement of health outcome – it might have been better to concentrate on fewer outcomes (just respiratory symptoms perhaps) and to document these more fully.

Example 2

Acute lower respiratory tract infections in infants: the influence of central heating systems (Scott and West, 1981).

Identification

Longitudinal study.

Checklist point 1: Is the cohort representative?

Yes. It concerns an unselected group of children from one general practice based on a housing estate in Cardiff.

Checklist point 2: Loss to follow-up

12% of children were lost to follow-up because parents moved. It is possible that this introduced bias, if those who moved were mainly those with symptoms due to hot air heating, although this bias must be small.

Checklist point 3: Documentation of exposure and outcome

Exposure measurement is obviously straightforward and reliable (hot air or radiator heating). Outcome data is less reliable; it is based on presentation of acute infection to a doctor and the prescription of an antibiotic for chest signs. Although it is unlikely that doctor behaviour was biased by heating type, presentation of symptoms to the doctor might have been.

Conclusion

The study conclusion, that severe respiratory illness is not related to type of central heating, is reasonably secure, although the study was fairly small and the power of the study to eliminate the possibility of a small effect is limited. More important, it is still possible that the 'rumours' that prompted the study are true and that hot air heating causes significant and important 'minor' respiratory effects such as persistent cough. (Such symptoms can be objectively measured by tape recording.)

Example 3

A prospective randomized trial of the value of rehousing on the grounds of mental ill-health (*J. Chron. Dis.*, 1986).

Identification

Intervention study.

Checklist point 1: Control group?

Yes.

Checklist point 2: Random allocation?

Yes – patients were allocated according to the order of entry into the study, which was effectively random.

Checklist point 3: Blind assessment?

No – the main outcome measure was a self-administered psychiatric questionnaire. It is impossible to 'blind' the occupant to their housing situation.

Checklist point 4: Small and negative?

Not applicable.

Conclusion

The main problem with this trial is, as the authors admit, that those not rehoused might be motivated to continue to demonstrate mental ill-health to justify eventual rehousing. The ethical justification for random allocation of medical priority was that the usual chances of rehousing of study subjects was considerably less than 50%.

1.9

Avoiding problems

Simplicity

Good research progresses by small, simple steps. Simple questions and careful specific measurement of outcomes reduce the need for complicated statistical analysis. Statistics are essential to indicate the (inevitable) uncertainty in any research measurement and (sometimes) to disentangle complex relationships. But the best research papers seldom need complex statistics and should be comprehensible, even to the layman.

The other advantage of simplicity of question is that it makes policy-making much easier. It is very difficult to know how to respond to a general statement that poor housing causes poor health. However, if a clear relationship can be demonstrated between respiratory disease, internal dampness and the insulational properties of the building, then the implications of the findings are apparent to everyone.

Scientific measurement

A major criticism of much research into housing and health is the lack of scientific measurement. Scientific measurement does not exclude qualitative research, but demands rigorous assessment of error and validity. In order to achieve this, medical researchers must involve Environmental Health Officers and other specialists in building construction to characterize the physical attributes of the dwelling. For the environmentalist, it means enrolling the help of social and medical researchers who have expertise and experience in measuring health outcomes. For all groups, it means that exposure and outcome must be measured independently.

Internal quality

Medical research has become better at objective measurement in recent years but ground has been lost by the failure to take account of health outcomes other than absence of bodily pathology. This requires qualitative techniques which in the past have been the preserve of the social scientist. However, social scientists will point out that qualitative research should be as rigorous (or, perhaps, even more rigorous) than biomedical research in its internal quality control. This means that questions of validity, internal consistency and repeatability of measurement instruments must be carefully assessed and documented. In some cases, this can be achieved in small studies by using previously validated questionnaires as survey instruments. In new areas of research, it means that pilot studies must be planned in which the survey instruments are carefully tested with prior agreement on acceptable limits of validity (and decision thresholds for starting again if necessary). These constraints may seem unnecessarily onerous, but unless they are rigorously adhered to, then the dogma that 'if you can't measure it with a ruler then ignore it' will continue to influence researchers and decision-makers.

Interagency collaboration

It must be obvious from the above comments that research into the relationship between housing and health must be an interagency task which involves experts in building construction and design, as well as environmental health workers and medical and social scientists. Research projects which harness all these agencies are usually better than those which do not. Nevertheless, different career structure and methods of funding, and even geographical barriers, have in the past discouraged these groups from working together. The development of a research institute concerned primarily with housing and health, with a firm academic base, would be a major step forward.

Overcoming depression

This short chapter will have failed if it did not induce some sense of depression at the enormity of the problems involved in research into the relationship between housing and health. This is an area where huge amounts of energy can be expended with very little return. However, it is also an area where there are a number of very important unanswered questions, and where there is the potential for influencing social policy to achieve major measurable improvements in the public health. It cannot be said too often that major improvements in the public health are invariably preceded by carefully written and well-documented descriptive reports of social ills. It is not important to try to prove causality if the description of circumstance is accurate and well illustrated.

The amateur researcher

The advantage of the descriptive study is that it is not necessary to be an expert to undertake it. The basic requirement is to be factual, to quantify and to make objective measurement as far as possible and to try not to sensationalize or to make causality claims beyond the evidence collected. It is also possible for relatively non-experienced research groups to carry out more sophisticated studies successfully, but much energy will be saved by deciding on an appropriate methodology at an early stage and seeking appropriate help from an established research group. It does not matter whether or not this group has previous experience of research in the same field (although, of course, it helps) so long as they have experience of working with that particular methodology. Again, the establishment of a network which would improve access to these points of expertise would help a great deal, and could be an important function in a centrally resourced agency.

A last word

The prerogative of the author is to have the last word. In December 1987, I ended a paper on the subject of research into housing and health by concluding that 'future research should be limited to examining the relationship between the specific quantified characteristic of the housing environment and a biologically plausible health outcome'. There is still much to be said for this approach, although I feel in retrospect that it was unnecessarily harsh. Researchers like to feel that they have special expertise but the word 'research' should not be used to make the activity inaccessible to the non-professional. Most of the problems outlined are ones of common sense and can be identified and solved without specific training. A local tenants' association can undoubtedly carry out a competent and necessary 'research' study into local problems and perceived needs. The constraint on the tenants' group is to ask themselves the key questions outlined here, and the duty of the expert researcher is to make themselves available to try to provide some answers. For specialized research groups, the way forward is to combine the skills and new technologies of measurement of attributes of the housing environment with the increasingly sophisticated qualitative and quantitative epidemiological research tools used in university departments of public health.

1.10
Further reading

For those interested in reading further, our 1986 review of housing and health commissioned by the Building Research Establishment (Mant and Gray, 1986) provides a very full bibliography of more than 200 studies ready to be critically appraised. There are a number of specialist texts on research method and three of the most readable are Kahn's text on epidemiological method (1983), Breslow and Day's text on case control studies (Breslow and Day, 1980) and Abranson's (1974) text on survey methods. A book with a strong medical flavour, but a very readable and authoritative approach to trial design, is Hulley and Cummings (1988). However, the best way to start to design research is to find out what has been done before and to learn from the mistakes (and successes) of previous workers. Re-inventing the square wheel is a common and wasteful process.

Bibliography

Abranson, J. H. (1974) – *Survey methods in community medicine*, Churchill-Livingstone, Edinburgh.

Breslow, N. E. and Day, N. E. (1980) *Statistical methods in cancer research, vol. 1. The analysis of case control studies*, IARC Publications, No. 32, Lyon, France.

Hulley, S. B. and Cummings, S. R. (1988) *Designing Clinical Research: An epidemiological approach*. Williams and Wilkins, Baltimore, Md.

Elton P. J., Packer J. M. (1986) A prospective randomized trial of the value of rehousing on the grounds of mental ill health. *J. Chron. Dis.* 39(3), 221–7.

Kahn, H. A. (1983) *An Introduction to Epidemiological Method*. Oxford University Press, London.

Mant, D. and Gray, J. A. M. (1986) *Building Regulations and Health: BRE Report*. HMSO, London.

Platt, S. D., Martin, C. J., Hunt, S. M. and Lewis, C. W. (1989) Damp housing, mould growth and symptomatic health state. *BMJ*, **298**, 1673–8.

Stott, N. and West, R. (1981) Acute lower respiratory tract infections in infants: the influence of central heating systems. *J. Roy. Coll. Gen. Pract.*, **31**, 148–50.

2

USING PUBLISHED DATA TO ASSESS HEALTH RISKS

COLIN THUNHURST

2.1

Social scientific investigation and the use of secondary data

The distinguishing feature of social scientific investigation is its inability to conduct controlled investigation. The (theoretical) method of the 'natural' scientist is to scrutinize hypothesized cause-and-effect relationships by performing pairs of matched experiments. To one group, the 'experimental group', an agent will be applied which is suspected of inducing a particular change. The group's progress will be monitored to see if the change does actually occur. To ensure that the change is not merely the product of the passage of time, or some other extraneous factor, progress will also be monitored in a 'control group'. That is, a group will be chosen whose characteristics have been, as far as is conceivably possible, matched to those of the experimental group in all relevant respects.

Thus a scientific investigation of the relationship between housing dampness and health would consist of taking two groups of residents matched according to their sex, age, occupations, health records, housing histories, etc. and allocating one group to housing that was damp. The other group would be given housing that was identical in every respect except that it was dry. Their respective health histories would be traced, with adequate checks that other matched characteristics had not changed significantly. Any differences in the health histories could be legitimately presumed to have derived from their differing housing circumstances.

Such an experiment is clearly neither practically nor ethically permissible. So the social scientist must adopt other methods. One such of these is the social survey. Examples of social surveys and their value in investigating the relationships between health and housing conditions are discussed and exemplified elsewhere in this book (see generally Chapter 3 and Part II, below). Given the inability to control the allocation of housing, the social scientist will investigate the differences in health circumstances that actually do exist in the population. By process of social survey, that is asking a range of questions concerning the respondents' social, demographic, environmental and other circumstances, the social scientist will analytically remove all other factors that might be related to variations in health experiences between groups (that is, controlling after the event, rather than before). When this has been done, what is left will be ascribed to varying housing circumstance.

Social scientists are inevitably on more dangerous ground than natural scientists because there is always the possibility that there is an extraneous intervening factor that they have failed to pre-empt and measure, and thus which is not adequately 'controlled for' in their post-survey analysis. Theoretically, the natural scientist has precluded this possibility by the precision with which he or she has matched experimental and control group members (ironically the best method of matching is generally to allocate by process of randomness). As a consequence of this, even the most laboriously and carefully designed social survey rarely presents totally conclusive evidence of the relationships between two factors. At best, they add to the weight of 'circumstantial' evidence.

Social surveys are costly and time-consuming. They can often be intrusive with very little real benefit to the participant; and for the reasons outlined above, they can often be inconclusive. Social scientists have not always used social surveys diplomatically. Investigators have not always been as energetic in feeding back the results of surveys to their 'subjects', as they have promised they would be when seeking prior co-operation. The subjects become objects, leading to a resentful feeling among certain 'interesting' groups within the population that they are overly surveyed, and treated like rats in mazes. This is not to say that social surveys are valueless. As is well illustrated elsewhere in this book, they can often produce revealing results, and may be worth conducting for other reasons than 'academic' social investigation. But there is a tendency to rely too heavily upon them.

Wherever possible, social investigators, before embarking upon large social surveys, should check that the information they are seeking is not 'naturally' occurring. Large amounts of data and information are already collected on individuals. Some are held as personal records (in hospitals, benefits offices, housing departments, etc.). Much more is available on groups in aggregate (cumulated by geographical location or by social grouping). Subject to obvious strictures on personal privacy and confidentiality, these may provide valuable sources. The sheer volume of secondary data already available would suggest that they might be more adequately exploited. To generate anything approaching such a quantity would require a very large number of purposefully designed social surveys.

In this chapter we look at the way that the rediscovery of inequalities in health has generated a renewed interest in the exploitation of secondary sources of data. Specifically, we consider the value of the local 'Black Report', a systematic investigation of the inequalities in health that exist within a specific locality. In particular, we consider whether the recent proliferation of local reports could provide us with a much-needed database for the further investigation of the relationships between housing circumstance and health condition.

2.2

The rediscovery of inequalities in health

The 1980s saw inequalities in health resurface as an item on the research, policy analysis and political agendas. The decade opened unpromisingly. In August 1980, the newly elected Conservative government surreptitiously attempted to 'suppress' the findings of the Working Party on Inequalities in Health, which had been established by their Labour predecessors (see 'Introduction' to Townsend, Davidson and Whitehead, 1988). At the time, they could hardly have been expected to have foreseen the *cause célèbre* that they were creating, the interpretations of their actions which would follow and, above all, the explosion of interest in the issues that was to come. However, twelve years on, with the benefit of hindsight, and several further attempts at the suppression of 'uncomfortable' findings later, it is hard not to draw the conclusion that they were perhaps only too well aware of the significance of the Working Party's report.

The government's handling of the publication of the Black Report, as it came to be known after the chair of the Working Party, Sir Douglas Black, has now been well chronicled (see Townsend, Davidson and Whitehead, 1988, which also includes a slightly shortened version of the original report). The irony of the report's reception is that the Working Party itself had essentially said nothing that was new; they produced no original research findings. What they, and their supporting research staff, had done was to collect together painstakingly, sift and re-present, evidence from a wealth of existing studies. They relied exclusively on secondary sources and secondary analyses. It was the cumulated weight of these that proved so overwhelming; and for a newly elected government firmly committed to the unqualified benefits of a capitalistic system of governance (and its necessary unevennesses) also proved so damning.

After carefully establishing their own conceptual framework, reviewing the available evidence on mortality and morbidity inequalities as they related to social class, reviewing similarly available evidence on systematic inequalities in the availability and usage of health services, and making some revealing international comparisons, the Working Party considered a range of explanations for the consistency of the relationships that they had exposed. What they did *not* do was to conclude their report with an abstract academic discourse on the nature of their general findings. Rather, they went on to offer a detailed strategy incorporating a specific action programme, which spelt out some concrete steps that could be taken to attempt a long-term rectification of the sorry picture that they had revealed. Within the overall strategy, there was necessarily a number of specific recommendations relating to the area of housing.

These recommendations were based on their conclusions that: 'Housing conditions are associated with health status in a variety of ways' (Townsend, Whitehead and Davidson, 1988, p. 188). This was an assertion they substantiated with reference to a wide range of studies which related to forms of heating, overcrowding, highrise living, homelessness, absence of facilities, forms of tenure, etc.

The publication of the Black Report proved to be the catalyst albeit somewhat slow-acting for an explosion of interest, and an explosion of attention to issues of inequality, poverty and health. The Working Party's offered strategy was less one for the health services than a strategy for social and economic services. Within this, it offered a newly invigorated role, indeed a *raison d'être*, for local authorities who were by the mid-1980s reeling under repeated central government measures aimed at condemning them to insignificance. Through the Black Report, health had been firmly placed back on the agenda of local government, though it did take a number of years for this realization to emerge.

Slowly, local authorities began to deliberate on the implications that the findings of the Black Report had for them. As they did, two important empirical questions necessarily followed: 'To what extent are the national inequalities reported within the Black Report replicated within our own area?'; and 'To what extent do these translate into geographical inequalities?'.

To answer these questions local authorities, and subsequently (often in collaboration) local health authorities, began to commission their own local 'Black Reports' (see e.g. Thunhurst, 1985a). As had the original Black Report, these local reports relied very strongly on secondary data sources.

The methods of analysis of the local reports have tended to be quite similar. They have normally been conducted at a ward level of aggregation using mortality data derived from primary mortality tapes (coded records of death certificates produced by the Office of Population Censuses and Surveys for regional health authorities) and social and economic data derived from the 1981 Census of Population. Where wards are inappropriate, the data will have been re-aggregated (for example, in view of the particular social geography of the City of Stoke-on-Trent, Thunhurst and Postma, 1989, re-aggregated wards into 'neighbourhoods' to highlight the systematic pattern of that city's internal health variations).

A range of different composite measures have been used to represent the more complex nature of 'social deprivation' or material poverty (see Thunhurst 1985b, 1989). Due to the absence of available morbidity data, the health side of the equation has generally been represented by mortality (death rates). Figure 2.1 shows the contrasting pattern of ward by ward inequality in mortality that has been revealed by a selected range of such local studies.

Alongside these studies based on the analysis of secondary sources of data, geographically targeted primary studies have also been conducted to investigate more rigorously the health problems of specific areas and estates (see e.g. Betts, 1985, and Ginnety, Kelly and Black, 1985). In the latter of these two studies, housing ranked

Target 1: By the year 2000, the actual differences in health status between countries and between groups within countries should be reduced by at least 25% by improving the level of health of disadvantaged nations and groups.

Target 6: By the year 2000, life expectancy at birth in the region should be at least 75 years.

Target 16: By 1995, in all member states there should be significant increases in positive health behaviour, such as balanced nutrition, non-smoking, appropriate physical activity and good stress management.

Target 27: By 1990, in all member states the infrastructures of the delivery systems should be organized so that resources are distributed according to need, and that services ensure physical and economic accessibility and cultural acceptability to the population.

Figure 2.1 Health for All Targets: examples.

as the principal concern of the investigators before and after conducting the study.

By 1986, new information was accumulating at such a rate that the then Health Education Council commissioned an update of the Black Report. The revision, entitled 'The Health Divide' (Whitehead, 1988 in Townsend, Davidson and Whitehead, 1988), drew upon a number of new sources: academic papers; the locally produced analyses; and the findings of the begrudgingly released analyses conducted for the 1979–83 Decennial Supplement on Occupational Mortality (OPCS, 1986). In many quarters, the form of the release of this latter source has been interpreted as another act of suppression (see Thunhurst, 1991). The publication of 'The Health Divide' was to prove to be the last act of the Health Education Council. It has been replaced by a newly constituted Health Education Authority. Thus throughout the decade discussion on the topic of health inequalities has been accompanied by a high level of political controversy.

2.3
Programmes of action

The Black Working Party offered the framework for analyses and the fragments of a programme of action, but the structural context for the development of a more comprehensive strategy was to be provided by the World Health Organization (WHO) and its European Regional Office. In 1977 the World Health Organization had adopted its global strategy of Health for All by the Year 2000. This was given a more concrete form in the Declaration of Alma Ata that followed in 1978. The European Region of the WHO moulded this strategy into a series of 38 targets that were adopted in 1984 (WHO, 1985).

The Targets were grouped under six headings: Health for all in Europe by the year 2000 (Targets 1–12); Life styles conducive to health (Targets 13–17); Healthy environment (Targets 18–25); Appropriate care (Targets 26–31); Research for health for all (Target 32); and Health development support (Targets 33–8). The Targets, examples of which are given in Figure 2.2, were based on the principles of equity, health promotion, community participation, multisectoral co-operation, primary health care and international co-operation, and were seen to relate as demonstrated in Figure 2.3. They incorporated time-scales that were defined accordingly.

Target 24, within the Healthy Environment group of targets, explicitly identifies problems of housing, *per se*, as problems of health. It states: 'By the year 2000, all people of the Region should have a better opportunity of living in houses and settlements which provide a healthy and safe environment.' This is expanded in the Targets report (WHO, 1985, p. 89), as follows:

The achievement of this target will require the acceleration of programmes of housing construction and improvements; the development of international health criteria for housing, space, heating, lighting, disposal of wastes, noise control and safety, while taking into account the special needs of groups such as young families, the elderly and the disabled.

In 1986, the WHO European Region launched its Healthy Cities Programme whereby exemplar cities throughout Europe were selected to pursue city-wide healthy strategies in pursuit of Health for All by the Year 2000 moulded broadly around the Region's 38 Targets (Ashton and Seymour, 1988). Within Britain an increasingly large number of cities and towns – inspired by the WHO European Region, but independent of it – have launched their own healthy city/healthy town programmes. Most have joined together under the umbrella of the UK Health for All Network, formerly the UK Healthy Cities Network.

Characteristic of the British adaptation of the Healthy Cities

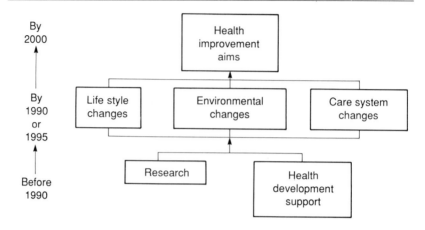

Figure 2.2 WHO European strategy for Health for All by the Year 2000.

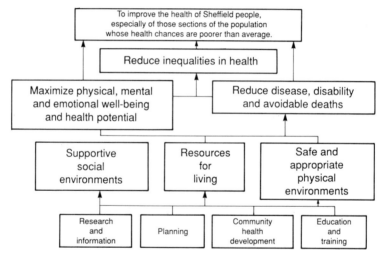

Figure 2.3 Healthy Sheffield 2000 strategy, working model: September 1989.

model has been an accentuation of the dimension of inequality, following the interest and concern that followed the publication of the Black Report. Thus the City of Sheffield, in their Healthy Sheffield 2000 Strategy, has taken the WHO's Target 6 (see Figure 2.2) and reformulated it. 'By the year 2000 the variation in life expectancy between the most and the least parts of Sheffield should be reduced by 50 per cent' (Healthy Sheffield 2000, 1987).

The overall strategy has been reconceptualized and reformulated

Table 2.1 Health Sheffield 2000: Target 24, Healthy homes

By the year 2000, significant progress will have been made towards ensuring that every citizen has a home which is in a satisfactory physical condition, of a design appropriate to the needs of those who occupy it and which is in an environment conducive to the development of a healthy, active and fulfilled community:

24.1: By the year 1990, substantial progress should have been made towards developing and implementing housing policies which enable service delivery to become more responsive to the needs and preferences of the users of the service

24.2: By the year 2000, over 60% of council dwellings currently identified as unsatisfactory (around 30 000 dwellings) should have benefited from substantial repair works, improvement or modernization

24.3: By the year 2000, approx. 60% of pre-1919 dwellings in the private sector currently identified as unfit, substandard or requiring substantial renovation (around 15 000 dwellings) should have been improved to give satisfactory accommodation by modern standards

24.4: By the year 1995, a substantial number of homes for rent, built to modern space and mobility standards, and of predominantly 2-storey traditional design should have been provided

24.5: By the year 1990, new or improved heating systems should have been installed to around 28 000 council dwellings

24.6: By the year 1995, suitable accommodation should be provided for 600 mentally ill and 200 mentally handicapped people who are to be discharged from hospitals and hostels under the Community Care initiatives

24.7: Up to 1990, adaptations to make existing dwellings more suited to the needs of people with disabilities should continue at least to their present level

within Sheffield to reflect this increased attention to inequalities, and to provide more substance to the facilitating structures on which the strategy is constructed (see Figure 2.4, taken from Healthy Sheffield 2000, 1989).

Again, reference to the topic of housing illustrates this reconceptualization and a more finely tuned attention to programmatic detail. The WHO Housing Target 24, has been substantially expanded in the Healthy Sheffield Targets (Table 2.1).

The Health for All by the Year 2000 approach, incorporating, as it does, explicit written targets, draws attention to the need to be able to carry out an accompanying monitoring process. This has prompted exercises, conducted both at the European regional level and within the UK, to establish a set of indicators which could be used to monitor progress towards achievement of the targets. And

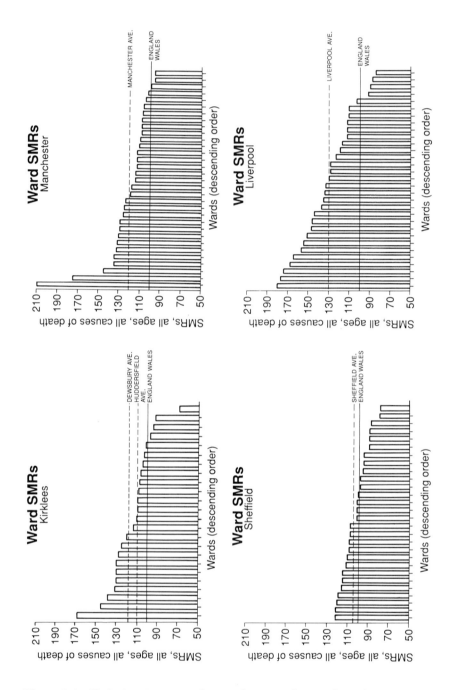

Figure 2.4   Variation in seasonal mortality rates by wards in four cities.

in the British context, the added emphasis on inequality has implied a need to monitor progress *within* towns and cities, as well as at a city-wide level.

It has always been anticipated that a number of the monitoring indicators would be 'soft' indicators, requiring primary data collection. But for regular monitoring, the repeated conduct of primary surveys is prohibitive. Thus the most effectively deployed data sources would need to be secondary ones, available only from routinely available data sources. In the light of this, the UK Healthy Cities Network commissioned a study on core indicators which highlighted, *inter alia*, steps that the members of the Network might take to improve the usefulness of secondary data sources for these purposes (Thunhurst, 1989).

2.4

Secondary studies: housing as an explanatory variable

The report of the Black Working Party was far from the first to employ secondary data to look at health inequalities. Nor was it the first to relate these to variations in the social and economic environment. There already existed a number of studies, some of which were referred to by the Working Party, which had employed secondary data sources, to endeavour to 'explain' variations in health status measures in terms of variations in the distribution of housing variables. Analytically, they tended to use techniques of multiple regression – these take a single 'dependent' variable (here, the health indicator) and find a weighted additive combination of 'independent' variables (here, the housing and related indicators) which statistically fits it most closely.

Brennan (1978) and Brennan and Lancashire (1978) analysed 1971 county borough data against mortality rates to investigate the effects of housing density, amenities and tenure, controlling for social class. Fryer *et al.* (1979) employed housing indicators, together with a wider range of other social and economic indicators derived from the 1971 Census in a similar analysis. These, and some subsequent studies, have endeavoured to isolate housing as a specific explanatory factor.

In contrast, other studies have employed a very wide range of non-purposefully selected Census indicators, which have included among them housing variables, in the hope that the analytic powers of the computer would somehow sort out the conceptual wood from the numerical trees. This approach has been criticized in the grounds that analysis and analytic computing power should not be deployed as a substitute for analytic thought – or to co-opt the now rather dated acronym: GIGO (Garbage In, Garbage Out). It has been further argued that Census variables should only be selected after a process of clear and explicit conceptualization of terms such as 'social deprivation', translated, as far as the range of topics in the Census permits, into identified direct and indirect indicators (Thunhurst, 1985b).

In either event, the empirical analyst is confronted with a methodological conundrum, derivative of the methods of the social scientist outlined above, which no amount of improvement in data sources can iron out. Housing is only one factor in the complex web of interacting forces that constitutes deprivation. Causally, housing deficiencies interact with other dimensions of poverty, such as poor employment, poor nutrition and poor access to transport, in such a way that it is impossible (some would say dangerous) to attempt to disentangle them. Apportioning blame (i.e. '45% of variations in ill-health are accounted for by variations in poor housing') will be interpreted to ignore the effect of these interactions. On the other hand, not to do so, and to lump everything into generic terms such as 'deprivation' will be interpreted as a failure to pinpoint contributory factors and thus also as a failure to make a significant contribution to policy debate.

The conundrum is well demonstrated by the results of the analyses that have contributed to the recent local 'Black Reports'. Thunhurst (1986), drawing upon the results of the Health and Poverty study in Sheffield, directs attention to the comparative statistical significance of 'direct' poverty indicators, such as unemployment rates, or 'indirect' poverty indicators, such as car ownership, in relation to the significance of housing variables. This is partly a product of the poor conceptualization of 'bad housing' which is possible employing Census indicators, but also a product of the complexities of the interacting relationships involved.

It should be stressed that the conundrum is only highlighted by analytic studies that employ secondarily derived data sources. It is not resolved only by studying or using housing variables.

2.5

Alternative views of the process of research

At one level, it could be argued that the conundrum exists only because of the reductionist assumptions that have become so deeply embedded in our understanding of what constitutes knowledge and thus also what constitutes research. Knowledge is typically seen as understanding small fragments of the world. Depth of knowledge is seen as a greater understanding of even smaller fragments. The method of achieving this knowledge is the prescribed process of scientific discovery, implicit in the method of the 'natural' scientist. This has been outlined above and has been most rigorously articulated by Sir Karl Popper (see e.g. Popper, 1972). Through a process of piece-by-piece isolated experimentation science aims to build knowledge in an incremental fashion. Thus, to demonstrate and isolate the health implication of housing, it is necessary to demonstrate, *ab initio*, the 'significance' of an isolated statistical relationship between a health variable and a housing variable. The process of research can easily degenerate into an undifferentiated trawl for significant statistics.

It is not an appropriate place to embark on a lengthy discourse on the nature of alternative philosophies and practices of science, nor the alternative statistical procedures that will be needed to accompany them. Social scientists have become increasingly disenchanted in endeavouring to mimic the natural sciences. And more recently, rather than attempting to adapt the methods of the natural scientist, social scientists have begun to develop more appropriate methods of their own. Methods of action or participatory research attempt to discover knowledge and theory which is 'grounded', that is rooted in the understandings of the social actors themselves, rather than aspiring to produce the more absolute 'objective knowledge' of the Popperian natural scientist (see e.g. Charmaz, 1990, or the various contributions in Reason and Rowan, 1981, or Mangham, 1987).

Alternative approaches to the production of knowledge demand appropriate analytic procedures. The classical method of statistical hypothesis testing incorporates Popperian assumptions that knowledge is the product of sequential one-off experiments. The Bayesian approach to statistics is incremental; experiments (or observations) produce new information which is taken with existing information (prior beliefs) to produce new knowledge (posterior beliefs). Thus methods of Bayesian statistics offer the potential, if not yet always the actual methods, to accompany this more progressive (in both senses) perspective on the process of accumulation of knowledge, while still maintaining sufficient rigour. (For a most useful illustrative discussion of the value of adopting a Bayesian perspective when studying the health effects of waste disposal see Sheldon and Smith, 1991.)

In addition, classical statistical methods incorporate assumptions about the process of accumulation of knowledge that bare little relationship to the way that knowledge does actually accrue. They are, as a consequence, inherently conservative. The method of hypothesis testing puts the burden of proof on disproving a null hypothesis. Thus it will be taken that there is no evidence of a health hazard unless there is overwhelming (typically, less than a one in 20 probability) that observed differences could have occurred as the mere product of chance. Thus given the very small samples that are often (necessarily) involved in the study of particular hazards (asbestos workers, people living near nuclear installations, etc.), critical limits will only be reached when at an intuitive level the health consequences have reached near-epidemic proportions. Repeatedly, classical statistical methods have been able to alert us to the existence of health hazards (e.g. the relationship between asbestos-related diseases and the asbestos mill at Hebden Bridge) at precisely that time when the last thing that was needed to identify them were sophisticated analytical procedures.

In practical terms, the implication is that while it is important to continue, cumulatively, to increase our understanding of the ways in which poor housing conditions affect health, programmatically, we should look to act on lower margins of 'proof' and in ways that see housing factors as intertwined in a network of social and environmental influences on health.

2.6

Strengthening the use of secondary sources

Within this perspective, the value of housing analyses based upon secondary sources is clearer. They will not provide a complete picture, not will they present scientific 'proofs' of the relationship between specific housing factors and specific health factors. They will add to the stock of knowledge. Before too long, it may be possible to conduct a housing-orientated Black Report which cumulates the fragments of health studies informing the housing debate. In the shorter term, what they can offer is simple mechanisms for geographical targeting, that is targeting of further investigation and, more importantly, targeting of action.

The potential in this direction could be greatly strengthened by a few simple steps – some pragmatic agreement on the common use of simple and composite indicators, the development of some common 'soft' indicators and the standardizing of analytic procedures; these are argued in more depth in Thunhurst (1989). The most urgent of these stem from the need to ensure that the opportunity of the next decennial Census – the only one that is due to be conducted before the appointed year 2000 – is not lost. It is proposed that that Census will contain, for the first time in many years, a question relating to long-term illness. It is not currently proposed that small area statistics recording data from this question will permit cross-interrogation with housing (or other social or environmental) factors.

To some degree, this limitation will be countered by an important innovation, which is to be introduced with the 1991 Census, to release, through the ESRC Survey Archive, a sample of anonymized records. This will enable researchers to retain more control over their studies based on the data collected at the time of the Census, as they will be able to produce their own cross-classifications, rather than simply relying upon those routinely produced by the OPCS in the small area statistics tabulations. Unfortunately, though, they will not permit detailed geographical disaggregation.

Also of increasing significance is the growing evidence accumulating from the OPCS's longitudinal survey. The Longitudinal Study has been tracing the record of various events held by the OPCS relating to 1% of the population of England and Wales. It has already permitted deeper analysis of a range of health-related social and environmental variables (OPCS and Social Statistics Research Unit, 1989) including issues of housing (Holmans, Nandy and Brown, 1987).

The new responsibilities of Directors of Public Health, particularly the reintroduction of the requirement to produce Annual Public Health Reports, and their previous unpreparedness for this assigned task, has prompted some creative thinking from this direction. Though the separation of local government and local health authority responsibilities, exacerbated by current reforms of the National Health Service, have undermined this potentially powerful source for informing the social and economic health debate.

Thus, in the short term, a degree of controlled eclecticism is called for – innovative local studies based upon a sense of shared purpose. The UK Health Cities Network (1990) has produced a very useful Core Health Measures Starter Pack which provides methodological supporting guidance, as well as suggestions on specific indicators.

Ultimately, though, the most substantial contributions will be made and the most interesting findings revealed when it is possible to 'tie' sequential secondary analyses – that is, when it is possible to take the secondary analysis conducted for a specific geographical area and to employ its findings as an incremental addition to the findings of analyses conducted for other geographical areas. To do this will necessarily involve researchers applying self-restraint to their more deeply instilled individualistic tendencies and will require Bayesian social statisticians to provide the supporting analytic framework. Some general agreement could be reached about standard procedures to be employed along the lines indicated above. These should meet both the needs of more research-orientated inquiry into specific housing/health relationships, as well as the more programmatic needs of Health for All. After all, social statisticians have merely modelled the world in various ways; the point, however, is to change it.

Bibliography

Ashton, J. and Seymour, H. (1988) *The New Public Health*, Open University Press, Milton Keynes.

Betts, G. (1985) *Report on a Survey on Health in Glyndon Ward, Greenwich*, Greenwich Health Rights Project.

Brennan, M. E. (1978) Patterns of mortality and the alienation of life: a study using census indicators, in: Armytage, W. H. G. and Peel, J. (eds) *Perimeters of Social Repair, Proceedings of the Fourteenth Annual Symposium of the Eugenics Society*, Academic Press, London, pp. 73–9.

Brennan, M. E. and Lancashire, R. (1978) Association of childhood mortality with housing status and unemployment. *J. Epidem. Comm. Health*, 32, pp. 28–33.

Charmaz, K. (1990) Discovering chronic illness: using grounded theory. *Soc. Sci. Med.*, 30 (11), 1161–72.

Fryer, J. G., Harding, R. A., MacDonald, M. D., Read, K. L. Q., Croker, G. R. and Abernathy, J. (1979) Comparing the early mortality rates of the local authorities in England and Wales. *J. R. Statist. Soc. A*, 142(2), 181–98.

Ginnety, P., Kelly, K. and Black, M. (1985) *Moyard: A Health Profile*, Eastern Health and Social Services Board, Belfast.

Healthy Sheffield 2000 (1987) *Sheffield Health for All by the Year 2000 – Draft Targets*, Sheffield City Council.

Healthy Sheffield 2000 (1989) *HS2000 Strategy*, Health and Consumer Services Department, Sheffield City Council.

Holmans, A. E., Nandy, S. and Brown, A. C. (1987) Household formation and dissolution and housing tenure: a longitudinal perspective, *Social Trends*, 17, 20–8.

Mangham, I. L. (ed.) (1987) *Organisation Analysis and Development*, Wiley, Chichester.

Office of Population Censuses and Surveys (OPCS) (1986) *Registrar-General's Decennial Supplement on Occupational Mortality 1979–83*, HMSO, London.

OPCS and Social Statistics Research Unit (1989) *Longitudinal Study, Newsletter No. 1*, LS Management Unit, OPCS, London.

Popper, K. R. (1972) *The Logic of Scientific Discovery*, Hutchinson, London.

Reason, P. and Rowan, J. (1981) *Human Inquiry – a Sourcebook of New Paradigm Research*, Wiley, Chichester.

Sheldon, T. and Smith, D. (1991) Assessing the health effects of waste disposal sites: issues in risk analysis and some Bayesian conclusions, in: Clarke, M., Smith, D. and Blowers, A. (eds) *Waste Location: Spatial Aspects of Waste Management, Hazards and Disposal*, Routledge, London, pp. 158–86.

Thunhurst, C. (1985a) *Poverty and Health in the City of Sheffield*, Environmental Health Department, Sheffield City Council.

Thunhurst, C. (1985b) The analysis of small area statistics and planning for health. *Statistician*, 34, 93–106.

Thunhurst, C. (1986) Poverty and ill health in Sheffield – the value of secondary data in exploring the relationship between housing and health, Proceedings of Conference on Unhealthy Housing – a Diagnosis, University of Warwick, 14–16 December 1986.

Thunhurst, C. (1989) *Core Health Measures for UK Cities*, UK Healthy Cities Network, Liverpool.

Thunhurst, C. (1991) What happened to the watchdogs? Information and public health, in: Draper, P. (ed.) *Health through Public Policy*, Merlin, London, pp. 122–30.

Thunhurst, C. and Postma, S. (1989) *Health Profile of the City of Stoke-on-Trent*, Environmental Health Department, Stoke-on-Trent City Council.

Townsend, P., Davidson, N. and Whitehead, M. (1988) *Inequalities in Health*, Penguin, Harmondsworth.

UK Healthy Cities Network (1990) *Core Health Measures Starter Pack*, UKHCN, Liverpool.

Whitehead, M. (1988) The health divide, in: Townsend, P., Davidson, N. and Whitehead M. (eds) *Inequalities in Health*, Penguin, Harmondsworth, pp. 215–356.

World Health Organization (WHO) (1985) *Targets for Health for All: Targets in Support of the European Regional Strategy for Health for All by the Year 2000*, World Health Organization Regional Office for Europe, Copenhagen.

3

HOUSING AND THE HEALTH OF THE COMMUNITY

DAVID BYRNE AND JANE KEITHLEY

3.1

Introduction

It is a cliché of socio-medical history to point out that the massive improvement in the health of populations of urban industrial societies during the past hundred years or so is far more a consequence of collective intervention in the environment than it is of the development, and even provision, of curative health care. However, in 1984 the editors of the *Journal of Epidemiology and Community Health* found it necessary to remind readers and contributors that community health meant something more than the study of the health states of individuals in a community and expressed considerable concern about the decline in work by doctors on issues of the health of the community as a whole. Blume (1982) has made a similar point about the subordination of epidemiology to the concerns and practices of case-centred curative medicine. In the light of these concerns, it is appropriate to ask what does make a difference to the health states of populations; and in the context of this book, what might be the influence of housing and health policies?

We want to pursue these questions in relation to the conceptualization of research dealing with the *social epidemiology* of housing and health, by which term we mean the social relationships between housing and health and the patterns of disease which result from those relationships. We would argue that the aggregate approach to issues of the aetiology (causal processes) of ill-health was not only relevant to the nineteenth and early twentieth century, but also crucial in contemporary research and practice.

We will argue that, while it is perfectly possible to relate housing conditions to the health of individuals resident in particular dwellings, it is far more important to conceptualize the impact of differential housing conditions on the aggregate health of whole communities, spatially and residentially defined. We think of housing conditions as operating at this level, that is at the level of the households which make up the communities and at the level of the individuals who form the households, although it is hard to construct any operational definition of housing conditions for individuals as opposed to households. We find it interesting and important that from the 1890s to the 1930s administrative mechanisms for slum clearance recognized the notion of the unhealthy area and used collectively organized epidemiological data in the legal representation of areas for clearance. This chapter will discuss the methodological questions associated with such a structural conception of the causal process of collective health.

3.2

Relationships between housing and health: the recent evidence

Let us begin by looking at recent research investigating relationships between housing and health, at some of the associated methodological debates and at the assumptions about the nature of health built into this research. Until recently, interest in the social origins of ill-health had been in decline in urban, industrial societies and there had been a particular neglect of the relationship between housing conditions and health. As has been described elsewhere (Byrne *et al.*, 1986), dramatic improvements in housing were accompanied by improvements in health, especially as measured by mortality at younger ages or by the growth and development of children, and by a decline in the incidence of those diseases most clearly associated with insanitary and overcrowded housing.

However, in recent years there has been something of a revival of interest in these relationships. This has sprung partly from an assertion that the construction of certain forms of housing (especially flatted accommodation), without regard to health criteria, nor to the needs and wishes of prospective residents, has had damaging effects on health. In addition, wider definitions of ill-health have been adopted, which include social and psychological as well as physical manifestations. Much of the recent research has been concerned with public sector housing, especially that which Dunleavy (1981) has described as 'mass housing'. It is ironic that local authority housing, a movement which had as one of its most important motivations a desire to improve working-class health through better housing conditions, has in recent decades produced the new slums and their associated health hazards.

What kind of health hazards do they produce? Smith (1989) has produced a recent review of the major studies. Most attention has been paid to respiratory disease (traditionally linked with bad housing), to mental illness, particularly of the depressive type, and to general stress-induced morbidity. In addition, studies have considered the influence of housing and estate design on the incidence of domestic accidents. Young children, their mothers and elderly people are the groups most often argued to be affected, simply because they spend more time in the home than others. Finally, with rising homelessness, more attention has been paid to the health implications of having no housing at all.

A number of studies have found links between damp housing, the presence of mould and high rates of asthma and respiratory illness, especially among children (Strachan et al., 1986; McCarthy et al., 1985; Blackman et al., 1989). In the case of elderly people, it has been argued that damp, cold houses are an important factor in excess winter deaths in Britain (Boardman, 1986) and not just in the extreme form of hypothermia, but also in increased susceptibility to coronary and cerebral thrombosis and respiratory disease (Smith, 1989, p. 26).

Other studies have asserted that there is for women especially a link between housing, mental health and stress-induced morbidity. Smith (1989, p. 29) classifies the housing circumstances which have been argued to play a role in design (often also referring to quality), density of occupation, location and locational change (i.e. moving house). Blackman et al. (1989) compared two areas of west Belfast which were both socially and economically deprived, but of which one consisted of very unpopular, high-rise, poor-quality dwellings and the other of traditionally built dwellings considered to be significantly better. They found marked differences in mental health between the two areas, for men and children, as well as for women. Ineichen (1986) reviewed the evidence up to the mid-1980s on the effect of high-rise housing on mental health. Although he concluded that the 'balance of evidence' suggests a damaging effect, especially for families with young children, his review demonstrates the variation in findings between studies. Thus McCarthy *et al.* (1985) argue that the location, environment and quality of construction of dwellings were more important than whether or not they were high-rise.

Smith, (1989) has recently completed an extensive review of the contemporary literature on housing and health and an indication of renewed interest is that the *British Medical Journal* has published a series of articles on this topic (Lowry, 1989/1990). However, throughout this literature arguments recur as to how this research should be done and the status of its findings.

First, there are issues of definition. How is 'bad housing' to be defined? How far should the traditional indicators relating to structural condition, possession of 'basic' amenities and density of occupation be updated and extended? How far should the location and environment of housing rather than just the condition of the individual dwelling be taken into account? Of what significance is the 'form' of the dwelling, for example, whether it is a house or a flat (for a discussion of some of these issues see Byrne *et al.*, 1986, pp. 32–9)?

Defining health and ill-health is, if anything, more contentious. In relation to morbidity, there is the question of how this is measured – e.g. by demand for medical services, by the detection of clinical symptoms by 'experts' or by asking people themselves? There is some evidence that different methods of measurement produce rather different pictures of the association between poor health and bad housing (Pike, 1981; Strachan *et al.*, 1986).

Secondly, even if ways of defining the quality of housing and the extent of ill-health can be agreed, the extent and nature of the relationship between the two remains difficult to establish. For example, how can the effects of housing be separated out from the effects of the many other factors which influence health and which are likely to co-vary with housing such as class, occupation, income, consumption habits, environmental pollution, and so on? Should housing effects be isolated from these other factors? For example, Burr (1986) argues that once passive smoking and social class are controlled for, the relationships between damp and mould and wheezing in infancy practically disappears. However, if smoking and social class are seen as part of housing (or vice versa), then this becomes clearly a case of 'partialling out' (see below).

Much of the literature is based on survey data linking household (or community) housing conditions and individual health, although the latter is frequently aggregated to give a measure of 'collective' health or ill-health. However, at the individual level the relationship is far from complete and, in addition, is extremely difficult to 'prove' not only because of the presence of so many intervening factors, but also because laboratory and other studies have often failed to demonstrate clear causal relationships in the positivist sense (see e.g. Byrne *et al.*, 1986, pp. 42–3). This is not a problem confined to housing and health. Laboratory studies have as yet failed even to establish the specific nature of a causal link between smoking and lung cancer. The issue is one of how far such demonstrations are necessary or even possible, both in order to assert that there is a link and also to be able to formulate policies to deal with it. Certainly, in the nineteenth century effective action on housing and health was not predicted on a correct understanding of causal mechanisms.

The disentangling of causal mechanisms may be further complicated by the probable time lag between living in poor housing and some of the health implications. Stress and depressive illness are likely to be linked with current housing conditions, as are frequent episodes of acute respiratory illnesses. However, long-term implications for health may be experienced many years later, perhaps at a time when current housing conditions are good. For example, there is growing evidence of an association between frequent or severe bouts of respiratory illness in childhood and lung function in later life (Smith, 1989; Yarnell and St Leger). The two ways of taking account of the importance of housing (and health) history, retrospective studies and longitudinal, cohort studies, each have their problems.

Despite these methodological debates, a common element which runs through most of the research is the concern to prove or disprove a link between housing conditions and the health of individuals. Health (and the lack of it) are seen as individual attributes rather than a property which can and should be measured at the level of the whole community. Let us now move on to consider whether this assumption is justified.

3.3

Health and illness: individual or collective attributes?

If we want to consider arguments for moving away from the notions of 'health' and 'illness' as solely individual attributes, we need to ask, first, whether it is appropriate to talk about the *health* of the community, and secondly, how far it is feasible to measure health and illness at this aggregate level.

The arguments for regarding health as a collective attribute are clear in a historical context, when the major causes of death were the infectious diseases. The individual's state of health at that time depended crucially and immediately on the health of others in the same community and on living standards and conditions in that community. It is now widely accepted that the reductions in mortality and morbidity, especially at young ages, in Britain and similar societies over the past century came too early to owe much to advances in modern, individualistic, curative medicine. McKeown (1979), for example, argues that it was better nutrition which made the largest contribution to improved health, followed by improvements in what he calls 'hygienic measures', including better water supplies and sanitation, disposal of waste and improvements in standards of food handling, processing and storage. Both were accompanied by changes in reproductive practices, leading to a fall in the birth rate which ensured that the improvements in health brought about were not reversed by rising numbers. Vaccination and immunization, he contends, had little impact on national mortality trends until the 1930s and have not been the most important influence even subsequently. To therapeutic and curative medicine, he assigns an even smaller role.

Most students of the subject, including doctors, would probably concur with McKeown's analysis of the past. The interpretation of the present and future in urban, industrial societies is more contentious, and the contemporary practice of medicine and the direction of resources within our health system rests on the assumption that the aetiology of ill-health has changed. The major causes of mortality and morbidity are no longer the infectious diseases, but illnesses of the cardio-vascular and respiratory systems and neoplasms predominantly affecting the middle-aged and elderly. These conditions are seen as matters of individual pathology, non-transmissible and thus not issues associated with the health or living conditions of the community as a whole. McKeown (1979) and others have pointed out that doctors have little interest in the origins, especially the social origins, of disease, but concentrate on its pathological manifestations. McKeown even contends that there is an inverse relationship between the interest and status of the disease to the medical profession and the usefulness of the treatment to the patient, contrasting high-status neurology with (pre-AIDS) low-status but effective venereology. The enormous improvements in living standards and the stark contrast between the advanced industrial countries and the Third World (which in some locales still has disease patterns similar to nineteenth-century Britain) support the view that what McKeown calls the residual diseases of contemporary industrial societies are not associated with the environment, including the housing in which the population lives.

However, even among those who argue that the environment is of continuing importance, there are two rather different views, leading to a difference in emphasis. McKeown, for example, suggests that today in countries like Britain the diseases of affluence predominate rather than the diseases of poverty. He does acknowledge that industrial societies have produced hazards of their own – e.g. air and water pollution and even the risks arising from medical investigations and treatment – but he contends that the major determinants of the 'diseases of affluence' lie in personal behaviours: the consumption of refined food, sedentary living, smoking and excessive consumption of alcohol. He emphasizes the role of individual choice in these behaviours and the importance of inducement and exhortations to individuals to change them. This is very similar to the recent emphasis in government rhetoric (although not in spending) on the importance of health education in the prevention of disease and promotion of health. Thus, in 1988, a government publication, *Public Health in England* (HMSO, 1988, p. 17) asserted that:

it is the growing awareness of the importance of individual behaviour in determining the patterns of health and disease in the population which represents perhaps the greatest single change affecting public health in recent years . . . Our ability to reduce . . . premature deaths is to a substantial extent dependent on social attitudes and individual understanding and behaviour.

On the other hand, some commentators have emphasized the constraints on individual behaviour and the wider social pressures and influences associated with detriment to health. Eyer (1984) points

out that the so-called diseases of affluence in fact affect disproportionately the poorer groups in affluent societies. He disaggregates
the overall decline in mortality in societies which have undergone
large-scale capitalist transformations. The death rates for infants,
children and women of child-bearing age have greatly declined, but
there is much less, if any, reduction for adult males and older people
generally. He relates this to the increase in a number of major risk
factors (smoking, excess alcohol, obesity, hypertension, etc.). So far
his analysis is very similar to that of McKeown but he then goes
on to argue that these are directly related to the stressful nature
of capitalist society which, in addition, through occupational and
environmental hazards has made an important direct contribution
to the increase in modern diseases. For Eyer, the health risks of
capitalism include the uprooting of people from stable communities
and the subjection of life to the constantly changing demands of the
market for labour. These risks fall heaviest on the least privileged in
society, so that the larger class differences in health are found
between the lowest urban class (social class 5 on the Registrar-
General's classification, for example) and all the others. Eyer contrasts this with the experience of societies which have benefited
from public health measures and improvements in nutrition without significant urban or capitalist transformation. Adult mortality
rates, for example, among the communal village peasantry of China
are lower than those in far richer industrial societies (Ashton and
Seymour, 1988).

Ashton and Seymour (1988, p. 21) in an optimistic book entitled *The
New Public Health*, attempt a synthesis of these two approaches:

The New Public Health is an approach which brings together environmental change and personal preventive measures . . . [it] goes beyond
an understanding of human biology and recognises the importance of
those social aspects of health problems which are caused by lifestyles.
In this way it seeks to avoid the trap of blaming the victim . . . What
are needed to address those problems are 'Healthy Public Policies'.

The implication of this type of analysis is that we must look beyond
individual choices and motivations, and the policies which seek
to change these directly, to the wider environmental hazards and
pressures which are conducive to certain forms of behaviour and
related to ill-health and at how these are differentially distributed.
There are a whole range and variety of possibilities in these analyses. One example which attracted national media attention was the

finding that tobacco product advertisements on Metro underground stations on Tyneside are heavily concentrated in those serving predominantly working-class areas. Another possible analysis could look at the relationship between poor housing and environmental conditions, a high incidence of psycho-depressive illness and propensity to smoke, leading to a high rate of smoking-related diseases. The work of Hilary Graham (1984) has contributed greatly to our understanding of the complex aetiology of apparently 'irrational' smoking behaviour, especially for women under stress. In the present authors' own study of housing and health in Gateshead, plenty of ethnographic material emerged to suggest that women explain their own smoking behaviour in terms of the miserable nature of their domestic environment. In other words, when conducting interviews, we have been offered cigarettes and refused as neither of us smoke, been congratulated on this by women who then explain how smoking helps them get through the day. Exhorting women such as these to give up smoking will not alter the predisposing factors and may actually increase the incidence and severity of depression. Smoking-related diseases then become issues of community health and living conditions, not just of the pathology or personal habits of the individual.

These diseases also become comprehensible only by accepting the impossibility of separating out the relative influence of different causal factors in explaining a phenomenon. Epidemiologists classically treat smoking as a purely individual variable deriving from individual choice. However, if living in particular housing or environmental conditions predisposes people to smoke, then smoking is a part of housing. This is the problem of 'partialling out'. Statisticians take indicators which may be different aspects of one structural element and look at their 'separate' contribution. For example, they treat both poor diet and bad housing as separate from class, when such life-chance inequalities are usually seen by sociologists as part of an individual's class position. In effect, they are cutting up what might be indivisible. In the case of the influence of smoking and bad housing on health, controlling for smoking would result in an underestimate of the importance of housing. If, as could be plausibly argued, other factors such as an excessive intake of alcohol or obesity are also part of housing (or even partly part of housing), then controlling for these would have similar (and cumulative) effects.

This undoubtedly has community health implications. However, the issues are different in crucial respects from those which predominated in the late nineteenth and early twentieth centuries. There is ample historical evidence to suggest that the government interest in public health which was so evident in that era stemmed from a dual concern to safeguard the current and future workforce and military force and to reduce the risk of the transmission of infectious diseases to the better-off sections of the population (Ashton and Seymour, 1988). More recently, poor environmental conditions have been directly or indirectly associated with a high incidence of disease, which are not infectious, and which are more likely to be associated with excess morbidity and premature mortality in middle age and beyond rather than among younger adults and children. It is hardly surprising, then, that they do not raise the same public concern. The recent attention paid to the growth of AIDS – an infectious disease to which younger age-groups are susceptible and which is no respecter of class (at least in the West), and to measures to contain it, take on a new meaning in this light (*ibid.*).

It was the spread of AIDS, together with outbreaks of Legionnaire's Disease and of salmonella food poisoning which spurred the government to set up a committee to review public health services (HMSO, 1988). It is not surprising therefore that the overwhelming emphasis in the subsequent report is on the control of communicable disease, with only scattered references to the role of public health measures in tackling non-communicable disease. AIDS and HIV infection are referred to as: 'Perhaps the greatest challenge to public health in recent years' (HMSO, 1988, p. 47). The clinical, bio-medical perspective on the aetiology of communicable disease is evident when the report refers to: 'the microbes which give rise to communicable disease and infection' (*ibid.*, p. 45). In line with this view of the primary importance of individual pathology, we have seen the decline of medical interest in the environment.

Blume (1982), in discussing the different approaches to explaining the considerable differences which remain in the health status of different socio-occupational groups in Britain, argues that epidemiology has become subordinate to a clinical, individualistic, medical perspective; and that although epidemiologists still study populations, their ultimate concern is with the health or ill-health of individuals and with how far linkages (for example, between health and housing) can be confirmed by, or are plausible in the light of, clinical and laboratory studies and biomedical theories. For Blume,

Table 3.1 Mortality rates: 1922–31

	Total death rate per 1000 living	TB death rate per 1000 living	Infant mortality per 1000 births
Tynemouth CB	12.77	1.4	83
Rudyerd Ward	16.31	1.9	109
Clive Street	20.8	4.8	143

Gateshead – i.e. 14.87 per 1000 population. In Barnes Close there were 90 – i.e. 33.93 per 1000 population (Byrne *et al.*, 1986, p. 20).

'epidemiology is at root no less individualistic than are the basic biomedical sciences with which it is linked in a common endeavour' (1982, p. 26), and 'epidemiologists see their field as serving to complement the insights gained from clinical and laboratory study in the understanding of disease aetiologies' (*ibid.*, p. 30). Blume quotes from Susser to the effect that: 'despite the epidemiologist's insistence on studying populations, his ultimate concern is with health, disease, and death as it occurs in individuals' (Susser, 1973, p. 59). The question we are asking is, whether this individualistic emphasis is necessary and whether it helps or hinders our understanding of relationships such as those between housing and health?

3.4
'Aggregate health' and housing

By way of illustration, we can look at how in the 1930s the concept of 'aggregate health' was used to justify action to improve housing conditions. Table 3.1 is taken from the evidence of the Medical Officer of Health for Tynemouth County Borough to the public enquiry dealing with the Clive Street Clearance Area, held in February 1933 (evidence held in Local Studies Centre, North Shields).

The important point is that this sort of evidence was aggregate and dealt with spatially defined collectivities; it was not 'individualistic'. If a Medical Officer of Health had asserted that the housing conditions of Barnes Close, in Table 3.1, caused any individual case of tuberculosis, then he would have been guilty of the 'ecological fallacy' to which we shall return. Subject to subsequent discussion about 'causality', he was on much safer ground when he said that the poor housing conditions caused the higher rate of tuberculosis in the area and went on to prescribe clearance as an effective treatment for the health of the residents in the area as a whole.

Here we want to explore this issue of 'aggregate health' in two ways. One will be by considering the real, as opposed to merely technical, implications of the issues which statisticians describe in terms of the 'ecological fallacy' and 'hierarchical data structures'; and the other is literary/historical, which we will address first.

In *Braided Lives*, a quasi-autobiographical novel by Marge Piercy (1982), the narrator's mother who is a working-class woman in Detroit warns her college student daughter to be careful in her dealings with her new social contacts because 'to the rich, we're just laying chickens'. This is a powerful and interesting metaphor. Suppose we were to think of the relationship between medicine and urban, working-class populations as being essentially veterinary in character, particularly before the introduction of the National Health Service (NHS), and certainly before the introduction of Health Insurance in 1912 (although the emphasis on the restoration of the health of the worker in that measure can also be interpreted in veterinary terms). In the nineteenth century urban, working-class populations were of interest to capitalists essentially as sources of labour power. Ill-health, as Chadwick showed in 1842, reduced the capacity for labour power's application — it stopped the chickens laying! What was to be done about it? If we continue this simplistic and very partial account (it ignores the capacity of working-class groups for collective action and assertion of their own interests), we could prescribe as veterinarians — better coops for more eggs. We would not be very much interested in the health of individual chickens, unless they were favoured pets whose owners paid for individual treatment, the historical essential for curative interventions by practitioners of medicine of all kinds. We would improve the health and hence productivity of the fowl yard as a whole by prescribing better coops. The foregoing is very simplistic, especially because the urban working-classes were not flocks of chickens and were perfectly capable of acting collectively to demand better public health for themselves. Such collectively orientated demands were far more important than demands for the provision of curative health services, not least because people had an accurate and cynical view of the potential contribution of such curative intervention. However, the metaphor is useful because in the use of veterinary science for normal agricultural production the individual has scant importance.

3.5

The ecological and atomist fallacies

Let us come at the same thing through a consideration of the 'ecological fallacy' which as Hammond (1973) has indicated, is 'short hand for . . . the use of aggregate data for inference to individuals'. In the early 1970s there was some debate in the *Transactions of the Institute of British Geographers* which derived from J. A. Gigg's studies of the spatial distribution of schizophrenics in Nottingham (Gudgeon, 1973; Giggs, 1973). In a subsequent article, R. A. Johnson (1976, p. 119) sought to distinguish between 'areal' and 'ecological' studies:

These investigations relating the 'contents' of social areas to the behaviour of the residents are termed areal studies of behaviour here . . . Areal studies are not able to discern the operation of structural or neighbourhood effects, since they make no reference to the internal set of forces, what we might term the individual effects . . . ecological studies require three data sets – referring to individual pre-dispositions towards certain behaviour, to the distribution of individuals with those pre-dispositions, and to the resultant behaviour.

Hakim (1978, p. 81) in explicit reference to Johnson's arguments, states that the linking of 'interview data on respondents to a survey . . . with information on their neighbourhood characteristics . . . is the only means of avoiding the ecological fallacy in testing causal hypotheses about environmental influences on social behaviour'.

From this point of view, the MOHs of the 1930s were clearly dealing with 'areal studies' and an epidemiologist with contemporary (i.e. mid-1980s) individualistic orientation (i.e. interest in the aetiology of disease in individuals) could dismiss their evidence in a consideration of the causes of diseases such as tuberculosis. Note we are not dealing here with the problems of spurious correlation, to which we shall return in a consideration of what J. A. Giggs calls the 'breeder versus drift' debate. We are dealing with issues of cross-level inference (Giggs, 1979).

However, the recommended solution to the problem (i.e. the writing of areal data to individual cases) raises a problem of equal magnitude to that of the 'ecological fallacy'. Indeed, the 'atomist fallacy' might be regarded as of far greater importance. This term refers to the way in which case-centred data distracts from the nature of social structure. Wright Mills (1959) criticized the work of American students of political behaviour by pointing out that their survey-based strategies required the assumption 'that the institutional structure of society, in so far as it is to be studied in this way, can be understood by means of such data about individuals'. Marsh, in her discussion of this problem, seems to suggest that it can indeed be resolved, simply by writing data from 'higher levels' to the individual case, although she recognizes that this is no strategy for coping with the relationships among cases. The problem is that it is these very relationships which constitute social structure (Marsh, 1982).

The issue can be illustrated with material from another field of study. Jencks's book, *Inequality*, drew on earlier research by Coleman (1966) about the causes of unequal educational attainment among US schoolchildren. In essence, the conclusion was that 'schools made no difference' (Jencks, 1973); however, Coleman had dealt with the effect of 'schools' by writing information about the average expenditure in each school district to the records of individual children. Bowles and Levin (1968) pointed out that: 'The averaging of expenditure among all the schools in a district imports a severe bias to the data, for the available evidence suggests that variation in expenditure among schools within a district is likely to follow a systematic pattern.' Feminists have made a very similar point about studies of individuals within households in which some household attribute (e.g. ownership of a car) is written to each individual regardless of the actual pattern of access contingent on power relations internal to the household. However, if the focus is on individuals, this strategy is the only one appropriate and we were forced to employ it ourselves (Byrne *et al.*, 1986).

J. W. B. Douglas (1973) criticized Jencks's work from another direction; he pointed out that Jencks was concerned with differences among individuals in relation to the determinants of educational attainment and not inequality between groups, but that for political and policy purposes, it was inequalities among groups that mattered. The error Douglas is identifying seems constantly to re-occur in quantitative social science. Given what we have had to say about the individualistic orientation of contemporary epidemiology, it is perhaps not surprising that a concept which is about relations among collectivities would be employed as an attribute of individuals in analyses. Jones and Cameron (1984) asserted that 'Social Class [is] an embarrassment to epidemiology'; they make a number of valid points about the nature of the process by which the Registrar-General's social class classification has been constructed, and say: 'If we wish to follow the course of changes in the health and ill-health of the working class in relation to the classes in society, we require a classification based on a set of principles which bring together a theoretical and practical tradition which is an expression of human history' (p. 44).

This, surely, is incontestable, and Jones and Cameron (1984) cite the ideas of Adam Smith and Marx as possible models; however, they then go on to say, 'If what is required is an analysis of society showing the importance of some circumstance which society can change for the better, and about which we have a theory on the genesis of this or that disease, then we should make the analysis of that circumstance central' (authors' emphasis, and so far so good):

We should identify in each case the status of each **individual**'s [emphasis added] educational achievement, subsistence level, degree of overcrowding in housing, or whatever conditions in which we are interested. If the analysis supports our theory we should make the appropriate recommendations for change. (*ibid.*, p. 45)

The reference to disease rather than health is worth flagging, but what we find most interesting is that even in this contribution, in which an approach to conceptualizing class is made, studies are to remain of individuals rather than collectivities. What we are saying is that it is possible to conceptualize health as a collective attribute of the household, of the spatially defined collectivity and of the (properly understood) social class. In practice, given the great importance of class as a demarcator of location in space and of (using a Weberian frame of reference) access to resources including housing, spatial and class location are very much interconnected. Out of this, we can construct an idea of 'community' and attempt to assess 'community health'.

3.6

The causes of health and illness

We will deal with how this might be done in the next section of this chapter, for there is one further 'theoretical' problem about the relationship between 'housing' and 'environment' which we have to get out of the way first. However, an example will serve to make the point and provide us with useful illustrative material.

In the construction of the Moyard Health Profile (EHSSB Working Party, 1986) it was found that the proportion of low birth weight babies whose mothers lived in Moyard, in west Belfast, was 'almost twice that for North and West Belfast District and over twice that of the proportion for the Eastern Board as a whole'. Low birth weight can be used as a modern alternative to infant mortality. It is an important indicator relating to maternal and child health which are closely associated with long-term poor health records. Given this simple (and as we shall see, easily obtained) piece of information, we can say that we have an indication of poor health in the aggregate of Moyard babies; and given the certainty of variation in individual birth weights among Moyard babies, this is far more appropriate as a way of looking at the situation than any analysis which wrote 'Moyard' to a variable set for each baby and explored the influences of location on birth weight.

Here it is worth making something explicit which has so far been left implicit. It is necessary to understand that our approach to social epidemiology (if not to other types of analysis: Byrne, 1989) is informed by a 'realist' rather than a 'positivist' epistemology. Epistemology can be defined as the way in which science 'knows what is real'. It is concerned with philosophical justification of our methods of understanding the phenomena we investigate. The dominant epistemological position in biomedical science has, in modern times, been positivist. We do not have space here for a developed account of the differences between positivism and realism, and readers are referred to Keat (1979), Sayer (1984) and Outhwaite (1987). However, one difference is of such importance that it does merit elaboration. In the positivist framework, the emphasis in understanding is on single causes with associated individual effects. The cause of an infectious disease, for example, is seen as a micro-organism. Bradbury (1933) in his classic investigation of the causes of TB acknowledged this positivist principle: 'In one sense there is only one cause of Tuberculosis, the TB bacillus.' However he promptly went on to be a 'realist' (before the term was coined) by saying that exposure to the bacillus was necessary for the development of clinical TB in a patient, but was not sufficient. Many who were exposed did not develop the disease. Why not? Bradbury attributed this to better housing, better nutrition and not being Irish. The last is interesting because what he was asserting was that those of Irish descent had had one generation less of exposure to the conditions of urban life and pandemic Tuberculosis and, in consequence, had not been as winnowed for natural resistance.

We have here, as with Graham's account of cigarette smoking, a multicausal account which involves a causal system rather than a single causal factor. The contraction of clinical tuberculosis did depend on exposure, but in an urban industrial era when the disease was pandemic, almost everyone was exposed. The likelihood of developing the disease was reduced by better genetic resistance (the consequence of winnowing over generations) and better phenotypical resistance (the consequence of better feeding and better housing conditions).

The exact mode of operation of housing conditions in relation to TB is worth considering further. Traditionally, of course, the emphasis was on overcrowding and consequent insufficient air. This reflected a recognition of the airborne mode of infection of the bacillus. However, it may be that this was not all that important in itself. Housing space standards, in terms of cubic capacity, were substantially reduced for new construction in the 1930s by a reduction in minimum ceiling heights, and this seems to have had no impact on the general decline in the incidence of and mortality from TB. This is probably because the new houses were better heated and less likely to facilitate general, debilitating respiratory infections. Other things being equal, generous internal space which is well ventilated (big, draughty rooms), are less likely to facilitate infection, but if resistance is the crucial factor, the well-fed, warm young adult without a childhood history of debilitating minor respiratory infection is better equipped to face the danger.

Realism deals precisely with causal systems of the kind described here. An understanding of the realist position gives us an explanation of why the greatest contributions made by scientifically informed measures to human health were in fact informed by scientific error. The introduction of public health interventions was informed by a miasmic theory of infectious disease. Get rid of the smells and the disease will go – and it did! Of course, what happened is that clean water, decent scavenging and effective sewers got rid of noxious micro-organisms along with the largely harmless ones which caused the rot. It was the 'urban ecology' which caused early nineteenth-century urban disease and public health interventions transformed that ecology. They changed the system.

Bio-mechanical medicine (Stacey, 1988) has mounted two challenges to the effective practical realism of sanitary primacy in public health. One of these, which has some force, is that associated with the emphasis on the contagious nature of infectious disease. It is the undoubted significance of contagion which underpins the proposals for the revival of a central medically controlled public health function in the health service as contained in the recent report *Public Health in England* (HMSO, 1988). Doctors matter here because what matters is disease transmission, and medical knowledge is required to identify the disease carriers prior to their isolation. This is the old principle of quarantine.

The contagion model has some claim to efficacy. The curative challenge to realist sanitation has almost none, but it is none the less the dominant one in contemporary medical understanding and practice and hence in health service organization. The historical record is clear – curative interventions have made little difference to human mortality. Their impact on morbidity is less certain: for example, it is very likely that the palliative procedures which are associated with much curative medicine have made many people feel a lot better and a holistic conception of health would rightly regard this as a reduction of morbidity. However, for most of the twentieth century the dominance of cure in medical practice has been very great. It still remains, although it is now under challenge in a way which it was not some 20 years ago.

There is a clear relationship between clinical dominance of the medical profession and the adoption of positivism by modern bio-mechanical medicine. If disease has a single cause, then elimination of that cause will eliminate the disease. With the addition of 'magic bullets', drugs which would kill the disease causing organisms without killing the patients, to the curative repertoire, clinicians could work effectively on a positivist basis. One must never forget that even if the application of such procedures made little difference to the general trend in human mortality, it did save many individual lives which would otherwise have been lost, and relieve much suffering which would otherwise have had to be endured. However, the effectiveness of that magic, with its positivist base, is not now universal. It is significant that in the wake of AIDS – the great expression of failure of the 'magic bullet' – the public health doctors are making a renewed bid for the importance of control over contagion. These factors at the intersection of history and the philosophy of science matter if we are to grasp how we might intervene

58

effectively in the future in the relationship between housing and health. It is interesting that some exponents of realism, and Sayer (1984) in particular, have developed an account of the realist position in relation to critical theory which:

means more than merely a different way of 'doing social science'. It implies a different view of the social role of this type of knowledge and of intellectuals. It means that social science should not be seen as developing a stock of knowledge about an object which is external to us, but should develop a critical self-awareness in people as subjects and indeed assist in their emancipation.

This leads us to the issue of how community health can be measured, and how policies to improve it can be put into practice.

3.7
Identifying community health and doing something about it

Carstairs in two interesting contributions first proposed the use of: 'an area base for environmental monitoring and epidemiological analysis' (Carstairs and Lowe, 1986), and then went on to explore the relationship between 'deprivation' (operationally defined through a composite index for post code areas based on male unemployment, households without cars, overcrowding in housing and low social class) and mortality. The essential finding was that: 'the classification of populations by their area of residence (in deprivation terms) appears to offer a superior basis for the explanation of differences in mortality between health boards than does social class' (Carstairs and Morris, 1989). Of course, this ignores the theoretical problems raised by considering 'deprivation' as something separate from social class. What is being dealt with is the relative efficiency of two sorts of index: an individual one based on occupation called 'Registrar-General's Social Class', and an areal one defined as outlined and called 'deprivation'. However, the existence of the areal effects is what matters for our argument. Carstairs and her co-workers are proposing, as we have, an areal epidemiology.

That is fine but we need to think about the causal processes which underlie measured relationships between 'residential' effects (the most important component of which are housing conditions, especially if defined to include effect of surrounding environment in residential areas) and morbidity. How does living in a deprived area make people ill? There are two perfectly compatible answers to that question. One involves a challenge to another aspect of positivist epistemology in bio-mechanical medicine – the theory of levels which asserts that we can explain the complex in terms of the simple but not vice versa. Biological status can influence psychological state, but psychological state cannot influence biological status. What we are referring to here is the health component of what Sennet in a most suggestive work calls 'The hidden injuries of class' (Sennet, 1973). Being down in a society which values being up does people damage. Low self-esteem, reflecting low social esteem, kills people.

However, this is probably far too radical for most health audiences, so we will concentrate here on the bio-mechanical component of areal effects. The argument is simple enough: it is based on the premise that a lot of minor ill-health adds up to serious problems. We await with interest the result of cohort studies which will provide us with firm information on this sort of model. Douglas's cohort has now reached the age of 44, and over the next 20 years we will start to see the patterns of premature mortality and the relations of these patterns with life experiences. We would place particular emphasis on low-grade respiratory infections in early life, but these are likely to be important throughout life. We may all be programmed to die at some point, but some of us suffer insults to our biology which pre-empt that programme. Even more important than early death is quality of life while alive. The quality of life is not good for chronic bronchitis sufferers. We need to know about associations here. How do these considerations translate into prescriptions for public health practice?

First, we need to expand our areal data base. A case can be made for the extension of the concept of 'notifiable disease'. The statutory obligation on practitioners to notify instances of a range of infectious diseases to the public health authorities was the clearest illustration of the nineteenth- and early twentieth-century concern with the health of the public as opposed to the cure of individuals. The main intention was to prevent the spread of epidemics. Notification was part of the armoury of doctors concerned with the 'contagion' model – which term, in this context, has a wider meaning than the literal one of diseases spread by touch. However, tuberculosis, which was then a pandemic disease, was also notifiable. Its

pandemic status meant that 'quarantine' was of questionable relevance. Of course, publicly funded sanatoria after the 1912 Health
Insurance Act were in part a quarantine measure designed to remove
sources of infection from the general community, but the evidence
suggests that their impact was relatively slight. It was always TB
incidence and mortality figures which were used in the interwar
period in the promotion of slum clearance schemes. The 'healthy
public policy' was based on good socio-epidemiological data.

It would be relatively easy to extend such notification. We originally suggested that a start might be made with low birth weight,
and it is interesting to see that this served as a key morbidity
indicator at the ward level in Townsend *et al.*'s (1988) study of
health in the Northern Region. We certainly agree with Carstairs
that the level to which data is coded on a spatial basis should be
the smallest possible, but post codes are probably good enough for
many purposes and can be easily employed. The real issue is not
what level to employ, but who is to collect the data?

For conditions requiring hospital admission, this should be simple
enough. All hospital records systems are moving towards electronic
storage systems. It is easy to construct such systems in such a way
as to record spatial information about events of interest. This is
precisely what insurance companies do in constructing the actuarial
information on which differential house and car insurance premiums are charged by post code of residence. This work in hospitals
is done by clerical employees (usually women, and thereby cheap),
employed as medical records staff.

The real problem lies with the general practitioners. Most morbidity is dealt with without reference to medical intervention, but
of that which does reach the health care system most is dealt with
by a GP. GPs are notoriously (by anecdote) poor at reporting what
they regard as the least serious of the notifiable diseases which they
are presently obliged to report. Can they be integrated into a wider
data collection system? This is a matter of persuading GPs to
become part of the medical record process in a more systematic
way. Again, this will become easier as GP practices also computer-
ize records. There are three ways of getting GP co-operation: the
first would be to extend the concept of notifiable disease by statute.
However, this will not be effective because it will not be enforceable. GPs will only do what they think is important. Medical education is changing as the limitations of the curative model become
apparent, but the re-education of all existing GPs is impractical,

without access to resources equivalent to those of the drug companies which continually re-educate GPs towards allopathic intervention. The second way would be to pay GPs to do this work, or
rather employ records staff to do it for them. This is probably the
best way of working. It is not necessary to have five years of full-
time and four of part-time medical education to code incidence to
area. GPs like being in charge of a 'team' and would co-operate with
this approach. The third and perhaps the ideal solution would be
to revive the idea of an integrated health service, with GPs working
from health centres for a salary as part of a local health team
including data collation staff. This would be a way of integrating
public health into the general administrative practices of public
policy but it is probably Utopian under present political conditions.

Consideration of two recent initiatives can take this discussion
forward. The first is the partial restoration of a Medical Officer of
Health under the guise of Director of Public Health at district and
regional level within the NHS. This results from the acceptance by
government of the recommendations of the report *Public Health in
England* (HMSO, 1988). This report was essentially a bid for a
restoration of power by public health doctors because of the
renewed importance of communicable disease in the form of food
poisoning, Legionnaire's Disease and AIDS. Any improvement in
public health's status is to be welcomed but these proposals are
largely limited to a concern with what we have called the 'contagion' model of public health, despite the much more inclusive
definition of public health as: 'the science of art of preventing
disease, prolonging life and promoting health through organized
efforts of society' (HMSO, 1988), adopted by the enquiry.

The RHAs and DHAs have been given a clear responsibility for
regularly reviewing the health of the population of their areas
through the appointment of a designated Director of Public Health
(DPH), and the DPH will in turn be required to produce an annual
report on the health of the area's population. This is fine as far as
it goes, but serious questions remain about the efficacy of a public
health function buried within a curative health service. It may well
be that community physicians have regained enough professional
status to make the contagion model much more central to health
authority practice than it ever has been before in the curative-
dominated NHS, but there are serious questions about the appropri-
ateness of the NHS as the agency for dealing with the promotion
of public health as the Committee itself defined it. Not only was

the relationship of Directors of Public Health with the local auth-
ority-based environmental health service scarcely discussed (and
this matters even for the contagion model), the role of public health
as a component and objective of wider public policy interventions
was not considered at all. This theme can be illustrated further by
a consideration of the objectives and content of the 'healthy cities'
programmes which Ashton and Seymour have identified as central
to *The New Public Health* (Ashton and Seymour, 1988; see also
Chapter 19 in this volume).

A full account of the development of these programmes, which
are an integral part of the World Health Organization's (WHO)
campaign for 'Health for All by the Year 2000' is given in Ashton
and Seymour (1988) but in summary the programmes are spatially
concentrated and deal with the three aspects of promotion of life
styles conducive to health, prevention of preventable conditions
and rehabilitation and health services. Targets 18–25 of the WHO
focus in Europe deal with 'producing healthy environments'; Target
24 relates to improving housing conditions; and Target 19 refers to
the monitoring, control and assessment of environmental risks. The
principles are sound but the actual practices described in Ashton
and Seymour's book place far more emphasis on modification of
consumption by individuals than on the inclusion of health as a
target in environmental policy in general. In this respect, in the UK
the Department of the Environment as the agency with central
responsibility for housing and planning ought to have at least as
much to do with 'healthy cities' as the Department of Health whose
main task is the administration of a curative service. This raises
the interesting question of the validity of the relatively recent separation of housing from the Ministry of Health. Indeed between the
wars the main agent of health at the disposal of the Ministry of
Health was housing policy.

Whatever may be the defects of healthy city campaigns which
have been sucked into the curative and individual centred system
of provision of health care, the assertion of the value of monitoring
is important. We have argued that such monitoring must be of the
health of communities and collectively based and spatially ordered.
What is to be healthy about the healthy cities if it is not the health
of the community which occupies them? Housing is not going to
be the only element in environmental determination of that health,
but it will be an important one and we need to pay systematic
attention to it.

Bibliography

Ashton, P. and Seymour, H. (1988) *The New Public Health*, Open University Press, Milton Keynes.

Blackman, T., Evason, E., Melaugh, M. and Woods, R. (1989) Housing and health: a case study of two areas of West Belfast. *J. Soc. Policy*, 1–26.

Blume, S. S. (1982) Explanation and social policy. *Jnl. Soc. Policy*, 11, 7–32.

Boardman, B. (1986) Seasonal mortality rates and cold homes. Paper presented at Conference on Unhealthy Housing: A Diagnosis, University of Warwick, December.

Bowles, S. and Levin, H. (1968) The determinants of scholastic achievement. *J. Human Res.*, Winter.

Bradbury, F. C. S. (1933) *Causal Factors in Tuberculosis*, National Association for the Prevention of TB, London.

Bradbury, F. C. S. and Byrne, D. S. (1989) *Beyond the Inner City*, Open University Press, Milton Keynes.

Byrne, D. S., Harrisson, S., Keithley, J. and McCarthy, P. (1986) *Housing and Health*, Gower, Aldershot, chapter 2.

Carley, M. (1981) *Social Measurement and Social Indicators*, Allen and Unwin, London.

Carstairs, V. and Lowe, M. (1986) Small area analysis: creating an area base for environmental monitoring and epidemiological analysis. *Community Medicine*, 8, 15.

Carstairs, V. and Morris, R. (1989) Deprivation and mortality: an alternative to social class. *Community Medicine*, 11, 210.

Coleman, J. (1966) *Equality of Educational Opportunity*, Washington, DC, US Government Printing Office.

Douglas, J. W. B. (1973) A blunt instrument. *New Society*, 20 September, p. 717.

Dunleavy, P. (1981) *Mass Housing in Britain*, Oxford University Press, London.

EHSSB Working Party (1985) *Moyard Health Profile*, EHSSB.

Eyer, J. (1984) Capitalism, health and illness, in: McKinlay, J. B. (ed.) *Issues in the Political Economy of Health Care*, Tavistock, London, pp. 23–59.

Eyer, J. and Giggs, J. A. (1973) the distribution of schizophrenics in Nottingham: a reply. *Trans. Inst. B. Geog.*, 38, pp. 55–76.

Giggs, J. A. (1979) Human health problems in urban areas, in: Herbert, D. T. and Smith, D. M. (eds) *Social Problems in the City*, Open University Press, Milton Keynes, pp. 84–116.

Graham, H. (1984) *Women, Health and the Family*, Harvester, Chichester.

Gudgeon, G. (1973) The distribution of schizophrenics in Nottingham: a comment. *Trans. Inst. B. Geog.*, 38, 148–9.

Hakim, C. (1978) *Secondary Analysis in Social Research*, Allen and Unwin, London, p. 81.

Hammond, J. L. (1973) Two sources of error in ecological correlations. *Am. Sociol. Rev.* 764–77.

HMSO (1988) *Public Health in England*, Cmnd 289, HMSO, London.

Ineichen, B. (1986) Mental illness and high rise living. Paper presented at Conference on Unhealthy Housing: A Diagnosis, University of Warwick, December.

Jencks, C. (1973) *Inequality*, Penguin, Harmondsworth.

Johnson, R. A. (1976) Areal studies, ecological studies and social patterns in cities. *Trans. Inst. Brit. Geog.* 1 (n. s.), 118–21.

Jones, I. G. and Cameron, D. (1984) *Social Class: An Embarrassment to Epidemiology, Community Medicine*, 6, pp. 44–50.

Journal of Epidemiology and Community Health (1984).

Keat, R. (1979) Positivism and statistics in social science, in: Irvine, J. *et al.* (eds) *Demystifying Social Statistics*, Pluto, London.

Lowry, S. (1989/90) Housing and health. Series of articles. *Br. Med. J.* 299, 1261–2, 1326–8, 1388–90, 1439–42, 1517–8 and 300, 32–4, 390–2.

McCarthy, P., Byrne, D. S., Harrisson, S. and Keithley, J. (1985) Housing type, housing location and mental health. *Social Psychiatry*, 20, 125–30.

McKeown, T. (1979) *The Role of Medicine*, Blackwell, Oxford.

Marsh, C. (1982) *The Survey Method*, Allen and Unwin, London.

Marsh, C., McCarthy, P., Byrne, D. S., Harrisson, S. and Keithley, J. (1985) Respiratory conditions: the effect of housing and other factors. *J. Epidemiol. Community Health*, 39, 15–19.

Mills, C. (1959) *The Sociological Imagination*, Oxford University Press, London, pp. 67–8.

Mills, C. W. and Outhwaite, W. (1987) *New Philosophies of Social Science*, Macmillan, London.

Piercy, M. (1982) *Braided Lives*, Penguin, Harmondsworth.

Pike, L. (1981) *Morbidity and Environment in an Urban General*

Practice, Birchfield Medical Centre/Department of Engineering Production, University of Birmingham.

Pike, L. and Sayer, A. (1984) *Method in Social Science – a Realist Approach*, Hutchinson, London.

Sennet (1973) *The Hidden Injuries of Class*, Vintage, New York.

Smith, S. (1989) *Housing and Health: A Review and Research Agenda*, Discussion Paper No. 27, Glasgow University Centre for Housing Research.

Smith, S. and Stacey, M. (1988) *The Sociology of Health and Healing*, Unwin Hyman, London.

Smith, S., Strachan, D., Burr, M., Hunt, S. *et al.* (1986) Papers presented at Conference on Unhealthy Housing: A Diagnosis, University of Warwick, December.

Susser, I. (1973) *Causal thinking in the health sciences*, Open University Press, Milton Keynes; quoted in Blume (1982), *op. cit.*

Townsend, P. *et al.* (1988) *Health, Deprivation and Inequality*, Croom Helm, London.

Yarnell, J. W. G. and St Leger, A. S. (1977) Housing conditions, respiratory illness and lung function in children in south Wales. *British Journal of Preventive and Social Medicine*, **31**, 183–8.

Part Two

The Identification and Evaluation of Hazards

4

DAMP AND MOULDY HOUSING: A HOLISTIC APPROACH

SONJA HUNT

4.1

Introduction

Until recently, most research aimed at investigating links between housing and health has been conducted according to a 'medical model' of disease which emphasizes individual diagnosis and individual treatment. This individualizing of health problems is reflected in the current focus on individual behaviour as a prime cause of ill-health, in spite of only weak evidence to support such a case. The application of the medical model in housing has meant an emphasis on professionally defined ill-health as opposed to a lay view; the use of diagnostic instrumentation rather than sufferers' reports; and has led to technical and moral fragmentation of the housing problem.

Professional definitions of ill-health depend upon a classification of symptoms according to accepted nosology with a view to making a diagnosis to guide treatment. There has thus been a preference for a case-finding approach, where diagnosed conditions can be linked to housing. There are three problems with this approach. First, there can be a great deal of disagreement on diagnosis between doctors. Such is the case, for example, with asthma and bronchitis. Some doctors have preferences in diagnoses and diagnostic categories are subject to fads and fashions (Allander and Rosenquist, 1975; Heasman and Lipworth, 1966). Secondly, for a person to get a diagnosis they first have to see a doctor. However, it is known that although at a given time the majority of the population suffers from some symptoms, these are but infrequently taken to health services since the decision to seek medical advice depends upon much more than the presence of a symptom (Mechanic, 1962). Thus a case-finding approach is bound to underestimate the extent of ill-health in a community. Thirdly, lay people are cast in the role of unreliable informants, even though (ironically) many diagnoses are in fact based upon reports by patients about their symptoms.

Reliance on diagnostic instrumentation, such as measures of respiratory function or other indicators of physiological function, is misplaced unless their application can be rigidly controlled with respect to timing, place and observer error. Instruments are notoriously subject to error, both in their readings and in the way they are read (Grasbeck and Saris, 1969; Bradwell, Carmalt and Whitehead, 1974; Hall *et al.*, 1976). In addition, many people are reluctant to comply with the procedures which are required for intrusive measures and lowered response rates lead to inevitable bias.

Technical fragmentation occurs when an issue is broken into separate parts and those parts separately studied. For example, the study of allergies as a consequence of exposure to mould is largely the province of doctors interested in respiratory medicine; identifying mould found in houses has been confined to building research and microbiology; measuring dampness in dwellings has been the task of Environmental Health Officers and surveyors; and investigating the reasons for the damp has been the concern of architects. These groups of 'experts' rarely work together or even pool their findings.

Moral fragmentation occurs when a collective problem is reduced to the characteristics of individuals, for example, blaming the residents of damp houses for the dampness; reporting a respiratory condition as due to an 'allergy', i.e. locating it in the individual rather than the environmental agent; or targeting individual behaviour for change rather than social conditions. A medical model of disease which emphasizes individual diagnosis and treatment has no room for the incorporation of social factors, unless, as in the case of tuberculosis, they can be shown to lead to the harbouring of pathological agents. Moreover, pointing to social factors may be regarded as a political act which lies outside the province of medical jurisdiction. Links between social problems and ill-health, which properly belong in the realm of public health, are thus reduced to the level of clinical medicine. This stance has also reinforced the tendency to do research *on* people rather than with them or for them. It is, for example, a common experience for individuals to form the 'objects' of research and never to know the outcome or even be thanked for their contribution.

An alternative approach to that of the medical model is provided by the notion of 'general susceptibility' which is founded on the hypothesis that people may become vulnerable to a variety of ills because of the social and economic strains under which they live. Geographically and historically, the poor get sick more than their more affluent compatriots from almost every known disorder, many of which have no association whatsoever with individual behaviour (RUHBC, 1989). Although the major causes of mortality and morbidity may change, for example, from acute infections to chronic diseases, the differential between the poorer and the more affluent remains relatively unchanged (Whitehead, 1988).

The most important question therefore is what is it that disadvantaged groups might have in common regardless of place or time? Obviously, lacking money, social and educational resources and without access to the power structure, less affluent people are less able to buffer themselves from the exigencies of life. In areas of social disadvantage, lack of employment opportunities, inadequate finances and bad housing are common experiences which impose daily strain. Often these problems are augmented by each other. For example, it is usually those on low incomes who live in the houses which are most hard to heat because of poor design and inadequate building materials.

Most people would regard their home as a place to relax, experience some peace and comfort and take shelter, both metaphorically and literally. Many of those who inhabit the lower rungs of the socio-economic ladder, however, do not have this luxury and are to all intents and purposes 'homeless', although they may have a place in which to live. The one place where they might reasonably expect to be comfortable imposes considerable mental and physical discomfort.

An unhealthy community may then impose a variety of strains on those who dwell within it. The well-known gradient of mortality and morbidity has been demonstrated to alter its slope according to where people live. Several authors, for example, Brotherston (1976) and Skrimshire (1978), have noted that the health experience of social class I people living in a deprived area is closer to that of social class III people living in affluent areas. Clearly, even the privileged position of the professional classes can be undermined by the disadvantageous nature of their living environment.

The medical model and the general susceptibility model are by no means incompatible. Taking tuberculosis as an example, the TB bacillus is the proximate cause, that is it must be present in order for the disease to develop, but measures like good sanitation, hygienic living conditions, light and space affect the ability of that bacillus to spread and survive. Moreover, not everyone exposed to tuberculosis will develop the disease. The great majority of illnesses find it easier to get a grip on vulnerable groups and there is mounting evidence that vulnerability is related to life circumstances (Jemmott and Locke, 1984). The treatment of individuals does nothing to alter the conditions which gave rise to the disorder in the first place. Indeed a person may be successfully diagnosed and treated, only to return to precisely the situation which created the problem in the first place. There need not be fragmentation in seeking for an aetiological agent, as long as the context in which that agent flourishes is taken fully into account.

Preventive measures aimed at socio-environmental conditions are not only efficacious in terms of long-term amelioration, but are likely to prevent not only a single disease, but a whole variety of disorders.

4.2

Housing as a health hazard

Almost all research in whatever field is initiated by a narrow range of people, usually those in positions of some power. Thus government departments may invite tenders for research of interest to them; research councils put out a list of topics they would be willing to fund (usually also of interest to the government); and commercial and industrial enterprises will also fund research from which they are likely to benefit. In addition, well-known or ambitious researchers may be able to attract funds for work they would like to do. What is extremely rare is for members of the general public, and especially disadvantaged members of the public, to be influential in setting up research of interest to *them*.

The first study

The inhabitants of damp dwellings have been largely disregarded in investigations of dampness and health, being useful only as objects of study, in spite of the fact that they might be regarded as participant observers on the topic of housing and health. Dampness has long been a concern of the Scots. In Glasgow, for example, about 70% of homes are known to suffer from dampness/condensation (Glasgow District Council, 1989). People living in damp houses tend to believe that this is bad for their health and that of their children.

However, it has been difficult for them to get any action for several reasons. First, there has not been any full-scale, methodologically sound research on the topic. Secondly, general practitioners have been reluctant on the whole to pronounce damp housing as a health hazard; and thirdly, local councils and governments alike have been alarmed at the prospect of the financial costs of ameliorating the problem, and it has been routine to blame dampness on the behaviour of the people living in the damp houses.

In 1983 a community development project was set up in an area to the north of Edinburgh, with the aim of assessing the perceived health needs of the community and involving local people in decision-making about their health. A major concern of women in a tenants' group was housing conditions, particularly dampness/mould and, in 1985, they made a slide/tape called 'Home, sweet home' which described the distress caused by living in damp and mouldy conditions and depicted the state of the houses, together with the unhelpful attitudes of housing officials and local doctors. The women were invited to give a presentation at a university seminar series and, after a sympathetic response, challenged the audience to 'do something'.

Accordingly, a small group of researchers got together with the tenants to discuss the issues and the possibility of carrying out a pilot project to assess the effects of damp, if any, on health status. It was evident that much previous research had been methodologically suspect for the following reasons:

1. It is difficult to separate effects of health due to housing, *per se*, from effects due to other variables such as low income, unemployment, selection of ill people into the worst housing, smoking, poor diet, overcrowding, and so on.

2. Investigator bias posed a problem for those studies where the same person or team had gathered data both on housing conditions and health.

3. Many epidemiological studies collect data on two sets of variables and look for correlations between them. However, most often it is not possible to forge these two sets of data into a causal model, because they apply only at the level of population. Such data are therefore subject to the 'ecological fallacy' – i.e. that a relationship which is demonstrated at population level will also be true at a less aggregated level. Such reasoning, for example, led to the focus on high fat diet as a causative factor in heart disease, because there was an association between total level of fat intake nationally and national mortality from heart disease. However, there is no way of knowing if it is the same people who eat the fat who have the heart attacks and in fact studies have shown that the equation does not apply at community or individual level.

(Kaplan, 1988)

This investigation therefore aimed to address these methodological issues and a double blind design was devised whereby data about health and data concerning damp would be collected from individual households within a defined community, by two co-ordinated but independent teams. An area, comprising one postal code sector, was chosen where the proportion of damp houses was known to be around 30% and where routine statistics showed the level of hospitalization for respiratory disease was unusually high.

Officers of the Environmental Health Department agreed to carry out a house survey which would assess dampness and record any visible mould growth. The Housing Department made records available and gave details about housing types in the area. An interview schedule was constructed with the assistance of local people similar to those who would be in the survey; this asked for information on the following topics:

1. Household composition.
2. Length of time in the house.
3. Symptoms and health problems in the previous two months.
4. Presence of long-standing illness.
5. Use of health services.
6. Sickness absence from work or school.
7. Smoking habits in the household.

8. Heating.
9. Problems with the house.
10. Employment and income.

A public meeting was held in the designated area at which the study was introduced to tenants and their co-operation asked for. An article appeared in a local paper and leaflets and posters were distributed in order that the community would be aware of the surveys. It was promised that the results of the study would be first given to the tenants concerned.

It is, of course, a basic tenet of scientific research that the subjects of the research should not be aware of the study hypothesis, lest they bias the results by falsifying or exaggerating the 'true' answers. Apart from this being insulting, by making the assumption that people are not faithful respondents, it is ethically questionable, especially where health issues are concerned. For the respondents to bias the results in favour of the study hypothesis would require a sufficiently large number of them to have implicit hypotheses about housing and health themselves, which were the same as those held by the investigators, and to be able to differentiate between those symptoms which might be linked to dampness/mould and those not linked and be aware of the existence of damp in their own house. They would then need to be motivated to give incorrect answers patterned in such a way as to support the study hypothesis. This set of circumstances is highly unlikely, even more so in view of the fact that, apart from those who are active in dampness campaigns, most people are *not* aware of hypothesized links between damp housing and symptoms. The study was conducted in the late winter and early spring of 1986. A one in four random sample of the 2180 dwellings in the area was drawn and a copy sent to the Environmental Health Department.

A team of trained interviewers visited residents at home and were instructed to interview a female, if possible, since women tend to have a more comprehensive knowledge of health problems in the family (Cartwright, 1983). During the same period, Environmental Health Officers (EHOs) surveyed houses, using protometers to measure relative humidity and damp in the categories severe, medium and slight; this was supplemented by observation. For most analyses, a composite measure of damp was derived whereby any sign of damp (i.e. damp, condensation and/or mould) was regarded as indicative of a damp house.

After both surveys were complete, the data were merged and comparisons made on a simple damp/not damp dichotomy. Because of no contacts, refusals and unoccupied houses, the final sample size of dwellings where both surveys had been completed was 300.

The results

The results showed a remarkable degree of agreement between the assessments of the EHOs and the tenants, with 83% agreement on whether or not the house was damp. Disagreement went in both directions – i.e. the tenant reported no damp, but the EHO did and vice versa. The presence of damp was found to be associated with particular streets and particular structures. Almost 80% of the damp houses were in only one-third of the streets. This was convincing evidence that tenants were not responsible for condensation/damp, which was found mainly in tenement buildings constructed between 1930 and 1936, where renovations to remove coal fires had cut down ventilation and where the new heating was expensive to run.

There were no differences between damp and not damp households in terms of duration of tenancy, weekly household income or smoking. They did differ, however, in that damp houses had more overcrowding, younger tenants and more children in them.

Health problems

There were no differences in reported symptoms of physical ill-health between adults in damp and dry houses, yet women in the damp houses did report significantly more emotional distress. Dampness was, however, strongly related to health problems in children. The mean number of symptoms was higher in children in damp houses, and children in damp houses were more often reported to suffer from aches and pains, diarrhoea, nervousness and headaches and to have had at least one respiratory problem in the past two months. These differences were statistically significant. Cigarette smoking was found to be independently associated with the reporting of respiratory symptoms. Log-linear analysis confirmed a significant main effect for dampness but not for smoking in the household. Identical results were obtained controlling for number of children in the household and overcrowding. In addition, where there was visible mould growth, there were significantly more reports of vomiting and sore throat in children.

Respondent bias was tested by comparing the reporting of health problems in relation to 'objective' and 'subjective' assessment of dampness/mould. Respondents who perceived their homes to be damp were *not* more likely to report symptoms for themselves or for their children. Differential bias in reporting by damp should result in general over-reporting of symptoms both in adults and children, but it was clear that differences in physical health were confined to certain symptoms only and to children. There was no association between respondents' emotional symptoms and tendency to over-report symptoms in their children.

This study was remarkable for several reasons: it was initiated by local people; it was the first to use a double blind study of individual households; it was a co-operative enterprise between tenants, council officials and academics; it exonerated tenants from the blame of causing damp; and it found strong evidence for a link between emotional distress in adults and damp housing and a link between selected symptoms of physical ill-health in children and dampness/mould. It was also very cheap at £2000; further details of this study can be found in Hunt, Martin and Platt (1986); Martin, Platt and Hunt (1987).

As promised, the results were released first to the tenants' groups in the area and a certain amount of publicity ensued, which generated a renewed interest in the topic of housing and health. However, the research team considered that there were still a number of unsatisfactory features of the study. For example, taking a random sample may not have been the best design, since it seemed likely that children were more susceptible to dampness/mould than adults, in whom symptoms due to housing conditions could be masked by previous health history. The study was also small and the number of children insufficient to make generalization possible. Moreover, it had been confined to one area of Edinburgh. There were many unanswered questions about the source of the symptoms and it was clear that more needed to be known about precisely why dampness/mould should be associated with certain symptoms.

4.3

Dampness, mould growth and health status

Damp conditions in a dwelling harbour several agents which might be damaging to health. Viruses which give rise to infection are more common in damp houses (Hatch *et al.*, 1976; Buckland and Tyrell, 1962). Bacteria too thrive in moist conditions, although very little work has been done in relation to their presence in domestic dwellings (Morris, 1989; Kingdom, 1960).

Dampness also encourages the house dust mite. (Voorhorst, Spieksman and Vareskamp, 1969) and surveys in Holland, South Wales and London have established links between house mites, dampness and symptoms of ill-heath (Burr *et al.*, 1980: Maunsell, Hughes and Wraith, 1970). The house dust mite population increases dramatically in damp conditions. Mites flourish in 40% or more humidity (Korsgaard, 1979) and their debris, particularly faecal pellets, act as allergens (Reed, 1981). The major problems caused by house dust mites are respiratory, especially wheeze and they are thus of particular concern in asthma (Dorward *et al.*, 1988).

Damp conditions particularly condensation, encourage the growth of mould. Mould is less likely to be found in conditions of penetrating or rising damp since the salts which emerge with the moisture tend to inhibit its growth. Condensation, on the other hand, contains relatively pure water which is highly conducive to the growth and proliferation of fungal spores, which live off the organic material on walls and in cavities, such as plaster, wallpaper and wallpaper paste. Once present, mould spreads easily to carpets, furniture and clothing. Fungal spores can give rise to three types of reactions; allergies, infections and toxic effects.

Moulds have long been known to be a source of respiratory allergens and there are case studies describing reactions so severe as to require hospitalization (Solomon, 1974; Kozak *et al.* 1980; Fergusson, Milne and Crompton, 1984). For example, a case described by Torok, De Weck and Scherner (1981) concerned a 23-year-old woman who developed severe symptoms of allergic alveolitis. Antibodies to two varieties of fungi were found in her blood serum. The symptoms were relieved after removal from her home and were eventually traced to a patch of mould on her bedroom wall. Similarly, a woman developed symptoms of headache, swollen and painful joints and breathlessness after moving into a damp house;

X-rays indicated nodes in her lungs. The symptoms disappeared spontaneously when she stayed away from the house and recurred on her return. Eventually the symptoms were traced to the presence of fungal spores in the air and on the walls (Pedersen and Gravesen, 1983).

Several larger-scale investigations have indicated that mould may be responsible for respiratory conditions which are a consequence of allergic reactions such as asthma, rhinitis, and alveolitis (Hosen, 1978; Maunsell, 1954; Fergusson, Milne and Crompton 1984; Strachan and Elton, 1986; Burr *et al.*, 1988). Fungi of the genera *Alternaria, Cladosporium, Penicillium* and *Aspergillus* appear to be the most significant in causing allergic reactions; and fungi from these genera have been found in domestic dwellings (Hunter *et al.*, 1988).

In addition to allergic effects, some varieties of fungus, for example, *Aspergillus fumigatus*, have characteristics which produce severe symptoms caused by direct lung infection. Responses to the inhalation of fungal spores can range from mild through acute and severe, with flu-like symptoms, to the causation of irreversible changes in lung function after chronic exposure. Systemic infections start normally in the lung, sometimes migrating to other organs, including heart, brain and kidneys. Such invasive diseases are rare and usually require both a high concentration of a particular fungus and a very susceptible individual (Tobin *et al.*, 1987).

Certain fungi produce metabolites which can be toxic. These mycotoxins are contained in the spores of toxigenic fungi and have been established as causes of illness in humans and animals (Smith and Moss, 1985). Reports of human reactions have been mainly associated with ingestion rather than inhalation and most reports have focused upon food contamination. However, food may become contaminated by fungi in domestic dwellings and spores may well be swallowed with mucus, especially where in the presence of respiratory problems there is a tendency for breathing to be done through the mouth.

Mycotoxins are readily absorbed through the membranes in the respiratory tract and enter the bloodstream causing damage to other parts of the body. Their presence in the lungs may interfere with immunity and contribute to diffuse alveolitis (Northup and Kilburn, 1978). Since mycotoxins can affect the immune system, they may also contribute to the severity of allergies and infections.

The development of reactions to fungi requires repeated exposure, which can be expected to occur where dwellings are damp. Since the severity of the effects may be related to the vulnerability of the person, young children, the elderly and those who are already ill may be particularly at risk.

The second study

It was decided to set up a second study which would address some of the unanswered questions associated with the first one. In addition, it was obvious that a larger study concentrating on vulnerable groups and carried out at several sites would have more power in terms of generalization of the findings. In view of the literature suggesting a strong relationship between fungal contamination of houses and varied symptomatology, the decision was made to investigate further the role of fungi in ill-health and to try to identify the domestic fungi responsible. As a direct consequence of the first study, Glasgow and Edinburgh district councils were willing to support a further project. In addition, it was possible to obtain money from the London Research Centre. Accordingly, the study was set up to take place in all three cities. Once again, tenants' groups declared their willingness to become involved and discussions about feasibility and the design of the study and the questionnaire were held with groups in Scotland and England; the objectives of the study were:

1. To establish the extent of dampness in a dwelling and grade each dwelling on a dampness scale.
2. To establish whether or not mould growth was present and to grade dwellings in terms of the extent and severity of surface mould growth.
3. To establish the air-borne fungal spore concentration.
4. Focusing on young families, to compare the physical and mental health of children in damp/mouldy housing with that of children in non-damp/mouldy houses.
5. To analyse samples of wall and air mould in order to identify specific genera of fungal spores present.
6. To identify and describe the building type, structural characteristics, heating arrangements and renovations to the building of the sample dwellings in relation to dampness/mould.

One of the major problems with studies of housing and health has been the lack of co-operation between various interested parties and the tendency to 'technical fragmentation' described earlier. Thus architects, housing officials, Environmental Health Officers, doctors, tenants and academic researchers, all with an interest in the same topic, have operated more or less independently of one another and there has been no avenue or indeed strategy for sharing relevant information.

Thus an important feature of this second study was the involvement and co-operation of workers from many different areas of interest. Architectural advice and practical assistance with the house survey was given by members of the Technical Services Agency, a tenant-owned architectural company in Glasgow. A lecturer in environmental health and some of his students devised the first-ever scales for the grading of dampness and mould. Microbiologists offered help with the identification of fungi, and a microbiologist was employed on the project. Officials from the various housing departments gave access to records and helped to provide contact with tenants' groups. Members of tenants' groups and community councils gave advice and information about their areas and proved invaluable in helping to identify the location of young families. A Community Health Resource Unit acted as a meeting-place and information distribution centre. Three research workers co-ordinated the study, arranged and designed the health survey and carried out the final data analysis.

Methods

Within each of the three cities, areas of council-owned housing were identified where there was a high proportion of families with young children (i.e. under 16 years of age) where there was known to be a high prevalence of damp housing and homogeneity in terms of socio-economic status, and where there existed information on housing types and any renovations.

Since official information is not held on family composition by address, the sample was identified in two ways: by tenants going out and identifying families on a list of addresses who met the study criteria, and where this was not possible, by interviewers identifying suitable families at the time of the health survey.

The study was carried out in the winter of 1988 and the procedure was approximately the same in each city at each site. Leaflets were distributed informing residents about a health survey, but not its purpose. Interviewers contacted families and carried out a health interview based upon a modified and expanded version of the schedule in the first study. In addition, questions were asked about the respondents' perception of any housing problems. The addresses where interviews had been successfully carried out were relayed to the surveying team which then visited the same addresses and surveyed the building, assessed levels of dampness, took samples of wall mould if present and took samples of air from each room. Petri dishes containing wall and air samples were taken each day to the laboratory, refrigerated and cultured. Air spore counts were calculated and fungi identified, where possible.

The study constituted a triple blind procedure, in so far as none of the three sets of data was put together until after the surveys were completed. The final sample size, based upon dwellings where both the health survey and the technical survey had been successfully completed, was 1124 adults and 1169 children.

Results of the second study

A comparison of the assessment of dampness/mould by respondents with that of the surveyors showed about 70% agreement with disagreements going in both directions. All the relationships between housing and health status reported here are based upon the surveyors' assessment of the house and not the respondents' assessments.

Initially, the respondents were divided into those whose homes had no dampness/mould, those with damp only and those with damp and mould, in order to ascertain any differences in the characteristics of the respondents. There were no differences between groups with respect to employment status (almost 50% of the whole sample were unemployed), marital status, income (approx. one-half of the sample had a household income of less than £80 per week), number of children in the house, respondent's sex, smoking in the household, overcrowding, or the amount spent on food and heating. Respondents did, however, differ by length of time at the address, but since the average time at any address was almost five years, this was not considered to be an important factor in respect of health experience.

A comparison of children in damp and non-damp dwellings showed significantly more vomiting, wheeze, irritability, fever and poor appetite under damp conditions, with significantly more wheeze, sore throat, cough, runny nose, headaches and fever in the presence of mould. Data were analysed for a 'dose–response' relationship between symptoms, dampness, visible mould and air spore count, by comparing number of symptoms reported at different levels of damp and mould (i.e. none, low, moderate and high). There was a significant dose–response relationship between aches and pains, wheeze, vomiting, headaches, sore throat, irritability, fever, poor appetite, cough and runny nose and dampness, with the likelihood of any symptom being present increasing as the dampness score increased. In relation to the amount of visible mould, six symptoms showed a dose–response relationship; these were wheeze, sore throat, irritability, headaches, fever and runny nose. For air spore count, there was a dose–response relationship with wheeze, fever and irritability. Since a number of other variables are known to produce some of these symptoms in children, analyses were carried out to assess the contribution of overcrowding, unemployment, income and smoking by the respondent and by anyone in the household. Regardless of the presence of smokers, symptoms were always higher in damp/mouldy houses. In the case of wheeze, cough and runny nose, both smoking and mould contributed to symptom levels, but for sore throat, headaches and fever symptom levels were *lower* in smoking households. It was thus concluded that smoking and mould have independent effects. Univariate analysis showed that when all other factors affecting symptoms were controlled for, a significant effect of dampness/mould remained for wheeze, sore throat, headaches and fever. Vomiting and diarrhoea were better accounted for by overcrowding and unemployment and emotional symptoms were clearly linked to unemployment. Runny nose was better accounted for by reports that the house was 'too cold'. The four relevant symptoms, that is wheeze, sore throat, fever and headaches, were consistent with the effects due to allergies and infections caused by fungi.

Four types of sources of error were considered in relation to interpretation of the results: investigator, respondent and selection bias and confounding variables. Investigator bias was ruled out in view of the triple blind nature of the study. Respondent bias is the feature which is most often attacked in investigations where symptomatology is based on reported, rather than clinically observed, health problems. This stance does, of course, raise the issue of whether doctors are more reliable observers of symptoms than parents and guardians, an issue which has never been resolved. There are good reasons to suppose that respondent bias could not account for the results of this investigation. First, it could be expected to be a general rather than a specific phenomenon, so that all or most symptoms would be over-reported by people who believed their homes to be damp. This was not the case. All analyses were based upon the relationship between surveyor observed damp-ness and mould levels and reported symptoms and this was in fact closer than relationships between symptoms and respondent perceived dampness/mould. There were significant dose–response findings which would have required respondents to be familiar with the grading system developed by the surveyors. This was imposs-ible. Finally, since the significant results were confined to four specific symptoms and these were consistent with effects of mould, respondent bias would have required familiarity with the relevant literature, an unlikely state of affairs.

Selection bias could have occurred where children already suffer-ing from the symptoms in question had come by some process to live in houses characterized by damp and mould. This could happen if the worst housing had been allocated to families most in need and the children of such families were more likely to be ill. However, in this investigation families in damp houses were not more likely to have moved from previously poor conditions, or to have moved for health reasons. Moreover, the average length of time in any dwelling was close to five years and many of the younger children had been born in that house.

Other factors such as the presence of pets, heating and washing arrangements, ventilation patterns and recent decorating were taken into account. These findings and analyses are reported in more detail in Hunt, Martin and Platt (1988); and Platt, Martin and Hunt (1989).

Mould analyses

The identification of moulds is a time-consuming and highly skilled task and it proved impossible to get through all the samples during the time span of the study, since each dwelling produced between three and seven samples, depending upon the number of rooms.

Altogether 404 moulds were identified, some rooms contained only one, others as many as seven. Species of *Penicillium* accounted for 50% of identified moulds, followed by *Ulocladium spp.* and *Cladosporium spp.* Other moulds were *Mucor, Acremonium, Chaetomium, Rhizopus, Aspergillus, Fusarium, Aureobasidium* and *Scopulariopus.* For those dwellings where surface moulds and air spores had been identified, an attempt was made to link the mould genera with children's symptoms reported in the dwelling. However, there were no consistent significant differences between symptoms and types of mould, although some trends were found and some of the fungi present had been implicated in other studies as allergenic and mycotoxic. This result is, perhaps, not so surprising in view of the simultaneous and prolonged exposure of the children, in most cases, to many different classes of fungi and the possible interactions between them. In order to assess the true significance of fungi for health problems, the relevant exposure time and 'dose' would need to be ascertained. However, this is very difficult for several reasons. First, different species of moulds have different effects and the meaning of relevant exposure is not clear, since a short period of exposure to one variety may induce adverse health effects, while for another variety a prolonged period of proximity might be necessary. For some moulds, a relatively low level of exposure may be harmful; for others, a high concentration may have minimal effects (Verhoeff *et al.* 1988).

It was concluded that different varieties of fungi probably cross-react and that the presence of many genera of fungi were responsible for the symptoms found (Hunt and Lewis, 1988). A study by Hyndman (1990) of dwellings in Tower Hamlets, which utilized both subjective and objective measures of both health status and housing conditions also found strong associations between dampness/mould and respiratory symptoms, diarrhoea and vomiting.

In general, available measuring techniques can give information about the presence of mould during short periods of time. However, the concentration of mould in dwellings can be expected to vary by room, by season and over time. Without a method of quantifying these variables, it is virtually impossible to establish mean exposure. Currently therefore the health consequences of long-term exposure to mould in the home have not been precisely established in uncontrolled environments. Nevertheless, the repeated findings of associations between the presence of mould and symptoms of ill-health, together with evidence from clinical assays, leaves little reason to doubt that exposure to some fungi can constitute a significant health hazard.

4.4

Longitudinal studies

Nevertheless, the most convincing evidence for a causal link between ill-health and dampness/mould would be a longitudinal study where health status could be assessed before and after the eradication of damp, using a suitable control group. Longitudinal studies are time-consuming and costly and require the investigator to be somewhat opportunistic in terms of taking advantage of changes planned by others (e.g. local authorities). Such changes take two forms: moving people from one set of housing to another, or effecting renovations, making significant repairs or implementing upgrading.

One of the earliest studies by Robinson (1955) in New Jersey suggested that moving people out of slums into more spacious and sanitary accommodation led to a decrease in the number of cases of tuberculosis and other childhood diseases. Wilner (1962) showed that families who had been rehoused into superior dwellings evidenced improved health with respect to lower rates of infectious and parasitic diseases, digestive disorders and accidents. The effects were significant only in the under 35-year-olds.

In Britain an investigation by Hopper (1962), in Rotherham, suggested that the residents of a new housing estate had less tuberculosis, bronchitis and accidents as compared with the area they had come from. Better health was strongly associated with better housing on a single estate in Liverpool, where improvements were being made to housing without decanting the residents. The findings were particularly significant with respect to mental health, but symptoms associated with damp, noise and security were also lower in those residents whose housing had been improved to the highest standard (McKenna and Hunt, 1990).

In 1988 an opportunity to carry out a longitudinal study on dampness eradication arose in Glasgow, when the South of Scotland Electricity Board and Glasgow District Council offered funding for the evaluation of a 'Heat with Rent' scheme and its effects on health and well-being. The site of the installation of the scheme was a single housing estate to the south of Glasgow, where a previous investigation had established that almost 80% of the houses suffered from dampness and were hard to heat (Glasgow District Council, 1986). The 'Heat with Rent' scheme involves the installation of a controlled heating system which responds to the outside temperature and where householders pay a fixed sum incorporated into their council rent. The scheme is not universally popular, especially with those on low income, since it limits the freedom to manipulate income, for example, saving on heat in order to buy food or clothes. The installation of the scheme is voluntary, although if tenants move out, the incoming resident has no choice.

The procedure by means of which the scheme was set up allowed for a 'natural' experiment, in so far as installation of the scheme proceeded on a rolling basis, with those who had opted for the scheme having it installed sequentially, allowing for comparison with those who had refused the scheme.

Due to limitations of funding, it was not possible to conduct independent surveys of the house and the health of the inhabitants. Instead the respondents were interviewed by means of a schedule similar to the one used in the two previously described studies. The design was a complex one, whereby several hundred respondents were contacted before the introduction of the scheme, followed up eight months later and re-interviewed and, subsequently, re-interviewed once more approximately one year after the first interview.

The results showed that the scheme was generally successful in eradicating dampness and mould. However, the health survey indicated that health status had declined over the period of the study in both adults and children and symptom reporting had risen in the whole sample, possibly as a consequence of rising unemployment in the area and financial problems. In those homes which had had the new system of heating involved, children were shown to have a less steep or no increase in some symptoms. Moreover, the symptoms in question were precisely those which had previously been associated with the presence of mould, that is sore throat, headaches and wheezing. The results were complicated by the fact that where other housing problems existed, such as noise and poor repair, and where financial circumstances were getting worse, this protective effect was less likely to be evident (Hunt and Hopton, 1988–9; Hopton and Hunt, 1990).

The complexity of the findings added weight to their validity, since it is highly likely that any straightforward links between symptoms and dampness/mould would be obscured by other factors which are known to contribute to ill-health, especially since strictly controlled experimental studies are not possible in the real world.

It could now be argued that the associations which have been found consistently between mould and the symptoms of ill-health, in different types of studies, in different places with different samples, meet the criteria for epidemiological association to be considered causal. That is, there is a strong specific relationship which is consistent across studies and substantially free of confounding variables.

In addition, there is reason to believe that damp conditions, regardless of the presence of mould, may be responsible for some health effects which could be a consequence of the tendency to harbour more bacteria and viruses. Some of the studies reported here have certainly given hints that there may be separable effects attributable to damp and to mould.

4.5
Long-term effects

The advancement of knowledge in the aetiology of health problems is but rarely of the type which makes dramatic headlines. More usually, it is the slow and painstaking accumulation of evidence which points us in the right direction. This stage has now been reached in respect of damp, mouldy and cold housing. It is still not possible to separate out the effects of each for certain. Most likely, since all three are found together, there are single, interactive and cumulative effects. However, the literature is scattered and general acceptance of the gravity of the situation has still to come.

If the findings of various studies reported here were to be duplicated throughout Britain, or indeed Europe, and there is little doubt that they would be, then there must be concern for the physical, emotional and social effects on the lives of millions of children. It is not solely the short-term experience of discomfort and illness, but the long-term consequences for chronic disorders and emotional distress which must receive attention. Folmer-Anderson (1984) found a strong link between housing conditions in childhood and later adult hospitalization. Barker and Osmond (1987), in their study of three neighbouring towns in Lancashire, suggested that the discrepancies in adult mortality rates between the towns could be largely explained by differences in housing conditions, overcrowding and sanitation during the period of infancy.

Early exposure to adverse living conditions is likely to increase vulnerability to illness and disease in later life. Interference with school and play activities can affect intellectual and social development. The child who is often feeling unwell will have few friends and may suffer emotional damage. Moreover, those children likely to be most at risk are already suffering from the consequences of belonging to a low-income family: they are in double jeopardy.

The links between housing and health have not been taken seriously enough by medical practitioners, local authorities or national government. Too often complaints about housing are seen as 'merely' an excuse to qualify for rehousing and general practitioners have been notoriously reluctant to lobby on behalf of their patients for what they perceive as a 'political' issue.

The dramatic improvements in health status in the past hundred years were largely a consequence of public health measures which created an environment conducive to good health. The only way for the problems created by bad housing to be tackled is for medical, housing, environmental health, research workers and tenants' organizations to co-operate in making the issue of housing a public health priority.

The cost of improving the housing stock will be high, but it can scarcely compare with the cost of allowing conditions to persist which are a constant drain on the resources of the health services and which, by affecting primarily the younger members of society, lead to the stunting of human potential and the perpetuation of social inequalities in health.

Bibliography

Allander, E and Rosenquist, U. (1975) The diagnostic process in outpatient endocrine care, with special reference to screening: further study of diagnostic patterns. *Scand. J. Soc. Med.* 3, 117–21.

Barker, D. and Osmond, C. (1987) Inequalities in health in Britain: specific explanations in three Lancashire towns. *BMJ*, 294, 749–52.

Bradwell, A. R., Carmalt, M. and Whitehead, T. (1974) Explaining the unexpected abnormal results of biochemical profile investigations. *Lancet*, ii. 1071–4.

Brotherston, J. Sir (1976) Inequality: is it inevitable? The Galton Lecture, 1975, in: Carter, C. O. and Peel, J. (eds) *Equalities and Inequalities in Health: Proceedings of the Twelfth Annual Symposium of the Eugenics Society*, Academic Press, London, 73–104.

Buckland, F. E. and Tyrell, D. A. J. (1962) Loss of infectivity on drying various viruses. *Nature*, 195, 1063–4.

Burr, M. L., Dean, B. V., Merrett, T. G. *et al.* (1980) Effect of anti-mite measures on children with mite sensitive asthma: a controlled trial. *Thorax*, 35, 506–12.

Burr, M. L., Mullins, J., Merrett, T. and Stott, N. (1988) Indoor moulds and asthma. *J. Roy. Soc. Health*, 108, 99–102.

Cartwright, A. (1983) *Health Surveys in Practice and Potential*, King Edward's Hospital Fund, London.

Dorward, A., Collof, M. J., MacKay, N. *et al.* (1988) Effect of house dust mite avoidance measures on adult atopic asthma. *Thorax*, 43, 98–102.

Fergusson, R., Milne, L. and Crompton, G. (1984) Penicillium allergic alveolitis: faulty installation of central heating. *Thorax*, 39, 294–8.

Folmer-Anderson, T. (1984) Persistence of social and health problems in the welfare state: a Danish cohort experience from 1948–1979. *Soc. Sci. Med.* 18, 555–60.

Glasgow District Council (1986) *House Conditions Survey*. Glasgow District Council, Lomond House, Glasgow.

Glasgow District Council (1989) *House Conditions Survey*. Glasgow District Council, Lomond House, Glasgow.

Grasbeck, R. and Saris, N. (1969) Establishment and use of normal values. *Scand. J. Clin. Lab. Invest. Suppl.*, 110, 62–63.

Hall, R., Horrocks, J., Clamp, S. and Dedombal, F. (1976) Observer variation in assessment of results of surgery for peptic ulceration. *BMJ*, 1, 814–16.

Hatch, M. T., Holmes, M. J., Deig, E. F. *et al.* (1976) Stability of airborne Rhinovirus Type 2 under atmospheric and physiological conditions. *Abstr. Ann. Meet. Am. Soc. Microbiol.*, Q18, 193.

Heasman, M. and Lipworth, L. (1966) *Accuracy of Certification and Cause of Death*, Studies on Medical and Population Subjects No. 20, General Register Office, London.

Hopper, J. M. (1962) Disease, health and housing. *Medical Officer*, 107, 97.

Hopton, J. and Hunt, S. M. (1990) Changes in health as a consequence of changes in housing. Paper presented at the Society for Social Medicine Conference. Glasgow, 12–16 Sept.

Hosen, H. (1978) Moulds in allergy. *J. Asthma Res.*, 15, 151–6.

Hunt, S. M., Martin, C. J. and Platt, S. P. (1986) Health and housing in a deprived area of Edinburgh. Paper presented at Conference on

Unhealthy Housing: A Diagnosis, University of Warwick, 14–16 December.

Hunt, S. M., Martin, C. J. and Platt, S. P. (1988) *Damp Housing, Mould Growth and Health Status: Part I*, Report to the Funding Bodies, Glasgow and Edinburgh District Councils.

Hunt, S. M. and Hopton, J. (1988–9) *Changing Housing Conditions in Relation to Health and Well-being*, Reports to the Funding Bodies, pts. I–III, SSEB/Glasgow District Council.

Hunt, S. M. and Lewis, C, (1988) *Damp Housing, Mould Growth and Health Status: Part II*, Report to the Funding Bodies, Glasgow and Edinburgh District Councils.

Hunter, C. A., Grant, C., Flannigan, B. and Bravery, A. F. (1988) Mould in buildings: the air spora of domestic dwellings. *Internat. Biodeterioration*, 24, 81–101.

Hyndman, S. J. (1990) Housing dampness and health among British Bengalis in East London. *Soc. Sci. Med.*, 30, 131–41.

Jemmott, J. B., II and Locke, S. E. (1984) Psychosocial factors, immunologic mediation and human susceptibility to infectious disease: how much do we know? *Psychol. Bull.*, 95, 78–108.

Kaplan, R. (1988) The value dimensions in studies of health promotion, in: Spacapan, S. and Oskamp, S. (eds) *The Social Psychology of Health: Claremont Symposium on Applied Social Psychology*, Sage, London, 207–36.

Kingdom, K. H. (1960) Relative humidity and airborne infections. *Am. Rev. Resp. Dis.*, 81 504–12.

Korsgaard, J. (1979) The effect of the indoor environment on the house dust mite, in: Fanger, P. O. and Valbjorn, O. (eds) *Indoor Climate: Effects on Human Comfort, Performance and Health*, Danish Building Research Institute, Copenhagen.

Kozak, P., Gallup, J., Cummins, L. H. and Gillman, S. A. (1980) Currently available methods for home mould surveys, II: examples of problem homes studied. *Anns Allergy*, 45, 167–75.

McKenna, S. P. and Hunt, S. M. (1990) *Better Housing, Better Health Report to Healthy Cities Project, Liverpool*, Galen Research and Consultancy, Manchester.

Martin, C. J., Platt, S. P. and Hunt, S. M. (1987) Housing conditions and ill health. *BMJ*, 294, 1125–7.

Maunsell, K. (1954) Sensitization risk from inhalation of fungal spores: 2. *J. Laryngol. Otol.*, 68, 765–75.

Maunsell, K., Hughes, A. and Wraith, D. G. (1970) Mite asthma: cause and management. *Practitioner*, 205, 779–83.

Mechanic, D. (1962) The concept of illness behaviour. *J. Chron. Dis.*, 15, 189–94.

Morris, G. (1989) Personal communication.

Northup, S. and Kilburn, K. (1978) The role of mycotoxins in human pulmonary disease, in: *Mycotoxic Fungi and Mycotoxicosis: Mycotoxicosos of Man and Plants*, Academic Press, London, Vol. 3.

Pedersen, B. and Gravesen, S. (1983) Allergic alveolitis precipitated by micro-organisms in the home environment. *Ugeskr. Laeger*, 145, 580–1.

Pitt, J. and Hocking, A. (1985) *Fungi and Food Spoilage*, Academic Press, Sydney.

Platt, S. P., Martin, C. J. and Hunt, S. M. (1989) Damp housing, mould growth and symptomatic health state. *BMJ*, 298, 1673–8.

Reed, C. (1981) Allergenic agents. *Bull. N.Y. Acad. Med.*, 57, 897–906.

Robinson, D. (1955) Slum clearance pays off. *Nat. Municip. Rev.*, 14, 461–5.

RUHBC (1989) *Changing the Public Health*, Wiley, Chichester.

Skrimshire, A. (1978) *Area Disadvantage, Social Class and the Health Service*, Social Evaluation Unit, University of Glasgow.

Smith, J. E. and Moss, M. O. (1985) *Mycotoxins: Formation, Analysis and Significance*, Wiley, Chichester.

Solomon, W. R. (1974) Fungus aerosols arising from cold mist vaporizers. *J. Allergy*, 54, 222–8.

Strachan, D. and Elton, P. (1986) Relationship between respiratory morbidity in children and the home environment. *Fam. Pract.*, 3, 137–42.

Tobin, R., Baranowski, E., Gilman, A. *et al.* (1987) Significance of fungi in indoor air: report of a working party. *Can. J. Pub. Health*, 78, Suppl. 1–14.

Torok, M., De Weck, A. and Scherner, M. (1981) Allergische Alveolitis infolge Verschimmelung der Schlafzimmerwand. *Schmeiz med Wschr.*, 111, 924–9.

Verhoeff, A., van Wijnen, J., Attwood, P. *et al.* (1988) *Enumeration and Identification of Airborne Viable Mould Propagules in Houses*, Landbouwuniversiteit, Wageningen.

Voorhorst, R., Spieksman, F. ThM. and Vareskamp, H. (1969) *House Dust Atopy and the House Dust Mite*, Staflein, Leiden.

Whitehead, M. (1988) *The Health Divide*. Health Education Council, London.

Wilner, D. M. (1962) *The Housing Environment and Family Life: A Longitudinal Study of the Effects of Housing on Morbidity and Mental Health*, Johns Hopkins Medical School, Baltimore, Md.

5

DAMPNESS, MOULD GROWTH AND RESPIRATORY DISEASE IN CHILDREN

DAVID PETER STRACHAN

5.1
Introduction

This chapter outlines the scope of epidemiological methods and their role in the assessment of environment hazards. The strengths and limitations of the epidemiological approach are illustrated with reference to studies of the relationship between dampness, mould growth and respiratory disease in children.

5.2
The scope of epidemiological research

Investigation of health hazards

Suggestions of a possible health hazard in the domestic, occupational or outdoor environment often arise from clinical observations of patients or laboratory experiments on animals or human volunteers. These observations are of great value in establishing that a risk to health *may* exist. They are of less use in measuring the extent to which a problem *does* exist in any given community. Evaluation of the importance to public health of a suspected environmental hazard requires on the one hand a detailed assessment of its distribution in the general population, and on the other hand a quantitative estimate of the amount of disease resulting from exposure. The latter information should properly be derived from epidemiological studies.

Epidemiology is the study of the distribution, determinants and control of disease in human populations. Epidemiological investigations are usually of an observational (non-experimental) design, seeking to exploit 'natural experiments' which lead to variations in the amount of disease within or between populations. These must be distinguished from experimental studies, where the effects of one factor can be investigated with other variables held constant. In the real world many socio-economic, cultural and environmental determinants of disease tend to cluster together. Epidemiologists may therefore require complex statistical techniques to disentangle the independent effects of the variables of interest from the possible *confounding* effects of other known or suspected causes.

Social and cultural background are also important influences upon the perception of illness, the diagnostic label applied and the uptake of medical services. Further, the experience of illness may affect recall of information by respondents. Any or all of these factors may influence comparisons between diseased and undiseased individuals. Thus a particular concern in epidemiological studies is the evaluation of sources of *bias* in the selection of diseased subjects, or in the information obtained from them. Bias is a feature of study design and is difficult to eliminate during data analysis. However, it is usually instructive to examine how potential sources of bias might have influenced the conclusions of a study.

In interpreting the results of an observational study, we may distinguish between internal validity (whether the findings accurately reflect the situation in the study sample), which is affected by bias and confounding, and external validity (whether the conclusions can be generalized to other geographical or cultural settings), which is influenced by the nature of the sample selected, including the effects of *chance* variations during random sampling.

Assessment of causality

Chance, bias and confounding offer spurious explanations for an association between environmental exposure and disease. The fourth possibility is that there is a causal relationship. There are few situations where the relationship between environmental exposure and disease is so clear-cut that all exposed individuals develop disease. More usually, exposure to a potential hazard increase the *risk* (or probability) of disease. This may be because there are a number of causes operating, or because the agent is only toxic to a subgroup of the population who are susceptible to its actions. A small increase in risk affecting a large number of exposed and susceptible individuals may present a more substantial public health problem than a greatly increased risk and applied to a small minority of the population.

Causes of disease may require investigation at an individual level, or at a population level. Thus a ubiquitous exposure to which only a susceptible subgroup develops disease (e.g. grass pollen and hay fever) would not be identified by comparisons of diseased and undiseased individuals within a population. Such studies would instead identify genetic factors or other determinants of susceptibility as the 'cause' of the disease. An unfortunate limitation of the epidemiological approach is that evaluation of the most widespread environmental hazards may require comparisons between populations, which are highly prone to confounding by social, cultural or other differences.

Epidemiological studies within a population are more useful for investigating the effects of an agent to which individuals are exposed in varying degrees. Associations between level of environmental exposure and disease outcome which are unlikely to be due to chance, bias or confounding may be further assessed by a number of criteria, elegantly discussed by Bradford-Hill (1965). Strong associations which are consistent with other studies (particularly studies of differing design and location), with a clear time-sequence between exposure and disease, evidence of a graded 'dose–response' relationship and a plausible biological explanation are those most likely to be causal.

However, none of these criteria should be regarded as prerequisites for a cause-and-effect relationship. In particular, the strength of an association will depend upon how precisely the degree of exposure to an environmental agent can be measured. In many circumstances, we are limited to single measurements as indicators of long-term exposure, or to indirect or surrogate measures of the agent (e.g. the presence of a gas cooker to indicate domestic exposure to nitrogen dioxide). Such indirect measures will tend to dilute associations and lead to misleading negative results from small-scale studies.

Evaluation of control measures

The acid test for determining whether an observed association is causal is to demonstrate that removal of the hazard reduces the amount of disease. This information is ideally collected by a controlled experiment, although more often it is derived from an observational evaluation of a control programme which must be justified in advance on the basis of non-experimental evidence, outlined above.

Proof of benefit in terms of reduction of one disease does not necessarily vindicate uncritical adoption of a control strategy. Measures which are effective in preventing one condition may have detrimental effects upon other diseases. If only a susceptible subgroup of the population stands to benefit, control measures may be more appropriately targeted to these individuals or their households, avoiding the risk of incurring unacceptable side-effects among the non-susceptible majority. The epidemiological evaluation of a public health strategy therefore needs to take a broad perspective.

5.3

Epidemiological studies of dampness, mould growth and respiratory disease in children

Background

The possibility that mould spores normally present in outdoor air might have a causal role in asthma and hay fever was first proposed before the Second World War and became widely accepted in the 1950s (Van de Werff, 1958; Hyde, Richards and Williams, 1956). However, as a review in 1981 pointed out (Salvaggio and Aukrust, 1981), much of the evidence was anecdotal and the literature was inadequate and controversial. Cutaneous hypersensitivity reactions to mould extracts were found among some asthmatic patients, suggesting the possibility of a causal relationship, but nasal provocation tests with the same extracts were often negative, even among the patients with positive skin tests. Furthermore, cutaneous reactions to mould extracts are generally associated with cutaneous hypersensitivity to pollen or house dust mites (Hendrick *et al.*, 1975), making it difficult to determine the independent contribution of mould exposure to the development of symptoms.

More recently, the focus has shifted to possible hazards from domestic exposure to indoor moulds. A comparison of 72 adult asthmatics and 72 control subjects of the same age and sex (Burr *et al.*, 1988) found that 19 asthmatics and 9 controls reported visible mould on the walls of their homes, a difference which just failed to reach conventional levels of statistical significance. However, there was a significantly higher proportion with immunological evidence of sensitization to *Penicillium* among the cases reporting mould growth in their homes. These and other results (Sherman and Merksamer, 1964) suggested that domestic mould spores may be capable of invoking species-specific hypersensitivity reactions in susceptible adults. However, in a detailed follow-up study of eight Dutch asthmatics who were known to be allergic to moulds (Beaumont *et al.*, 1985), pulmonary complaints were more common when the outdoor mould spore concentrations were high, but no association was found with indoor concentrations.

Against this somewhat confusing scientific background, dampness and associated mould growth have emerged over the past decade as a political focus for more general discontent about the quality of Britain's public housing stock. A number of local surveys designed to highlight the high prevalence of dampness in certain public sector housing estates have found a higher prevalence of respiratory complaints among the tenants of damp or mouldy homes. Indeed, residents in these estates often perceive housing as one of the more important determinants of their health (McCarthy *et al.* 1985; Martin, 1987).

These public concerns served to emphasize the paucity of epidemiological research into the contribution of damp housing conditions to ill-health, particularly diseases of the respiratory system. My study in Edinburgh was one of several investigations that attempted to fill this gap.

5.4
A population survey of damp housing and childhood asthma

A random sample of one in three primary schools in Edinburgh were chosen, and the parents of all children in their third school year (aged 6 to 7 years) were contacted by post in November 1986. A questionnaire asked about respiratory symptoms experienced by the child in the past year, and the past month, and information was sought about conditions in the home, including the rooms affected by 'condensation or dampness on walls' and 'patches of mould or fungus'. The response rate was 92% (1012/1095), with complete information on respiratory symptoms and housing conditions for between 926 and 1004, depending upon the detail required.

Table 5.1 shows the relationship between 'lower' respiratory symptoms and various aspects of the home environment, in terms of the prevalence (proportion of affected children) of each symptom by each housing variable. Relationships with upper respiratory symptoms such as running nose, hay fever, ear trouble and sore throat, are presented elsewhere (Strachan, 1988). The prevalences of wheeze and chesty colds were higher, by a factor of two or three, among children from homes reported to be affected by dampness or mould growth. The higher prevalences among children sleeping in mouldy bedrooms might be interpreted as a graded dose–response relationship. Cough, both during the day and night, was also more common among the children sleeping in damp bedrooms.

Tests for chance variations

Conventional tests of statistical significance confirmed that none of the above relationships was likely to have occurred by chance alone. For instance, associations of this magnitude between mouldy bedrooms and wheeze or chesty colds would occur by chance alone less than once in 1000 comparisons. The asterisks in the table indicate the degree of statistical significance for each association; those with no asterisks could easily have occurred by chance.

Table 5.1 Prevalence (%) of 'lower' respiratory symptoms, by features of the home environment

		Wheeze (past year)		Chesty colds (past year)		Night cough (3+ nights in past month)		Day cough (3+ days in past month)	
Tenure	own	10.7	(75/702)	13.5	(93/690)	7.8	(54/692)	13.2	(91/689)
	rent	*16.3	(49/301)	‡27.4	(80/292)	‡22.5	(66/293)	‡22.0	(63/286)
Persons	<1.0	11.5	(39/338)	15.6	(52/334)	8.0	(27/336)	13.4	(45/335)
per room	1–1.5	13.3	(66/496)	17.2	(84/487)	*13.0	(63/486)	17.1	(83/484)
	1.5+	11.1	(14/126)	*25.0	(31/124)	†18.7	(23/123)	15.4	(18/117)
Smokers	0	12.1	(64/530)	14.8	(77/519)	9.0	(47/523)	13.9	(72/519)
in	1	12.1	(37/307)	18.4	(55/299)	*14.0	(42/301)	16.5	(49/297)
household	2+	13.4	(22/164)	‡25.3	(41/162)	‡19.5	(31/159)	20.4	(32/157)
Gas	no	13.0	(55/422)	21.0	(87/414)	13.5	(56/415)	15.3	(63/411)
cooker	yes	11.7	(68/579)	*15.2	(86/566)	11.2	(64/569)	16.0	(90/563)
Bottled	no	12.4	(114/920)	16.8	(151/901)	11.9	(108/905)	15.8	(141/895)
gas stove	yes	12.8	(10/78)	*27.6	(21/76)	13.2	(10/76)	14.3	(11/77)
Paraffin	no	12.4	(121/974)	17.6	(168/953)	11.8	(113/958)	15.6	(148/949)
heater	yes	12.5	(3/24)	16.7	(4/24)	21.7	(5/23)	17.4	(4/23)
Coal	no	12.5	(117/937)	17.5	(161/918)	11.7	(108/921)	15.2	(139/912)
fire	yes	11.5	(7/61)	18.7	(11/59)	21.7	(5/23)	17.4	(4/23)
Damp	none	10.6	(90/853)	15.3	(128/839)	10.7	(90/841)	14.7	(123/834)
	other room	†20.9	(18/86)	*25.6	(21/82)	11.1	(9/81)	18.5	(15/81)
	child's bedroom	†24.6	(15/61)	‡37.3	(22/59)	‡31.1	(19/61)	*25.9	(15/58)
Mould	none	10.5	(96/911)	15.6	(140/895)	11.7	(105/896)	15.3	(136/889)
	other room	*23.4	(11/47)	†32.6	(15/46)	12.8	(6/47)	17.0	(8/47)
	child's bedroom	‡38.1	(16/42)	‡43.6	(17/39)	21.4	(9/42)	26.3	(10/38)

Notes:
Significance of difference from prevalence in uppermost category:
* p<0.05   † p<0.01   ‡ p<0.001
(number of children in parentheses).

Investigation of confounding

The association between damp, mouldy housing and wheeze was remarkable in view of the lack of variation of wheeze with other environmental factors in the home (Table 5.1). Compared to rented homes, owner-occupied homes were less likely to be affected by dampness (8% vs 30%) or mould growth (5% vs 19%), and this accounted for the difference in the prevalence of wheeze by housing tenure. Among homes unaffected by damp or mould, the prevalence of wheeze was similar in the rented sector (11.1%) and in the owner-occupied homes (10.6%).

Possible confounding effects were investigated further by the statistical technique of multiple logistic regression modelling, of which a detailed account is given elsewhere (Strachan, 1988). These analyses confirmed that the threefold difference in prevalence of wheeze between mouldy and non-mouldy homes was essentially unaltered by adjustment for the effects of housing tenure, parental smoking, household crowding and use of gas for cooking. This was because none of these factors were strongly related to wheeze, independent of their associations with mould in the home. However, the weaker associations of night cough and daytime cough with mouldy housing were entirely explained by the confounding effect of tenure, smoking and housing density. Chesty colds showed an intermediate pattern, the association with mouldy housing being partially accounted for by other housing variables.

Evaluation of bias

The findings of the questionnaire survey appeared to support a relationship between mould growth and asthma. The next step was to consider whether a spurious association could have arisen as a result of systematic differences in the information obtained from the groups to be compared. Objective evidence of both disease and environmental exposure was obtained in order to investigate two types of reporting bias:

1. Parents who were concerned about the presence of dampness or mould growth in the home might report respiratory symptoms at a lower threshold of severity than other parents. There was a suggestion from a preliminary study of general practice records that this might be the case (Strachan and Elton, 1986).
2. Parents who were aware of their child's asthmatic tendency might seek possible explanations for the disease and thereby become more aware of putative hazards in the home, including dampness and mould growth.

Table 5.2 Prevalence (%) of wheeze in past year, by mould in the home and exercise-induced bronchial liability

		No mould		Mould (any room)		Total	
Tested on treatment*		100.0	(8/8)	100.0	(3/3)	100.0	(11/11)
Exercise-	> 20%	48.6	(17/35)	60.0	(3/5)	50.0	(20/40)
induced	10–20%	11.1	(7/63)	44.4	(4/9)	15.3	(11/72)
reduction	0–10%	8.9	(34/383)	33.3	(10/30)	10.7	(44/413)
in FEV1	increase	6.6	(20/303)	14.7	(5/34)	7.4	(25/337)
Total		10.9	(86/792)	30.9	(25/81)	12.7	(111/873)

Note:
* Eleven children on regular treatment with inhaled steroid preparations or oral anti-asthma drugs. All other asthmatic children were tested at least 6 h after their last dose of inhaled therapy (number of children in parentheses).

5.5
Objective measurement of asthma

Many asthmatic children become wheezy after exercise, and the response of the airways to exercise has been used for many years as a measure of asthma in hospital out-patient practice. This physiological challenge was considered to be an appropriate choice for an objective test for asthma in the community survey. With parental consent, airflow was measured in 873 children before and after a period of 6 min running in a corridor or classroom. The volume of air forcefully expired in 1 s (FEV1) was used to measure airflow, and increasing degrees of reduction in FEV1 after exercise were taken to indicate increasing severity of exercise-induced asthma.

Table 5.2 shows the prevalence of wheeze in the past year by degree of exercise-induced asthma and presence or absence of mould in the home. As expected, among all homes the proportion of wheezy children rose sharply with increasing degrees of exercise-induced airflow reduction, but less than one-third of the 111 children with a history of wheeze had measurable exercise-induced asthma (more than 10% reduction in FEV1). This discrepancy is not surprising if we consider that the exercise test was measuring the presence of asthma on the day of examination, whereas the questionnaire inquired about episodes over a one-year period. One in ten children without a history of wheeze also 'reacted' to the exercise challenge with more than a 10% reduction in FEV1. This may reflect a subclinical asthmatic tendency or technical difficulties with spirometric measurements in this age-group (Strachan, 1989).

At any given level of exercise-induced asthma, children from mouldy homes had a substantially increased prevalence of wheeze (Table 5.2). This objective measurement of disease was only weakly associated with mouldy housing; indeed exercise-induced airflow reduction 'explained' hardly any of the association between reported mould growth and reported wheeze (Strachan, 1988). This would be surprising if there were a true relationship between mould growth and asthma, but it is consistent with an increased awareness of wheeze by parents in mouldy homes.

The use of exercise challenge as a test for asthma can be criticized, but it is difficult to explain the different relationships between reported wheeze and exercise-induced asthma in children from mouldy and non-mouldy homes unless exposure to mould resulted in a syndrome (or a subtype of asthma) which caused wheeze but was not associated with airways reactivity during exercise. This proposition is, by its nature, difficult to test objectively, but it is unlikely to fit with an allergic mechanism because cutaneous hypersensitivity to airborne allergens in children is associated with higher levels of airways reactivity to non-allergic challenges (Peat *et al.*, 1989).

An alternative argument might be that exercise-induced airflow reduction reflects an underlying susceptibility to wheeze in response to environmental stimuli, including airborne allergens. In this case, the prevalence of symptoms might depend upon both host factors (reactive airways) and the 'dose' of trigger factors in the environment (including, perhaps, mould spores). However, such a distinction between host and environmental factors is called into question by observations that when patients with an allergy to house dust mites are removed to an environment free of mite allergens, they lose responsiveness of their airways to non-allergic stimuli such as the pharmacological agent histamine (Platts-Mills *et al.*, 1982).

Monitoring bedroom temperature and relative humidity

One aspect of 'dampness' in the home which was susceptible to objective measurement was the humidity of the indoor air. All families whose child was eligible for inclusion in the respiratory examination survey were included in a screening survey to identify the children's bedrooms with the highest relative humidity. Details of the methods are described elsewhere (Strachan and Sanders, 1989). During a four-month period from January to April 1987, an attempt was made to visit the homes of 377 children, comprising all those in eight schools, those in the top fifth of the distribution of relative humidity (as estimated from the screening survey) and the remainder of the homes reported to be affected by dampness or mould growth. The temperature and relative humidity of the child's bedroom were monitored for six days using a Casella thermohygrograph; the charts were then digitized and the weekly mean temperature and relative humidity were correct for external climatic variations (details are described elsewhere, Strachan and Sanders, 1989). Usable recordings were obtained from 317 (84%) of the homes.

There was a poor correlation between measured humidity and reported dampness in the child's bedroom; only 17 of 37 damp bedrooms were in the top quarter of the distribution of adjusted relative humidity, and 9 were below the mid-point of the distribution. Thus, if the association of respiratory symptoms with reported dampness and mould growth (Table 5.1) were a reflection of effects related to humid indoor air, we would expect that direct measurements of the air would correlate much more strongly with measures of disease.

In fact the differences in adjusted temperature and adjusted humidity between the bedrooms of children with and without respiratory symptoms were small and none were greater than might have been expected by chance (Table 5.3). They were generally in the expected direction, with cooler, more humid conditions in the bedrooms of the symptomatic children, but these differences were very slight by comparison with the substantial variations between homes, the range of adjusted temperatures being more than 7 deg C and the adjusted relative humidities spanning a range of 26%. There were no correlations between bedroom conditions and the measurements of ventilatory function before or after exercise obtained in the examinations at school.

Table 5.3 Mean temperature and relative humidity in bedrooms of children with and without respiratory symptoms, adjusted for climatic variations during the period of the study

Symptom	Mean adjusted temp (°C)			Mean adjusted RH (%)		
	No symptoms	With symptoms	(t)	No symptoms	With symptoms	(t)
Night cough (in past month)	17.94	17.51	−1.9	52.74	53.34	+0.7
Day cough (in past month)	17.91	17.55	−1.5	52.65	53.65	+1.2
Wheeze (in past year)	17.88	17.51	−1.3	52.73	53.87	+1.1
Chesty colds (in past year)	17.88	17.65	−0.9	53.00	52.53	−0.5

Notes:
Student's t-tests for differences between means (t) have 315 degrees of freedom; all differences are non-significant (p>0.05).

These studies used similar methods to those of Melia et al. (1982), who reported generally higher levels of relative humidity in their study in north-east England. They found a significant excess of lower respiratory complaints in the children with the most humid bedrooms. However, only 44% of their sample had complete data, and they did not control for climatic variation. In both studies, we need to question the validity of airborne humidity as an indicator of biologically relevant exposure.

The discrepancy between reports of dampness and measurements of airborne humidity was not unexpected, as the questionnaire referred to 'damp patches on walls', which are a function of the temperature of the wall (reflecting the efficiency of the insulation) as much as the humidity of the air in the room. The relative humidity of the cold or moist micro-environments suitable for mould growth may be poorly represented by measurements of the air in one room of the house. On the other hand, airborne humidity is likely to be more important than local condensation as a determinant of exposure to house dust mites, which thrive in humid mattresses and carpets (Blythe, 1976) and which are a common source of allergic sensitization in children (Sears et al., 1989). Similarly, direct effects of cold, damp air on the respiratory tract should relate more closely to temperature and relative humidity than to patches of condensation.

5.6

Measurement of airborne mould spores

Since the thermohygrograph survey was unable to measure condensation, dampness and mould growth directly, further studies were
conducted to explore the relationship between mould growth and
wheeze as reported in the questionnaire. The aim was to determine
whether the reporting of mould in the home differed according to
whether the child had a wheezing tendency – i.e. whether there
was evidence of reporting bias in the questionnaire information
relating to mould growth.

A subsample of the 317 homes included in the thermohygrograph
survey were selected: all homes with reported mould growth, all
homes where the index child was wheezy, and a random one in
eight samples of the remaining 247 homes. The target sample was
114 homes, of which 88 (77%) were satisfactorily monitored during
the winter of 1987–8. Each home was visited four times at monthly
intervals for air sampling in three rooms, including the child's
bedroom. Details of the survey methods and the subsequent culture
and identification of mould spores from the air samples are
described elsewhere (Strachan *et al.*, 1990).

There was substantial variation in the concentration of spores
cultured from air samples, with considerable differences between
rooms in the same house and different visits to the same room.
Spore counts ranged from 0 to 41 000 spores per cubic metre of air,
although most were in the range of 50–1500 m^{-3}. Surprisingly, there
was almost no difference in the distribution of counts obtained
from homes reported to be mouldy or free from mould, nor was
there any difference between the average count or spread of counts
from homes of wheezy and non-wheezy children. For instance, the
mid-point values (medians) of the distribution of spore counts
obtained from the child's bedroom were 200 m^{-3} for wheezy children
in reportedly mouldy homes, 212 m^{-3} for wheezy children in non-
mouldy homes, 224 m^{-3} for non-wheezy children in mouldy homes
and 247 m^{-3} for non-wheezy children in non-mouldy homes. These
small differences should be compared to the very wide variation in
the individual counts from different samples, mentioned above.

Considerable detail regarding the quantity of different types of
viable airborne mould spores was obtained. Nearly 50 categories of
fungi were identified, but spores of *Penicillium* species and *Clados-*

Table 5.4 Geometric mean* airborne mould counts (CFU per cubic metre), all visits combined, by history of wheeze and degree of exercise-induced bronchial liability during 1986–7

Room sampled	Mould species	Wheeze in past year			Bronchial liability >10%		
		Yes	No	(t)	Yes	No	(t)
Living	All species	304	311	−0.08	381	282	+1.52
Child's	All species	223	229	−0.07	285	206	+1.28
Other	All species	309	314	−0.04	407	278	+1.67
Pooled	All species	276	281	−0.07	354	253	+1.63
Pooled	Penicillium species	39	55	−0.78	62	49	+0.75
Pooled	Cladosporium species	16	12	+0.46	12	13	−0.30
Pooled	Sistotrema brinkmanii	5.1	3.4	+0.63	3.1	3.8	−0.18
Pooled	White-rot Basidiomycetes	2.5	1.3	+1.45	1.0	1.7	−1.70
Number of children		34	54		26	62	

Notes:
Student's t-tests for differences between means have 88 degrees of freedom.
* Logarithms of the mould spore counts were weighted for the different sampling fractions among 'no mould, no wheeze' homes and other homes.
† Reduction in FEV1 of more than 10% of pre-exercise value, at either five or ten min after a 6 min free running exercise challenge.

porium species accounted for about half of the total spore count and were identified on every occasion in at least one room of all the homes. Table 5.4 shows a measure of the average spore count (a weighted geometric mean, Strachan et al., 1990) obtained by pooling the data from all rooms and all visits, for the most commonly isolated types of fungi. The total spore count was slightly lower in the homes of the wheezy children, but somewhat higher in the homes of the children with exercise-induced airflow reduction. None of the principal fungal types were strongly related to wheeze; all the differences shown were well within the range expected from chance variations.

These studies of indoor moulds offer no support for the association between reported mould growth and childhood asthma being due to substantially higher levels of exposure to mould spores in the mouldy homes. This contrasts with a recent study by Platt et al. (1989) of nearly 600 homes in Glasgow, Edinburgh and London. They found significant correlations between wheeze in children and assessments of dampness and mould growth by surveyors, and a weaker (but statistically significant) association of wheeze in children with total mould spore counts obtained on a single visit. Interestingly, no relationship was found between dampness, mould growth or spore counts and respiratory symptoms in adult respondents.

The findings described here do not provide direct evidence of differential reporting of mould growth because the mould spore counts correlated so poorly with the questionnaire information obtained from the parents of both the wheezy and the non-wheezy children. This may be partly a reflection of the degree of natural variation in airborne mould spores within any given home over time. Platt *et al.* (1989) also found a poor correlation between total spore counts and self-reported dampness and mould growth. They report a disagreement between subjective (self-reported) and objective (surveyor) evaluations of the state of dampness and mould growth in nearly one-third of the dwellings studied. These observations suggest that there is potential for differential reporting of dampness and mould growth, although the degree of reporting bias cannot currently be specified in any detail.

Although these mycological investigations are of limited value in explaining the association between mould and wheeze which was reported in the questionnaire, they do provide useful background information which, taken together with the published literature, helps us to assess whether a causal relationship is likely to exist between domestic mould exposure and asthma in childhood. This will be discussed in the next section.

5.7
Assessment of causality

At first sight, the association demonstrated here between domestic mould growth and wheeze in childhood meets many of the conventional criteria for considering an epidemiological association to be causal. It is strong, relatively specific when compared to other respiratory symptoms, consistent with other studies and free of substantial confounding by other factors studied. Assuming the duration of exposure was greatest when the child's bedroom was affected, there is evidence of a graded dose–response relationship. If it were interpreted causally, this association between mould and wheeze would be strong enough to account for 6% of all wheeze among children in owner-occupied homes and 26% of all wheeze among children in rented homes. It would therefore be of considerable public health importance.

Nevertheless, attempts to validate reported symptoms and housing conditions by objective measurements cast doubt upon the reality of the association, and provided some indirect evidence of differential reporting, at least of respiratory symptoms. Unfortunately, in this context the more objective the data, the less clearly do they relate to the everyday experience of children and their parents. Hence in evaluating reporting bias as an alternative to a causal explanation it is appropriate to question, as we did earlier, the validity of the objective indices chosen. We also need to consider the strength of additional evidence for or against the causal association between domestic mould growth and asthma. This supplementary evidence combines clinical, epidemiological and mycological observations.

Causal mechanisms

A causal relationship between airborne moulds and respiratory symptoms in children might operate in either of two ways. In the first model, which applies to other allergic diseases such as hay fever, everybody might be exposed to high concentrations of airborne spores which cause disease only in a susceptible minority. This situation would not result in any difference in the proportion of children with asthma among families from mouldy and non-mouldy homes. On the other hand, domestic mould growth might influence the cumulative burden of airborne spores, causing sufficient variation in individual exposure to result in differential rates of disease. This second model, which is consistent with the observations, would imply:

(a) that reported indoor mould growth was an important determinant of overall exposure; and

(b) that a substantial proportion of all children were prone to wheeze in the presence of high concentrations of spores.

Indoor mould growth and exposure to mould spores

The viable mould spore counts obtained by air sampling may not adequately reflect peaks and troughs of exposure but, to put them into perspective, only three of the samples in our samples in our study approached the levels of 10 000–50 000 spores per cubic metre which are typical of a summer garden (Lacey, 1962; Hudson, 1969). Occupational exposures, such as the handling of mouldy hay, are associated with airborne spore burdens of a different order of magnitude, reaching 1 600 000 000 m^{-3} at times (Lacey and Lacey, 1964). The somewhat higher average mould spore counts which other studies (Hunter et al., 1988) have obtained from visibly mouldy homes in the winter are modest by comparison with summer, outdoor concentrations. The air in all homes contains a variety of mould spores and many of the types isolated indoors are similar to species normally found out of doors (Richards, 1954; Adams and Hyde, 1965). There is little evidence of the proportion of the British population with an allergy to moulds, but studies from other countries suggest that cutaneous hypersensitivity to extracts of mould fungi is uncommon, and certainly much rarer than an allergy to pollen or other domestic allergens such as house dust mites or pets. A population survey of over 3000 people of all ages in Arizona (Barbee et al., 1976) found only 8% with cutaneous hypersensitivity to a mix of common local moulds. Among 714 13-year-old children in New Zealand (Sears et al., 1989), 6% had cutaneous hypersensitivity to the outdoor mould *Alternaria*, 3% to *Cladosporium* and 2% to *Penicillium*, whereas 30% reacted to house dust mites. A survey of 372 primary school children in Vienna (Studnicka) found only three (1%) with positive skin reactions to a mixed mould extract, whereas 7% had cutaneous hypersensitivity to house dust mites. Asthmatic subjects are known to have a high probability of associated allergy, yet among asthmatic patients of all ages attending an immunological out-patient clinic in London (Hendrick et al., 1975), only 18% had positive skin reactions to moulds other than *Aspergillus fumigatus* (which is rarely found in the domestic environment). In contrast, four out of five patients had multiple positive skin reactions, including hypersensitivity to grass pollens and house dust mites. These observations suggest that only a small minority of children in the general population are likely to have clinically significant allergic reactions to mould spores.

Alternative to mould allergy

'Mould allergy' provides a superficially attractive causal explanation for the observed association between damp, mouldy housing and childhood asthma, but one which looks less convincing on more rigorous examination. This chapter has deliberately focused in some detail upon this particular mechanism, because it is often quoted in support of a link between housing conditions and ill-health. Alternative mechanisms can be proposed such as allergy to house dust mites which thrive in humid environments. In the light of the discussion above, this would appear to be a more promising line of inquiry because of the higher prevalence of allergy to house dust mites in the general population, particularly among asthmatic patients.

Similar causal models to those discussed above would apply to house dust mite allergy, so it will be necessary to demonstrate that the natural variability of domestic exposure to mite antigens between damp and dry homes is sufficient to influence the degree of allergic sensitization and the prevalence of asthmatic symptoms. Technical developments in the measurement of mite allergens (as distinct from live mites) now make sure studies feasible (Platts-Mills and Chapman, 1987; International Workshop Report, 1988). There is some evidence from Scandinavia that children with house dust mite allergy are exposed to higher levels of mite allergens in their homes (Nordvall *et al.*, 1988) but a study in South Wales (Burr *et al.*, 1988) found no relationship between mite allergen exposure and wheeze in infants, despite an association between wheeze and reported dampness in the home. The absence of a strong relationship between wheeze and indoor relative humidity in our Edinburgh study argues against an important role for house dust mites in explaining the association between childhood asthma and damp patches reported on walls.

In the meantime, the absence of a coherent biological explanation suggests that greater credence should be given to the possibility of a spurious relationship between damp housing and childhood asthma, arising from differential reporting of either symptoms or housing conditions, or both. This conclusion should be reassessed periodically in the light of further epidemiological studies and accumulating evidence of the levels of airborne allergens and other chemicals in the domestic environment.

5.8

Conclusion

The relationship between asthma and domestic mould growth highlights the methodological difficulties posed by a disease which is episodic and poorly characterized between attacks, and an exposure which is visible and about which there is deeply engrained public opinion. As such, it is a useful illustration of the potential pitfalls which may be encountered in observational research. Not all epidemiological investigations are subject to such limitations. For instance, the possible hazards of nitrogen dioxide emissions from gas cookers have not been widely recognized by the general public. Thus it would be improbable that substantial variation in symptom reporting would occur between homes with and without gas cookers, or that considerable bias would arise in the reporting of the fuel used for cooking. Studies of clearly defined outcomes, such as registered cases of cancer, may largely avoid concerns about differential case ascertainment, but they need to address the possibility of bias in the reporting of housing conditions by cancer patients and healthy control subjects.

The focus of this investigation has been on respiratory disease, for which clear prior hypotheses existed to suggest a link to damp or mouldy housing conditions. Conclusions about the presence or absence of effects upon the respiratory system do not exclude the possibility of adverse influences on other aspects of health, including subjective well-being and psychological distress (Platt *et al.*, 1989). Measurement of these effects may prove even more difficult than objective assessment of childhood asthma. Valid indices of health and disease will be an essential prerequisite for any experimental studies of the effect of rehousing on health, given that the intervention cannot be concealed from the residents involved.

This chapter has also demonstrated the contribution that clinical science and environmental monitoring make to the collection and causal interpretation of epidemiological data. Clearly the detailed requirements of any given investigation will vary, but the epidemiologist can often play a key role in drawing together elements of medicine (measurement of disease), environmental hygiene (measurement of exposure) and statistics (analysis of aggregate data). Epidemiological evidence relates to statistical statements comparing average risk among groups, and cannot adequately describe idiosyncratic reactions to an environmental exposure among a few highly susceptible individuals. Thus clinical and laboratory evidence pertaining to a particular patient may be more useful when the focus of action is at the individual level such as in medical or administrative decisions about the need for rehousing or legal proceedings relating to a particular household.

Epidemiological evidence is of greater relevance to public policy such as the development of building standards and regulations. In concluding, therefore, it is appropriate briefly to cross the boundary between scientific investigation and policy development. Public concern has focused attention on the possible health hazards of damp housing, but these should not be viewed in isolation. There are forceful arguments for improving the standards of heating and insulation throughout the housing stock on grounds of general comfort and global energy conservation, quite apart from any benefits to health. Given the current limitations of the clinical and epidemiological data, it may be unwise to place too great an emphasis upon risks to health when making the case for eradication of dampness in houses.

Acknowledgements

These studies could not have been contemplated without the extensive collaboration of Dr Christopher Sanders, Building Research Establishment, Scottish Laboratory, East Kilbride (thermohygrograph survey), and Dr Brian Flannigan, Department of Biological Sciences, Heriot-Watt University (mycological survey), nor without research funding from the Asthma Research Council (respiratory examinations and thermohygrograph survey) and the Building Research Establishment (mycological survey). I am also indebted to Ms P. Ross, Ms B. Somerville, Ms A. Chanterelle, Ms E. McCabe and Ms F. McGarry, for their diligent assistance in various aspects of the surveys; to Dr M. Fulton, for epidemiological advice; and to Dr A. F. Bravey and Dr C. Hunter, for comments on the mycological studies. However, I alone take responsibility for the views expressed here.

Bibliography

Adams, K. F. and Hyde, W. A. (1965) Pollen grains and fungus spores indoors and out at Cardiff. *J. Palynology*, 1, 67–9.

Barbee, R. A., Lebowitz, M. D., Thompson, H. C. and Burrows, B. (1976) Immediate skin-test reactivity in a general population sample. *Ann. Internal. Med.*, 84, 129–33.

Beaumont, F., Kauffman, H. F., Sluiter, H. J. and de Vries, K. (1985) Sequential sampling of fungal air spores inside and outside the homes of mould-sensitive asthmatic patients: a search for a relationship to obstructive reactions. *Ann. Allergy*, 55, 740–6.

Blythe, M. E. (1976) Some aspects of the ecological study of the house dust mites. *Br. J. Dis. Chest.*, 70, 3–31.

Bradford-Hill, A. (1965) The environment and disease: association or causation? *J. Roy. Soc. Med.*, 58, 295–300.

Burr, M. L., Miskelly, F. G., Butland, B. K., Merrett, T. G. and Vaughan-Williams, E. (1989) Environmental factors and symptoms in infants at high risk of allergy. *J. Epidemiol. Community Health*, 43, 125–32.

Burr, M. L., Mullins, J., Merrett, T. G. and Stott, N. C. H. (1988) Indoor moulds and asthma. *J. Roy. Soc. Health*, 108, 99–101.

Hendrick, D. J., Davies, R. J., d'Souza, M. F. and Pepys, J. (1975) An analysis of skin prick test reactions in 656 asthmatic patients. *Thorax*, 30, 2–8.

Hudson, H. J. (1969) Aspergilli in the air spora at Cambridge. *Trans. B. Mycological. Soc.*, 52, 153–9.

Hunter, C. A., Grant, C., Flannigan, B. and Bravery, A. F. (1988) Mould in buildings: the air spora of domestic dwellings. *Biodeterioration*, 24, 81–101.

Hyde, H. A., Richards, M. and Williams, D. A. (1956) Allergy to mould spores in Britain. *B. Med. J.*, i, 886–90.

International Workshop Report (1988) Dust mite allergens and asthma: a worldwide problem. *Bull. WHO*, 66, 769–80.

Lacey, J. and Lacey, M. E. (1964) Spore concentrations in the air of farm buildings. *Trans. B. Mycological. Soc.*, 47, 547–52.

Lacey, M. E. (1962) The summer air spora of two contrasting adjacent rural sites. *J. Gen. Microbiol.*, 29, 485–501.

McCarthy, P., Byrne, D., Harrison, S. and Keithley, J. (1985) Respiratory conditions: effect of housing and other factors. *J. Epidemiol. Community Health*, 39, 15–19.

Martin, C. J. (1987) Responding to public need: a study of housing and health. *Radical Community Medicine*, 30, 28–34.

Melia, R. J. W., Florey, C. D. V., Morris, R. W., Goldstein, B. D., John, H. H., Clark, D., Craighead, I. B. and Mackinlay, J. C. (1982) Childhood respiratory illness and the home environment, II: Association between respiratory illness and nitrogen dioxide, temperature and relative humidity. *Int. J. Epidemiol.*, 11, 164–9.

Nordvall, S. L., Eriksson, M., Rylander, E. and Schwartz, B. (1988) Sensitisation of children in the Stockholm area to house dust mites. *Acta Peadiatr. Scand.*, 77, 716–20.

Peat, J. K., Salome, C. M., Sedgwick, C. S., Kerribijn, J. and Woolcock, A. J. (1989) A prospective study of bronchial hyperresponsiveness and respiratory symptoms in a population of Australian school children. *Clin. Exp. Allergy*, 19, 299–306.

Platt, S. D., Martin, C. J., Hunt, S. M. and Lewis, C. W. (1989) Damp housing, mould growth and symptomatic health state. *Br. Med. J.*, 298, 1673–8.

Platts-Mills, T. A. E. and Chapman, M. D. (1987) Dust mites: immunology, allergic disease and environmental control. *J. Allergy Clin. Immunol.*, 80, 755–75.

Platts-Mills, T. A. E., Tovey, E. R., Mitchell, E. B., Moszoko, H., Nock, P. and Wilkins, S. R. (1982) Reduction of bronchial hyperreactivity during prolonged allergen avoidance. *Lancet*, ii, 675–8.

Richards, M. (1954) Atmospheric mould spores in and out of doors. *J. Allergy*, 25, 429–39.

Salvaggio, J. and Aukrust, L. (1981) Mould-induced asthma. *J. Allergy Clin. Immunol.*, 68, 327–46.

Sears, M. R., Herbison, G. P., Holdaway, M. D., Hewitt, C. J., Flannery, E. M. and Silva, P. A. (1989) The relative risks of sensitivity to grass pollen, house dust mite and cat dander in the development of childhood asthma. *Clin. Exp. Allergy*, 19, 419–24.

Sherman, H. and Merksamer, D. (1964) Skin test reactions in mould sensitive patients in relation to presence of moulds in their homes. *N. Y. J. Med.*, 64, 2533–5.

Strachan, D. P., Flannigan, B., McCabe, E. M. and McGarry, F. (1990) Quantification of airborne moulds in the homes of children with and without wheeze. *Thorax*, **45**, 382–7.

Strachan, D. P. (1988) Damp housing and childhood asthma: validation of reporting of symptoms. *B. Med. J.*, 1223–6.

Strachan, D. P. (1989) Repeatability of ventilatory function measurements in a population survey of seven-year-old children. *Thorax*, 44, 474–9.

Strachan, D. P. and Elton, R. A. (1986) Relationship between respiratory morbidity in children and the home environment. *Family Practice*, 3, 137–42.

Strachan, D. P. and Sanders, C. H. (1989) Damp housing and childhood asthma; respiratory effects of indoor temperature and relative humidity. *J. Epidemiol. Community Health*, 43, 7–14.

Studnicka, M. (1989) Personal communication.

Van de Werff, P. J. (1958) *Mould Fungi and Bronchial Asthma: A Mycological and Clinical Study*, Charles C. Thomas, Springfield, Ill.

6

COLD- AND HEAT-RELATED ILLNESSES IN THE INDOOR ENVIRONMENT

K. J. COLLINS

6.1

Introduction

Indoor climate embodies those aspects of the hygrothermal environment, lighting, noise and air quality that influence requirements for comfort, health and safety. Interactions occur between the physical elements of the environment such that each component has to be critically considered in relation to its effect on the others, and this is so particularly when devising standards. For example, increasing window area with the intention of improving natural lighting can result in over-heating by increasing thermal gain from solar radiation, and conversely there will be increased heat loss from the built environment in cold external conditions. Another common example is the effect that thermal insulation of a building by draught-proofing can have in reducing ventilation and affecting air quality. Inevitably a 'trade-off' has to be made between such competing demands when setting comfort and health standards in housing design and construction. A satisfactory indoor climate also has a bearing on home safety; accidents are less likely to occur in well-lit, thermally comfortable surroundings. There now exists a considerable body of evidence to show that the design of buildings and features of the quality of the indoor environment exert a significant influence on the health of the occupants (Mant and Gray, 1986).

A basic requirement of housing is that it should provide appropriate protection from excessive changes in external ambient temperature, as well as other environmental hazards. The efficiency with which this requirement is attained varies considerably in different geographical regions and socio-economic groups within the same region. Marked fluctuations in indoor hygrothermal conditions can, and do, occur, which pose a threat to health, especially for certain vulnerable groups such as the elderly, infants, the sick and disabled who spend much if not all of their time indoors. It is, for example, widely accepted that living in damp housing is unhealthy and may be associated with respiratory diseases, though not all studies have found simple relationships between damp housing and poor health. The potential dangers of very low indoor temperature for inducing hypothermia in old people, especially those living in 'fuel poverty' has been well recognized. The concept that cold indoor conditions are deleterious to health is also supported by the finding of excess morbidity and mortality in winter, in Britain, a fact not applicable to many European countries with much colder winters but universally warm and well-insulated houses. It is apparent, as will be discussed later, that excess winter mortality can arise from the combined effects of acute exposure to cold outdoors, as well as more chronic though less severe cold indoors. It is not possible to forecast accurately the safe temperature limits for health, for there are wide individual variations. In part of this chapter, we consider the limited evidence at present available that indicates the health risks as house temperatures fall.

In Britain, health effects of excessive ambient heat inside dwellings are, for most practical purposes of minor significance. However, there is ample evidence of the hazards of heat stress and heat-related disorders suffered by residents in urban conurbations in the USA during heatwaves. Similar effects are seen only occasionally in Britain which does not have the large temperature swings of the continental climate. The effects of excessive heat in the summer should not, however, be too readily dismissed in view of the prospects of global warming and its potential effects on health (WHO, 1990). Again, the evidence for deleterious health effects of significant increases in indoor temperatures will be discussed below.

6.2

Thermal factors and health

Four environmental factors affecting thermal equilibrium of the body are relevant in the indoor climate: ambient air temperature (dry-bulb temperature), radiant temperature, air humidity and air movement. These factors interact in producing thermal stress, and between them, they determine the combined thermal load on the body and whether undue body heating or cooling will occur. Given appropriate weightings, the four physical parameters can be combined to indicate the level of environmental thermal stress. Such an index should incorporate the important modifying effects of physical activity level and degree of clothing insulation of the occupants (McIntyre, 1980).

The best single index of the indoor temperature environment in cold conditions appears to be the dry-bulb (air) temperature or, in normal indoor spaces, the 'operative temperature' (Gagge, 1940) which can be taken to be the mean of air and wall (radiant) temperatures. In warm conditions the wet-bulb globe temperature (WBGT) is one of the most widely applied indices of heat stress and, in the indoor climate, is calculated from 0.7 wet-bulb temperature, plus 0.3 globe (radiant) temperature.

In still or slow-moving air, which is the condition found in most houses, relative humidity and air movement tend to play only a minor role in determining the indoor thermal climate and its acceptability in cool conditions. When excess water vapour is released into the indoor environment, particularly in bathrooms and kitchens, or when gaps in the fabric of the building allow draughts into living spaces, then the factors of humidity and air movement assume greater importance. Cold air may more easily become saturated and cause condensation indoors and provide a more favourable environment for the growth of micro-organisms and moulds.

In warm countries it may be desirable to introduce some mechanism of cooling the dwelling to maintain a satisfactory healthy environment. It is possible in some areas to introduce cool air at night in order to lower the temperature of the building structure. Increased ventilation in warm conditions may be produced by natural means by manipulating openings to secure maximum benefit of prevailing breezes, or by using mechanical ventilation. In areas where cooling of buildings is likely to be desirable, it is good planning to orientate buildings in such a way as to reduce the effects of excessive solar radiation. Appropriate use of shades over windows is also an important measure to reduce radiant heat gain. Increased humidity indoors in warm climates causes a significant increment in heat stress, and under these conditions, dehumidification is extremely effective in relieving the thermal impact.

The planning of housing construction to meet these thermal requirements obviously needs to take account of, at an early stage, the relevant range of outdoor (dimensioning) temperatures, and specifications should be drawn up according to local environmental conditions.

6.3
The comfort zone

In a 'healthy' residential environment an individual will usually perceive that he or she feels 'comfortable'. This may be because health involves normal body functioning and the absence of physiological or psychological stress. Appropriate thermal conditions for comfort, really an absence of sensation of discomfort, may therefore be a precondition of a healthy environment, and temperature stress outside the comfort zone would contribute to an unhealthy one.

Human thermal comfort is determined by a number of environmental, physiological and psychological factors which may be defined, but there is also a component of individual idiosyncrasy. It is necessary to take into account a person's physical activity and clothing insulation, as well as the thermal factors prevailing, but it is claimed that thermal comfort standards are little altered by acclimatization, age, gender or race (Fanger, 1982). Generalizations from surveys of thermal comfort carried out in individuals' homes are not always reliable because preferences are often biased by personal circumstances which may have little to do with the sensation of thermal comfort.

The Centre Scientifique et Technique du Bâtiment (CSTB), Paris, recommended that during the winter the operative temperature in housing should be between 18°C and 22°C (65–70°F), with a relative humidity greater than 30% and an air movement not exceeding 0.1 m s^{-1} (WHO, 1961). In Russia the recommendation was 18–22°C also, and in the USA a minimum indoor temperature of 18°C operative temperature for normally vigorous people wearing normal clothing at rest.

Recently a WHO Working Group (WHO, 1984) concluded that an indoor environment between 18°C and 24°C offers little thermal threat to appropriately clothed sedentary individuals where there is also an air movement of less than 0.2 m s⁻¹, a relative humidity of 50% and a mean radiant temperature within 2 degC of indoor air temperature. Because elderly people have, in general, a more sedentary life style, it has been recommended that dwellings inhabited by elderly people should be heated, or be capable of being heated, to 2–3 degC higher than for young people. Surveys in the UK have, however, shown that houses occupied by elderly people are slightly colder than the average (Collins, 1986). The question of adaptation to the indoor environment has been little studied in the elderly. Expectations for heating in the home by old people may be lower than in younger people who have been brought up in centrally heated surroundings. Physiological responses may also change with continuous or repeated exposure to cold indoor environments, though at present there is little consistent evidence for physiological acclimatization to mildly cold conditions in either young or old.

In temperature-controlled environments thermal comfort has been found to be the same in both young and old groups in a range of ambient temperatures above 20°C (Collins, 1986). The normal range of room temperatures in the UK tends to fall below 20°C and it is therefore important to determine thermal comfort in the lower range (Collins and Hoinville, 1980). Studies in temperatures ranging from 12°C to 24°C have shown that elderly people did not differ substantially from the young in their temperature preferences, even in the low range. However, a small number of elderly with poor temperature discrimination showed a preference for lower temperatures. Conversely, a person suffering from hypothyroidism and producing subnormal internal heat may feel cold even in a temperature of 24°C and suffer stress.

In the summer, the CSTB recommended that the operative temperature should not exceed 26°C (79°F) when the relative humidity is 30% or 24°C (75°F) at 60% relative humidity. The recommended maximum operative temperature in the USSR is 25°C (77°F) with 50% relative humidity and an air movement not exceeding 0.2 m s⁻¹. In the USA it was suggested that the operative temperature should not exceed 24°C (75°F).

In warm surroundings, excessive humidity will decrease the tolerance to higher temperatures, and air movement will increase it if the air temperature is not above body temperature. The principal effect of high humidity on comfort is due to inhibition of sweat evaporation. When indoor temperatures are normal for comfort and sweating is absent, the influence of high humidity is slight. Physical activity that produces sweating may lead to discomfort. Some authors have linked high humidity to stuffiness and it is possible that high humidity may be associated with poor ventilation and odours (McIntyre, 1980). One of the main reasons for limiting humidity levels in buildings is to limit condensation and mould growth which may have harmful effects on health.

6.4
Temperature requirements and morbidity in children

The thermal comfort of children has been studied extensively in the schoolroom, particularly in secondary school children. There appears to be little difference in the temperature preferences of adults and children. Young children generally have a higher metabolism than adults; they have different restrictions on clothing, and engage in different and usually more energetic activities. All of these factors will affect the measurement of thermal comfort in housing surveys. On the whole, thermal comfort in children will principally reflect the relatively high levels of habitual activity.

Several studies have found an association between damp housing and respiratory disease, particularly wheeze in children (Burr et al., 1989), and there is an association between asthma and sensitivity to allergens from moulds in the housing environment (Strachan and Elton, 1986). But there is often a poor correlation between reported wheezing and recorded consultations with general practitioners, and no apparent association between the report of mould in the housing environment and objective measurements of bronchial reactivity. There may be a strong element of bias in reporting respiratory conditions in children living in poor housing that needs to be controlled for.

For newborn babies, the need to provide a thermally neutral environment is important during the first few weeks of life; 21–24°C (70–75°F) provides neutral conditions for a full-term cot-nursed baby more than 2 days old, but for a 1 kg baby in the first few days of life, a temperature of 31°C (88°F) might be required if the baby is nursed in a cot instead of an incubator. The indoor thermal environment is important for the health and safety of older infants too. A carry-cot placed on an uninsulated floor with under-floor heating may produce conductive heating of the baby; and similarly, a toddler in closer proximity to a heated floor will be more affected than the parent.

There are between 1500 and 2000 deaths annually in children less than 12 months old in the UK in whom a thorough post-mortem examination fails to demonstrate an adequate cause for death (Sudden Infant Death Syndrome, SIDS). 'Cot deaths' occur in about one in 500 live births in the UK, and two-thirds are in children between the ages of 1 and 6 months. The incidence is greater in winter months between October and March and at night. Many of these babies, approx. 60%, have had minor, often non-specific, symptoms in the days before death. Since the peak incidence of SIDS occurs in winter, it has been suggested that a cold environ-ment may have a direct effect, or perhaps acts by producing con-ditions where respiratory tract infections are more common. A significant correlation has been reported between minimum daily environmental temperatures and the incidence of SIDS four days later (Murphy and Campbell, 1987).

In Australia and New Zealand there is an increased incidence of SIDS with increasing latitude in these countries, which also sug-gests the involvement of environmental factors for some infant deaths. The effect appears to be most obvious in infants over 3 months old, and there is the added suggestion that certain respirat-ory virus infections may be responsible (Bacon, Scott and Jones, 1979). The seasonal and annual incidence of SIDS, for example, correlates with the incidence of brochiolitis in a community, and with isolations of respiratory syncytial virus (RSV) and, to a lesser extent with influenza and para-influenza viruses (Nicholl and Davies, 1986); RSV is a very important cause of bronchiolitis in infants in winter, often extending to pneumonia. These viruses can be isolated from the respiratory tracts of a significant number of infants aged over 3 months with SIDS.

It does not appear to be simply the direct effect of a cold indoor environment that is important; SIDS babies have sometimes been described with presenting symptoms of fever, shock and con-vulsions with no obvious cause, the only constant finding being that all had been excessively covered with bedding or exposed to external heating (Williams and Fraser, 1990). This led to the proposal that excessive wrapping and mild infection could produce potentially fatal heat stroke in infancy. Clothing and bedding selected by parents often appeared to depend on the external rather than room temperature, so that on a cold night extra blankets would be put on the baby, even though the room temperature might be warmer than in summer (Uren *et al.*, 1980).

Young infants have a higher heat storage rate than adults when exposed to warm conditions and their body temperature may be expected to rise at about twice the rate of adults and develop hyperpyrexia more rapidly. The face is an important source of cooling, so that the prone positioning of a baby may reduce heat loss and increase susceptibility to hyperthermia. There are strong suspicions therefore that thermal environmental factors may contribute to the development of SIDS, though most research on the subject has led to the view that a single cause is unlikely.

6.5

Humidity, cold and respiratory disorders

In cold air temperatures, in winter, the moisture content (absolute humidity) of the outside air is low, even though the relative humidity (RH) may approach 100%. When this air infiltrates the indoor environment and becomes warm, it will usually create naturally low RH conditions, though in the UK this will usually not be much below 35% RH. Where outside temperature conditions are much lower in winter in regions like North America and northern Europe, and indoor heating is generally more efficient, RH in the indoor environment can be very low and irritant effects of a dry environment noticed by occupants.

There are many additional sources of water vapour in the indoor environment and adequate ventilation is necessary to prevent humidity rising to unacceptable levels. In the 18–24°C comfort range of indoor climate, RH between 20% and 70% is regarded as being compatible with health, the preferred RH being between 40% and 50%.

The 1978 UK Field Survey of House Temperatures (Hunt and Gidman, 1982) found that the average dwelling temperature was 15.8 ± 2.9 degC dry bulb (60 ± 1.6 degF) and 12.2 ± 2.2 degC wet bulb (54 ± 1.2 degF) resulting in an average RH of 67 ± 11%; 46% of respondents had a condensation problem somewhere in the home, and this occurred in 50% of non-centrally heated homes and 43% of centrally heated homes. Homes with condensation problems were 0.5°C (1°F) cooler on average, mostly due to a 0.7°C (± 1.3°F) difference in upstairs temperature. In the homes of 20% of respondents, mould growth was reported in the house. The findings of this survey are in broad agreement with the usually accepted view that 70% RH indoors is sufficient to sustain mould growth.

Respiratory illnesses usually show an annual peak in winter and a minimum in summer, a fact that has been attributed partly to the decrease in indoor RH when house temperatures are kept high in winter (Green, 1982). Evidence from several studies in humidified and non-humidified buildings tends to support the view that the occurrence of upper respiratory tract infections increases when indoor RH is low. The most commonly suggested cause for this is the increased transmission of infection because of a greater survival of airborne micro-organisms at lower humidities. Higher humidities produce larger airborne particles which, it is claimed, are less infective. The simplistic nature of these propositions is obvious when it may be found that the environmental and behavioural factors involved are all strongly correlated and the statistical requirements of investigations then become difficult to satisfy.

Although the incidence of the common cold increases in winter, cold winter temperature does not in itself appear to be the cause. Isolated communities in cold climates may be completely free from colds and upper respiratory tract infections for the whole of the winter, but epidemics occur when first contact is made with visitors. The view that resistance to infection is lowered by 'chilling' in cold conditions is not supported by experimental work (Tyrrell, 1965). Objective data are lacking of a causal relationship between body chilling and a subsequent respiratory illness. Another reason sometimes given for the high incidence of winter colds is that low indoor humidity predisposes to infection by drying the oral and nasal mucosa. The flow rate of the mucous bed of the nose appears to be slowed by low humidity, but this observation was not confirmed when longer exposures to dry air were investigated (Anderson *et al.*, 1973).

The temperature of the respiratory airways in very cold air temperatures can fall enough to impair the function of the bronchial epithelium and encourage respiratory infections. The thermal capacity of respired air is much increased in the presence of water mist such as occurs in fog. Thus in a cold misty environment the temperature of the airways may fall sufficiently to impair the function of the ciliated, goblet, and mast cells in the bronchial epithelium. Such a situation occurred in the London Smog in December 1952 when deaths from bronchitis in the elderly increased ninefold and there was a two or three times increase in deaths from heart attacks. Cold air is also seen as a principal cause of asthma, especially when combined with exercise (Deal et al., 1979). Lesser degrees of cold in low indoor temperatures may damage the lungs indirectly by reducing the resistance of the body to infections secondary to colds and influenza. This effect is believed to be prevented by heating the indoor environment to a minimum of 16°C (60°F) and by ensuring that RH is in the middle range and that there is adequate but not excessive ventilation (Jones, 1975). The factual basis on which this 'lower' limiting temperature for respiratory and thermal health was originally defined is difficult to uncover. It was enshrined in the *Offices, Shops and Railways Premises Act 1963*, which proposed that 'where a substantial proportion of work done does not involve severe physical effort, a room temperature of less than 16°C after the first hour shall not be deemed a reasonable temperature'.

The effect of high rather than low RH in the indoor climate also creates special problems for those with respiratory disease. Some individuals may suffer from asthma or allergic rhinitis because of house dust mites, and the occurrence of these mites is partly related to the water vapour content of indoor air. The highest concentration of mites is found in RH above 40% at 22°C (71°F) (Korsgaard, 1979). Allergic reactions occurring as the result of moulds and fungi growing in damp areas of building interiors is discussed elsewhere in this volume (Chapter 5).

6.6
Cardiovascular responses in the cold

Below the comfort zone, cold-induced responses may take many forms among which, the effects on the heart and circulation are serious. With air temperatures as low as 6°C (43°F), it is known that cardiovascular reflexes can be initiated by cold air on the face and hands resulting in changes in heart rate and blood pressure. A seasonal pattern of blood pressure variation has been recognized for some time (Rose, 1961), the difference between the winter peak and summer trough being on average 5 mm Hg for both systolic and diastolic pressures. However, it was observed that the February–April peak in blood pressure did not coincide with mortality from ischaemic heart disease which showed a peak in January–February during the lowest average seasonal air temperatures. Confirmation of the seasonal variation in blood pressure has come from the MRC Treatment Trial for mild hypertension (Brennan *et al.*, 1982), where it was also found that the seasonal variation was greater in older subjects.

Increases in blood pressure due to cold may be initiated by a sympathetic nervous reflex derived from skin cooling in accordance with the known response of the 'cold pressor' test based on hand immersion in cold water. In an indoor investigation involving young and old subjects exposed at rest for 4 hours a day, in temperatures as low as 6°C (43°F), it was found that cold extremities and slightly lowered core temperature could lead to short-term increases in blood pressure. This, of course, could be damaging to people suffering from hypertension. After 2 h at rest in 6°C while wearing thick indoor clothing (1.5 clo), the mean increase in systolic blood pressure was greater in old subjects (24 ± 4 mm Hg) than in young (14 ± 6 mm Hg). A small rise in blood pressure occurred in older men after 1 h in 12°C (54°F) increasing further after 2 h, but not in young adults. At 15°C (59°F) there was no increase in blood pressure in either group (Collins *et al.*, 1985).

There is a negative association between the fall in deep body temperature and the systolic blood pressure increment, and in the tests described above, the mean fall in body temperature in young people was about 0.1 degC compared with 0.3 degC in the elderly in 6°C. There does not appear to be an appreciable adaptive change in the blood pressure response to cold after 7–10 days' repeated exposure to 6°C for 4 h each day. It suggests that old people living at home in cold surroundings are not likely to acquire significant acclimatization to the effects of cold on the cardiovascular system.

Raised blood pressure in the cold may have a long-term effect on the development of arterial thrombosis. In young adults who had received mild surface convective cooling for 6 h, there was an increase in blood platelet and red cell counts as well as increased blood viscosity (Keatinge *et al.*, 1984). The change in blood composition can be attributed to haemoconcentration following peripheral blood-vessel vascoconstriction, and there is evidence that new platelets are added to the circulation. Whole-blood viscosity rises by 20% after 6 h surface cooling with the major changes occurring after the first hour. Thus, in addition to raised arterial pressure, severe indoor cold could increase blood viscosity and induce changes in platelet number. These factors could contribute to the increase in arterial thrombosis in cold conditions, especially in elderly people with atheromatous blood vessels. Elderly and other patients with angina pectoris fare badly in cold weather when the oxygen requirement of the myocardium increases during exercise.

6.7
Urban hypothermia

While there are many clinical and accidental conditions where deep body temperature becomes subnormal, in clinical usage hypothermia means a deep body temperature below 35°C (95°F). During the past three decades, health workers have become increasingly concerned with the occurrence of hypothermia in urban surroundings. It has become a topic popularly recognized, and it is sometimes used as a political yardstick with which to measure social neglect. In the urban setting, concern naturally focuses on the elderly, who are known to be particularly vulnerable to the effects of cold because of a less-efficient body temperature regulating mechanism (Collins, 1983). Accidental hypothermia, when extreme cold stress overwhelms the body's thermal defences, can occur at any age if unexpected exposure to severe cold and exhaustion occurs during outdoor activities. But accidental exposure to cold may also occur in well-populated urban areas. For example, it is not unusual for an isolated elderly person to venture from a warm bed into icy-cold rooms forgetting to put on warm clothing. An accidental fall resulting in a broken limb and thus immobilization in cold surroundings is a typical setting for urban hypothermia.

As might be expected, statistics show that most deaths associated with urban hypothermia occur during the coldest winter months, but there is a general pattern of high risk of hypothermia in the elderly and the newborn throughout the year. Since 1971, records have been kept by the Office of Population Censuses and Surveys of the number of deaths where hypothermia is mentioned on the death certificate. In recent years, statistics have been based on deaths where hypothermia is considered to be an underlying cause,

Table 6.1 Outdoor temperatures and hypothermic deaths in England and Wales for the March quarter: 1979/90

| Year | Mean monthly temperature (°C) | | | Mean quarterly temperature (°C) | Hypothermia deaths for March quarter† |
	Jan.	Feb.	March		
1979	0.9	1.9	5.3	2.7	293
1980	3.1	6.3	5.4	4.9	137
1981	5.2	3.7	8.3	5.7	151
1982	3.6	5.5	6.6	5.2	225
1983	7.0	2.6	7.0	5.5	121
1984	4.3	4.2	5.3	4.6	145
1985	1.0	2.3	4.6	2.6	277
1986	3.8	−0.7	5.1	2.7	294
1987	1.4	4.1	4.6	3.6	152
1988	5.8	5.2	6.6	5.9	91
1989	6.7	6.4	7.8	7.0	64
1990*	7.1	7.8	8.7	7.9	74

Notes:
* Provisional figures.
† Hypothermia as underlying cause of death.
Sources:
Office of Population Censuses and Surveys
London Meteorological Office.

and total deaths where there is mention of hypothermia on the certificate (about two or three times as numerous as for underlying cause). Certification of hypothermia deaths may be expected to vary from year to year but are more stable for the underlying cause category. The highest number occur in the March quarter (January–March) when the mean quarterly ambient temperature is lowest. There is thus a clear association with ambient temperature (see Table 6.1). There has been a remarkable reduction in these deaths in the past three years during the unusually warm winters of 1988–1990.

A scheme of classification is helpful in diagnosis and notification. Primary hypothermia may occur when there is an inherent impairment in the thermoregulatory system itself, which can occur when there are congenital defects in the central nervous system. Secondary hypothermia is much more common and may be found when hypothermia is a symptom of underlying disease rather than the primary event. Secondary hypothermia often accompanies alcoholism, brain disease and metabolic disturbances such as in diabetes mellitus.

Many commonly prescribed drugs can, under certain circumstances, induce hypothermia by depressing the central nervous system and involuntary thermoregulation. A potentially dangerous situation exists when a central nervous system depressant, such as alcohol taken in excess, is combined with exposure to a cold environment. Even when there is no immediate threat of cold, hypothermia often accompanies deliberate self-poisoning with drugs such as phenothiazines, barbiturates and hypnotics.

Hypothermia has been reported in most parts of the world including those normally considered to be tropical. The condition is observed acutely in refugee camps in the developing countries, especially in groups of severely ill, undernourished people at the end of a cold night. The combination of intercurrent infections, such as in pneumonia or gastro-enteritis in frail undernourished infants, is often associated with hypothermia.

The principles of preventing the development of hypothermia in urban situations should be recognized by those attending elderly people living in any degree of social or physical isolation. Of primary importance is the early detection of incipient hypothermia by regular surveillance. There are key factors to alert suspicion – i.e. low temperatures in the living space and bedroom and lack of potential heating sources, poverty combined with social isolation and a general deterioration in well-being. In an attempt to conserve resources by reducing expenditure on costly fuel, some old people may keep the temperature of their living accommodation too low for comfort, encouraging a state of 'voluntary hypothermia'. The provision of adequate space heating in the dwelling is obviously the most important measure. There is a need also to ensure that nutrition is of a good standard, for sometimes elderly people feel that extra expenditure on fuel in the winter can be balanced by less spent on food. Severe hypothermia (below 30°C (86°F) deep body temperature) carries a high mortality, especially in the elderly. In published series of hypothermia cases mortality varies between 30% and 80%, depending on the severity and duration of the fall in body temperature.

6.8

Winter mortality and cold homes

In the UK there is a pronounced increase in mortality mainly from cardiovascular and respiratory disease during the winter. Hypothermia causes about 1% of excess deaths in the winter quarter of the year, and only 0.05% as the underlying cause. A seasonal or winter mortality ratio can be used to describe changes in excess winter deaths by the ratio between the annual equivalent death rate for the January–March quarter and the average rate for the whole calendar year. During the 1960s and 1970s, the UK had the highest winter mortality ratio for temperate and cold countries in North America and Europe. This high trend for the UK now appears to be declining, but there still remains a large discrepancy between the UK and countries such as Canada and Scandinavian nations which have a much colder winter climate than Britain. There is a strong negative correlation between winter mortality and indoor temperatures in different European countries (Boardman, 1986) and the indication is that high winter mortality ratios may be linked to cold homes and lack of central heating.

An analysis of recorded monthly deaths in England and Wales for the years 1962–7 clearly showed the strong relationship that exists between external environmental temperature and death rates (Bull and Morton, 1978). In people older than 60 years the slope of the regression of death rates on ambient temperature is steeper than in young adults. The length of time that passes between the onset of a cold spell and an increase in mortality is found to be one to two days for myocardial infarction, three to four days for strokes and one week for pneumonia and bronchitis.

About half the excess winter deaths were certified as being caused by coronary or cerebral thrombosis (Bull and Morton, 1978). One of the underlying causes for this may be an increase in blood viscosity and haematocrit in the cold. This was shown in many early studies (Burton and Edholm, 1955), and again more recently with mild surface cooling (Keatinge *et al.*, 1984). Although none of these studies has been applied to elderly people, it can be speculated that older people with increased atherosclerosis may be susceptible to platelet deposition and thrombus formation in the cold. Another factor that could be involved is the change that occurs in cardiovascular reflexes in the elderly (Collins *et al.*, 1985).

Influenza epidemics also contribute markedly to winter mortality, and in severe epidemics (e.g. in the winter of 1969–70) respiratory deaths were reported to increase by 50%. A reduction in air pollution in urban areas has contributed to the reduction in respiratory morbidity in recent years. Air pollution tended to fall in the 1950s and probably ceased to be a major factor in regions

Table 6.2 Seasonal variation in mortality and percentage of households with central heating in England and Wales in 1982, for persons over 75 years (Alderson, 1985)

Region	Percentage households with central heating	Seasonal mortality ratio
North	63.4	0.519
Yorkshire and Humberside	56.4	0.581
East Midlands	65.3	0.637
East Anglia	66.5	0.537
South-east	63.2	0.509
South-west	58.2	0.462
West Midlands	56.7	0.599
North-west	54.6	0.610
Wales	57.8	0.481
England and Wales	60.2	0.508

like London after about 1964, although well into the decade, winter bronchitis remained a major phenomenon in those affected.

Although the suggestion that low indoor temperatures contribute to morbidity and mortality especially in elderly people (Collins, 1986) has received wide support, some uncertainty has been expressed about the effect that can be expected from maintaining warm temperatures indoors (Keatinge, 1987). For example, in eight English regions and in Wales no difference was found between the proportion of people over 75 years of age living in centrally heated homes and the seasonal variation in mortality (Table 6.2).

Another study found that seasonal mortality in the elderly living in centrally heated homes where daytime temperatures could be maintained, did not differ from the general population of England and Wales (Keatinge, 1986). The conclusion drawn from these studies is that cardiovascular deaths in winter may be caused predominantly by brief excursions outdoors and not by low indoor temperatures. It does not explain why excess winter mortality is much less pronounced in countries with warmer homes and colder outdoor winter conditions unless there are large behavioural and clothing differences which prove to be critical.

The use of central heating in households in Britain has increased from 13% in 1964 to 66% in 1984, and with it excess winter mortality has declined. Excess mortality from respiratory disease in winter has decreased by 69% during this period, even when adjusted for the varying coldness of winters (Keatinge et al., 1990). Part of the improvement in the mortality figures from respiratory disease may be explained by a decline in influenza epidemics, in cigarette consumption and the availability of better antibiotics.

In contrast, excess winter mortality from coronary and cerebrovascular disease has not fallen significantly as home heating has improved. The present evidence therefore suggests that changes in the respiratory mortality in the elderly in winter is most closely related to improvements in home heating and to the occurrence of influenza epidemics. The effects of outdoor cold may be more dominant in causing excess coronary and cerebrovascular deaths, though there may be an indoor factor if the home environment is particularly cold.

6.9

Heat-related illnesses in the urban environment

The morbidity and mortality associated with cold winters described in the preceding sections are well recognized in the UK but there is less awareness of the effects of hot summers. Heatwaves have no precise meteorological definition, but might be regarded in Greater London as consisting of periods of three days or more when the maximum daily temperature exceeds 27°C (80°F) dry bulb. When such conditions do occur, or when there are prolonged periods of hot weather, they are accompanied by a significant increase in morbidity and mortality (MacFarlane and Waller, 1976).

In the USA some 4000 deaths each year have been attributed to the effects of heat, and 80% of these deaths occur in persons over 50 years of age (Heslop, Beard and Sainsbury, 1985). For the UK, the annual total of deaths registered as due directly to excessive heat is usually only in single figures, but in a summer with a prolonged heatwave such as occurred in 1976, 37 such deaths were recorded. In addition, there were 500 excess deaths per week from all causes in the same period of 1976, predominantly in those over 65 years of age, and increased hospital admissions of patients with cardiovascular illnesses. There is thus a significant effect of increased ambient temperature on health, though, as with the effects of cold, it is difficult to judge what contribution is made by the indoor temperature environment. In a world which has warmed up during the present century, and which may be expected to warm up even more during the next, there is a need to evaluate the short-

133

term and long-term effects of increasing heat stress in the urban environment.

Changing hygrothermal conditions in the home may be expected to influence human health in proportion to the degree of heat stress. Within certain limits of climatic stress, for example, with a projected global warming average increase of 3 degC (5.4 degF) in middle and lower latitudes, human thermal comfort can probably be maintained by appropriate behavioural responses and greater use of air conditioning. Natural heat acclimatization will develop after several days of heat exposure which will help to limit increases in deep body temperature. Severe heat stress can, however, result in deterioration in health and give rise to heat illness with effects ranging from mild cardiovascular disturbances to tissue damage and death due to heat-stroke (Weiner, Collins and Rubel, 1984). Of primary concern are the high-risk groups in whom even mild heat stress may produce abnormal heat strain. The critical groups will be determined by the potential environmental, social and behavioural, and biological and medical, risk factors (Kilbourne *et al.*, 1982).

The risk factors listed in Table 6.3 are all positively correlated with heat illness. Very high levels of physical activity in the heat are clearly associated with greater risk of heat illness, but conversely habitual physical activity may bring about an improvement in physical fitness and acclimatization which will improve ability to withstand heat stress. At risk are those generally less able to take care of themselves: the elderly, infants under 1 year, the chronic sick, the mentally and physically disabled and low socio-economic groups. It is important to recognize that many commonly prescribed drugs may have adverse effects under heatwave conditions (British Occupational Hygiene Society Technical Guide, 1990).

The majority of heat-related illnesses in hot weather prove to be minor – e.g. heat syncope, or skin disorders, such as prickly heat, which occurs when sweat is allowed to accumulate on unventilated skin regions. In urban societies, even in heatwaves, it is unlikely that the more serious conditions, such as water or salt deficiency heat-exhaustion, will arise where it is possible to restrict physical activity, to seek shelter and have ready access to fluids. Heat-exhaustion syndromes and heat intolerance can, in the extreme, lead to heat-stroke which is characterized by hyperthermia with a deep body temperature of 41°C (106°F) and above, central nervous system

Table 6.3 Factors promoting heat illness in urban areas*

Environmental

Lack of natural or artificial air conditioning indoors
High indoor humidity
Low air movement/building ventilation
High radiant heat load
High density of living units in building/high occupation density
Dwellings constructed of heat-absorbent materials
High-rise buildings

Social and behavioural

High physical activity level
Poor socio-economic situation and education
Social isolation
Lack of facilities for baths/showers
Unable to care for self/disabled

Biological and medical

Age of individual
Physically unfit
Obesity
High alcohol consumption
Previous history of heat disorder
Cardiovascular, pulmonary, renal, endocrine disease
Skin disease associated with decreased sweating
Febrile illness
Dehydration
Mental illness
Drugs, e.g. neuroleptics, anti-cholinergics, anti-depressants, sedative-hypnotics, diuretics

Note:
* Modified from Kilbourne *et al.* (1982), pp. 3332–6.

disturbances leading to convulsions and coma and often a hot, dry skin.

For most vulnerable unacclimatized people in cities and urban areas, increased cardiovascular strain is the major threat imposed by environmental heat. Recorded deaths from coronary or cerebral thrombosis rise markedly in heatwaves. This may be partly explained by increased blood viscosity and the effects of heat on the blood clotting system during moderate heat exposure.

The constructional dimensions, building materials and conditioning of the indoor environment play an important part in determining the health of the occupants. Heatwaves present special problems because of the retention of heat by buildings, especially if ventilation for cooling at night is impaired. The measurement of average hygrothermal conditions may not provide a full indication of the degree of heat stress in the built environment, the effects on health may depend largely on the duration of hot weather. Forced air movement is generally beneficial, but it may be associated with increased thermal strain when ambient temperature exceeds 37°C (98°F). Fully air-conditioned houses with windows which cannot be opened (already the building practice in many large stores and public buildings) are at the mercy of the power supplies and could become hazardous for some if there were power cuts during a heat-wave.

Early behavioural signs of prolonged heat stress in densely populated areas include increasing discomfort, social intolerance and irritability. These signs are frequently observed in 'heat islands' formed in the centres of cities. Those suffering from poor mental health may be particularly affected by unaccustomed heat stress and the indirect effects of high indoor environmental temperature on sleep patterns.

There is much current debate on predictions of climate change in the coming decades and the likelihood of significant global warming. The impact on ecosytems throughout the world could be enormous; given even the highly developed human potential to adapt both physiologically and behaviourally to increased temperatures, there is still the possibility of short-term and long-term effects and both direct and indirect threats to human health (WHO, 1990).

6.10
Accident rates and ambient temperature

Tests on office workers have shown little change in accident rates and performance in the range of temperatures within acceptable comfort values. Investigations of accident rates during the First World War clearly demonstrated a relationship between accidents and ambient temperature in factories (Chrenko, 1978). In munitions factories the lowest accident rates occurred in temperatures between 18°C and 20°C (65°F–68°F). Investigations among coal-miners showed that accidents were, to some extent, age related, with the highest rates in temperatures of 26°C (79°F) or above and in those workers in the extremes of the age range.

In the USA it is reported that the number of accidents increase in hot and humid environments (Ellis, 1972). More accidental deaths were found to occur in June and July than in any other month, though what proportion of domestic accidents was included was not stated. The possibility that non-climatic causes during the vacation period of the year, rather than summer warmth, accounted for the increase in the numbers of deaths, is supported by the increase in deaths recorded as the result of accidents in motor vehicles, accidental falls and drowning during July.

Individual performance can also be affected by thermal stress and may contribute to accidents. A number of investigations have found that subjects perform better in laboratory tests when they are uncomfortably warm, rather than comfortable, suggesting that heat has an arousing effect. At very high temperatures, concentration again becomes difficult.

During manual performance in the cold, the critical skin temperature at which the onset of numbness occurs is about 6°C (43°F) (British Occupational Hygiene Society Technical Guide, 1990). Manual dexterity decreases with decreasing temperature due to a combination of numbness and joint stiffness. In Britain, accidents, often resulting in a fatal outcome, are more common in winter; and domestic accidents increase as well as those outdoors. There is an impairment in sensory function, co-ordination and muscle function in the cold, and the impact of severe cold on cerebral function may result in increasing errors. Reduced core temperature, such as may occur with the development of hypothermia in elderly people, is likely to affect brain function. Under these conditions, susceptibility to accidents will be increased, particularly if reduced brain functioning is combined with muscle weakness.

Bibliography

Alderson, M. R. (1985) Season and mortality. *Health Trends*, 17, 210–24.

Anderson, I. *et al.* (1973) Human responses to 78-hour exposure to dry air. *Arch. Environ. Health*, 29, 22–7.

Bacon, C. J., Scott, D. J. and Jones, P. (1979) Heat stroke in well-wrapped infants. *Lancet*, i, 422–5.

Boardman, B. (1986) Seasonal mortality and cold homes, in: *Unhealthy Homes: A Diagnosis*, Institution of Environmental Health Officers and Legal Research Institute, University of Warwick.

Brennan, P. J., Greenberg, G., Miall, W. E. and Thompson, S. G. (1982) Seasonal variation in arterial blood pressure. *B. Med. J.,* 285, 919–23.

British Occupational Hygiene Society Technical Guide (1990) *The Thermal Environment,* No. 8, Science Reviews Ltd, Leeds.

Bull, G. M. and Morton J. (1978) Environment, temperature and death rates. *Age and Ageing,* 7, 210–24.

Burr, M. L., Miskelly, F. G., Butland, B. K., Merrett, T. G. and Vaughan-Williams, E. (1989) Environmental factors and symptoms in infants at high risk of allergy. *J. Epidemiol. Community Health,* 43, 137–42.

Burton, A. C. and Edholm, O. G. (1955) *Man in a Cold Environment,* Edward Arnold, London, pp. 129–30.

Chrenko, F. A. (ed.) (1978) *Bedford's Basic Principles of Ventilation and Heating,* H. K. Lewis, London.

Collins, K. J. (1983) *Hypothermia, the Facts,* Oxford University Press, London.

Collins, K. J., Easton, J. C., Belfield-Smith, H., Exton-Smith, A. N. and Pluck, R. A. (1985) Effects of age on body temperature and blood pressure in cold environments. *Clinical Science,* 69, 465–70.

Collins, K. J. (1986) Low indoor temperatures and morbidity in the elderly. *Age and Ageing,* 15, 212–20.

Collins, K. J. and Hoinville, E. (1980) Temperature requirements in old age. *Building Services Engineering Research and Technology,* 1, 165–72.

Deal, E. C., McFadden, E. R., Ingram, R. H., Strauss, R. H. and Jagger, J. J. (1979) Role of respiratory heat exchange in production of exercise-induced asthma. *J. Appl. Physiol.,* 46, 467–75.

Ellis, F. P. (1972) Mortality from heat illness and heat-aggravated illness in the United States. *Environment. Res.,* 5, 1–58.

Fanger, P. O. (1982) *Thermal Comfort,* R. E. Kleiber, Malabar, Fla.

Gagge, A. P. (1940) Standard operative temperature, generalized temperature scale applicable to direct and partitional calorimetry. *American Journal of Physiology,* 131, p. 93.

Green, G. H. (1982) The positive and negative effects of building humidification. ASHRAE Transactions, 88, Part 1.

Heslop, H. E., Beard, M. E. J. and Sainsbury R. (1985) Heat-related illnesses in the elderly. *Geriatric Medicine Today,* 4, 21–4.

Hunt, D. R. G. and Gidman, M. I. (1982) A national field survey of house temperatures. *Building Environment,* 17, 107–24.

Jones, W. T. (1975) *The Health and Safety at Work Act: A practical Handbook*. Graham and Trottman, London.

Keatinge, W. R., Coleshaw, S. R. K., Cotter, F., Mattock, M., Murphy, M. and Chelliah, R. (1984) Increases in platelet and red cell counts, blood viscosity and arterial pressure during mild surface cooling: factors in mortality from coronary and cerebral thrombosis in winter. *B. Med. J.*, 289, 1405–8.

Keatinge, W. R. (1986) Seasonal mortality among elderly people with unrestricted home heating. *B. Med. J.*, 293, 732–3.

Keatinge, W. R. (1987) Winter mortality: warm housing offers cold comfort. *Geriatric Medicine*, 17, 65–9.

Keatinge, W. R., Coleshaw, S. R. K. and Holmes, J. (1990) Changes in seasonal mortalities with improvement in home heating in England and Wales from 1964 to 1984. *Int. J. Biometeorol.*, 33, 71–6.

Kilbourne, E. M., Choi, K., Jones, T. S. and Thacker, S. B. (1982) Risk factors for heat-stroke: a case control study. *J. Am. Med. Assoc.*, 247, 3332–6.

Korsgaard, J. (1979) The effect of the indoor environment on the house dust mite, in: Fanger, P. O. and Valbjorn, O. (eds) *Indoor Climate*, Danish Building Research Institute, Copenhagen, pp. 187–205.

MacFarlane, A. and Waller, R. E. (1976) Short term increases in mortality during heat waves. *Nature*, 264, 434–6.

McIntyre, D. A. (1980) *Indoor Climate*, Applied Science, London.

Mant, D. C. and Muir Gray, J. A. (1986) *Building Regulations and Health*, Department of the Environment Building Research Establishment, London.

Murphy, M. F. G. and Campbell M. J. (1987) Sudden Infant Death Syndrome and environmental temperature: an analysis using vital statistics. *J. Epidemiol. Community Health*, 41, 63–71.

Nicholl, A. and Davies, L. (1986) How warm are babies kept at home? *Health Visitor*, 59, 113–14.

Rose, G. (1961) Seasonal variation in blood pressure in man. *Nature*, 189, 235.

Strachan, D. P. and Elton, R. A. (1986) Relationship between respiratory morbidity in children and the home environment. *Family Practice*, 3, 137–42.

Tyrrell, D. A. J. (1965) *Common Colds and Related Diseases*, Edward Arnold, London.

Uren, E. C., Williams, A. L., Jack, I. and Rees, J. W. (1980) Association of respiratory virus infections with Sudden Infant Death Syndrome. *Med. J. Australia*, i, 417–19.

Weiner, J. S., Collins, K. J. and Rubel, L. R. (1984) Heat-associated illnesses, in: *Hunter's Tropical Medicine* (6th edn) (ed. G. T. Strickland) W. B. Saunders, Philadelphia, Pa., pp. 873–9.

Williams A. L. and Fraser, J. (1990) Illness preceding sudden infant death, *B. Med. J.*, 300, 1584.

World Health Organization (WHO) (1961) Technical Report series No. 225, Expert Committee on the Public Health Aspects of Housing, WHO, Geneva.

WHO (1984) *The Effects of the Indoor Housing Climate on the Health of the Elderly*, WHO, Copenhagen.

WHO (1990) *Potential Health Effects of Climatic Change*, Report of a WHO Task Group, WHO, Geneva.

7

COLD, CONDENSATION AND HOUSING POVERTY

THOMAS A. MARKUS

7.1
Introduction

A number of studies have shown the links between cold houses, condensation dampness, climate and poverty – not only of the general kind, but in its special form of 'fuel poverty'. Others have shown the effects of these on both morbidity and mortality. This chapter examines these factors in the context of Glasgow but the analysis and its conclusions will have general application in cold climates.

One definition of a house is a place where, at a cost which the occupants can afford, comfortable and healthy conditions can be maintained, independently of external climatic conditions. The definition of 'healthful housing' by the World Health Organization, (WHO), though much more elaborate, refers to protection from the 'elements' rather than climate and makes no mention of economic factors (WHO, 1961).

7.2
Material factors

Condensation

The indoor atmosphere is a mixture of air and water vapour. The latter is generated by the presence of bodies and by such activities as clothes washing and drying, bathing and showering, cooking and the combustion of certain fuels. Water vapour from the external atmosphere also contributes.

The amount of water vapour which can be held by a given volume of air depends on the air temperature – the warmer it is, the more moisture can be held. As moisture is added, eventually saturation is reached and any further moisture will condense out in the form of liquid water. Similarly, for a given air/vapour mixture, as it is cooled, a temperature is eventually reached where it is saturated and below which the excess will condense out. This is known as the 'dewpoint temperature' for that air/vapour mixture; the relative humidity is then 100%. As heating or cooling occurs, unless moisture is added or removed, while the *relative humidity* falls or rises, the *absolute humidity*, measured, say, in pressure units such as Pascals, remains constant.

These relationships are shown in psychrometric charts such as that illustrated in Figure 7.1. Point (a) represents an absolute humidity of 4.4 Pascals, at a temperature of 5°C, giving a relative humidity of 80%. If this air/water mixture is warmed, with no change to the absolute moisture content, to 20°C, the relative humidity, shown at point (b), drops to 29.5%. If the same mixture is cooled till it reaches the 100% relative humidity curve at point (c) it will be seen that its dewpoint temperature is 1.7°C.

The inside surface temperature of building elements depends on their insulation. The less adequate the insulation, the colder will be that surface in cold weather. When it drops to the dewpoint temperature of the room air, condensation will form on it. It is normal for the inside surface of single glass to be the first to drop to this point, which is not to say that such condensation is harmless – it can cause timber rot, metal corrosion and destruction of paint, wallpaper and flooring materials unless provision is made for its drainage. On large glass window areas the volume of water can be considerable.

When external or internal conditions are changing, due to weather changes or intermittent use of heating, it can occur that elements with insulation higher than that of window glass first drop to dewpoint. The inner surface of a massive element, such as a concrete or brick wall which has cooled down, may take longer to heat up when the room heating is turned on than that of a lighter element such as glass. When double glazing is introduced, it may then be more frequent for other surfaces to suffer condensation. Single glass acts to remove water vapour from the air, just as the freezer plates

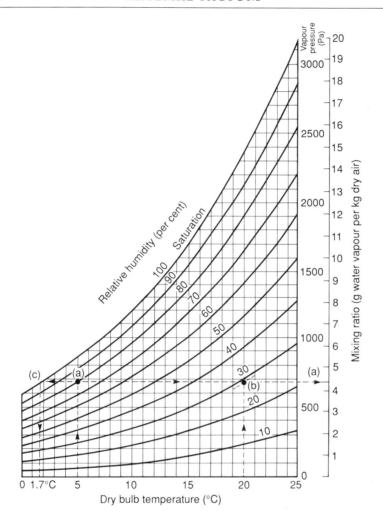

Figure 7.1 Relationship between relative humidity, temperature and vapour pressure.

in a refrigerator do (here the condensate freezes and forms ice). In this sense it is useful in condensing out moisture which might otherwise cause more damage on other surfaces, including those which support mould growth.

If a massive element is lined with a lightweight material, such as insulating dry lining, this gives that element a much quicker response under dynamic room conditions and will also make the

143

underlying mass even colder. So the lining material must incorporate a vapour check or barrier to reduce or prevent the permeation of moisture in to the structure, otherwise interstitial condensation within the fabric can occur. Alternatively, the airspace between the lining and the massive element can be ventilated to the exterior, drier atmosphere. This is also a necessary feature where loft insulation is placed on the ceiling, which then makes the underside of slates and tiles on the roof much colder.

If the fabric gets wet through rising or penetrating damp, due to defective damp proof courses or joints, or construction cracks or gaps, then the insulation value of porous materials drops, their inside surfaces will become colder and condensation will therefore take place more readily. A vicious circle between other forms of damp and condensation can thus be set up.

Insulation and mass

The *thermal resistance* of a building element, together with the resistance of its two surfaces, will determine the rate at which heat flows from the warmer to the colder side. The reciprocal of this is known as the *thermal transmittance*, or U-value (expressed in units of W m^{2}K^{-1} – i.e. the heat flowing through an element, measured in watts per square metre of surface area, per degC difference between the inside and outside air temperatures). Special problems occur in non-homogeneous construction where elements such as concrete columns or slabs penetrate through cavities or insulation and act as *cold bridges*, rapidly conducting heat through an otherwise insulated element (Figure 7.2).

Corners, and the under or top side of access decks which form ceiling or floor surfaces in rooms on one side and are exposed to external air on the other are also frequent trouble spots.

Two elements of identical U-value but different mass can have different internal surface temperatures under dynamic conditions, for the reasons already described.

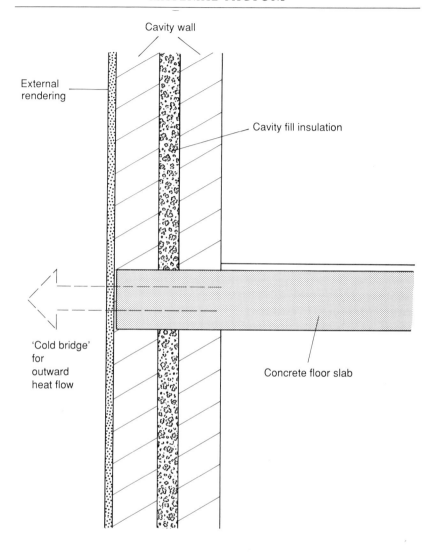

Figure 7.2 'Cold bridge' created by concrete slab penetrating through insulating wall.

Ventilation

All houses have paths of air leakage between the inside and outside (e.g. gaps around opening windows and doors, construction cracks, flues and ventilators). As the heated air is exchanged for cold, outside air, heat is lost. In a house insulated to modern standards this

145

heat loss can be well over half the total. A certain amount of air change is required to control the build-up of moisture and to give fresh air. Too little will increase the risks of condensation and also risk smells, other pollutants and lack of fresh air. Too much will excessively cool the inside air and, in turn, the room surfaces and will thus also increase the risks of condensation, even though the amount of water vapour may have diminished. So there is an optimum rate of air change, the computation of which under specified conditions requires a good thermal model. However, even relatively little ventilation, such as takes place through trickle vents in windows, is normally adequate, expect in spaces where a lot of moisture is produced such as kitchens and bathrooms. These should have extractor fans, preferably humidistat-controlled, and self-closing doors to cut them off from the rest of the house.

Heating systems

It is evident that, beside the fabric and ventilation losses, it is the heating system, the fuel and the control system which will determine whether or not a house can be economically heated. There is a huge technological choice available today, but the retrofitting to older and thermally deficient housing is severely constrained by space and the availability of suitable fuel (e.g. gas). The system also has to possess the right response characteristics which match the demand of the users and the thermal response of the fabric.

Where there is an inadequate heating system, it is usual for all members of the household to congregate in the one heatable space, often the living-room. Elderly and sick people, with official encouragement, often move their beds into this space in cold weather (e.g. leaflet issued jointly by Age Concern Scotland and South of England Electricity Board, 1990).

House density and usage

The amount of moisture generated in a house is in some proportion to the number of its occupants which, in turn, relates to the volume they occupy, and to the period of occupancy. If the volume occupied is too small, the condensation risks increase – as it will in a house continuously used, for example, by a parent with under-school-age children or a sick, disabled or elderly person. But an excessively large house also poses risks, in that some rooms will remain unused or underheated, and in these condensation will more readily occur. So there is an optimum house density for a given size of household, and it should form an important part of good housing management that houses should be matched to households.

7.3
Material effects

Both cold and condensation can affect the fabric of a house. Between fabric which is cold and other, warmer, parts stresses can be set up which can cause excessive temperature gradients and cracking.

Condensation moisture can affect plaster, wood, metal and room decorations. If it supports mould, there can be serious health risks (see Chapter 4).

7.4
Personal and social effects

Comfort

Thermal comfort depends on two personal and four environmental variables. The two personal ones are the level of activity and the amount of clothing worn. Clearly inactive people, or people wearing less clothing, require warmer environments than active ones or those wearing more (see Chapter 6). Of the four environmental variables, the first is air temperature. Since the surface temperature of the body or its clothing is about 34°C, air warmer than this will heat the body and air colder will cool it. The second variable is the radiation environment. The body will lose heat to surfaces colder than itself and gain heat from those that are warmer. Most surfaces in a room are colder than the air. Provided this is only by 1–2 degC, then it is not too critical. But if the differences are greater than this, then the heat loss to them has to be compensated for by higher air temperatures.

The third environmental variable is air movement. The faster this is, the greater will be the heat gain from warming air or heat loss to cooling air. Again, this is not too significant indoors if there are no strong air movements. But if there are draughts from doors,

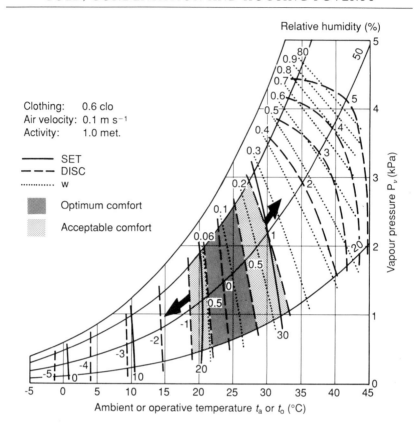

Figure 7.3 Typical thermal comfort chart.

windows, underfloor voids or downdraughts from falling streams of cold air near large, cold surfaces such as windows, then the increased heat loss will have to be compensated for by air temperature or radiation adjustments.

The fourth variable is humidity, which controls the rate of evaporative cooling. In cold and temperate climates this is not sufficiently large for humidity to be critical. It becomes important, however, in warm environments where high humidities may limit necessary evaporative cooling.

The relationship between the six variables is well understood (Markus and Morris 1980), and a variety of indices have been developed which attempt by means of a single figure to describe the thermal environment. Among these are Standard Effective Temperature (SET) and Resultant Temperature (Tres). Figure 7.3 shows, on a psychometric chart, the relationship between the variables for one specified level of air movement, clothing and activity. On it are shown values of SET and the zones in which comfort would be predicted.

Survival and hypothermia

(a) Death

Normal deep body temperature is about 37°C. A sensitive thermoregulatory system enables this to be maintained in a wide variety of environments. If it drops to less than 36°C, muscular weakness and eventually death results. It may rise to 40°C during heavy activity, or even 42°C for short periods in a fever. But such temperatures over longer periods cause the thermoregulatory system itself to break down and start a vicious circle which ends in heat-stroke and death.

In all cold climates there are some hypothermic deaths in winter. These usually make the headlines, but many more occur from a combination of hypothermia with other illness such as heart, circulatory and chest disease. The relationship between hypothermia and death has been well studied. (A comprehensive review of literature on hypothermia and other temperature effects in housing appears in Mant and Gray, 1986; since then Coleshaw *et al.*, 1986, have added a useful work.) Figure 7.4 shows the seasonal variation of deaths in Scotland for the years 1981–7 in which hypothermia is mentioned as a cause (General Register Office for Scotland, 1987).

The winter increases are very marked. Table 7.1 gives the figures per 1000 of the population for the years 1981–6 for the over-65s and the over-80s and sets them beside the comparable figures for England and Wales; it can be seen that the Scottish ones are three to four times higher. This cannot be explained by the climatic differences alone, which are much smaller. There is a presumed interaction with differences in clothing, nourishment, general health and, probably, house heating.

(b) Winter deaths in general

Without reference to hypothermia, there is a well-known excess of deaths in winter over the summer or year average rate. Table 7.2

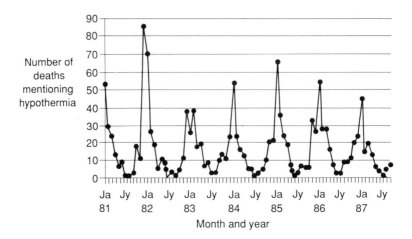

Figure 7.4 Deaths mentioning hypothermia, Scotland: 1981–1987. Source: Registrar General for Scotland.

Table 7.1 Mortality rates per 1000 population for deaths mentioning hypothermia

Year	Age	Scotland 65+	Scotland 80+	Total	England and Wales 65+	England and Wales 80+	Total
1981		0.269	0.663	0.049	0.076	0.232	0.014
1982		0.222	0.536	0.038	0.072	0.220	0.013
1983		0.191	0.563	0.035	0.060	0.174	0.011
1984		0.195	0.461	0.034	0.062	0.165	0.011
1985		0.277	0.756	0.045	0.093	0.259	0.017
1986		0.230	0.580	0.041	0.091	0.268	0.017

Source:
Registrar-General for Scotland

shows the excess for Scotland for the years 1958–87; it ranges from about 18% to 63%. Table 7.3 gives the same information for five-yearly averages; this shows a consistent drop over the same period, even though the final figure is still 24.5%. Keatinge (1987) argues that winter excess mortality is due to the elderly being exposed to cold outdoor air, and uses as evidence the fact that there is no difference between a group living in fully heated, sheltered housing and those in the population at large. However, the fact that in other countries (some with much more severe winters than those of the UK), where elderly people presumably also go out and where the excess is far smaller, weakens this argument. Moreover, many

Table 7.2 'Excess' winter mortality: Scotland, 1958–87

Year	Winter deaths	Summer deaths	Differences	Percentage excess
	A	B	A − B	(A − B) × 100
				B
1958	18 622	12 667	5 955	47.0
1959	21 048	12 900	8 148	63.2
1960	17 194	13 705	3 489	25.5
1961	18 752	13 514	5 238	38.8
1962	18 516	13 460	5 056	37.6
1963	20 711	13 775	6 936	50.4
1964	16 510	13 644	2 866	21.0
1965	17 806	13 860	3 946	28.5
1966	19 471	13 655	5 816	42.6
1967	15 834	13 365	2 469	18.5
1968	19 264	13 482	5 782	42.9
1969	18 148	13 970	4 178	29.9
1970	19 271	14 157	5 114	36.1
1971	16 712	14 145	2 567	18.1
1972	19 108	14 349	4 759	33.2
1973	18 171	14 303	3 868	27.0
1974	17 093	14 490	2 603	18.0
1975	17 338	14 114	3 224	22.8
1976	19 780	14 071	5 709	40.6
1977	17 049	13 859	3 190	23.0
1978	19 112	14 433	4 679	32.4
1979	18 810	14 580	4 230	29.0
1980	17 304	14 246	3 058	21.5
1981	17 293	14 269	3 024	21.2
1982	19 364	14 165	5 199	36.7
1983	18 108	14 245	3 863	27.1
1984	17 225	13 831	3 394	24.5
1985	17 466	14 354	3 112	21.7
1986	18 456	14 273	4 183	29.3
1987*	16 878	14 088	2 790	19.8

Note:
* Provisional.
Source:
Registrar-General for Scotland

elderly in the UK do not move out during cold spells, following official advice not to do so. Boardman (1985), in a survey of activity patterns, has shown that the elderly only spend about 3.2 hours per day out of the house, presumably much of that in other indoor environments.

Table 7.3 Excess winter mortality, Scotland for 5 year periods 1957–1987

Five-year period	Percentage excess Winter mortality
1958–62	42.1
1963–7	32.3
1968–72	32.0
1973–7	26.2
1978–82	28.2
1983–7	24.5

Source:
Hansard, 17 February 1988, p. 65.

Table 7.4 Weekly hospital admissions: 1970–80

		Heart disease	Acute respiratory	Pneumonia	Bronchitis
Glasgow	Mean	137	3.4	37	35
	Min.	39	0	3	2
	Max.	196	19	145	102
	Corr.	0.32	0.32	0.42	0.44
	Slope	0.20	0.03	0.23	0.19
Turnhouse	Mean	71	43	16	16
(Edinburgh)	Min.	34	0	3	5
	Max.	103	22	61	38
	Corr.	0.23	0.43	0.42	0.44
	Slope	0.10	0.05	0.11	0.09

Source:
Tagg (1987).

(c) Cold-related illness

An analysis of hospital admissions for four cold-related illnesses in Glasgow and Edinburgh for the years between 1970 and 1980 shows correlations between weekly Degree Days and admissions in the order of 0.44 for bronchitis, and only a little lower for pneumonia and other acute respiratory diseases, while for heart disease, with the lowest correlation, it was still 0.32 in Glasgow and 0.23 in Edinburgh (Tagg, 1987); the result is shown in Table 7.4. Even at the lowest correlations, the weather explained at least 10% of the admissions. Another analysis used five disease categories for the years 1980–5, and the results are shown in Table 7.5. Here again, the two cities show correlations ranging from 0.44 to 0.25, the highest being for bronchitis/emphysema.

As in the case of hypothermic death, and general winter mortality

Table 7.5 Weekly hospital admissions and Degree Days: 1980–5

		Ischaemic heart disease	Other heart diseases	Acute respiratory	Pneumonia/ influenza	Bronchitis/ emphysema
Glasgow	Mean	77	58	2.8	25	14
	Min.	35	19	0	10	4
	Max.	112	86	14	59	29
	Corr.	0.30	0.40	0.41	0.54	0.41
	Slope	0.13	0.14	0.03	0.15	0.07
Turnhouse	Mean	52	33	5	15	12
(Edinburgh)	Min.	24	3	0	3	2
	Max.	86	58	26	37	27
	Corr.	0.25	0.29	0.41	0.51	0.44
	Slope	0.09	0.07	0.05	0.10	0.07

Source:
Tagg (1987).

excess, it is difficult to prove that house conditions have significantly affected the findings on hospital admissions. But since every survey shows large numbers of houses below safe temperature limits, it is a fair working assumption until more definitive data become available that there is a significant contribution from housing thermal deficiencies. One survey (Primrose and Smith, 1981) found in a mild winter between mid-November and mid-December that 96% of the over-65s surveyed lived in living-rooms below the recommended 21.1°C; 84% were below the 1961 recommendation of 18.3°C, while even 16°C failed to be met by 64%.

(d) Mould-related illness

Damp surfaces, from whatever cause, form suitable breeding areas for a variety of moulds. It has been shown that the spores released by such moulds are associated with a number of illnesses, especially children's asthma and other chest diseases (among the many recent reports are those by Martin, Platt and Hunt, 1987; Martin *et al.*, 1989; Strachan, 1986; and Burr *et al.*, 1988). The evidence is accumulating and it is beginning to be accepted even in legal cases for damages.

(e) Mental and emotional illness

There is evidence that presence of damp, mouldy and cold conditions causes anxiety and depression (see Chapter 14). This is all the more serious since these conditions often prevail in households where these psychological stresses are already present from other social and economic causes. Moreover, occupants of such houses are often reluctant to invite friends, or even friends' children, into their homes as they feel embarrassed by the sight of the damp and deteriorating surfaces, and by the associated smells. Thus they become lonely and isolated.

7.5
Climate

The severity of the climate fully explains the variations in heat loss between two identical houses, used in a similar manner and heated to the same standards. It is usually external air temperature which is used as measure of climate, and certainly it is important. The index used is normally the Degree Day: this is a concept based on the finding that an unheated house maintains an internal temperature several degrees above that of the outside as a consequence of activities, shelter from wind and the heat gains from solar radiation through windows (even from overcast skies). The exact difference in temperature depends, naturally, on the specifics of all these variables. It is often of the order of about 3 degC, which means that if, for instance, an internal temperature of 20°C is to be attained, the house will not require heating until the external air temperature drops to 17°C or below; this is known as the 'base temperature'. If the average external temperature drops for one day by 1 degC below the base, this is known as 'one Degree Day'; if it drops by 2 degC for one day, or by 1 degC for two days, this is known as 'two Degree Days' and so on.

In the UK, 15.5°C is often taken as the base and Figure 7.5 is a Degree Day map using that figure. Table 7.6 shows the Degree Days for 17 UK regions, both for the whole year and for the September–May heating season. If the mildest place, in south-western England, is given an arbitrary index of 100, it will be seen that Glasgow, in the west of Scotland, has Degree Days 33% and 30% higher for the two values. This means that a house in Glasgow would require about one-third more fuel per annum to maintain the same internal conditions as the identical house in Bristol.

But the severity of the climate with regard to heat loss is greater than Degree Days indicate since they exclude the effects of wind,

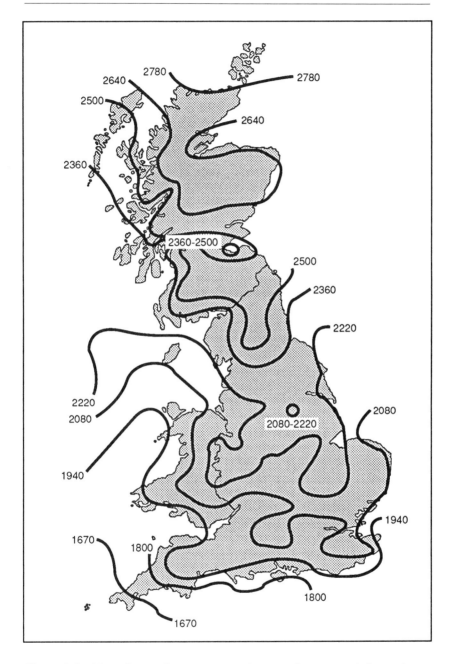

Figure 7.5 Map of annual Degree Days for period 1921–50, below a base temperature of 15.5°C. Source: BRE

Table 7.6 Degree Days for 17 UK regions the whole year and for the September–May heating season

	Whole year	%	Sept–May 'Building Services' and CIBS	%
Thames Valley	2137	= 109	2019	= 111
South-eastern	2445	= 124	2258	= 124
Southern	2286	= 116	2110	= 116
South-western	1966	= 100*	1825	= 100*
Severn Valley	2235	= 114	2088	= 114
Midlands	2527	= 129	2329	= 128
West Pennines	2389	= 122	2209	= 121
North-western	2556	= 130	2335	= 128
Borders	2727	= 139	2453	= 134
North-eastern	2534	= 129	2331	= 128
East Pennines	2398	= 122	2221	= 122
East Anglia	2468	= 126	2289	= 125
West Scotland	2615	= 133	2374	= 130
East Scotland	2744	= 140	2474	= 136
North-east Scotland	2903	= 148	2602	= 146
Wales	2276	= 116	2066	= 113
Northern Ireland	2544	= 129	2310	= 127

* South West as mildest = 100
Notes:
Seventeen regions defined by Department of Energy.
CIBS Annual Total for 20 years, 1959–78 *almost* the same (Guide A2.4).
Building Services: 1984
(Meteorological Office data, 15.5° base, 20 years to 1979). Also *Energy Management*, April 1983.

sunshine and rain, all of which will affect the heat loss. Rain, by wetting porous external walling materials, will reduce their insulation value; but in a wall insulated to modern standards this will be of little importance. In older, poorer constructions, say, an 11 inch cavity brick wall with no insulation, it begins to be significant.

Wind will determine the rate at which leakage of air between the inside and outside takes place. In a house insulated to modern standards heat loss resulting from such leakage – which clearly depends on the airtightness of the house – could be over half the total heat loss. Solar radiation falling through windows onto floors and walls, or heating roof and wall surfaces, can considerably reduce energy demand, provided that the heating system is sufficiently responsive to such gains and reduces its output when they occur rather than wasting them. Such energy can also be used in solar heating systems – either active, with air or water collector panels,

Table 7.7 Climatic Severity Index (CSI)

Year		(1) Kew	(2) Aborporth	(3) Eskdalemuir	(4) Lerwick
1,	2, 3, 4				
1964	1976	3834	3743	5872	5798
1965	1977	3599	3603	5550	5612
1966	1978	3452	3794	5525	5832
1967	1979	3143	4172	6029	6325
1968	1980	3477	3783	5594	5991
5-year average		3501	3819	5714	5912
Index		100*	109	163	169
Degree Days		2000	2040	2600	2900
Index		100*	102	130	145

* South west as mildest = 100
Notes:
Degree Days based on base temperature 15.5°C, 20-year average, Lacy and Shellard, interpolated on contours at 144 DD intervals.
Developed at Strathclyde University under contract to Scottish Development Department.
Combined effect of: air temperature
                     radiation
                     wind
Annual consumption (kWh) for one sample house (type 16), for 18 months (September–April).

pumps and heat exchangers, or passive, with conservatories, glazed spaces and rooflights into roof voids.

The University of Strathclyde, sponsored by the Scottish Development Department, has developed a Climatic Severity Index (CSI) which combines into a single figure the effects of air temperature, wind and solar radiation for any place where these data are available or can be estimated (Markus *et al.*, 1984). The CSI can be calculated for any kind of house design and construction and will be proportional to its heat loss; the procedure has been computerized.

Table 7.7 shows the CSIs for four places in the UK (chosen because measured solar radiation dates are available) for the five years 1976–80, and the five-year averages; alongside the five-year averages, the Degree Days for the four locations are also given. If the mildest of the four, Kew, is given an arbitrary index of 100, the index for Lerwick measured by CSI is 169, whereas measured by Degree Days it is only 145. For Eskdalemuir the two figures are 163 and 130, and for Aborporth 109 and 102. That means, then, that the true difference in fuel expenditure is much greater than Degree Days suggest; for instance, in the case of Eskdalemuir, CSI gives an increase over twice as high as that given by Degree Days.

7.6

Cold and poverty

A number of researchers have examined family fuel expenditure in the UK and reported no significant variations with climatic severity, whether assessed by Degree Days or CSI (Hutton and Bradshaw, 1983); Figure 7.6 explains the reasons for this finding. In Figure 7.6 the assumption is made that the fuel consumption and internal thermal conditions, whether measured by an index such as SET or Tres, or simply by air temperature averaged over space and time (as is done in the figure), are linearly related. On the Figure sloping lines representing this relationship are drawn for two houses – a thermally 'poor' one (low insulation, draughty, inefficient heating system) and a thermally 'good' one. Naturally, the correlation is stronger, that is the slope is steeper, for the 'poor' house. For each of the two houses, three lines are shown, representing that house in a severe, average and mild climate. Also shown is a horizontal base line, representing the fuel consumed for hot water, cooking, lights and equipment – at 100 kWh per week – on the assumption that this does not vary either with the thermal quality of the house or with climate.

On the y-axis in Figure 7.6 is a scale of fuel consumption in energy units (kWh), as well as two in cash units (£s/week) representing two different fuel costs, or different tariffs for the same fuel. For most low-income families, there is an inelastic limit to what can be spent on fuel and the households achieve whatever thermal conditions that expenditure will purchase. There are two horizontal lines representing a weekly expenditure of £9 (averaged over the entire year), which gives two different energy consumptions according to which of the two fuel costs is operational. In one case, it buys 240 kWh per week, at an average cost of 3.75p per kWh and in the other 300 kWh per week at average cost of 3p per kWh.

Figure 7.6 demonstrates two effects: the first is specific to low-income families. It is the case that they tend to live in thermally 'poor' housing. This is not only true in the private rented or owner-occupied sector, where one would expect it, but also in the public sector, where a kind of 'market force' is at work. So if the two horizontal lines are projected across to meet the slopes of the three 'poor' houses and then projected vertically down on to the x-axis, they show the kind of (inadequate) house temperatures that such a

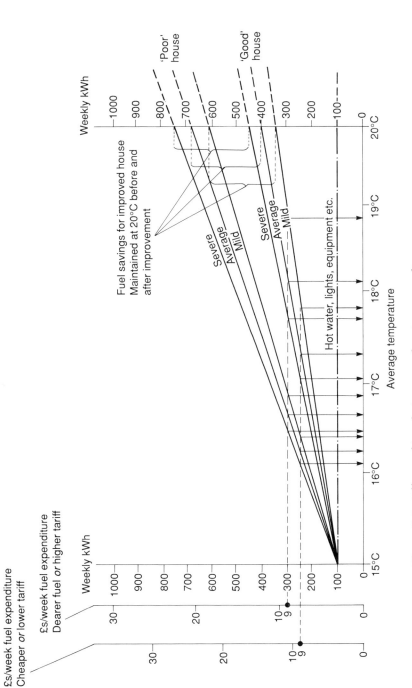

Figure 7.6 Effects of insulation upon heating expenditure or temperature.

low-income household could expect to meet; clearly they are slightly higher in a warmer climate.

There is accumulated evidence that if a thermal improvement to this house takes place, the household will not make fuel or cash savings, but will continue to spend to its budgetary limit and meet higher standards. This can be seen if the two horizontal lines are projected to the second set of three sloping lines, and then projected vertically down on to the x-axis. Since there is now a perception that fuel expenditure is a worthwhile investment, it may even *increase* somewhat.

The second effect is specific to middle- to high-income households. If they occupy a 'poor' house, but are able to meet full thermal comfort standards, investment in thermal improvements in their case will have real fuel or cash benefits, as can be seen in Figure 7.6 by projecting six horizontal lines across on to the y-axis on the right-hand side and measuring the drop in fuel expenditure between pairs of corresponding lines, which have been bracketed together.

There are two general conclusions: first, that for low-income families expenditure surveys cannot indicate the effect of climatic variation – only massive surveys of house thermal conditions, carried out on the size of sample used for the expenditure surveys, would reveal that, as the climate gets colder, so do the houses; and secondly, that investment in thermal improvements benefit the well-off in cash terms much more than the poor. That does not mean that they should not be made – far from it – but that the returns are more difficult to quantify since they consist of a diminution of misery and suffering; nor, in their case, will the effects be significant in terms of reducing the national energy bill or the 'greenhouse' effect. But it does have implications for public policy – that resources for subsidies should be transferred to the poorer housing stock and households since, in any case, the better-off can afford to finance substantial improvements themselves.

There is a further point about fuel bills and poverty. All the fuel Boards have a variety of 'easy payment' schemes – 'fuel direct', uniform weekly or monthly payments, tokens and 'heat-with-rent'. Certainly these avoid the crises of fuel debt, arrears and disconnections caused by large two- or three-monthly bills. But by making payments 'easy', at a steady trickle, the iniquity of the total annual bill can be camouflaged. The payments become a first call and diminish available money for food, clothing and entertainment. An analogy with cigarette smoking is relevant. Many people on low incomes can 'afford' to smoke because cigarettes are available in small, daily packages. If they were only available in bulk packages of two- or three-monthly supplics, many smokers would give up, reduce smoking or incur 'cigarette debts'!

7.7
The Glasgow dimension

The situation in general

For Scottish houses, in general, the fuel poverty problems were first described by Markus (1979). Glasgow's housing problems relate to fabric, disrepair, climate, external estate environment and socio-economic factors. The *Housing Enquiry* highlighted these in a concise form and the issues of cold, underheated and damp houses were identified as central (Grieve *et al.*, 1986). The *Glasgow House Condition Survey*, in five volumes with a surveyor's manual (City of Glasgow, 1987–90), is the most extensive document of its kind ever published for a British city. Included is a wealth of data on house heating, condensation and dampness. Volume 1 shows the overall size of the problem in 1985, at the time of the survey, though conditions have not changed greatly in five years. The stock was 287 195 units, of which the local authority sector, the largest in Europe, was 165 057 units. There was a mixture of late-nineteenth-century tenements, terraces and villas; pre-1919 two- and three-storey blocks; inter-war four-in-a-block and other low-rise houses; and post Second World War high-rise blocks of flats and two-storey maisonettes, as well as two- and three-storey housing. About 60% of the houses had external fabric repairs to be made, 20% of a major type.

Only 46% of the houses had any kind of partial or full central heating, much of it in the form of electric underfloor systems or older electric storage systems, which had either ceased to be operational or were completely uneconomic to run and hence not used. Many of these houses, as well as those without any system, use paraffin or LPG for all or part of their heating requirements with the associated problems of extra moisture generation. Moreover, these fuels, together with full tariff electricity, are over three times as expensive as gas used in a reasonably efficient central heating system.

About 29% of Glasgow's houses are affected by some kind of dampness, condensation or mould growth, 19% having condensation only and 15% suffering from mould growth. Since the survey took place in relatively warm summer weather, the extent of these problems has been significantly underestimated. The figures for the local authority stock are worse than those for the city as a whole. Here 28% have condensation, 8% 'substantial', and 22% have mould growth. Some types, such as tower blocks and those with deck access, have worse performance than the average. The highest incidence of condensation was in houses where there were children in the household and the worst affected households, despite the conditions they meet (or fail to meet) spend more of their income, as a percentage, on fuel than others.

Volume 5 shows that the percentage of family income spent on heating varied from 23.9% for the poorest families to 3.2% for the wealthiest. The actual sums had a much smaller range – from £478 to £720 per annum, the former being for the poorest households and the latter for the second wealthiest group.

Some examples

On a Glasgow estate at Darnley (Markus *et al.*, 1985) some general measurement and analysis was carried out as well as continuous monitoring over the heating season of conditions, activities and fuel expenditure in nine individual houses. The room temperatures recorded in living-rooms, bedrooms and kitchens are shown in Figure 7.7. In bedrooms and living-rooms none of the houses' average temperatures reached recommended levels, and in kitchens only two. Apart from kitchens, even the highest temperatures reached, at the extreme ends of the range, were below recommended levels. Many readings of 8–14°C were recorded. Fuel expenditures (Figure 7.8) show great variations and the large inter-house differences did not correlate significantly with house temperatures; there were too many intervening variables of household size and composition, house size, use patterns and income.

House densities varied from 1054 to 7323 cubic metres per person – a ratio of about 1:6. Moisture production was quite highly related to these densities but, even more strikingly, to the actual number of occupants, as is shown in Figure 7.9. Only house 6, with two occupants but a rather high moisture production, departs from what

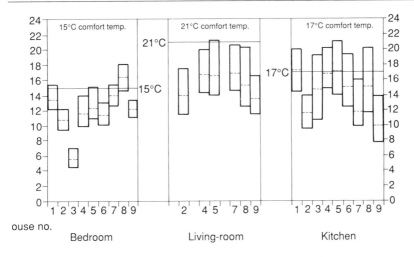

Figure 7.7 Darnley: mean maximum, mean average and mean minimum temperatures of three rooms in nine houses.

is virtually a linear relationship. The figure also shows how significant a part is played by clothes drying as a proportion of the total moisture produced.

In a study (Porteous, 1988) and practical project in Easthall, in the Easterhouse estate in Glasgow, for thermal upgrading including the use of passive solar energy, supported by the European Community and Glasgow District Council, the existing houses had a precast concrete block external wall with an inbuilt cavity and bridging concrete ties. The houses were draughty, cold, damp and mouldy. The improvements reduced the calculated weekly fuel bill required to maintain comfort standards from around £25.00 to £6.50 in the worst case. Another study of a 1960s house on the Castlemilk estate (Heatwise, 1988) showed a tenant who spent, in 1988, £836 per annum on fuel, still achieving only a very cold house. To achieve recommended comfort conditions would have required an annual expenditure of £1160. Thermal improvements costing around £2500 (insulation, draughtproofing and improved heating system) would have enabled these conditions to be achieved at an annual fuel expenditure of £650. This represents a payback period of around four years. But there is no need to labour the point as every study undertaken in Glasgow produces the same findings. Of course, none but the comfortably-off household could reap the full benefits since others will use all or some of the improvement in achieving higher

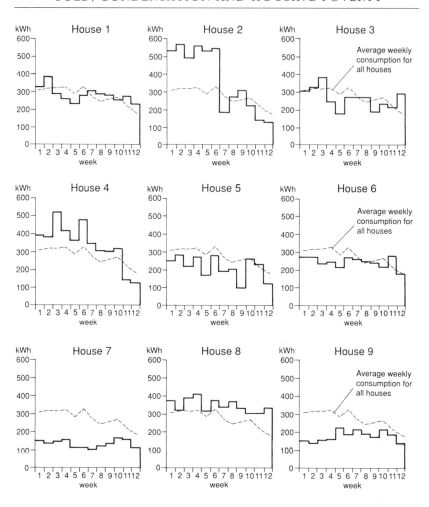

Figure 7.8 Darnley: weekly total fuel consumption – all fuels.

standards. The consequences of that in comfort, health and improved social life are immense, though difficult to quantify. Given adequate resources, and their intelligent use, what better programme for national investment could be found?

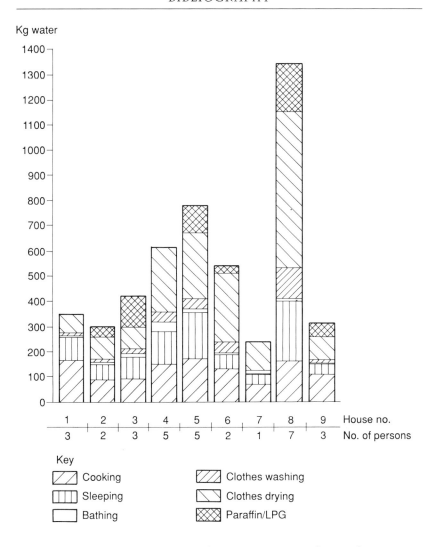

Figure 7.9 Darnley: moisture production over 13-week period.

Bibliography

Age Concern Scotland and South of Scotland Electricity Board (undated, c. 1990) *Hypothermia: What is it?*, SSEB, Glasgow.

Boardman, B. (1985) Activity levels within the home. Paper presented at Joint Meeting of CIB W17/77, 'Controlling Thermal

Environments', Budapest, 18–20 September 1985; Science Policy Research Unit, University of Sussex, Brighton.

Burr, M. L., Mullins, J., Merrett, T. G. and Stott, N. C. H. (1988) Indoor moulds and asthma. *J. Roy. Soc. Health*, 108, 99–100.

City of Glasgow (1987–90) *House Condition Survey*; 5 vols plus Surveyor's Manual.

Coleshaw, S. R. K. *et al.* (1986) Hypothermia in emergency admissions in cold weather. *Clinical Science*, 70, Suppl. 13, 93.

General Register Office for Scotland (1987) Vital Events Report, No. 30 (November), in: *Registrar-General's Vital Statistics Return*, Weeks 41–44, Edinburgh.

Grieve, R., Sir *et al.* (1986) *Inquiry into Housing in Glasgow*, Glasgow District Council.

Heatwise, Glasgow (1988) Kate's icy castle. *Scottish Energy News*, 2 August, 5.

Hutton, S. and Bradshaw, J. (1983) *Regional Variation in Domestic Fuel Expenditure*, DHSS, 169, 10/83, from Social Policy Research Unit, University of York, York; and Hutton, S. (1985), Regional variation in fuel expenditure using Climatic Severity Index, private communication from Social Policy Research Unit, University of York.

Keatinge, W. R. (1987) Winter mortality: warm housing offers cold comfort. *Geriatric Medicine*, December, 65–9.

Mant, D. C. and Muir Gray, J. A. (1986) *Building Regulation and Health*, Building Research Establishment/Department of the Environment, Watford.

Markus, T. A. (1979) Fuel poverty in Scottish homes. *Architects' Journal*, 23 May, 1077–82.

Markus, T. A. and Morris, E. N. (1980) *Buildings, Climate and Energy*, Pitman, London, chapter 3.

Markus, T. A., Clarke, J. A., Morris, E. N. and Collins, T. G. (1984) The influence of climate on housing: a simple technique for the assessment of dynamic energy behaviour. *Energy and Buildings*, 7, 243–59.

Markus, T. A. and Nelson, I. *et al.* (1985) *An Investigation of Condensation Dampness*, Glasgow District Council/University of Strathclyde, Glasgow.

Martin, C. J., Platt, S. D. and Hunt, S. M. (1987) Housing conditions and ill health. *B. Med. J.*, 294, 1125–7.

Martin, C. J., Platt, S. D., Hunt, S. M. and Lewis, C. W. (1989) Damp housing, mould growth, and symptomatic health state. *B. Med. J.*, 298, 1673–8.

Porteous, C. (1988) Calculations in 'Passive solar retrofit of thermally sub-standard housing at Glasgow, Easthall' (submission to European Community).

Primrose, W. R. and Smith, L. N. (1981) Urban hypothermia. *B. Med. J.*, 7(2), 282, 474.

Strachan, D. P. (1986) 'Damp housing and childhood asthma: validation of reporting of symptoms, *B. Med. J.*, 297, 1223–6.

Tagg, S. K. (1987) Report on weather and hospital admissions, internal draft report presented to Age Concern (Scotland), University of Strathclyde, Glasgow, November.

World Health Organization (WHO) (1961) *Expert Committee on the Public Health Aspects of Housing: First Report*, World Health Organization Technical Report Series No. 225, WHO, Geneva.

8

MENTAL HEALTH AND HIGH-RISE HOUSING

HUGH FREEMAN

8.1

Introduction

High-rise housing represents one specific and important case in which the general relationship of the environment to mental health needs to be examined scientifically. This is far from easy, though, because every aspect of the subject is immensely complex, while up to now social psychiatry has failed either to construct a credible environmental offshoot or to demonstrate that it can intervene usefully in public issues of this kind. For their part, planners, architects and others whose decisions affect the fabric of people's lives have shown little interest in looking at the long-term human effects of their activities – a task which for psychiatrists is considered to be one of the basic tools of the craft.

However, knowledge of this kind is beginning to be obtained (Freeman, 1985). It is now generally accepted scientifically that the aetiology of virtually all psychiatric disorders is multi-factoral, so that the environmental contribution to their origins (however expressed) must be part of a wider causal whole. It would be wrong therefore to make simplistic statements such as that 'high-rise housing causes depression'. Furthermore, any environmental factor will have widely varying effects on the different people exposed to it, these variations depending on the individuals' genetic constitution, previous experience, bodily health, cultural background, etc. If a high rate of a particular form of morbidity is coincident with a particular kind of environment, all that can be said with confidence is that a meaningful connection between the two *could* exist; but this connection may be only very tenuous and the direction of causality uncertain. For instance, where high-rise housing is mainly occupied by the poor, these residents may have had a worse than average level of health – both mental and physical – *before* they lived in that particular accommodation. For understandable practical reasons most research on environmental effects up to now has been cross-sectional (i.e. at a single point in time) but only longitudinal studies can eventually reveal whatever significant interactions there may be between these effects and psychiatric disorders (Quinton, 1988).

When looking at the psychological aspects of the environment, a basic question that needs to be asked is: what models or concepts should be used in the attempt to identify the processes of interaction between factors at the community level and health or behaviour at the individual level? One of these models is social support, maintained through social networks (e.g. Brown, 1990), and different environmental forms can greatly influence the extent to which this support is likely to be received. For instance, because of the differences in ease of access and in opportunities for informal encounters, those living in high-rise flats may on the whole be less socially supported than those in terraced houses. Another important general model is that of stress, though demonstrating its effects in any specific terms has proved to be difficult (Freeman, 1988). Other than the study of Cohen *et al.* (1986), in California, there have been few attempts to examine either the interplay between multiple environmental stressors themselves or the influence that these may have on health. In fact the direct effects of such stressors either on behaviour or bodily physiology may be less harmful than the consequences of individuals' coping responses to these forces (Evans, 1982).

8.2
Historical background

From the British point of view, the high-rise question is dominated by the special historical experience of the nation's urban communities. As the first industrial country, Britain was also the most highly urbanized until late into the nineteenth century, but this rapidly growing working-class population was not housed mainly in densely packed blocks of tenements and flats, as was the case in most comparable parts of Europe and America. By 1900, almost 90% of English people were living in terraced houses; however small, they were predominantly for single families (Muthesius, 1982), and this was true both of the middle and working classes. Rasmussen (1934) pointed out that the 'scattered city' of England, where each family tended to have a separate house, was in marked contrast to the 'concentrated city' typical of Europe. The situation was rather different, however, in Scottish cities, where four-storey tenements were fairly common, as they were to some extent in the East End of London. Philanthropic developments there, such as those of the Peabody Trust, provided a model for local authorities when these began to take on housing responsibilities after 1918. The benefits of craftsmanship, good-quality materials and traditional building methods then produced 'the last generation of multi-storey housing to weather well' (Esher, 1981).

However, the huge volume of interwar housing, both private and public, was very largely made up once again of single-family homes, and mostly in the form of that peculiarly British structure, the 'semi'; only 5% of the housing output of local authorities between the two world wars was in the form of flats (Ash, 1980). Over eight million people, the great majority of them of upper-working- or lower-middle-class status, were then rehoused in an environment where the density was, on average, about one-third that of the pre-1918 cities. Building was all by conventional methods and, except for some very large developments such as Manchester's Wythen-shawe and London's Dagenham, mostly with little involvement of architects or planners; on the whole, it has stood the test of time remarkably well. In Scotland this period saw a picture much more like that of England developing on the edges of its cities, but nothing comparable was to be found then in any other European country or – for working-class tenants – in North America. There was indeed some movement in industrialized cities everywhere from central flats to suburban villas, but only for a middle-class élite, who were becoming able to take advantage of the new mobility of the private car. Where improvements did occur outside Britain in working-class housing – as in the Karl Marx Hof, Vienna – these were almost without exception of a multi-storey kind.

These developments in Britain were strongly influenced by the Garden City ideology that had been formulated around the turn of the century by Ebenezer Howard; it had found its first embodiment in the Letchworth new town. Like Patrick Geddes, who inspired the British school of environment planning, Howard had reacted strongly against the uncontrolled, congested and unhealthy environment of the nineteenth-century industrial city (Hall, 1988). But there was a fundamental difference between the actual suburbia or large municipal estate of the 1930s and the designs of these visionaries: what was actually built was essentially a series of unplanned dormitories, whereas their theories had envisaged comprehensive, designed communities.

Britain therefore developed a cultural tradition of housing in which multi-storey accommodation seemed an aberration, only to be tolerated by people until a 'normal' single-family home should become available to them. In 1964 only 7% of households in England were living in purpose-built flats, compared with over 50% in some other European countries including Sweden and France (OPCS, 1973). The advantages of the semi, particularly for those who came from a nineteenth-century terraced house with no modern amenities, were immediately apparent. As well as the conveniences of the dwelling itself, there was a safe, supervised play area for children in the garden (increasingly important as streets became dangerous through traffic), 'defensible' space round the house (Newman, 1972) which discouraged intruders and a reasonable balance between privacy and proximity of neighbours. The British people developed an affection for the semi which shows little sign of cooling (Coleman, 1985); if it wants a change, it is only to more of the same – a detached house with garden all around.

That percipient chronicler of proletarian life, Richard Hoggart, writes (1988) that: 'English working-class people like horizontal urban villages, not European-style high-rise flats.' Thus, Quarry Hill Flats in his native Leeds, modelled on the Karl Marx Hof, 'had become a noxious slum' by the 1970s and was totally demolished, while the original is still regarded by the Viennese as a highly desirable place to live.

However, the disadvantages of the 1930s environmental form are less tangible (though no less real) and took longer to emerge. They include the disorientating sameness of the suburban landscape, the loss of all local or regional identity in the houses themselves, reduced access to services through low population density and geographical sprawl, and the possible attenuation of family and friendship ties (at least initially) from the dispersal of established communities – though wider ownership of cars and telephones has since reduced this problem. However, since neither private nor public initiative offered any real alternative for most people (i.e. affordable accommodation with modern amenities, near urban centres), a 'normal' home increasingly came to be regarded as one that was characteristic of the suburb. Except in London, the tradition of urban living virtually died out in Britain among those who had the resources to exercise any choice – but with baleful consequences for the health of cities. As Newman (1980) has described: 'A very high price has been paid . . . in abandoned residential neighbour-hoods, business areas and social and cultural institutions . . . in the high cost of commuter travel [and] in the disappearance of urban life-style.'

In the period after the Second World War, many different factors, including population growth and wartime damage and neglect, pro-duced an enormous increase in the demand for new housing in Britain. Even before 1939, much of the nineteenth-century indus-trial terraced housing had been legally 'condemned' as unfit for further use and a quarter of a million homes were subject to 'slum clearance'. Meanwhile, a planning system had come into being which held it as axiomatic that urban population densities must be greatly reduced and that there was a 'shortage of land' for homes in all urban areas. For their part, architects mostly believed that traditional building methods, based on brick and stone, were now too slow, too expensive and generally too outdated for large-scale use. Small-scale housing had tended to become synonymous with overcrowding because much of the nineteenth-century accom-modation had come to be occupied by far more people than it had been designed for (Sherlock, 1990). Both national and local authorities therefore became increasingly attracted to the possi-bility of a 'quick technological fix' which would be in tune with the general ethos of the time, restrict urban sprawl and 'solve' the housing problem once and for all. As a result, within only five years – 1969 to 1973 – more than one million people in Britain were housed in high-rise blocks (Cochrane, 1983). Many of these were put up very quickly by industrialized methods, with low-quality materials, poor workmanship and minimal environmental plan-ning. Far from being cheaper to build, as was claimed, their average cost was 50% higher than houses, and they consistently took longer than houses to complete for occupation (Willmott and Murie, 1980). Furthermore, as McCarthy *et al.* (1985) have pointed out, when overcrowded, inner city slums were replaced by tower blocks, 'The result was that most of the existing social problems – poverty, unemployment, large families, delinquency – remained. In addition, new problems were created.'

8.3
Methodological issues

General methodological issues which arise in the investigation of the relationship between mental health and the environment will not be considered further here (for discussion of these see Freeman, 1985). Examining the effects of high-rise housing, though, involves a number of confounding variables, and the failure to resolve these adequately accounts to some extent for the very unsatisfactory state of knowledge on the subject at present.

The most fundamental question to be asked about high-rise housing is: does the height of a dwelling from the ground have any effect in itself on the mental health of those living in it? An answer to this will require controlling for every other factor that might be associated with height and which might itself have an independent effect on mental health. Yet it is known that such factors have a tendency to cluster in either a positive or a negative direction, so that their separation in any study is likely to be extremely difficult.

Some of the main associated factors which could independently influence mental health are the following:

1. *Social class*: in particular, high-rise dwellings may be largely restricted to the poor (as in much British public housing), be largely for the rich (parts of Manhattan, New York) or include much of the population (Israel). Thus, even if people living in high-rise homes appear to show changes in mental health that are related to the residential experience, such findings may not be generalizable to the whole population from which the residents are drawn, if their social class distribution or other characteristics are not representative of that population.
2. *Size and quality of the dwelling*: these parameters may be much the same as residents would be likely to experience outside, or may be entirely different. For instance, the incoming tenants to British high-rise flats in the 1960s often came from old terraced houses which were very small and had no modern facilities, so that these people may well have been glad to 'trade-off' inconvenient height from the ground for a better standard of accom-

modation. Jephcott (1971) points out that with working-class people, 'it is easy to drum up an opinion on the fitness of a new bathroom, but less so to weigh up and then put into words such a nebulous matter as the influence of life in a high flat on one's social contacts'. On the other hand, many of the flats soon became incurably damp or impossible to heat economically, whereas such problems were unusual in other types of public housing. Vint and Bintliff (1983) suggest that if there are risks associated with technical changes in building, the costs of these should be accepted by the industry and by public authorities – not by the tenants, as has usually been the case.

3. *Stage in the life-cycle*: the nature of the experience of a high-rise home may be related to whether or not the residents have children or adolescents in the family. At the same time, the experience of other residents, who have no such dependants, may also depend to a significant extent on how many children or adolescents are present in that block or immediate neighbour-hood, for instance, because gangs of teenagers cause vandalism and harass older people by hanging around entrances. It would be wrong therefore to make comparisons of the mental health status of residents in different kinds of accommodation, if their age-group distributions were different. It seems likely that high-rise blocks restricted to single, childless or retired people may function well if the surroundings are tolerable (Ineichen, 1979). Williamson (1981) studied a large sample of relatively young, upwardly mobile people living in high-rise flats in two German cities, finding a much better level of adjustment than among working-class samples in similar accommodation in the UK.

4. *Structural features of the block*: Coleman (1985) found that indi-cators of social malaise all had a direct relationship (of worsen-ing) against an upward trend of four design variables – dwellings per entrance, dwellings per block, number of storeys and number of overhead walkways; clearly number of storeys is a direct function of height. Newman (1972) had previously found that the number of dwellings per entrance was the most important factor affecting the rate of crime in the block – i.e. the more dwellings, the more crime. Though crime levels are not a direct proxy for mental ill-health, fear of crime and the psychological and social consequences of having been exposed to it should represent two important elements in any overall measure of such morbidity. Other structural features that can be relevant to

mental health include: sound insulation (rarely adequate), basic services (lifts, rubbish disposal, etc.), spatial opportunities for informal meetings and the presence of 'dead' spaces that encourage vandalism or crime (e.g. unused garages). Lifts and rubbish chutes will tend to be more problematic at greater heights from the ground, but can still cause concern in medium-rise blocks.

5. *Immediate surroundings of the block*: both Newman and Coleman have identified features of the immediate environment which show a direct relationship with crime and malaise; for instance, unobserved entrances, unfenced territory and excessive ease of access from outside the site. In practice, high-rise blocks in Britain are often surrounded by a no-man's land of dereliction, with uncollected rubbish, ill-maintained grass and a profusion of dog excrement. Yet as Sherlock (1990) points out, 'open space in central areas which has no particular purpose simply attenuates the concentration of people and activities that is necessary for urban life'. On the other hand, some blocks are certainly to be found which are situated in pleasant surroundings, mixed with lower-rise housing of good quality (McCarthy *et al.*, 1985); in practice, these have tended to be occupied mainly by single people or by couples without children, so that it becomes difficult to separate the influence of this environmental factor from that of factor 3, above.

Both Newman and Coleman have been accused of 'architectural determinism', and also of promoting no more than a 'target hardening', which would simply move on the problem. However, Newman (1972) never proposed that 'the forms of the built environment directly affect the social structures and values of society ... or create "moral attitudes" ', nor claimed that crime is inevitable if certain structural features are present. Management and social problems usually co-exist with deficiencies of design, and it would be unreasonable to expect life in a particular environment to improve significantly if all these are not confronted at the same time (Wilson and Hunter, 1978). For her part, Coleman (1985) has stated that 'bad design does not determine anything, but it increases the odds against which people have to struggle'. Her research also indicated that design features which are bad from the human point of view tend to be found clustered together in the same scheme and so reinforce each other.

Vandalism is a factor of constantly increasing importance. Ash

(1980) states that its growth from the late 1960s 'exacerbated the deterioration of hard-to-let estates in particular, and high-rise estates generally. Vacancies and vandalism were mutually reinforcing since empty flats attracted vandals and vandalism put people off from accepting vacancies.' Why this growth should have occurred is unlikely to have a simple explanation, but the replacement of more traditional environments by large-scale redevelopments in which high-rise buildings were usually prominent must almost certainly have been relevant.

In an empirical study of the complex interaction between social and structural factors in a New York public housing development, Newman and Franck (1980) found that the rates of actual crime, fear of crime and instability of resident population were related to four major factors. These were: the size of the building; its accessibility for unauthorized entry; a combined factor of low incomes and proportion of one-parent families; and the ratio of teenagers to adults. The tenets of 'defensible space' theory were confirmed in the indirect effects of the size of the building on rates of burglary, personal crime and fear of crime, for which residents' control of the space outside their flat was found to be an important intervening variable. The conclusion to be drawn from this and similar work is that a complex, anonymous environment, combined (as this often is) with poor building maintenance and social instability of the resident population, will adversely affect the quality of life of residents. One aspect of this process may well be a poorer level of mental health, though this has not often been directly examined.

However, an important research approach which has sought to relate psychiatric morbidity to environmental circumstances is the work of Brown and his colleagues on depression (e.g. Brown and Harris, 1982). While accepting that certain people are vulnerable to depression, they see this as essentially a social phenomenon, whose occurrence is highly related to the presence of severe, long-term life events, mostly distinguished by the experience of actual or threatened major loss ('severe events'). Relevant examples of these include having to move to escape difficult neighbours, the failure of arrangements to obtain a new flat or receiving notice to quit one's home. A second group of aetiological factors are 'major difficulties', which are defined as being severe, lasting at least two years and not involving health. An example is poor housing, which featured in 28% of the reported cases of chronic depression; the indices of poor housing used here were: overcrowding, physical deprivation, exposure to noise and insecurity of tenure. Severe events and major difficulties were aggregated as 'provoking agents'. The third psychosocial group of factors are of vulnerability, and this is related to the support received from social relationships.

This model was mainly developed on the basis of data obtained from working-class women living in two deprived areas of inner London, though some comparisons have been made with other samples. The generalizability of its conclusions have been questioned, though: Werry and Carlielle (1983) asked whether 'results of studies in London and other huge cities are typical of anywhere except themselves and whether or not some of the ominous findings would also be true of the millions of women who live in less crowded and less insecure circumstances'. This raises the further question of how social class is related to psychiatric disorder, and though the conventional wisdom is that morbidity increases steadily with lower status, any such relationship is probably far more complex than has generally been assumed. For instance, the risk of experiencing a burglary or an accident to a child is probably much greater for a working-class woman, who may also have to cope with such experiences as enforced rehousing, debt, unemployment or police trouble, which are not on the whole encountered by middle-class women.

However, if this aspect of the environment/mental health equation is considered from the point of view of high-rise accommodation, it seems impossible to separate the housing variable from the effects of social class. In the samples studied by Brown *et al.*, a significant proportion of the women were living in that kind of accommodation because public housing in those areas contained many tower blocks. A proportion of the severe events and major difficulties which these subjects experienced (e.g. vandalism, lift failures, uncollected rubbish) could be specifically related to high-rise living, but these would be very unlikely to be experienced by middle-class women living at the same height. At the same time, though, a proportion of each of the three types of proposed aetiological factors are not directly related to environment or social class, and these may be expected to affect women from all classes at similar rates. In fact, when rates of only mild depression were compared, no significant social class differences were found.

Longitudinal research, although so essential to provide any useful responses to the questions at issue here, is extremely difficult, not least because of the mobility of high-rise residents, at least in Britain. The study by Ineichen and Hooper (1974) seems to have been prevented from obtaining any possible positive findings of adverse effects from high-rise living by the fact that few residents likely to have shown such changes remained long enough to appear in the sample at 18-months follow-up; by then, 60% of the flat-dwellers had moved. It is, in any case, difficult to disaggregate the effects of a particular kind of home from the effects of moving, though the latter is unlikely to produce any significant psychiatric disorder in a person of previously stable personality (Hall, 1966). Among those that do stay, an 'adjustment effect' has been reported, whereby symptoms decrease after a year or more in residence (Ineichen and Hooper, 1974), but this would presumably depend on environmental conditions not deteriorating greatly.

The particular British attitudes to high-rise accommodation, referred to above, indicate that any conclusions about its effects will need to take account of cultural differences. There appear to be widespread feelings in Britain, not to be dismissed because they are difficult to define, that tower blocks are somehow an offence against the natural or traditional order of human habitation. Hoggart (1988) writes of medium-rise blocks, constructed in Leeds in the 1970s, that if their planners had understood the pattern of life of the demolished old streets, the message conveyed to them would have been 'not a general heartless appearance such as this, not several storeys like this, not stairways like these and above all not enclosed bare-arsed courts like these'. Such attitudes to multi-storey housing are not universal, though, and the variations between different populations in this respect no doubt reflect not only different cultural histories, but the objective reality which most people face in their search for decent living accommodation. With the collapse of communist regimes in Eastern Europe in 1989, for instance, evidence emerged that waiting-lists there, even for small flats in tower blocks, could be for more than 20 years, and in urban areas there was virtually no alternative, except for the few people inheriting a dwelling that had escaped state ownership. In Israel the alternative to a high-rise flat for middle-class people would be one in a four-storey, multi-family dwelling, which presumably is much less attractive as an option than a single-family house (Churchman and Ginsberg, 1984) (see above, 'Methodological issues').

To some extent, cultural differences will also be related to feelings on crowding and available space per person: though Brown and

Chombart de Lauwe (1959) reported that rates of illness and social disorganization were then above average in France, with less than 8–10 m² per person in a dwelling; under half that space in Hong Kong was associated with low rates of mortality, morbidity and overt criminality. The effect of the mediating social structure seems to be evident in this contrast, since in Chinese culture privacy is defined in terms of groups rather than individuals; although having a particular number of people in a house might result in negative effects if they were non-kin, this does not generally occur when they are defined as kin (Anderson, 1972). Similarly, the level of external noise that should be acceptable within a dwelling probably depends much more on cultural factors than on any absolute standards. Noise may also be tolerated to varying extents according to its source: aircraft or traffic noise may be regarded as unavoidable, whereas that from neighbours' sound systems arouses stress and resentment.

Three matched groups of families, each with two very young children, living respectively in high-rise flats, low-rise flats and houses, all rented from the council in the same London borough, were compared by Richman (1974). She found that the children might spend most of the day isolated in a flat with their mother, so that the resulting boredom and irritation could well lead to tension and strained relationships; this was particularly the case when children were at the toddling stage or able to run about, but could not safely be left on their own. Since contact with neighbours might only be by chance, when entering or leaving, flat life seemed to exacerbate the inherent difficulties of women who were poor mixers, and to increase the problems of isolation and restriction to the home experienced by many mothers of young children. Depression of moderate-to-severe extent was found in 41% of the mothers and more marked among those living in flats; surprisingly, though, the highest prevalence was among the women in low-rise flats, which did not necessarily allow the mother more mobility or the children more freedom than high-rise accommodation (whose residents produced the most complaints). Psychiatric problems in the mothers tended to be associated with behavioural problems in the children. Richman concluded that depression, loneliness and dissatisfaction with accommodation affect a high proportion of mothers with young children who live in flats; she also suggested, as have others, that some of the differences between families in different kinds of accommodation might have been obscured by the number of those who had moved out of high-rise flats in the previous year.

8.4
Empirical studies of high-rise housing

The first relevant study was that of Fanning (1967), comparing the health of service families in low-rise flats in Germany with that of similar families in houses; measured by medical consultation rates, the flat-dwellers showed 57% more morbidity. The six disorders for which higher rates in flats were most marked included neurosis (especially for young married women), but Fanning speculated that emotional stress might also have contributed to the largest group of cases in flat-dwellers, which was of respiratory illness. Living in flats, though, was only one of the stresses affecting these subjects, in addition to those caused by service overseas, such as disruption of the extended family. However, as Ineichen (1979) pointed out, the wives living in flats were generally younger than those in houses, had more recently moved to Germany and had husbands of lower rank, so that the two populations were not fully matched.

Moore (1974, 1975, 1976) carried out a series of similar studies, including residents of one tower block; he found no increased prevalence of psychiatric disorder among the flat-dwellers, even when questionnaire scores were added to the consultation rates. Although flat life was responsible for sufficient stress to cause some increase in clinical psychiatric illness for those of neurotic personality, this did not produce an overall level which was significantly greater than that of the house-dwellers.

Among civilian populations in Britain, Reynolds and Nicholson (1969) investigated the prevalence of neurotic symptoms in women living in six council estates in London and Sheffield, mostly in high-rise accommodation. These symptoms were very frequent in the sample, but showed no relationship to the type of housing, height above the ground or population density of the estate. In Bristol, Ineichen and Hooper (1974) found that women living in houses in a redeveloped central area reported more neurotic symptoms than those in high-rise flats or maisonettes (which had the lowest rate). However, the number of children living in flats considered by their mothers to present behavioural problems was relatively almost double that in either of the other groups; loneliness and isolation were significant complaints among these women. In Brighton, Bagley (1973) compared a random sample of women living in a 12-storey block of flats with a control group in houses on a prewar council estate; the house-dwellers emerged as significantly less neurotic and consulted their general practitioners significantly less often for 'nervous illness'. The women living in flats complained significantly more about housing and environmental matters. Gilloran (1968) concluded from a study in Edinburgh that the outstanding problem of family life in high flats was isolation; the fact that young mothers were usually separated from relatives and established friendship networks meant that they were never free of the responsibility of child-minding: 'Never previously anywhere have mothers been expected to undertake this task entirely alone.' McCarthy *et al.* (1985) interviewed 383 families on eight housing estates in Gateshead, of whom 174 lived in medium- or high-rise blocks; although there was a non-significant trend for flat residents to report more symptoms than those living in houses, no overall relationship was found between levels of symptoms and types of dwellings. Stewart (1970) found that mothers with young children in high flats were particularly likely to show symptoms of psychiatric disorders, though this was not true of mothers with teenage children. Littlewood and Tinker (1981) reported that two-thirds of mothers with children under 5 who were rehoused from flats said that their emotional health was better since the move, and most said that their children were better behaved.

Studying parents with children, living in rented public flats in a Canadian city, Gillis (1977) found that women, but not men, showed more psychological stress the higher up they lived. It was speculated that these women felt it difficult to fulfil the traditional role of wife-mother in such an artificial, non-traditional environment. In Glasgow, Hannay (1981) found a significant correlation between residence in high flats and an increased prevalence of psychiatric symptoms; in particular, those on the fifth floor and above had twice the prevalence, compared with those on the lower floors or those living in houses. Littlewood and Tinker (1981) found that families moving out of high-rise dwellings reported fewer symptoms of depression after the move, compared with before.

McCarthy *et al.* (1985) compared rates of psychological distress in residents of eight different types of housing situation within a metropolitan district in the north-east of England. Although high-rise flats located in inner city, 'problem' estates were found to be associated with high levels of psychological distress, similar dwellings located in the suburbs were associated with low levels of distress. It was concluded that the type of area in which people live is more closely associated with levels of psychological impairment than is the type of housing which they inhabit; household social class and age, on their own, did not have a significant effect on psychological distress.

The basic problem of all such research, though, is that large effects from changes in housing variables could only be expected, 'If the whole package of poverty, illness, and social problems could be unravelled into a single long causal chain with housing as one of the early links', but instead, 'residential variables [are] richly embedded in a large matrix of individual and social variables that condition and attenuate the impact of the residential environment' (Kasl *et al.*, 1982). These authors point out that the 'meaning' of housing needs to be understood in the experiential rather than just in the physical sense, and that poor housing is an obstacle to well-being and self-fulfilment, but remedying only poor housing is not enough'. They also consider it undesirable to take a particular residential parameter, such as persons per room, translate it into a specific psychological construct, and so commit us to a single intervening process between that and behavioural outcomes or human experiences. Because of the many ways in which different psycho-social variables can alter the effects of such processes in subgroups of the population, Kasl *et al.* consider that the main effort of research should be directed towards disentangling these various influences and outcomes.

Birtchnell, Masters and Deahl (1988) screened for depressive symptoms of all young married women on a London housing estate; they lived in a variety of accommodation, some of which was high-rise. A disproportionate concentration of depressed women was found in the least desirable areas of the estate; the interiors of their dwellings were significantly poorer in appearance, compared with those who had low scores for depression; and they made significantly more complaints about the estate, which were only partly explicable in terms of their worse accommodation. Birtchnell *et al.* concluded that although the innate vulnerability of the depressed women may have influenced their location there, the accommodation itself is also likely to have played a part in the development and maintenance of their depression.

We have already referred to the specific relationship established by Coleman (1985) between indices of social malaise and specific design features of high-rise flats (dwellings per block, number of storeys per block, etc.). Psychiatric morbidity was not included in the model because of lack of suitable data, which would indeed require a very complex epidemiological exercise. However, one aspect of the study which seems open to criticism is the inclusion of the number of children in care as one of the measures of social malaise of a public housing area. Apart from its sensitivity to the effects of local ideologies or administrative policies (particularly in some of the areas that were mapped), this variable was not of the same nature as the others – litter, graffiti, and fouling with urine or faeces. Furthermore, its place in the chain of causality is uncertain; the rate of children in care is a multi-factorially determined product that raises complex questions about incidence vs prevalence, length of time spent living in a particular environment, or the age and sex structure of that particular population.

Ash (1980) has pointed out that the cycle of research, design, construction and evaluation has been too slow for conclusions to emerge when they were needed, particularly when government departments were involved. A survey by the Ministry of Housing and Local Government of families living at high density was complete in 1963 but not published until seven years later.

8.5
High-rise living as a pathogenic factor

In view of the generally modest level of positive evidence that has emerged from the literature reviewed above, why does high-rise living continue to receive so much attention in studies of housing and health, and why is there such a widespread and persistent feeling that it must be inherently stressful?

One answer is to be found in the physical risks associated with this kind of accommodation which, if relatively rare, are far from unknown. The Ronan Point disaster showed that solidity of construction could not always be assumed, particularly when relatively new prefabricated building methods were being used, as they were on a wide scale in Britain in the 1950s and 1960s. Also gas explosions, which can never be completely eliminated, are likely to be much more dangerous in a high-rise than in a low-rise building.

Secondly, there is the danger of falling, particularly for children and where there are balconies; this may result in mothers especially developing compulsive fears about their children's safety (Stewart, 1970). Coroners' records for England and Wales showed that in 1973–7 children living above the first* floor were 57 times more likely to be killed by falling from their homes than were children in lower accommodation, so that these fears are by no means groundless. Associated with this problem is that of how to supervise play for children young enough to require constant adult observation. For families in any accommodation above ground level, there are only three possibilities: (a) keep young children in the flat; (b) have a parent always present when they are outside; or (c) arrange a rota with other parents. The first two have obvious drawbacks of their own, while the third is likely to be hampered by a generally less than close state of neighbourly relationships in high-rise blocks. For school-age children, high-rise estates are usually lacking in environmental interest, deprived of the informal supervisory care of adults, and more vulnerable to damage, compared with traditional streets.

Thirdly, there is the danger of fire which may spread (e.g. along ducts which run through tower blocks). Although fire-escape doors may be provided, these are often bolted or nailed up because they provide easy access to burglars. Fire brigades are not always as well equipped as they should be with the extending ladders needed for high-level rescue.

Fourthly, Freedman (1975) concluded from his studies of crowding that if a social situation is initially unfavourable (e.g. through poverty, racial tension or crime) feelings of fear, suspicion and isolation are likely to be increased by the experience of living in a high-rise building with many other families. Similarly, Jephcott (1971) suggested that high-rise living is particularly hard on those who are below average in social assets, since the support which might be expected from neighbours and friends in a traditional environment is much less likely to be received, in view of the large numbers of people involved and the physical isolation of individual flats. It is probably unreasonable to expect such people to show the methodical habits, self-restraint and social competence that are required to make satisfactory use of multi-storey housing. Furthermore, unlike the better-off, they do not usually have the safety valves of holidays, outdoor sports or car travel.

* Second floor in American usage.

Fifthly, there are the large maintenance costs (often ignored in the original calculations) of such a high-technology environment, which is only successful when enough money is available indefinitely to ensure that all the mechanical aspects are functioning and that the communal areas are clean and free from crime. Throughout the world, though, housing authorities have built high-rise developments on a scale far beyond their capacity to maintain them adequately; essential services soon break down and building faults occur which tenants themselves are powerless to improve. The personal freedom and opportunities for choice and self-expression of residents are also restricted in such matters as keeping pets, making adaptations to the home and having any outside space in which to potter about. As the quality of structure and maintenance falls with inadequate resources, so vandalism, crime and the general despoiling of the environment tend to escalate. This results in respectable families making every possible effort to get out, being replaced by 'difficult' clients on the waiting-list, who may include former long-stay patients of psychiatric hospitals. In this vicious circle of environmental deterioration, those who were already disadvantaged may find themselves trapped in dirty, dangerous, noisy and incomprehensible living conditions, which can certainly be described as 'stressful'.

Finally, there is the aesthetic aspect; although not generally regarded as significant from the point of view of health, and although virtually impossible to study scientifically, this is unlikely to be without significance. Tower blocks and other megastructural forms of housing, as well as giant shopping-centres, seem to overwhelm the human environment, wiping out the intimate scale of a traditional street or square, the flowering trees of a suburb in the spring or the view of hills or sky beyond an urban area. Jephcott (1971) describes tower blocks as

inescapable. [They] dwarf everything, important public buildings, trees, humans . . . They also diminish the pleasantness of city parks and public gardens since their prodigious height dispels the illusion of rural things . . . And any house or garden lying alongside a multi-storey block suffers drastically from the overshadowing of this cold and concrete wing.

High-rise blocks owe their appearance almost entirely to the architectural Modern Movement, inspired by Le Corbusier. This, as Bauman (1990) has pointed out, 'was afflicted from the start with a death-wish, a nostalgia for paralysis and silence, a self-incapacitation that in its terminal stages measured its success by the emptiness of a canvas, the semantic blankness of the page and the dehumanized geometry of our human habitat.' It cannot be proved that high-rise residents, as well as those around them, have suffered in mental health from these aesthetic phenomena, but the argument that they have done so deserves to be taken seriously.

8.6
Conclusion

Analysis of the available information on the high-rise/mental health relationship therefore does not produce a clear picture. Apart from any other consideration, it is a situation that is likely to change over time; technical progress could well allow some of the more troublesome features of high-rise accommodation to be improved, but only if money is spent, both in building and in later maintenance. It would be entirely wrong, though, to see any problems of high-rise living as stemming from high overall density; low-density suburbanization 'could be as damaging to the urban areas as the tower blocks of the 1960s' (Sherlock, 1990). Cochrane's (1983) conclusion is that blaming an increased use of psychiatric services on the physical environment is 'a very tempting simplification of reality'; shifts in attitudes have greatly changed people's expectations of, and tolerance of, levels of distress. He believes that these changes, 'with changes in family structure, sex role definitions and the availability of treatment, far outweigh the impact of residential effects except in extreme circumstances or where vulnerability already exists'.

All the factors identified by Cochrane (1983) are undoubtedly important, and he is right to warn against the attempt to establish cause-and-effect relationships on a simplistic basis. Suedfeld (1991) has emphasized that the environment has in fact no *direct* effect on human beings: rather it is filtered through their psychological and physiological information-processing systems. But this is no reason to regard the home and surrounding environment as having little influence in the aetiological model. When allowance has been made for all likely confounding variables, the effects of height from the ground seem to have some independent role within this general influence.

The methodological caveats that were raised at the beginning of this chapter will also need to be supplemented by current changes in the notion of causality. Individual exposures (e.g. to a type of housing) often act as a 'component cause' rather than as a 'sufficient cause' of an effect (Rothman, 1986). An effect is likely to arise from the interaction of component causes, but very often most (or all) of these are unknown. When mental states are component causes, their meaning will have a mediating role, and this meaning may vary according to the social characteristics of the people concerned. To call for more reliable and longer-term research may seem an evasion of the questions posed earlier, but without such work any answers can only be tentative. From the common sense point of view, though, high-rise living – particularly where imposed – must be regarded as at least under suspicion of adversely affecting the mental health of many people. As Mitchell (1976) has pointed out, though housing investment may not be justified simply on the basis of research data, 'the extent to which a country adequately houses its population is an indicator of the nation's political maturity'.

Acknowledgement

The helpful comments on this manuscript of John Birtchnell, Peter Willmott and Jim Connelly are greatly appreciated.

Bibliography

Anderson, E. N. Jr (1972) Some Chinese methods of dealing with crowding. *Urban Anthropology*, 1, 141–50.

Ash, J. (1980) The rise and fall of high-rise housing in England, in: Ungerson, C., Karn, V., Huttman, E. and Fara, S. F. (eds) *The Consumer Experience of Housing*, Gower, Aldershot.

Bagley, C. (1973) The built environment as an influence on personality and social behaviour: a spatial study. In D. Canter, T. R. Lee (eds) *Psychology and the Built Environment*, Architectural Press, Tonbridge.

Bauman, Z. (1990) Living with indeterminacy. *Times Literary Supplement*, 11 May, p. 501.

Birtchnell, J., Masters, N. and Deahl, M. (1988) Depression and the physical environment. *B. J. Psychiatry*, 153, 56–64.

Brown, G. W. (1990) Depression in the community, in: Bennett, D. H. and Freeman, H. L. (eds) *Community Psychiatry*. Churchill Livingstone, London.

Brown, G. W. and Harris, T. (1982) *Social Origins of Depression*, Tavistock, London.

Chombart de Lauwe, P. M. (1953) *Famille et habitation*, Centre National de la Recherché Scientifique, Paris.

Churchman, A. and Ginsberg, Y. (1984) The image and experience of high rise housing in Israel. *J. Environ. Psychol.*, 4, 27–41.

Cochrane, R. (1983) *The Social Creation of Mental Illness*, Longman, London.

Cohen, S., Evans, G. W., Stokols, D. and Krantz, D. S. (1986) *Behaviour, Health and Environmental Stress*, Plenum, New York.

Coleman, A. (1985) *Utopia on Trial: Vision and Reality in Planned Housing*, Hilary Shipman, London.

Esher, L. (Lord) (1981) *A Broken Wave*, Allen Lane, London.

Evans, G. W. (1982) General introduction, in: Evens, G. W. (ed.) *Environmental Stress*, Cambridge University Press, Cambridge.

Fanning, P. M. (1967) Families in flats. *BMJ*, **ii**, 382–6.

Freedman, J. L. (1975) *Crowding and Behaviour*, W. H. Freeman, San Francisco, Calif.

Freeman, H. L. (1985) Housing in *Mental Health and The Environment* (ed. Freeman, H. L.), Churchill Livingstone, London.

Freeman, H. L. (1988) Psychiatric aspects of environmental stress. I. *J. Mental Health*, 17, 13–23.

Gillis, A. R. (1977) High rise housing and psychological strain. *J. Health Social Behaviour*, 18, 418–31.

Gilloran, J. L. (1968) Social health problems associated with 'high living'. *Medical Officer*, 120, 117–18.

Hall, P. (1966) Some clinical aspects of moving house as an apparent precipitant of psychiatric symptoms. *J. Psychosom. Res.*, 10, 59–70.

Hall, P. (1988) *Cities of Tomorrow*, Basil Blackwell, Oxford.

Hannay, D. R. (1981) Mental health and high flats. *J. Chron. Dis.*, 34, 431–2.

Hoggart, R. (1988) *A Local Habitation*, London.

Ineichen, B. (1979) High rise living and mental stress. *Biol. Human Affairs*, 44, 81–5.

Ineichen, B. and Hooper, D. (1974) Wives' mental health and

children's behaviour problems in contrasting residential areas. *Soc. Sci. Medicine*, 8, 369–74.

Jephcott, P. (1971) *Homes in High Flats*, Oliver and Boyd, Edinburgh.

Kasl, S. V., White, M., Will, J. and Marcuse, P. (1982) In: Baum, A. and Singer, J. E. (eds) *Advances in Environmental Psychology*, Lawrence Erlbaum, Boston, Mass., Vol. 4.

Littlewood, J. and Tinker, A. (1981) *Families in Flats*, HMSO, London.

McCarthy, P., Byrne, D., Harrison, S. and Keithley, J. (1985). Housing type, housing location and mental health. *Social Psychiatry*, 20, 125–30.

Mcarthy, D. and Seagert, S. (1976) Residential density, social control and social withdrawal. *Human Ecology*, 6, 297–330.

Mitchell, R. E. (1976) Cultural and health influences on building, housing and community standards. *Human Ecology*, 4, 297–330.

Moore, N. C. (1974) Psychiatric illness and living in flats. *B. J. Psychiatry*, 125, 500–7.

Moore, N. C. (1975) Social aspects of flat dwellings. *Public Health*, 89, 109–15.

Moore, N. C. (1976) The personality and mental health of flat dwellers. *B. J. Psychiatry*, 128, 259–61.

Muthesius, S. (1982) *The English Terraced House*, Yale University Press, London.

Newman, O. (1972) *Defensible Space*, Collier, New York.

Newman, O. (1980) *Community of Interest*, Anchor, New York.

Newman, O. and Franck, K. A. (1980) *Factors Influencing Crime and Instability in Urban Housing Developments*, US Department of Justice, Washington, DC.

Office of Population Censuses and Surveys (OPCS) (1973) *Social Trends*, HMSO, London.

Quinton, D. (1988) Urbanism and child mental health. *J. Child Psychol. Psychiatry*, 29, 11–20.

Rasmussen, S. (1934) *London: The Unique City*, MIT Press, Cambridge, Mass.

Reynolds, I. and Nicholson, C. (1969) Living off the ground. *Architects' Journal*, 34, 150–4.

Richman, N. (1974) The effects of housing on pre-school children and their mothers. *Development. Med. Child Neurology*, 16, 53–8.

Rothman, K. (1986) *Modern Epidemiology*, Little Brown, Boston, Mass.

Sherlock, H. (1990) *Cities are Good for Us*, Transport 2000, London.

Stewart, W. F. R. (1970) *Children in Flats – a Family Study*, NSPCC, London.

Suedfeld, P. (1992) Groups in isolation and confinement: environments and experiences, in: Harrison, A. A., Clearwater, Y. A. and McKay, C. P. (eds) *The Human Experience in Antarctica*.

Vint, J. and Bintliff, J. (1983) Tower blocks: the economics of high rise housing. *Soc. Pol. Admin.* 17, 118–29.

Werry, J. S. and Carlielle, J. (1983) The nuclear family, suburban neurosis, and astrogenesis in Auckland mothers of young children. *J. Am. Acad. Child Psychiatry*, 22, 172–9.

Williamson, R. C. (1981) Adjustment to the high-rise: variables in a German sample. *Environment and Behaviour*, 13, 289–310.

Willmott, P. and Murie, A. (1988) *Polarisation and Social Housing*, Policy Studies Institute, London.

Wilson, S. and Hunter, J. (1978) Updating defensible space. *Architects' Journal*, 43, October, 11.

9

WOMEN, CROWDING AND MENTAL HEALTH

JONATHAN GABE AND PAUL WILLIAMS

9.1

Introduction

Despite the widespread belief that housing affects health, scientific research over the past two decades has failed to demonstrate this relationship convincingly (Kasl, 1974; Kirmeyer, 1978; Cohen, Glass and Phillips, 1979; Loring, 1979). The research has generally been of two kinds: ecological studies investigating the relationship between measures of population density in geographically defined areas and indirect indicators of health status (e.g. hospital admissions) (Galle, Gove and McPherson, 1972; Levy and Herzog, 1974; Collette and Webb, 1977), and studies relating individuals' housing circumstances to measures of ill-health (Taylor and Chave, 1964; Moore, 1974, 1976; Booth and Cowell, 1976; Booth and Edwards, 1976).

Both these approaches can be criticized on methodological grounds. The first uses a unit of analysis (i.e. geographical areas) that makes it difficult to draw meaningful inferences about the effects of household or neighbourhood crowding on individuals (Kasl and Harburg, 1975; Baldassare, 1979). The second approach, although taking the individual as the unit of analysis, fails to acknowledge that individuals are, first and foremost, members of particular social groups (Davies and Roche, 1980; Graham, 1983), who differ in their use of, and control over, the available household or neighbourhood space because of their position in the social structure (Gabe and Williams, 1986). This failure to acknowledge the importance of social groupings would seem to reflect the popularity of 'methodological individualism' and 'abstract empiricism' among many epidemiological and sociological researchers (Mills, 1959; Paterson, 1981; Bryant, 1985).

We have chosen to work at the individual rather than ecological level but to treat individuals primarily as members of specific social groups. From this standpoint, it is particularly important to consider the effects of housing on the health of those groups that because of their social position are most tied to the house and immediate neighbourhood, and hence are most likely to highlight a relationship between housing and health. This chapter is concerned with one such social category – namely, women.

9.2
Women, household crowding and health

It is widely assumed that poor housing conditions exert a deleterious effect on the health and well-being of household members. One aspect of housing that is generally considered to be important is internal density, or the degree of crowding in the home. Women's subordinated position in society (Barrett, 1980; Oakley, 1981; Burton, 1985), and the nature of the demands placed on them in the home as a result of the unequal division of labour (in terms of child-rearing and housework – see Hunt, 1974; Oakley, 1974; Brittan and Maynard, 1984; Allan, 1985), make it likely, a priori, that they would suffer more from household crowding than men. Yet the effects of such crowding on women's health have rarely been considered; this is a further example of women's invisibility in the social sciences generally (Oakley, 1974; Tivers, 1978; Smith, 1979; Stacey, 1981), and urban studies in particular (Duvall and Booth, 1978; Gamarnikow, 1978; McDowell, 1983).

In Britain the only empirical research considering the significance of internal crowding for women's health was undertaken in the 1930s by Spring Rice (1939). Using qualitative methods, she investigated the health and social conditions of 1250 married, working-class women in various parts of Britain. She provided a graphic description of their housing conditions that were thought by the women to influence their health. Her respondents were in no doubt that overcrowding, and other features such as poor structural conditions (e.g. damp, inadequate sanitation) and neighbourhood noise, had a direct and damaging effect on their physical and mental well-being. In many cases, this was thought to be compounded by the problems of fulfilling domestic responsibilities in such conditions.

To our knowledge, quantitative research on this topic has not previously been undertaken in Britain. However, such work has been conducted in North America: Duvall and Booth (1978) selected a subsample of married women with dependent children from a study conducted in Toronto (Booth and Cowell, 1976), and explored the relationship between perceived crowding (not objective crowding measured as persons per room) and indicators of emotional well-being (regular sedative-hypnotic drug use over past year; index of psychiatric impairment) and physical health (e.g. stress-related illness reported; uterine disorders). They found that perceived crowding was positively, if modestly, associated with the mental health measures but not the physical health indicators.

Two other studies have used individual-level data to consider the relationship between women's health and internal crowding. Baldassare (1981) used US survey data to consider the relationship between internal density (persons per room) and measures of health (satisfaction) and mental health (worry about a nervous breakdown). He found that women with young children living in high-density homes were more likely to be dissatisfied with their health.

Gove and Hughes (1983), analysing survey data on Chicago house-holds, found that the relationship between internal crowding and health of the women respondents varied according to household composition and marital status. For example, the effect of crowding on the mental health of married women was greater if children and other adults (in addition to the spouse) were present in the household.

In most of these studies women have been conceptualized primarily as household members with certain roles to fulfil. As Connell (1985) and Stacey and Thorne (1985), among others, have pointed out, however, reducing gender relations to sex roles has the effect of playing down the extent to which people are structurally constrained to adopt certain patterns of behaviour. Furthermore, it minimizes the degree of conflict within the household stemming from the asymmetrical power relationship between men and women.

Thus we have chosen to conceptualize women as, first and foremost, members of a subordinate social group. Given this starting-point, one can hypothesize that women, being in a subordinated position in the household (Brittan and Maynard, 1984; Allan, 1985), are less able to control household space and less able to achieve a desired level of privacy for themselves than male members. Consequently, they are more likely to suffer the adverse psychological effects of household crowding. These deleterious consequences are likely to be compounded by, among other things, the presence of preschool children (Brown and Harris, 1978) and the sense of isolation and separation from the mainstream of life that tends to be experienced by those not employed outside the home (Coyle, 1984; Gabe and Thorogood, 1986). This may apply particularly to working-class women, as a consequence of limited material resources (Stacey and Price, 1981).

Before we therefore present a report of a study in which we explore the relationship between housing and the psychological ill-health of women, as members of a subordinate social group. In the light of the argument we have developed, particular attention will be given to the extent to which this relationship is mediated by the women's employment status, social class position and responsibility for preschool children. The extent to which these women's satisfaction with their housing is an intervening factor will also be considered.

9.3
Methods

The survey from which the present data were extracted was conducted in 1977 primarily to investigate the effects of aircraft noise on health in west London (Tarnopolsky and Morton-Williams, 1980). The present study is concerned with a subsample selected to be representative of the population of UK-born women between the ages of 25 and 45 years (Gabe and Williams, 1986). These women have been selected for consideration because they are more likely to spend time at home and are hence more likely to be exposed to the effect of internal crowding.

Every respondent was interviewed by an agency interviewer, and supplied information about a variety of social factors, including marital status, social class, presence of one or more preschool child(ren) in the household and employment status. Social class was categorized according to the socio-economic groupings (SEGs) within the Registrar-General's Classification of Occupations (Office of Population Censuses and Surveys, 1970). For the currently employed (whether full-time or part-time), this was done on the basis of the respondent's own main occupation; for the housewife and the otherwise not-employed, classification was on the basis of her last known main occupation. It can be argued that classification on such a basis is superior to deriving women's class position from the (usually male) head of household because: (a) intellectual sexism is thereby avoided (Acker, 1973; Allen, 1982); (b) women's own occupation may have an important influence on their own and their families' standard of living, security and well-being (West, 1978; Stanworth, 1984); and (c) it recognizes that there are a significant number of contemporary households in which the class positions of the partners are different (Stanworth, 1984; Heath and Britten, 1984).

In addition, respondents were asked to enumerate the household members. Also each was asked: 'How many rooms do you have in your present accommodation (not including kitchen and bathroom) for the sole use of your household?' An index of crowding was then calculated by dividing the number of persons in the household by the number of rooms: this simple index, the person-to-room ratio, has been widely used (Collette and Webb, 1977; Gillis, 1977; Baldassare, 1981) and has been validated by Gove and associates (Gove, Hughes and Galle, 1979; Gove and Hughes, 1983) as a good objective index of crowding. Each woman also assessed her satisfaction with her accommodation on a five-point scale, and indicated how long she had lived at that particular address.

Respondents also completed the 30-item version of the General Health Questionnaire (GHQ) (Goldberg, 1972, 1978), which is a commonly used self-completion questionnaire designed to measure minor psychological symptoms in a wide variety of settings. Examples of the questions include: 'Have you recently been getting scared or panicky for no good reason?'; 'Have you found everything getting on top of you?'; and 'Have you felt that life isn't worth living?'. The GHQ score can be interpreted in a number of ways (Tarnopolsky, 1979); in the present study, it is regarded as a measure of the *number* of symptoms (i.e. the score is the number of symptoms that the respondent indicates that she has experienced 'recently') rather than as an indicator or estimator of psychiatric 'caseness'.

9.4

Findings

The sample on which the analysis is based comprised 452 UK-born women between the ages of 25 and 45 years, inclusive (mean age, 33.1 years); 321 (71%) were married, and 110 (24%) had one or more preschool child(ren) living at home. Nearly half were in full-time employment, and a further quarter were employed part-time; 23% belonged to SEGs 1 and 2, while only 9% were members of SEGs 5 and 6; only 3% of the women remained unclassified. The sample is therefore skewed towards SEGs 1 and 2. This is partly due to the characteristics of the survey area – according to the 1971 census, 16% of the population were in SEGs 1 and 2 – and partly due to our having defined a population subgroup (i.e. UK-born women between the ages of 25 and 45) for the study.

The mean number of psychological symptoms, as measured by the GHQ score, was 3.23 (SEM, 0.25): 202 (45%) of the respondents scored zero, and 107 (24%) had a score of 5 or more. This threshold, or cut-off point, yields a dichotomous classification that agrees well with clinical psychiatric opinion (Goldberg, 1972, 1978). A person with a score of 5 is referred to as a 'probable case', since there is a high probability that she or he will be regarded as ill if seen by a psychiatrist. In this chapter we do not report on the proportion of 'probable cases'; this is because we wish to avoid undue medicaliz-ation of emotional distress. Differences that result from these alter-native methods of using GHQ responses (i.e. scores vs proportion of 'cases') are, in general, small (Williams, 1985) and due entirely to differences in the power of different statistical techniques (Pesco-solido and Kelley, 1983).

The 32 women who had lived in their present accommodation for less than six months were then excluded. For the remaining 420, there was a trend towards a J-shaped relationship between household size and mean GHQ score, with women living alone or in large households having higher scores than those living in households of intermediate size. This relationship did not reach statistical significance, nor did the inverse relationship between GHQ score and number of rooms.

It is now accepted that persons living alone should be excluded from the analysis when indexes of crowding are being considered because their presence biases the distribution of the person-to-room

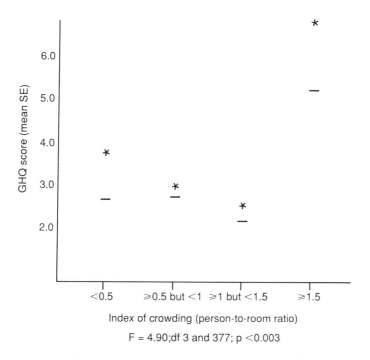

Index of crowding (person-to-room ratio)

F = 4.90;df 3 and 377; p <0.003

Figure 9.1 Relationship between crowding and psychological symptoms (as measured by GHQ score, persons living alone excluded).

ratio (Booth and Cowell, 1976; Gove, Hughes and Galle, 1979; Gove and Hughes, 1983; Magaziner, 1983). Removing these 39 women from the present sample (leaving 381 women) made no substantive difference to the relationships between GHQ score, household size and number of rooms.

The association between GHQ score and the index of crowding (the person-to-room ratio) was then investigated. Preliminary inspection showed that the relationship was curvilinear, so the values of the person-to-room ratio were aggregated into four categories (<0.5; 0.5 but <1; ⩾1 but <1.5; and ⩾1.5) for analysis. Figure 9.1 shows that this highly significant relationship was J-shaped: the highest mean GHQ score occurred in the highest crowding category (⩾1.5 persons per room), but the second highest score was found in the lowest category (<0.5 persons per room).

The relationship between GHQ score and the crowding index was assessed in subcategories defined according to employment status,

Table 9.1 Relationship between crowding, other variables and psychological symptoms (as measured by GHQ score)†

| | Index of crowding (persons/rooms) | | | |
	<0.5	≥0.5 but <1	≥1 but <1.5	≥1.5
Employment status				
Employed	4.16	2.85	1.95	4.66
	(1.36)	(0.41)	(0.37)	(1.77)
Not employed	3.27	2.92	3.80	8.53
	(1.90)	(0.68)	(0.93)	(2.34)

2-way ANOVA: independent effect of crowding, F=4.12; df 3 and 406; p<0.007

Social class				
SEGs 1 and 2	3.00	2.21	2.10	10.00
	(1.81)	(0.63)	(0.83)	(4.94)
SEGs 3 and 4	3.79	3.38	2.24	6.12
	(1.26)	(0.50)	(0.39)	(1.75)
SEGs 5 and 6	−‡	1.83	5.06	4.75
		(0.93)	(2.04)	(2.29)

2-way ANOVA: independent effect of crowding, F=4.57; df 3 and 399; p<0.005

Preschool children				
None	3.74	2.81	2.42	3.69
	(1.01)	(0.40)	(0.47)	(1.12)
One or more	−‡	3.38	2.71	9.92
		(0.86)	(0.70)	(2.64)

2-way ANOVA: independent effect of crowding F=4.40; df 3 and 415; p<0.005

Satisfaction with housing				
Satisfied	3.18	2.75	2.42	4.93
	(0.99)	(0.37)	(0.44)	(1.04)
Dissatisfied	8.50	5.13	3.04	9.30
	(4.48)	(1.60)	(0.86)	(3.36)

2-way ANOVA: independent effect of crowding, F=3.94; df 3 and 374; p<0.01

Notes:
† GHQ scores shown with SE in parentheses; persons living alone excluded from the analysis.
‡ Only one respondent in each of these groups.

social class and the presence or absence of preschool children. The J-shaped relationship was found in all except SEGs 5 and 6 (there was only one respondent from these SEGs in the lowest crowding category), and this was confirmed by two-way analysis of variance (Table 9.1).

Finally, a dummy-variable hierarchical multiple regression analysis was carried out. Following the approach of Baldassare (1979), the three socio-demographic variables were fitted first, then satisfaction

Table 9.2 Psychological symptoms, crowding, and other variables: hierarchical multiple regression*

Employment status	B(SE)	F;df;p	Multiple r^2
Not employed	0.630 (0.620)	3.50;1 & 360;<0.05	0.010

Children
  presence of
  preschool children
	0.357 (0.657)	0.53;1 & 359;n.s.	0.011

Social class
  SEGs 3 and 4
  SEGs 5 and 6
	0.492 (0.648)
	0.525 (0.967)
		0.16;2 & 357;n.s.	0.012

Satisfaction with housing Dissatisfied	1.826 (0.771)	7.94;1 & 356;<0.005	0.034
Number of persons	0.573 (0.437)	0.73;1 & 355;n.s.	0.036
Number of rooms	−0.414 (0.429)	0.14;1 & 354;n.s.	0.036

Index of crowding
  ≥0.5 but <1
  ≥1 but <1.5
	−2.605 (1.302)
	−3.468 (1.919)
		4.19;3 & 351;<0.01	0.069

≥1.5	−0.681 (2.680)		
Constant	4.175		

Note:
* Persons living alone excluded from analysis.

with housing, the two components of the crowding index (number of persons and number of rooms) and, finally, crowding itself. The seven variables together accounted for 6.6% of the variance in GHQ score. Table 9.2 shows that even after allowing for the effects of the background variables and the two components of the index, the effect of crowding remained significant, accounting for an increment of 3.3% in the explained variance – i.e. almost half the explained variance was due to the independent effect of crowding. The proportion of variance accounted for is small in real terms; however, it is of a similar order of magnitude to that often reported in studies that relate social factors to psychological ill-health (see e.g. Cochrane and Stopes-Roe, 1980).

9.5

Conclusion

The results can be succinctly summarized. We found a significant and strong J-shaped relationship between crowding in the home and psychological distress among the women. The relationship persisted even when three socio-demographic variables (employment status, presence of children and social class), satisfaction with housing and the two components of the crowding index were controlled for. This association accounted for half of the explained variance in psychological symptoms.

These findings should be interpreted with caution. The data are cross-sectional, and the problems of drawing causal inferences from such data are well known (Susser, 1973). Furthermore, it can be argued that the social survey method is insufficiently sensitive to explore fully the ways in which people experience housing and its effects on their health. This may be the case particularly for women, because their experiences as housewives and mothers inside the home are interrupted and fragmented (Smith, 1979), a state of affairs that cannot adequately be tapped, except through more qualitative research methods (Graham, 1983).

Also we have not, at this stage, taken into account other attributes of housing (e.g. structural and non-structural deficiencies), experiential aspects of crowding or social interaction outside the home. Furthermore, the measure of social class that we used – the Registrar-General's socio-economic groupings – is open to criticism both on theoretical (Nichols, 1979; Oakley, 1981; Graham, 1984) and empirical grounds (Dale, Gilbert and Arber, 1985), even though the woman's *own* occupation (and not that of the usually male head of household) was used to define her class position.

Despite these limitations, we believe the findings presented here are both interesting and important, especially in view of the absence of previous quantitative research on this topic emanating from Britain. Our findings, in so far as they demonstrate a positive relationship between high levels of crowding and psychological distress, confirm the findings of Gove and his associates (Goldberg, 1972; Gove and Hughes, 1983) rather than those of Baldassare (1979, 1981). There are a number of possible explanations for this relationship. It may be that the crowding/health relationship is spurious. Such an interpretation is not supported by our data since the crowding variable exerted an effect on psychological symptoms *additional* to the effect of household size.

We suggest that women in high-density housing may find difficulty in controlling the desired amount of social interaction with other members of the household and that this has consequences for their psychological health (Stokols, 1976). Related to this, it may be difficult for a woman in crowded conditions to achieve the degree of privacy necessary to maintain such a state of health (Altman, 1975), especially given the lack of clear demarcation between the domestic work for which she is generally responsible and leisure (Brittan and Maynard, 1984). Furthermore, access to and space for household objects may be experienced as constraining.

That women living in the most crowded conditions with preschool children should be particularly likely to experience psychological distress is not surprising and is similar to the findings of Brown and Harris (1978). They reported that women in south London who were at home with small children and lived in poor overcrowded conditions were particularly likely to be depressed. Women in such conditions are likely to find meeting their small children's constant needs particularly difficult, especially when this is compounded by a sense of physical isolation (Oakley, 1974; Hobson, 1978; Griffen *et al.*, 1982) and restricted opportunities for leisure (Deem, 1982; Griffin, MacIntosh and McCabe, 1982; Allan, 1985).

While this relationship between high levels of crowding and psychological symptoms was not altogether unexpected, the additional finding that *low* levels of crowding were also detrimental was somewhat surprising. Together, these results suggest that there is an optimal level of density in the home for psychological health (Altman, 1975).

Possible explanations for this effect of spaciousness in the home include the following. Women with an ample amount of space may find that they have insufficient opportunities for casual interchange and other forms of interaction with significant others in the home (Smith, 1971). Many may experience this as distressing (Magaziner, 1983) since there are considerable individual differences in preference and need for social interaction. In addition, the perception of space itself, quite apart from the presence or absence of others, may engender a sense of loneliness. Further, the amount of housework to be done in such spacious accommodation may be experienced as a burden (Ungerson, 1985) since women are likely to shoulder the major responsibility for this, given the unequal division of labour in the household (Hunt, 1974; Oakley, 1974; Brittan and Maynard, 1984; Allan, 1985). Also space may create childcare supervision problems, in so far as children's activities might be more difficult to monitor (Smith, 1971), thereby making these women's lives more stressful. Finally, it may be that in a small proportion of households spaciousness may result from a recent loss (for example, of a partner of a child), which may in itself give rise to emotional distress (Brown and Harris, 1978).

Three implications arise from this relationship between housing and health. These are substantive, theoretical and political. From the substantive point of view, the heightened distress experienced as a result of too much or too little space may compound the risk of accidents in the home among women already vulnerable to such accidents because of the physical inadequacies of their accommodation (Austerberry and Watson, 1981; Doyal, 1983). It may also encourage them to turn to resources such as cigarettes, alcohol and tranquillizers to get by (Stacey and Price, 1981; Graham, 1984, 1985), even though such resources can be harmful for health as well as sustaining.

Furthermore, it seems possible that the psychological ill-health experienced by women as a result of particular levels of density in the home will also affect their ability to function as health workers in the home, giving emotional support and encouragement to other members of the household and creating the domestic conditions necessary for the maintenance of their health (Graham, 1984, 1985). This has implications for the present British government's attempt to place a greater burden of health care on the family and therefore on women, who are the first-line providers of health care within the family (Finch and Groves, 1980; Graham, 1985).

This analysis also has theoretical implications. It suggests that the relationship between crowding and health for women needs to be explained within the context of the social organization of household space. Within sociology, the theory of space has not been adequately developed (Giddens, 1979); furthermore, such work as there is has focused primarily on landscape rather than on social relationships within buildings (Prior, 1986; Stimson, 1986). In particular, there has been little sociological research on the way in which gender inequalities within the household affect the distribution of space between men and women (or between other household members), or on the kinds of meaning that women from different social backgrounds or at different stages in the life-cycle give to the space that is available. There is also a lack of empirical evidence concerning the strategies that women develop to manage household space in order to achieve a desired level of privacy. It can be hypothesized that when such strategies fail and/or when the optimal level of privacy is not experienced, a woman's sense of self and hence well-being is likely to be undermined. Excessive privacy starves a person of the social contact that can confirm her sense of worth (Altman, 1975), whereas insufficient privacy limits opportunities for 'off-stage' or 'back region' behaviour (i.e. behaviour free from normative constraints), which may be essential for a person in a subordinate position in order to sustain her personal identity and ontological security (Goffman, 1959; Altman, 1975; Giddens, 1985).

Finally, it would appear that our research has implications for housing policy and design. If density within the home has an optimal level for psychological well-being, this should be acknowledged in state design guidelines to architects. This is unlikely to occur in the near future, however, if the present government's decision in 1981 to abolish compulsory space standards (for council housing), first established in the Parker Morris Report (Ministry of Housing and Local Government, 1961), is anything to go by (Austerberry and Watson, 1981; Matrix, 1984). In addition, our findings provide empirical justification for the view that official housing design guidelines, such as *Housing the Family* (Department of the Environment, 1974), should acknowledge that 'a room of one's own' (Woolf, 1929) is as much a right for women as for other members of the household. At the present time, it seems that guidelines to architects assume that women should only spend their time servicing the family in the kitchen or 'master' bedroom (Matrix, 1984).

Acknowledgements

This study was part of a research programme funded by the Department of Health and Social Security, under the direction of Professor Michael Shepherd. Data collection was funded jointly by the Medical Research Council and the Department of Trade. Thanks are due to Dr Alex Tarnopolsky, for access to the data; and to Mike Bury and an anonymous referee, for their comments on an earlier draft of this chapter.

Bibliography

Acker, J. (1973) Women and social stratification: a case of intellectual sexism. *Am. J. Sociol.*, 78, 936–45.

Allan, G. (1985) *Family Life*, Blackwell, Oxford.

Allen, S. (1982) Gender inequality and class formation, in: Giddens, A. and Mackenzie, G. (eds) *Social Class and the Division of Labour*, Cambridge University Press, Cambridge.

Altman, I. (1975) *The Environment and Social Behaviour*, Brooks Cole, Monterey, Calif.

Austerberry, H. and Watson, S. (1981) A woman's place: a feminist approach to housing in Britain. *Feminist Rev.*, 8, 49–62.

Baldassare, M. (1979) *Residential Crowding in Urban America*, University of California Press, London.

Baldassare, M. (1981) The effects of household density on subgroups. *Am. Sociol. Rev.*, 46, 110–18.

Barrett, M. (1980) *Women's Oppression Today*, Verso, London.

Booth, A. and Cowell, J. (1976) The effects of crowding upon health. *J. Health Soc. Behav.*, 17, 204–20.

Booth, A. and Edwards, J. (1976) Crowding and family relations. *Am. Sociol. Rev.*, 41, 308–21.

Brittan, A. and Maynard, M. (1984) *Sexism, Racism and Oppression*, Blackwell, Oxford.

Brown, G. W. and Harris, T. (1978) *Social Origins of Depression*, Tavistock, London.

Bryant, C. G. (1985) *Positivism in Social Theory and Research*, Macmillan, London.

Burton, C. (1985) *Subordination: Feminism and Social Theory*, Allen and Unwin, Sydney.

Cochrane, R. and Stopes-Roe, H. (1980) Factors affecting the distribution of psychological symptoms in urban areas of England. *Acta Psychiatr. Scand.*, 61, 445–60.

Cohen, S., Glass, D. and Phillips, S. (1979) Environment and health, in: Freeman, H., Levine, S. and Reeder, L. G. (eds) *Handbook of Medical Sociology*, Englewood Cliffs, NJ.

Collette, J. and Webb, S. (1977) Urban density, household crowding and stress reactions. *Aust. N.Z. J. Sociol.*, 12, 184–91.

Connell, R. W. (1985) Theorising gender. *Sociology*, 19, 260–72.

Coyle, A. (1984) *Redundant Women*, The Women's Press, London.

Dale, A., Gilbert, G. N. and Arber, S. (1985) Integrating women into class theory. *Sociology*, 19, 384–409.

Davies, C. and Roche, S. (1980) The place of methodology: a critique of Brown and Harris. *Sociol., Rev.*, 28, 641–56.

Deem, R. (1982) Women, leisure and inequality. *Leisure Studies*, 1, 29–46.

Department of the Environment (1974) *Housing the Family*, MTP Construction, Lancaster.

Doyal, L. (1983) Women, health and the sexual division of labour: a case study of the women's health movement in Britain. *Int. J. Health Serv.*, 13, 373–87.

Duvall, D. and Booth, A. (1978) The housing environment and women's health. *J. Health Soc. Behav.*, 19, 410–17.

Finch, J. and Groves, D. (1980) Care and the family: a case for equal opportunities? *J. Soc. Policy*, 9, 487–511.

Gabe, J. and Thorogood, N. (1986) Prescribed drug use and the management of everyday life: the experiences of black and white working class women. *Sociol. Rev.*, 34, 737–72.

Gabe, J. and Williams, P. (1986) Is space bad for your health? The relationship between crowding in the home and emotional distress in women. *Sociol. Health Illness*, 8, 351–71.

Galle, O., Gove, W. R. and McPherson, J. M. (1972) Population density and pathology: what are the relationships for man? *Science*, 176, 23–9.

Gamarnikow, E. (1978) Introduction to women and the city. *Int. J. Urb. Reg. Res.*, 2, 390–403, 1978.

Giddens, A. (1979) *Central Problems in Social Theory*, Macmillan, London.

Giddens, A. (1985) Time, space and regionalisation, in: Gregory, D. and Urry, J. (eds) *Social Relations and Spatial Structures*, Macmillan, London.

Gillis, A. R. (1977) High-rise housing and psychological strain. *J. Health Soc. Behav.*, 18, 418–31.

Goffman, E. (1959) *The Presentation of Self in Everyday Life*, Doubleday, Anchor, New York.

Goldberg, D. (1972) *The Identification of Psychiatric Illness by Questionnaire*, Oxford University Press, London.

Goldberg, D. (1978) *Manual of the General Health Questionnaire*, National Foundation for Educational Research, Windsor.

Gove, W. R. and Hughes, M. (1983) *Overcrowding in the Household: An Analysis of Determinants and Effects*, Academic Press, New York.

Gove, W. R., Hughes, M. and Galle, O. R. (1979) Overcrowding in the home: an empirical investigation of its possible pathological consequences. *Am. Sociol. Rev.*, 44, 59–80.

Graham, H. (1983) Do her answers fit his questions? Women and the survey method, in: Garmarnikow, E. *et al.* (eds) *The Public and the Private*, Heinemann, London.

Graham, H. (1984) *Women, Health and the Family*, Wheatsheaf Books, Brighton.

Graham, H. (1985) Providers, negotiators and mediators: women as the hidden carers, in: Lewin, E. and Olesen, V. (eds) *Women, Health and Healing*, Tavistock Publications, New York.

Griffin, C., MacIntosh, S. and McCabe, T. (1982) Women and leisure, in: Hargreaves, J. (ed.) *Sport, Culture and Ideology*, Routledge and Kegan Paul, London.

Heath, A. and Britten, N. (1984) Women's jobs do make a difference. *Sociology*, 18, 475–90.

Hobson, D. (1978) Houswifes: isolation as oppression, in: *Women's Subordination*, Women's Studies Group, Centre for Contemporary Cultural Studies, University of Birmingham, Hutchinson, London.

Hunt, P. (1974) *The Sociology of Housework*, Martin Robertson, London.

Kasl, S. (1974) Effects of housing on mental and physical health. *Man. Environ. Syst.*, 4, 207–22.

Kasl, S. and Harburg, E. (1975) Mental health and the urban environment: some doubts and second thoughts. *J. Health Soc. Behav.*, 16, 268–82.

Kirmeyer, S. (1978) Urban density and pathology: a review of research. *Environ. Behav.*, 10, 247–26.

Levy, L. and Herzog, A. (1974) Effects of population density and crowding on health and social adaptation in the Netherlands. *J. Health Soc. Behav.*, 15, 228–40.

Loring, W. (1979) Introduction, in: Hinkle, L. and Loring, W. (eds) *The Effect of the Man-Made Environment on Health and Behaviour*, Castle House, Guildford.

McDowell, L. (1983) City and home: urban housing and the sexual division of labour, in: Evans, M. and Ungerson, C. (eds) *Sexual Divisions, Patterns and Processes*, Tavistock, London.

Magaziner, J. (1983) Density, living alone, age and psychopathology in the urban environment. Unpublished paper.

Matrix (1984) *Making Space: Women and the Man-Made Environment*, Pluto Press, London.

Mills, C. W. (1959) *The Sociological Imagination*, Oxford University Press, New York.

Ministry of Housing and Local Government (1961) *Homes for Today and Tomorrow* (Parker Morris Report), Her Majesty's Stationery Office, London.

Moore, N. C. (1974) Psychiatric illness and living in flats. *B. J. Psychiatry*, 125, 500–7.

Moore, N. C. (1976) The personality and mental health of flat dwellers. *B. J. Psychiatry*, 128, 259–61.

Nichols, T. (1979) Social class: official, sociological and Marxist, in: Irvine, J. *et al.* (eds) *Demystifying Social Statistics*, Pluto Press, London.

Oakley, A. (1974) *The Sociology of Housework*, Martin Robertson, London.

Oakley, A. (1981) *Subject Women*, Martin Robertson, Oxford.

Office of Population Censuses and Surveys (OPCS) (1970) *Classification of Occupations*, HMSO, London.

Paterson, K. (1981) Theoretical perspectives in epidemiology: a critical appraisal. *Rad. Comm. Med.*, 8, 21–9.

Pescosolido, B. and Kelley, J. (1983) Confronting theory with data: regression analysis, Goodman's loglinear models and comparative research. *Sociology*, 17, 359–79.

Prior, L. (1986) The architecture of the hospital: a study of space and medical knowledge. Paper presented at the British Sociological Association Medical Sociology Conference, York.

Smith, D. E. (1971) Household space and family organisation, in: Davies, D. and Herman, K. (eds) *Social Space: Canadian Perspectives*, New Press, Toronto.

Smith, D. E. (1979) A sociology for women, in: Sherman, J. and Peck, E. (eds) *The Prism of Sex: Essays in the Sociology of Knowledge*, University of Wisconsin Press, Madison, Wis.

Spring Rice, M. (1939) *Working Class Wives: Their Health and Conditions*, Penguin, Harmondsworth.

Stacey, J. and Thorne, B. (1985) The missing feminist revolution in sociology. *Soc. Problems*, 32, 301–16.

Stacey, M. (1981) The division of labour or overcoming the two Adams, in: Abrams, P. *et al.* (eds) *Practice and Progress: British Sociology 1950–80*, Allen and Unwin, London.

Stacey, M. and Price, M. (1981) *Women, Power and Politics*, Tavistock, London.

Stanworth, M. (1984) Women and class analysis: a reply to Goldthorpe, *Sociology*, 18, 159–70.

Stimson, G. (1986) Place and space in sociological fieldwork. *Sociol. Rev.*, 34, 641–56.

Stokols, D. (1976) The experience of crowding in primary and secondary environments. *Environ. Behav.*, 8, 49–86.

Susser, M. (1973) *Causal Thinking in the Health Sciences: Concepts and Strategies in Epidemiology*, Oxford University Press, New York.

Tarnopolsky, A. *et al.* (1979) Validity and uses of a screening questionnaire in the community. *Br. J. Psychiatry*, 134, 508–15.

Tarnopolsky, A. and Morton-Williams, J. (1980) *Aircraft Noise and the Prevalence of Psychiatric Disorders*, Social and Community Planning, London.

Taylor, S. and Chave, S. P. (1964) *Mental Health and the Environment*, Longman, London.

Tivers, J. (1978) How the other half lives: the geographical study of women. *Area*, 10, 302–6.

Ungerson, C. (ed.) (1985) *Women and Social Policy*, Macmillan, London.

West, J. (1978) Women, sex and class, in: Kuhn, A. and Wolpe, A. M. (eds) *Feminism and Materialism*, Routledge and Kegan Paul, London.

Williams, P. (1985) Minor psychiatric morbidity in West London. MD thesis, University of London.

Woolf, V. (1929) *A Room of One's Own*, Hogarth Press, London.

10

CROWDING AND MORTALITY IN LONDON BOROUGHS

JOHN M. KELLETT

10.1

Introduction

The growth of urban civilization, though familiar in Britain, also has profound effects in the less developed world. Infectious diseases, which ravaged such concentrations of population in previous centuries, are now under control, but evidence continues to emerge that crowding is a potent cause of disease. Studies on animal population (Christian, 1964; Calhoun, 1973; Ratcliffe and Snyder, 1962) have demonstrated a wide range of physical and psychological effects from crowding, including diminished stature, hypertrophy of the spleen and adrenal glands, glomerulohephritis, reduced immunological reactivity, delay in sexual maturation, increased sensitivity to alloxan-induced diabetes, and premature atheroma. Studies on human populations have come up with similar findings, though open to alternative interpretations.

I have recently reviewed these findings, while Gove and Hughes have debated the issue with Booth and colleagues in the pages of the *American Sociological Review* (Gove and Hughes, 1980a, 1980b; Booth et al., 1980a, 1980b). Much of the debate centres around the degree to which crowding is the pathogenic variable or whether it is statistically associated with other more potent factors. We may conclude that despite marked associations of crowding with social pathology, the relation between crowding and mortality remains uncertain, and there is little evidence to relate it to individual diseases.

The unit chosen for analysis was the London borough , of which there are 33. Their population ranges from 140 000 to 307 000, with the one exception of the City of London whose population contains only 4245 residents. The total population of Greater London is seven and a half million which comprises an area of 158 000 hectares. Mortality is expressed as a ratio of the deaths of the residents in the borough to the deaths from an age-matched sample in the nation as a whole. Only correlations reaching a significance of 0.01 have been considered to allow for the assumption that each borough is independent from the other, and one which is invalid for neighbouring boroughs.

Population density is probably the closest one can come to measure the frequency of life events for large groups of the population. It may be measured in one of three ways: (1) population per hectare ('density'); (2) persons per room ('crowding'); and (3) population potential. Only the first two are used in this study, reflecting as they do a stable environmental influence. One should, however, bear in mind that the population per hectare may underestimate density if, for example, a large part of the borough was occupied by industry and the population was accommodated in one corner. Similarly, population per room takes no account of the size of the room: large Victorian terraced houses may register higher crowding than purpose-built flats, though space in the former is much greater. Persons per room also does not take account of the geometrical progression of possible interactions that can occur when the number of a household increases.

Whereas a high population density is likely to reflect the stresses of inner city areas, including an increase of largely non-personal interaction, measures of crowding are likely to increase the experience of events like bereavement and the making and breaking of relations. It may therefore be more prone to excite symptoms of anger than the anxiety aroused by non-personal interaction.

Clearly the measures of crowding could exert their effects through associated social factors. The relation of these factors one to another are displayed in Figure 10.1, which displays the factors plotted against their loading on the first two factors which account for three-quarters of the variance. It will be seen that factor 1 related closely to indices of overcrowding, and crime, New Commonwealth immigration and non-possession of a car. Perhaps surprisingly, mea-

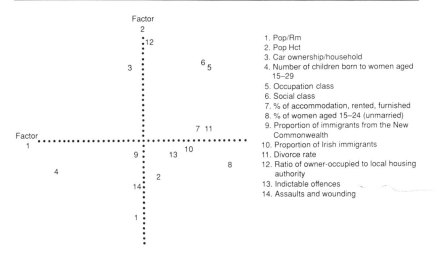

Figure 10.1 Demographic indices plotted against the first two factors of factor analysis.

sures of social class are much more closely related to factor 2. Though correlations are controlled for the effects of social class, they are not controlled for crime which may be the result rather than the cause of overcrowding.

10.2
Total mortality

Death is, of course, a normal phenomenon but in this study one was concerned with premature death which could not reasonably be attributed to genetic programming. One therefore selected mortality statistics for males and females separately between the ages of 15 and 54, and 55 and 64, henceforth called 'younger' and 'older' respectively.

Population density seems to exert its effect on the older of both sexes (Table 10.1). The influence of crowding on total mortality is compounded by a strong inverse relationship between mortality and car ownership (which may reduce the effects of such crowding) and a direct relation to the percentage of single females aged 15–24, which might leave these younger single people more vulnerable to personal encounters. This hypothesis is also supported by the negative associations of mortality to the numbers of children born to

Table 10.1 Correlations with mortality (controlling for social class)

| | Males | | | | Females | | | |
	15–54		55–64		15–54		55–64	
Pop/room	0.31	(0.37)	0.73	(0.64)	0.31	(0.29)	0.82	(0.74)
Pop/Hct	0.16	(0.16)	0.51	(0.47)	0.13	(0.10)	0.70	(0.70)
Social class	−0.01		−0.45		−0.12		−0.54	
Own car	−0.43	(−0.47)	−0.81	(−0.76)	−0.45	(−0.44)	−0.78	(−0.78)
% single women	0.62	(0.66)	0.57	(0.85)	0.61	(0.69)	0.19	(0.47)
Own house	−0.59	(−0.71)	−0.77	(−0.69)	−0.61	(−0.67)	−0.56	(−0.36)
Assaults wound	0.19	(0.19)	0.57	(0.51)	0.16	(0.12)	0.82	(0.81)

Note:
Statistical significance: $>0.40 = <0.01$; $>0.50 = <0.001$

mothers aged 15–29 ($r = 0.37$, $p <0.02$) suggesting that the presence of such children exerts a protective influence on the health of both younger males ($r = 0.40$, $p<0.01$) and females. Other strong associations with mortality include the percentage of indictable offences and assaults, and lower social class, both of which exert their main effect in the older groups. Controlling for social class does not reduce the effect of density and crowding.

10.3
Specific mortality

One might, however, expect that the less specific the disease under study, the more likely would its death rate reflect general social factors, while individual disease might only relate to a single pathogen. The effect of adding them together would cancel out these specific associations and leave only the general.

Certain deaths, such as violent and accidental deaths in younger groups, have long been associated with mental stress. These show no association with crowding in females until controlled for social class, though there are strong associations with density and crime. More than half such deaths are suicides, and in this group of younger females there is the familiar association with proportion of rented accommodation ($r = 0.78$), unmarried status ($r = 0.54$) and crime ($r = 0.74$). Violent deaths in younger males show a more convincing effect with crowding ($r = 0.62$), although in other respects they are similar to the younger females. It is noticeable, however, that the association with crowding increases for both males and females when the effects of social class are controlled.

Diseases which are traditionally considered psychosomatic rarely cause death (possibly because their long course has emphasized psychological influences to their caring physicians) but some, like peptic ulcer, still figure as a cause of premature mortality. Here only females show an effect of crowding (r = 0.54). Vascular diseases show a more convincing effect of population pressures. Myocardial infarction correlates 0.55 and 0.66 with younger and older females, and 0.63 with older males which remain significant after controlling for social class. Similarly cerebrovascular accidents in younger females (r = 0.43) and males (r = 0.61) show a good correlation with crowding, though the figure for females loses significance when controlled for class.

Certain cancers are known to reflect personal habits, and one may not be surprised that carcinoma of the bronchus shows an association with crowding. Similarly, carcinoma of the cervix has often been associated with poor personal hygiene, and it shows a sharp association with population density, crime and larger families. Most endocrine diseases are not specified as causes of death, but diabetes does feature quite frequently. This was found to be positively associated with crowding in younger and older females, and younger males, but only in the younger females does the significance remain above the 0.01 level after controlling for class.

The last group of diseases associated with crowding are respiratory diseases. Chronic bronchitis is associated with crowding in older males (r = 0.85) and younger and older females (0.65 and 0.52), while bronchitis, asthma and emphysema, a larger category, shows

Table 10.2 Causes of death with no significant correlations with indices of social deprivation above the p = 0.01 level (excluding diseases where n = <250)

Males	Carcinoma	colon	15–54	359
		rectum	55–64	511
		pancreas	15–54	273
		prostate	55–64	351
	Motor vehicle accidents (correlates +0.38 with car ownership)		15–54	1427
Females	Carcinoma	colon	55–64	794
		rectum	55–64	401
		pancreas	55–64	398
		breast	55–64	2532
		uterus	55–64	305
	Hypertension		55–64	371
	Motor vehicle accidents		15–54	497

Source:
OPCS.

highly significant associations with crowding in the older groups of both sexes, although as expected they also related to class.

Table 10.2 indicates those conditions where social deprivation seems of no importance. This would suggest that most cancers are in this category which may indicate genetic loading or exposure to environmental factors which are independent of deprivation. Though the length of survival in breast cancer has been related to psychological factors (Greer, Morris and Pettingale, 1979), this would seem to play little part in its origin. The only surprise is the presence of hypertension in older women, which also reflects the results for the younger women, though here the numbers dying of this were too few for analysis. Possibly this is an odd category as deaths from hypertension are usually the results of strokes or heart attacks. Motor vehicle accidents, a major cause of death in young males, clusters in the wealthier boroughs and presumably reflects access to a car.

Any epidemiological study has to balance the effects of choosing too large an area such that specific effects in a small part of the area are submerged in the data from elsewhere, or too small an area where the variables under study are so infrequent as to be impossible to relate significantly to each other. Studies of the latter kind can best be performed on predictors of mild illness like the effect of cholesterol on the incidence of ischaemic heart disease rather than on the tighter but rarer category of death. Even for an area as large as a London borough, deaths between the ages of 15 and 54 are rare, and to derive adequate numbers it was necessary to combine the results of five years. It may be argued that the social indices at the midpoint of those years do not reflect the social indices at the midpoint of the illness developed, but simply concern the environment sought by the sufferers of the disease. Thus an association of bungalows with arthritis is much more likely to be the choice of those with arthritis avoiding staircases than a pathogenic influence of houses without stairs on the joints. Certainly in some diseases the environmental factors would have to be present for many years to exert their effect. Nevertheless, it is likely that the environmental factors present in 1971 will reflect those present for at least the previous 15 years.

10.4
Death certification

While figures for total mortality are likely to be accurate, one can question the validity of the data in individual diagnostic categories. For example, Heasman and Lipworth (1966) concluded that only 45% of death certificates were accurate when compared with information available from necropsy and hospital records. A more recent study from the Royal College of Physicians (1978) showed 39 major discrepancies in 191 death certificates of patients who died before the age of 50. However, even these major discrepancies usually left the cause of death within the same general group. Thus cerebral haemorrhage was recorded instead of subarachnoid haemorrhage, and cardiac arrest instead of myocardial infarction. If inaccuracies were spread randomly throughout London, this would tend to reduce the significance of the correlations found, which might suggest that the results are even more significant than they already appear.

However, there remains the possibility that death certification might be less accurate in boroughs with high mortality, and might artificially expand the larger categories of death such as cerebrovascular accidents and myocardial infarction. To test this, the correlation between deaths from subarachnoid haemorrhage and cerebrovascular accidents was calculated. If in areas with high mortality the former were misclassified as deaths from cerebrovascular accidents, there would be a negative correlation between the deaths from the two conditions whereas if, as one might expect, they derived from similar pathology and would occur more frequently in similar environments, there would be a positive correlation, which there was. Furthermore, Robertson, Bloor and Samphier (1987) have examined the accuracy of death certification by social class and found that the disagreement was most common for the non-manual group and conclude that: 'class mortality gradients in the neoplastic, cerebrovascular, and digestive chapters might be steeper if they were based on pathologists' rather than clinicians' diagnoses; only in the respiratory chapter might the effect be towards a levelling of the gradient; and the gradients in cardiovascular disease would be unaltered.' It is likely therefore that with the broad categories used in this study, death certificates are sufficiently reliable to draw valid conclusions.

10.5

Aetiological hypothesis

The finding of a correlation is a long step from finding the nature of that connection. At its simplest there are three possibilities:

1. That the disease induces a move to more crowded domicile (e.g. from financial difficulties).
2. That crowding produces the disease.
3. That a third factor causes both crowding and disease (e.g. boroughs which attract polluting industries may have different housing policies, including high-density accommodation, or poverty may be the third factor).

Whereas chronic diseases could indeed produce a loss of income and a move to poorer surroundings (a major defect of studies attributing psychosomatic diseases to stress), it is difficult to sustain the hypothesis when the disease concerned is more acute, such as carcinoma of the bronchus and acute myocardial infarction. It could, however, account for some of the associations with chronic bronchitis. The third hypothesis is more difficult to dismiss. Several social measures are used, and one can argue that their association with both the mortality rate and population density accounts for the association of density with that disease. The Black Report (1980) drew attention to the relation between social class and mortality but did not consider the effects of population density as the intervening variable. Morris (1979) suggests that the social inequalities in health are due to poverty, poor education, childhood illness, etc., but does not consider crowding. Marmot and McDowall (1986) have shown how this mortality differential is increasing, though Moser, Pugh and Goldblatt (1988) have shown that car ownership and type of ownership of housing have independent effects. Clearly social class by itself does not cause death and an aetiological hypothesis has to postulate a pathogenic mechanism. The relative importance of overcrowding will be discussed later.

One obvious pathogenic influence is the intake of tobacco. Unfortunately, figures for this are not broken down by London borough. However, a survey of London broken into three regions, Central, North and South, showed very similar percentages of smoking adults in 1971 (68%, 69%, 65%). By 1971, smoking was more frequent among the lower classes but 13 years earlier there was no class effect for women, and the class gradient was small for men (65% for class I, 77% for Class V).

Other pathogenic factors include hardness of water (Crawford, Gardner and Morris, 1968) and diet. The water supply to London differs little in hardness ranging from 276 mg l^{-1} of calcium from Thames-derived water to 302 mg l^{-1} from water which is mixed with river water such that it is unlikely that average hardness will extend beyond 375 mg and 325 mg. Other pathogenic factors, such as diet and physical exercise, are likely to be more related to social class than population density, so we have controlled for this variable. However, the effects of social class on total mortality are not particularly marked, especially in those below the age of 55.

Where many of the social variables are closely correlated, there is no watertight statistical technique to separate them into primary and secondary factors. Although previous studies have attempted to separate the effects of crowding and density (e.g. Galle, Gove and McPherson, 1972), this is not practical in London where the correlation between the two reaches 0.79. Crowding correlates best with low car ownership (0.88), and low numbers of owner-occupiers (0.65), though the correlations with density are less (0.86, 0.32). Presumably the former mitigates the effects of crowding, while the latter increases autonomy. Clearly these social indices exert their effect on mortality by altering the behaviour and experience of individuals within that borough. To attempt to dissect the effects of one social variable from another would only serve to remove the effects altogether. Thus Booth and Cowell (1976) controlled not only for age, occupation, education, ethnicity and health of parents, but also for the three indices of crowding apart from that under test, and not surprisingly, found that none retained their significance.

The significance of crowding as a pathogenic influence should not blind one to the dangers of isolation. Welin *et al.* (1985) show a marked reduction in mortality of middle-aged Swedish men with increasing numbers per household. If crowding is pathogenic, one may ask why humans migrate to cities like moths to a flame. Certainly there are situations where most people value close social contact with others such as in a near-empty restaurant or at the beginning of a party. Women, in particular, feel more secure if they are surrounded by other women (Sundstrom, 1978), though men are more sensitive to the restriction on their space. The migration to the city is largely caused by economic factors. Though city life is associated with increased density, crowding is as common in rural communities. Man as the supremely successful mammal has little threat from animal predators, and his battle for territory is as much with his own kind, as it is for the robin. Fanning has drawn attention to the stresses deriving from flat-dwelling where the lack of neutral space prevents people from being able to maintain good relationships with their neighbours, who need to be friends but not intimates. This is more reflected by measures of density, and relations with neighbours are clearly increasingly important the more time is spent out of the house. This could explain the greater importance of density in hot climates like Honolulu (Schmitt, 1966). Crowding, however, exerts its effects within the home. Our society expects adults to have enough privacy to make love, and nurse their infants, for children to play games and study, and teenagers to create their den and establish their independence. A strict social convention of silence and hierarchy can replace the privacy of walls, at some cost to self-expression. Just as agonistic encounters between animals lead to murder if escape routes are cut, so being forced to live cheek by jowl with your antagonist, whether spouse or brother, can lead to intolerable strain. The greater ease by which males can leave the house is balanced by their greater physical vulnerability to strain, so that the correlations with total mortality remain very similar for men and women. The size of the correlation is much greater in the 55–64 age-group reflecting, in part, the length of time humans tolerate strain before they succumb. While I am postulating a direct effect of interpersonal conflict on disease as has been shown by animal work, there remains a possibility that the connection is through the stress-related habits like smoking, drinking, gluttony and risk taking.

One would not expect all diseases to be the result of the same psychological strain. Cancers, for example, may result from exposure to carcinogens, whereas other rarer diseases have such genetic loading that they overwhelm any environmental effects (e.g. Down's Syndrome, Huntington's Chorea, Neurofibromatosis).

Several studies have addressed the relationship of crowding and density to mortality which are summarized in Table 10.3. The finding of strong associations with vascular disease fits well with the psychosomatic hypothesis. However, one could conclude that the association with respiratory disease and bronchial carcinoma is more likely to be a direct effect of smoking, though as I have argued above, this is not supported by the evidence on

Table 10.3 Studies of the correlation of mortality with crowding and density

Author	Date	Sample	Findings (figures in parenthesis controlled for social class)
Schmitt	1966	42 census tracts metropolitan Honolulu	r = 0.66 (0.59) density r = 0.37 (0.15) crowding Uncontrolled for age
Galle, Gove, McPherson	1972	75 Community Areas Chicago	r = 0.78 crowding r = 0.28 (−0.18) density Strong correlations of class/ ethnicity and measures of density/crowding made distinction between density variables and class impossible
Factor, Waldron	1973	10 Community Areas Chicago	r = 0.19 density. No measure of crowding. Also compared mortality in countries of same wealth and different density and showed no relationship
Levy, Herzog	1974	125 economic geographical regions Holland	r = 0.19 density r = 0.19 crowding r = 0.40 economic deprivation heart disease males r = 0.47 density r = 0.11 crowding
Fox, Goldblatt	1982	UK 1971 Census + mortality 1971–5	crowding correlated with deaths from neoplasms and respiratory disease in males, and circulatory and respiratory disease in females
Townsend, Simpson, Tibbs	1985	28 wards Bristol	Aged 15–64 r = 0.55 also high correlations with households without car, unemployment, and low income. No measure of density and no control for other variables
Alexander, O'Brien, Hepburn, Miller	1987	Women aged 45–64 in 78 general practices Edinburgh 47 334 women years	r = 0.61 overcrowding r = 0.57 class r = 0.55 no car

smoking. The correlations with suicide are quite different and coincide with those originally reported by Sainsbury (1955), namely indices of isolation and discord.

10.6
Conclusion

The growth of population and urbanization will inevitably lead to increasing density. The capacity of large populations to create wealth may make this inevitable, though here again, one should not ignore the ability of wealth to draw large populations. In other words, the finding of wealth creation and urbanization together does not necessarily mean that urbanization produces wealth, but could indicate that wealth produces urbanization. We can, however, control crowding and create cities where the design is deliberately tailored to meet the biological needs of its inhabitants. The family environment needs defensible space, good sound-proofing, and sufficient rooms to provide privacy on demand. Surrounding the family environment are the inner tribe, the residents of the street, the block of flats, the hamlet. Here the neutral space of Fanning comes into its own and a central social focus of the community becomes important, be it the church hall or the pub, where everyone is mutually recognized. Beyond this is the wider tribe where membership is demonstrated by markers like the scarf of the football team, the crest of the town. So often the distinctions between the hamlet and the town are lost in the urban plan that the inner tribes are constantly adjusting to newcomers. The Georgian square whose central garden provides the neutral meeting area, and whose enclosed structure gives clear limits to its size and membership, may well turn out to be the most sophisticated model of a townscape built for man.

Clearly the stable village does not suit everyone. The minority groups, like homosexuals, might find the atmosphere stultifying, though in a large city there is always the possibility of the minority taking a hamlet for itself. Indeed by designing self-contained hamlets residents would have more choice as to their tribe.

Ninety-five people were killed on one afternoon at Hillsborough, due to crowding at a football match. How many more people are now dying for the same reason?

Bibliography

Alexander, F. E., O'Brien, F., Hepburn, W. and Miller, M. (1987) Association between mortality among women and socio-economic factors in general practices in Edinburgh: an application of small area statistics. *BMJ*, 295, 754–56.

Black Report (1980) *Inequalities in Health*, DHSS, London.

Booth, A. and Cowell, J. (1976) Crowding and health. *J. Health Soc. Behaviour*, 17, 204–20.

Booth, A., Johnson, D. and Edwards, J. (1980a) In pursuit of pathology: the effects of human crowding. *Am. Soc. Rev.*, 45, 873–8.

Booth, A., Johnson, D. and Edwards, J. (1980b) Reply to Gove and Hughes. *Am. Soc. Rev.*, 45, 870–3.

Calhoun, J. B. (1973) The explosive growth and demise of a mouse population. *Proc. RSM*, 66, 80–5.

Carstairs, V. and Morris, R. (1989) Deprivation: explaining differences in mortality between Scotland and England and Wales. *BMJ*, 299, 886–9.

Christian, J. J. (1964) Physiological and pathological correlates of population density. *Proc. RSM*, 57, 169–73.

Crawford, M. D., Gardner, J. M. and Morris, J. N. (1968) Mortality and hardness of local water supplies. *Lancet*, i, 827–31.

Factor, R. and Waldron, I. (1973) Contemporary population densities and human health. *Nature*, 242, 381–4.

Fanning, D. M. (1967) Families in flats. *BMJ*, 4, 382–6.

Fox, A. S. J. and Goldblatt, P. (1982) *Longitudinal Study: Sociodemographic Mortality Differentials*, OPCS, London.

Galle, O. R., Gove, W. R. and McPherson, J. M. (1972) Population density and pathology: what are the relations for man? *Science*, 176, 23–30.

Gove, W. R. and Hughes, M. (1980a) The effects of crowding found in the Toronto study: some methodological and empirical questions. *Am. Soc. Rev.*, 45, 864–70.

Gove, W. R. and Hughes, M. (1980b) In pursuit of perceptions: a reply to the claim of Booth and his colleagues that household crowding is not an important variable. *Am. Soc. Rev.*, 45, 878–86.

Greer, H. S., Morris, T. and Pettingale, K. W. (1979) Psychological response to breast cancer: effect on outcome. *Lancet*, ii, 785–7.

Heasman, M. A. and Lipworth, L. (1966) *Accuracy of Certification of Causes of Death*, HMSO, London.

Kellett, J. M. (1989) Health and housing. *J. Psychosom. Res.*, 33, 255–68.

Marmot, M. G. and McDowall, M. E. (1986) Mortality decline and widening social inequalities. *Lancet*, ii, 274–7.

Metropolitan Police Office (1982) Personal communication.

Morris, J. N. (1979) Social inequalities undiminished. *Lancet*, i, 87–90.

Moser, K., Pugh, H. S. and Goldblatt, P. O. (1988) Inequalities in women's health: looking at mortality differentials using an alternative approach. *BMJ*, 296, 1221–4.

Office of Population Censuses and Surveys (OPCS) (1971a) Census Data for London, GLC.

OPCS (1971b) *Census 1971*, Economic Activity, Greater London, HMSO, London.

OPCS (1969–73) Mortality data, unpublished.

Ratcliffe, H. L. and Snyder, R. L. (1962) Patterns of disease, controlled population and experimental design. *Circulation*, 26, 1352–7.

Robertson, C., Bloor, M. J. and Samphier, M. L. (1987) Social class gradients, specific cause mortality and accuracy of diagnosis of cause of death. *Lancet*, ii, 576–7.

Royal College of Physicians Study Group; Death Certification and Epidemiological Research Study Group (1978) *BMJ*, 2, 1063–5.

Sainsbury, P. (1955) *Suicide in London*, Chapman and Hall, London.

Schmitt, R. C. (1966) Density, health and social disorganisation. *J. Am. Inst. Planners*, 32, 38–40.

Sundstrom, E. (1978) Crowding as a sequential process: review of research on the effects of population density on humans, in: Baum, A. and Epstein, Y. M. (eds) *Human Responses to Crowding*, Lawrence Erlbaum, New Jersey.

Townsend, P., Simpson, D. and Tibbs, N. (1985) Inequalities in health care in the City of Bristol: a preliminary review of statistical evidence. *Int. J. Health Services*, 15, 637–63.

Wald, N., Kiryluk, S., Bardby, S., Doll, R. and Pike, M. (1988) *UK Smoking Statistics*, Oxford University Press, Oxford.

Welin, L., Tibblin, G., Svardsudd, K., Tibblin, B., Ander-Perciva, S. and Larsson, B. (1985) Wilhemsen prospective study of social influences on mortality. *Lancet*, ii, 1915–18.

11

ACCIDENTS AT HOME: THE MODERN EPIDEMIC

RAY RANSON

11.1

Introduction

Home accidents are now a leading cause of death and injury, especially to young children and the elderly. For example, 3.2 million accidents occur in the home every year in the UK, with no sign of diminuation. More effective systems of accident recording, monitoring and investigation, together with enforcement, collaboration and education, are urgently needed to redress the current epidemic. More attention needs to be given to preventive safety design in professional training and adoption of home safety design standards and legislation. The major threat to public health which home accidents represent must not go unchallenged.

11.2

Scale of the problem

Deaths and injuries caused by accidents in the home presents one of the biggest public health challenges of this century. Quarterly statistics by the World Health Organization (WHO) in 1984 stated that accident injuries of all kinds now rank fifth among the leading causes of death; in the case of young children and the elderly, it is often higher than for infectious diseases (WHO, 1984) (Figure 11.1).

The long-term trend for *fatal* home accidents in the UK shows a steady improvement from some 7500 deaths per annum in 1966 to just over 5000 per annum by 1991. However, this has been levelling out over the past few years and the progress of improvement now appears to have bottomed out (Barrow, 1987). According to the latest estimates of the UK Home Accident Surveillance Scheme (HASS), 3.2 million accidents occurred in the home during 1988. Of these, 5149 were fatal and represent about 40% of all fatal accidents and a third of all accidents treated in hospital (DTI, 1991) (Figure 11.2).

The trend in *non-fatal* accidents is less satisfactory. Here the number has stayed constant at around 3 million per annum through-out the 10 years of HASS – i.e. according to HASS, there has been no improvement at all in non-fatal accident rates over this period (Barrow, 1987).

The cost of treating home accidents is enormous. Apart from unquantifiable human and social costs and lost working time, etc., the National Health Service spends over £300 million each year treating the victims of accidents (DTI, 1989). The cost of childhood accidents alone is greater than the cost of treating cancer for all age-groups. The DTI Home Accident Surveillance System estimates that there are approx. 750 000 accidents to children aged under 16 in and around the home each year. In fact home-related accidents are the cause of a quarter of all deaths of children aged between 10 and 14 and result in about 5000 children being permanently disabled each year (CAPT, 1989). Elderly people are another group vulnerable to accidents particularly in and around the home. It is estimated that more than 300 000 people aged 65 and over require hospital attention each year as a result of home accidents and another 176 000 require attention for leisure accidents. These figures could increase by 100 000 over the next three decades due to ageing of the population alone (DTI, 1991).

Policy-makers and practitioners in the UK are therefore faced with a major health hazard, which unlike other twentieth-century ailments has reached epidemic proportions and shows no signs of diminishing. The tragedy is that these human deaths and resultant misery are, in the main, entirely preventable since we already have detailed knowledge of causation and safety design measures which can limit both the incidence and severity of home accidents.

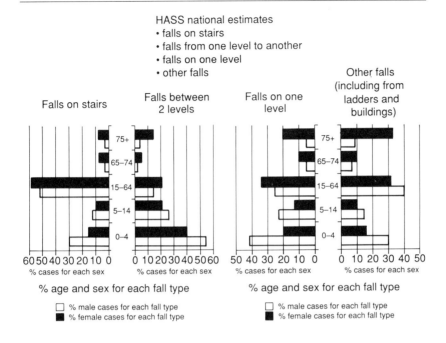

Figure 11.1 Leading causes of death, by age.

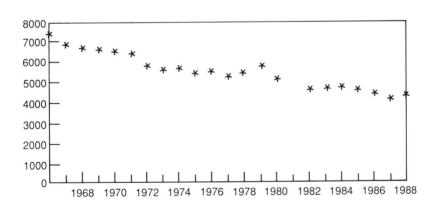

Figure 11.2 Trends in fatal home accidents: England and Wales. 1981 statistics were not available due to industrial action.

Source:
Twelfth Annual Report, Home Accident Surveillance System.

11.3

Vulnerable groups and epidemiological characteristics

(a) Age and sex

Examination of accident returns show a fairly standard morbidity pattern by age and gender (Backett, 1965). Children have a relatively high injury rate but a fairly low risk of death. Home accidents gradually rise to a peak in the toddler and 1–3 years age-group dropping somewhat in the 15–24 age-group, steady in middle age and, finally, rising sharply in the elderly. The elderly suffer fewer accidents than children, but more of the accidents end in serious injury or death. Adult females have a slightly higher number of fatal home accidents than males, probably because they spend more time in the home, are often distracted by young children and may be subject to the often destabilizing effects of premenstrual tension.

About three-quarters of a million children suffer injuries from home accidents every year in the UK, and another 1.2 million children outside the home. In all age-groups, and in all countries where accident statistics are available, boys are roughly twice as likely to have an accident as girls (Martin, 1971). There is some evidence to show that girls have increased hazards perception and increased fine motor co-ordination in comparison with boys which might help explain this phenomenon (Langley, Silvap and Williams, 1980). Other relevant factors may include differences in play patterns, child behaviour and treatment of boys and girls by adults in risk management and supervision.

A review of home accidents in children shows that the pattern of accidents also changes with the hazards of the environment and the stage of child development. Young babies are totally unable to protect themselves and rely entirely on adult guardians for their safety. Toddlers aged 2–5 years (who have the largest number of home accidents of any age-group) also are incapable of recognizing dangers, are physically immature and yet, at the same time, are actively exploring their environment; consequently, they are at greater risk of minor accidents. For babies, the greatest hazards are to be found in the bedroom, kitchen, bathroom or any room where he or she is unattended; falls are the most common type of accident. However, for children aged 2–5 years the places where accidents most frequently occur are the living-room, kitchen, nursery and bedrooms: falls, scalds, poisoning and burns predominate. For some-what older children, the pattern of accidents is more varied with dangers in the immediate vicinity of the home becoming more commonplace. For example, according to the first report of the Leisure Accident Surveillance Scheme (LASS), sports and play activi-ties accounted for approx. 80% of leisure injuries to children aged 5–14 years in 1988 (DTI, 1991).

Home accidents can have very serious consequences for the elderly, such as invalidity, extended periods of medical care and even death. In addition, pathological factors, such as acute and chronic illnesses, compound the effects of accidents. The tendency of the elderly to tire easily, to be forgetful, absent-minded and fearful of modern surroundings and equipment increases environ-mental hazards (WHO, 1986). Physiological effects of ageing also affect elderly people to different degrees. The side-effects of medi-cation for geriatric ailments or mental illness also interfere with normal reasoning abilities, thus increasing accident risks. Depression, lack of self-confidence or boredom also may disincline the elderly to take safety precautions.

The main cause of accidents to elderly people are falls. In 1987 it is estimated that there were 203 450 falls to people over the age of 60 requiring hospital treatment (19.3 falls per 1000 of the population aged 60+). About a quarter of these accidents result in fractures and dislocations, and another quarter in cuts and lacer-ations. Most studies including the HASS data, substantiate that the risk of falling increases with age. Falls account for 82% of all fatal accidents in the home to people over the age of 75; a lot of these fatalities are not caused by the injuries themselves but are a result of subsequent trauma and shock. Stairs and uneven and slippery floors feature strongly as implicating factors in falls, but medical problems may also play an important part. Disturbances of gait, vision and handgrip strength can all be associated with falls. Sec-ondly, there are health problems which may increase the probability of falling, including cardiovascular and neurological problems and possibly psychological factors (DTI, 1991).

A study undertaken by the Age Concern Institute of Geratology recommends that further research needs to be done to prevent such falls. This would mean looking at the environment, medical prob-lems and type of people having falls. The same study shows the importance of evaluating innovatory schemes to reduce falls and the need for professionals to share experiences.

(b) Socio-economic characteristics

There is a lot of evidence in the UK linking social class with accidental deaths – e.g. research by Constantinides *et al.* (1986) showed a close correlation between the number of home accidents and socio-economic factors such as income and class. Socially neglected families generally live in substandard housing that is overcrowded, unduly cluttered with equipment and household belongings (because of limited storage space) or has inadequate cooking facilities, all of which are likely to play some part in home accidents. For instance, an information paper by the Building Research Establishment in England noted that a number of housing and social indicators are statistically correlated with fire incidence in dwellings. Research showed a higher incidence of fires in areas of non-owner-occupied and presumably thus poorer areas (Chandler, 1960). In poor housing, accidents are related to the higher number of hazards present and also, perhaps, to less understanding of hazard risks. Such misunderstanding may be increased in groups where there are language and communication barriers. A point worth noting since ethnic minorities, for example, frequently occupy the worst housing.

Families from the lower social classes, particularly SEG 4 (the group which suffers most from child accidents), have little opportunity for upward mobility to better accommodation. This is due, in part, to the lack of access to low-cost housing and the decrease in availability of council housing. The sale of council properties, the massive reduction in local authorities capital programmes for new build and rehabilitation have also played a part in confining thousands of families in the lower social groups to unsafe and otherwise unhealthy housing.

A study by Wedge and Prosser (1973) identified 'deprived' children (those coming from one parent or very large families, in poor housing and on low income) as being at increased risk of serious accidents. They found that by the age of 11 years, 'deprived' children were more likely than others to have received a burn, scald and serious flesh wounds as a result of an accident at home. One in seven children had suffered a burn or scald, compared with one in 11 other children, and four times more had received a flesh wound requiring ten or more stitches.

Brown and Davidson (1978) found that both social class and the mother's psychiatric state were highly associated with accidents.

Of one hundred working-class women with possible or known psy-chiatric diseases, a reported accident rate in children of 19.2% was observed, compared with 9.6% in a sample class control group. The figures for middle-class women were 5.3% and 1.5% respectively.

Low income may also contribute to home accidents, by reducing the amount of finance available to remedy an unsafe physical environment, or to buy safer but more expensive equipment and goods. Poorer families do not usually own their homes and usually live in privately rented or council housing and have less mobility compared with owner-occupiers.

Children of one-parent families also appear to have a higher number of accidents. Single parents generally have less income, and tend to live in poorer, less safe housing. There may also be less opportunity for supervision. Working, single parents usually have to leave their children in the supervision of a childminder. The responsibility for safety is therefore passed on to a third party at least during working hours. The relationship between home acci-dents and housing type (owner-occupied, private or publicly rented) is not known, but from 1991 OPCS deaths data will be available by housing type. Unfortunately, mobility data will not be available.

(c) **Homeless families**

There is a direct correlation with class, race, income, social depri-vation and other socio-economic characteristics with homelessness. The potential for home accidents in accommodation for homeless families is therefore enormous and likely to increase as more famil-ies are placed into temporary accommodation. According to a report of the National Audit Office, the number of households accepted as homeless by local authorities has doubled from 53 000 in 1978 to over 126 000 in 1989, representing 300 000 or more people. Between 1982 and 1989 the number of households in all types of temporary accommodation quadrupled, while those in bed-and-breakfast accommodation increased sixfold, the heaviest usage being in London (Audit Commission, 1989). A recent report by the Child Accident Prevention Trust (CAPT, 1991) concludes that much of the temporary accommodation allocated to homeless famil-ies (with children) by local authorities and others is ill-designed, ill-equipped and ill-maintained.

Statistics on the numbers of accidents to children and families living in temporary accommodation are unavailable, but the accumulated weight of anecdotal, non-statistical data and the application of findings from many studies indicate that homeless families are at an increased risk of home accidents compared with other groups. That is, poor housing, overcrowding and lack of facilities and services, increased risk of fire, combined with family stress and social deprivation, make children more vulnerable not just to accidents, but to a wide range of health-related problems. In the case of fire, Home Office statistics show that residents of houses in multiple occupation (which includes most temporary accommodation) are ten times more likely to die in a fire than other occupancy dwellers (Home Office, 1989). Thomas and Niner (1989) found that satisfactory means of escape were absent in 56% of bed-and-breakfast hostels, and despite the fact that 80% of the properties surveyed had been issued with a fire certificate, only 43% had adequate means of escape overall.

All children need space in which to play safely, yet in Thomas and Niner's study 72% of families in bed-and-breakfast hostels had no safe place to play. The same study showed that 30% of parents reported a deterioration in their children's behaviour while homeless, mostly that they were cheekier and harder to control and subject to wildness and tantrums. A study carried out in Manchester comparing the health of families in temporary accommodation with those re-housed supports this finding (Minogue, 1989).

Marcus *et al.* (1964) have suggested that accidents occur more often to children who rely on action as a mechanism to cope with their anxiety. It may be that behavioural changes such as over-activity, aggression, impulsiveness and daring expose children to hazards and that family disturbances associated with homelessness and resettlement into temporary accommodation are likely to increase children's insecurity, anxiety and resultant accidents.

(d) State of health

Another important epidemiological factor in the etiology of home accidents concerns the state of health of the occupants. Studies of fatal accidents carried out by the Consumer Safety Unit of the UK Department of Trade (Poyner, 1980) suggest that many accidents in the home occur because of the physical and mental condition of the casualty and the characteristics of the social setting. Relevant

Table 11.1 UK accidents to children under 15 years involving architectural features (DTI, 1991)

Constructural features (stairs, steps 85 000) (glass, 14 000)	187 000
Heating and ventilation (radiators, hot water pipes, 10 000)	18 000
Fixtures (fireplace and grates 10 000)	31 000
Articles and features of the outside environment (terraces and yards 15 000)	81 000
Wall and floor furnishings (vinyl flooring 4000)	12 000
Other	2 000
Total	331 000

factors include alcohol, drugs, mental and physically disabling illness, tiredness, stress and inadequate supervision of children because a parent, or parents, are in poor health. Very low intelligence also is correlated with increased accident liability, but other disabilities in the form of decreased sight, hearing, sense of smell, skeletal deformity and spasticity also make people more vulnerable to accidents. For example, arthritis and osteoporosis (particularly of the neck of the femur) make a fall that might not seriously injure a healthy limb more likely to result in a fracture. Also the relative immobility of the arthritic lower limb makes tripping and falling more probable.

(e) Constructional features

The environment in which home accidents occur is highly related to causation and type of injuries incurred. Accidents associated with (but not necessarily caused by) constructional and architectural features account for the majority of all accidents in the home: 15.4% or 419 000 per annum in total. For example, analysis of HASS data show that almost half of all accidents to children (i.e. 331 000 out of 750 000) are associated with architectural features in and around the home (DTI, 1991) (Table 11.1). It is not known how many of the accidents shown in the table are associated with other factors, such as lack of parental supervision, but clearly improvements in the integral design, housing environment and building materials are likely to make a major impact on accident prevention and subsequent injuries.

11.4

Conception of the problem

Before addressing approaches and strategies for reducing home accidents, it is necessary to discuss the contexts in which the terms 'accident', 'injury', 'safety' and the 'home' are commonly used.

There are many definitions of 'accident' in common use such as the following.

Rosenfield (1956): 'Any suddenly occurring unintentional event which causes injury or property damage.'

Tuyns (1960): 'A chance event producing identifiable bodily damage.'

Marcusson and Oehmisch (1971): 'An accident is an event which is caused by some rapidly acting force, independent of man's will – manifests itself in physical or mental damage.'

World Health Organization (1975): 'An unpremeditated event resulting in recognisable injury.'

For recording purposes, HASS define as accident as 'any unintentional injury or suspected injury no matter how caused, except deliberately self-inflicted injuries/suspected suicides or injuries resulting from physical attacks by other persons' (DTI, 1991).

Three important features emerge from these definitions:

1. Accidents by definition cannot be premeditated. They occur as a result of chance or 'fate'.
2. Accidents are only counted if they result in measurable physical injury and, to a lesser extent, mental damage. (They therefore exclude the vast majority of 'accidents' which do not cause injuries.)
3. They exclude self-inflicted or intentional injuries (including attacks against the person).

There is considerable variation in the way in which accidents (where they are monitored at all) are collated across the world making any comparisons meaningless. Some countries, for example, include suicides in their accident statistics, others only keep statistics on fatalities or do not record severity of injuries.

The term 'injury' includes cuts, lacerations, bruises, fractures, dislocations, sprains, burns, scalds, poisonings, suffocations and choking by foreign bodies, etc.

The term 'home' is generally regarded as synonymous with the word 'house', 'flat', 'apartment' or 'dwelling' – i.e. the physical structure for providing shelter against the elements serving as the focus of household life. In the UK the HASS definition of a 'home' includes the outside environs, not just the building. In some countries (not the UK) where the 'home' is also the base for cottage industries, home accident statistics may include injuries caused by occupational accidents. The UK also does not count 'homes' to people who live in and work in hotels, shops and farms. These are regarded as commercial or industrial establishments.

'Safety' is generally perceived as a state in which accidents are unlikely to occur, and if they were to occur, would limit injuries to the person. 'Home safety' is typically used to describe circumstances which limit accident occurrence and resultant injuries within the confines of the shelter. The first aspect of this relates to environmental considerations – i.e. the state in which the home environment, and products used in the home, are so designed, maintained and supervised as to be considered 'safe'. Secondly, the term is used in relation to the 'safe' management of household activities and domestic operations. Finally, 'home safety' is concerned with regulating or supervising the behaviour of people who live in or visit the home. However, this classic interpretation is both simplistic and limited.

First, by confining the home to the physical shelter, the immediate residential environment is, by definition, excluded. It is accepted that there are difficulties defining the boundaries of the residential environment and, in any case, these vary with age, but it is important to recognize that the home is part of a much wider physical, social and community infrastructure which people closely associate with their housing. People do not spend all of their time indoors. Children, for example, spend a lot of time outside the shelter playing in gardens and communal areas within the immediate environs of the home. As children get older they play in the streets, or in estate playgrounds and nearby outbuildings (sheds, garages, etc.). Adults and elderly people frequently use community and recreational facilities which form an integral part of their housing.

Indeed in many regions (e.g. Mediterranean countries) very little time is spent indoors; meals and social activities, for example, are usually spent in cafés, bars and restaurants.

My own view is that 'home safety' must include the 'residential environment', which has been described by the WHO (1972) as 'the physical structure that mankind uses for shelter and the environs of that structure including all necessary services, facilities, equipment and devices needed or prescribed for the physical and social well-being of the family'.

Inclusion of the environment would certainly mean including leisure activities, safety of play areas and pedestrian and road safety, at least in the immediate surroundings of the home. It may also include water safety (pools, canals, ponds, etc.).

The second interpretational constraint concerns the attitudes of professionals who often have chosen to take a very narrow interpretation of the term 'safety'. Not only have they failed to recognize the relationship between safety and health, but they have virtually hi-jacked home safety from other public health policies and activities. The WHO (1961) defines 'health' as 'not merely the absence of disease and infirmity, but a state of complete physical, mental and social well-being'. Since the outcome of recorded accidents is, by definition, *always* physical injury of some kind and therefore impairment of physical and usually mental health (shock, etc.), it seems patently obvious that safety is but one facet of health and should be included in public health policies and programmes.

Another consequence of these semantics has been confusion in adjudicating what constitutes 'health' and 'safety', often resulting in a very limited approach to safety auditing and housing inspections, culminating in prioritization of some home safety features while ignoring others of equal importance. For example, home safety practitioners may confine safety audits to appliances, number of power points, furnishings and products used within the home while ignoring structural and design elements of the property itself – i.e. giving attention to fixtures, fittings and domestic appliances which they regard as the householder's responsibility to maintain (e.g. loose carpets, old kettle flexes, oil heaters, fireguards and overloaded electrical points).

A 'holistic' home safety policy would take a much wider view. For example, it would: examine the condition of flooring to which loose carpets are attached; examine the design and layout of the kitchen in which the kettle is situated; and look at available benefits to enable householders to use a safer form of heating and opportunities for improvement grants or legal remedies to deal with under-provision of electrical points. Such a policy would also put aside any institutional barriers between safety and health during auditing. For example, safety might include the 'accidental' ingestion of asbestos fibres from asbestos building materials or 'accidental' inhalation of indoor air pollutants emitted from building products or 'accidental' lead poisoning caused by children chewing lead paintwork. From this perspective, any distinction between 'safety' and 'health' is arbitrary and meaningless.

11.5
Responding to the challenge

There are several key elements to any effective home safety prevention strategy. These embrace policy considerations, preventive countermeasures, institutional approaches, interdisciplinary collaboration, monitoring and evaluation.

(i) Policy considerations

The classical approach to policy development is based on a logical sequence of events: the collection and analysis of information on accidents and their resultant injuries, identification of practical measures to reduce accidents or their injuries, the implementation of these measures and an assessment of their effectiveness. At each stage, there has to be an assessment of what is achievable within a given time-span and available resources. An alternative approach is for policy to develop organically from experiential initiatives – i.e. based on incremental pragmatism rather than the synoptic approach, described earlier. However, in both cases, there must be an active willingness to put home safety into a proactive programme, that is, safety needs to be on the political agenda. Policies by themselves do not reduce accidents: they have to be actually implemented.

Research carried out by the Child Accident Prevention Trust showed a wide variety of local approaches towards child accident prevention work (CAPT, 1991b). In some cases, accident prevention was being carried out under the umbrella of a tightly structured policy, while in other cases there was no policy at all and work was proceeding in an *ad hoc* fashion. The CAPT concluded that these differences were mainly due to the degree of political support, enthusiasm, motivation or otherwise of the people involved, the availability of resources and the extent to which interdisciplinary and community collaboration, etc. had been developed.

What also emerged was that groups working in accident prevention activities often did so with no clear targets of what they wanted to achieve. That is, they had no framework in which to carry out accident prevention work or to measure the success or otherwise of what they were doing.

The WHO's strategy document *Health for All by the Year 2000* (1986) makes specific reference to a number of targets for safety in the home and environment. For example, Target 11 states that by the year 2000, deaths from accidents in the European Region should be reduced by at least 25%; Target 24 requires that all people in the region should have a better opportunity of living in houses and settlements which provide a healthy and safe environment. These targets thus provide an opportunity to re-examine existing policies, standards, legislation and attitudes towards accident limitation at a national and local level. In the UK compliance with these targets would mean reducing deaths from home accidents by 1200 per annum. A further reduction of 800 000 non-fatal accidents each year would be needed if we were to apply the same targets as for fatal accidents. These are challenging but not unrealistic goals, given political will and support, which has so far been largely unforthcoming.

(ii) Countermeasures

There are the following categories of countermeasures:

Primary prevention: measures aimed at preventing an accident happening at all (e.g. a window lock will prevent a child from falling out of a window).

Secondary prevention: measures aimed at reducing or minimizing the effect and severity of accidents such as the use of soft surfaces (e.g. vegetation) outside windows to lessen the impact of falls.

Tertiary prevention: measures aimed at minimizing the severity of the final outcome of the injury (e.g. the immediate provision of first aid or treatment following an injury).

In all cases, three main approaches are utilized: (a) education; (b) engineering; and (c) enforcement.

These approaches should not be seen in isolation, for example, provision and public acceptance of safety legislation (enforcement) is dependent upon raising awareness of the necessity for the legislation (education) and the ready availability of design means (engineering) to achieve it.

(a) **Home safety education**

This is concerned with increasing knowledge of the problem and its solution resulting in a change in attitude towards it and, in some cases, an actual change in behaviour. Such educational approaches may be directed at the individuals themselves or at people who have a responsibility for supervising others (e.g. parents, childminders).

Research has repeatedly shown that education is the main (usually the only) approach adopted by field professionals towards accident prevention. For example, a survey by CAPT showed that while virtually all respondents used educational means in child accident prevention work, only 7% (of 144) were involved in environmental approaches in relation to housing schemes (CAPT, 1991b). However, regardless of the fact that other approaches might be more appropriate, it is nevertheless important that any educational approach is effective in achieving stated objectives.

Given the view that home safety is a branch of preventive medicine (i.e. that it has a public health foundation), then it follows that home safety education should be administered on the same principles as other health education initiatives. These are generally developed along three main lines: (i) raising individual competence and knowledge about health and illness and about prevention and coping with a given situation; (ii) raising competence and knowledge in using the health care system and to understand its functions; and (iii) raising awareness about social, political and environmental factors that affect safety. There are several elements to achieving these objectives. Most of these revolve around targeting the right information to the right people and optimizing the right communication vehicles to ensure that this is achieved.

Regarding targeting, home safety education is similar to other health education initiatives in institutionalizing 'individual responsibility in making informed safety choices'. This concept is partly misguided because it assumes that everybody is in a position to make these choices and is reliant upon securing changes in life styles which are extremely difficult to achieve, particularly in the very young and old. There is no doubt that life styles which incorporate risky behaviour can be hazardous to safety. However, this is not because people choose to act dangerously: taking risks is sometimes the only way people can survive in a given situation or adapt to the unsatisfactory physical and social environment in which they live. In these cases, didactic styles of safety education which blame people for putting themselves or others at risk only serves to enforce the powerlessness which poor people, ethnic minorities, single-parent families, the chronically sick and the elderly already face.

Local authorities in the UK have generally failed to target home safety education to those groups who would most benefit from it. Most have ignored social, cultural, economic and ethnic considerations in their safety campaigns. Unfortunately, safety statistics show that it is precisely these groups which have the most accidents. The downside of this policy is that Home Safety Education Officers waste time and effort preaching to the converted. Safety education has therefore come to be regarded very much as a middle-class institution.

Another application of safety education is aimed at those in a position to change the physical environment in which hazardous life styles take place (e.g. the politicians, the policy-makers and the professionals). This really is the third aspect of health education: raising awareness about social, economic and environmental factors which underpin home safety policies. A few local authorities have successfully taken up these issues through interprofessional health promotion teams and home safety committees but many have not tackled the issue at all.

Education of professionals, such as Environmental Health Officers, GPs, health visitors, midwives, district nurses, Housing Officers, etc., on home safety would probably be a much more effective approach than current initiatives. There are signs that this is beginning to happen. New developments in national vocational qualifications (NVQ) include safety as a core theme in their objectives and competences. Thus a new generation of well-trained, safety-aware practitioners is emerging. Other educational approaches include those aimed at people with direct supervisory responsibility for the safety of others – e.g. nursery nurses, childminders and carers. Education methods which involve active participation of the groups concerned are more likely to ensure that home safety responses are based on what can actually be achieved (i.e. empowerment for change) within the short or medium term. Methods of communication should be used to the fullest to ensure that a relevant message gets across. Local press, radio, television, and video can be used to support poster campaigns or lecture-based teaching. Such campaigns need to be constantly reinforced if home safety is to be kept on the agenda. Finally, the national curriculum makes provision for home safety education to be included in teaching programmes for schools.

(b) Engineering

In the context of home safety, engineering is the approach used for implementing safety design criteria in the home environment. Its primary purpose is to prevent accidents through the design of building elements used in the construction of the home and products used during household activities. Its secondary role is to minimize the effects of injuries following an accident.

Much is known about the safe design of building materials, products and their application in the home environment. The Department of the Environment booklet *Safety in the Home* (DoE, 1971), and the Child Accident Prevention Trust book *Child Safety and Housing* (CAPT, 1966), gives detailed information on safety design measures in housing. British Standards and Codes of Practice incorporate considerable safety criteria and the Building Regulations, where they apply, are also relevant. However, for these to be applied there needs to be an awareness of the importance of the issue and implicit responsibility to implement safety in design briefs. However, architects and planners, for example, are often ignorant about home safety design criteria which are not even specifically included in their training programmes, and often evade responsibility for safety by blaming the commissioning agencies (who may also be ignorant about safety design) for not specifying safety in the design brief.

Commissioning agencies, local authorities, architect/planning professional bodies, building agencies and societies all have an opportunity to ensure that safety design criteria are incorporated into new housing schemes, estate upgrading programmes and area improvement initiatives. There are many examples where such implementation would result in a marked reduction in accidents. For example, in the UK during 1988 there were 27 000 accidents attributable to the use of non-safety glass in doors and windows (DTI, 1991). According to Sinnot (1987), 'the elimination of glass in doors and the relocation or modification of windows so that they are unlikely to be contacted accidentally would virtually eliminate injuries caused by architectural glass'. Where this cannot be achieved, Sinnot recommends use of a safety glazing material in all glazed panels in doors, side-panels and low-level windows. However, Sinnot believes that existing British requirements (BS 6262) for glass are 'inadequate'; in any case, compliance with British Standards is not statutorily required by current Building Regulations. This is another example where education could be used as a means of facilitating better design through an engineering approach. Virtually every other building element used in home construction could be assessed to ascertain accident risk and the means for reducing such risks.

To help, some agencies have produced design checklists for architects and designers when originating plans and specifications; one example is presented in a document entitled *Healthy Housing Guidelines*, produced for the WHO (Ranson, 1988). The following requirements relate directly to home safety and can be used as a basis for policy formulation and implementation: (i) protection of neighbourhoods against the hazards of vehicular traffic; (ii) avoidance of unsafe conditions in the housing environment, in outbuildings and surroundings of the home; (iii) protection against the risks and effects of falls; (iv) provision of adequate facilities for enabling means of escape in case of fire and control and removal of conditions likely to cause or promote fire; (v) protection against burns and scalds; (vi) protection against asphyxiation or gas poisoning from faulty heating and cooking appliances and services; (vii) protection against electrical shocks from defective appliances and services; (viii) protection against bodily injuries from lacerations and similar injuries; (ix) protection against poisoning from dangerous drugs, medicines and household chemicals; (x) protection against poisoning from plants; and (xi) protection against poisoning from soil.

The basis of these principles is that they provide a framework in which home safety can be incorporated into a much wider healthy housing strategy (Ranson, 1991). The Appendix to this chapter provides an example of a checklist which an architect or commissioning client might use when designing new housing. Alternatively, a similar checklist could be used as the basis of evaluation when inspecting a property or as part of a home check scheme. However, there is no substitute for locally relevant appraisal schemes properly targeted to match achievable goals, legislation, types of property, etc., as applicable.

(c) Enforcement

There is no overall national legislative framework for home safety prevention work. Such legislation as there is is scattered among Housing Acts, Building Regulations, consumer legislation, Health and Safety at Work Acts and other relevant miscellaneous legislation. There are also various common law and public liability rights which may be applicable. In addition, tenancies, leases and landlord and tenant legislation may incorporate provisions relating to home safety – e.g. repair obligations and stipulations regarding usage and permitted activities.

There is no single agency responsible for enforcing those statutory provisions which do exist. In general, Environmental Health Departments are responsible for enforcing Housing Acts which make some provision for rectifying structural safety defects in the home. These include, to some extent, provisions relating to fitness for human habitation. However, there are now very limited statutory controls to deal with items which are dangerous because of inherent design features and there is virtually no legislation to cope with hazards in the residential environment.

Local Authority Building Control Officers are responsible for enforcing Building Regulations which incorporate a number of requirements directly or indirectly affecting safety in new housing or conversions and certain other building works. However, the Building Regulations have been considerably diluted as part of the government's strategy of 'lifting the bureaucratic burden' from builders and house designers. For example, builders no longer have to seek prior approval for building work or, in some cases, necessarily to submit plans.

In general, there is much better legislation to deal with safety of consumer goods used in the home. Trading Standards Officers enforce a plethora of consumer legislation relating to household products, furnishings and appliances (as well as building products in some cases).

The only piece of legislation which is specifically dedicated to home safety is the *Home Safety Act 1961*. This one-page piece of legislation enables local authorities to carry out safety education work, although it is left up to individual local authorities to decide how far they wish to implement this. In most cases, Environmental Health Departments administer it, although home safety education is often tagged on to the work of Road Safety Officers. These officers often do not have a background in building or housing. Whoever administers it, the Home Safety Act has tended to direct local authorities' home safety activities towards education rather than an enforcement approach. For example, the vast majority of Environmental Health Officers' work is concerned with enforcement activities, but in the case of home safety this approach is discarded in favour of education. The reasons for this are largely conceptual, partly caused by the lack of priority or specificity of home safety in housing and other legislation which they enforce. In any case, home safety is poorly resourced and has a very low priority in local authorities' overall activities.

Health authorities have virtually no enforcement powers in relation to home safety, although health visitors have an advisory role when visiting premises where children under the age of 5 years are living. The need for an effective legislative and enforcement framework for home safety prevention work is therefore becoming increasingly apparent. Home accidents account for nine times more deaths, and 16 times more injuries, than all occupational accidents put together, yet there is no comparable machinery for tackling home-accidents. Occupational safety is governed by the provisions of the Health and Safety at Work, etc. Act and Regulations and Orders made thereunder. Guidance notes covering almost every conceivable aspect of occupational safety are available to employers and employees alike. A Health and Safety Commission oversees the work of a Health and Safety Executive, who along with local authorities, employ inspectors to visit workplaces regularly to check on safety. All occupational accidents have to be recorded and notified to the respective enforcement authority. These are then investigated and remedial action taken. Prohibition and improvement notices can be served to rectify hazards either immediately or within a specific time-scale. This may be followed by court action where substantive fines and even imprisonment can be imposed upon calcitrant offenders. In the workplace, safety is actively encouraged through safety representatives and safety committees and every year the Health and Safety Executive issues a report detailing trends on accidents, preventive initiatives and recommendations for improvements. There is a need for a similar legislative and institutional framework to be set up for home safety. At the present time, local authorities are not even notified of major home accidents within their districts (although they *are* notified of major road traffic accidents). There is virtually no liaison between accident and emergency departments, general practitioners, etc. with local authorities. Accident investigations and possible remedial or secondary preventive action is therefore not carried out and opportunities for primary preventive work in situations and housing environments where similar hazards may exist is also lost. There has been little or no leadership or guidance on this issue from government departments or professional bodies or proposals for changing the status quo. This reflects the very low priority which home safety has within the general order of other public safety work.

(d) Collaboration

Home safety initiatives cannot be administered by any one authority, agency or profession; they cut across too many boundaries and disciplines. The need for intersectoral collaboration and community involvement is therefore patently apparent. Despite this, recent research shows that good communication and liaison between the different agencies with a role in accident prevention is badly lacking (CAPT, 1991b). Poor communication was found both within and between agencies. This was attributed to a variety of factors including incompatible structures, overlapping geographical boundaries, interagency and interdepartmental rivalry, professional and bureaucratic hide-boundness and a simple lack of practice. This resulted in a very poor shared information base, a poor understanding of what other agencies do, or are in a position to do, and confusion about ways to develop better liaison. There are, of course, many different levels in which intercollaboration can be applied: at the design and construction stage, it may involve consultation and liaison between architects, planners, Environmental Health Officers (EHOs), Building Control Officers and the fire authority. Tenants' associations or residents' groups, where they exist, could also be consulted for their inputs. Such intercollaboration could be formalized through local housing groups with representatives from all the main agencies and community.

For existing housing, intercollaboration may involve joint visits to certain properties (for example, temporary accommodation for homeless families) by the local EHO and the health visitor. Health authorities, GPs and family practitioner committees could liaise directly with local authorities on accident notification and monitoring, particularly in areas where housing is poor and more likely to result in accidents. Directors of Public Health could co-ordinate some of these activities. Interdisciplinary health promotion teams or accident prevention teams could initiate home safety campaigns or co-ordinate initiatives. This could involve local schools and voluntary organizations, as well as local press/radio, etc.; in fact opportunities for involvement of local organizations and institutions in home accident prevention work are endless. What is needed is a new approach towards collective working, dispelling of entrenched attitudes towards other agencies and more understanding of each other's work and roles in relation to home accident prevention. A start on this has already been made in some areas, but more central direction and resources are needed to enable these activities to produce meaningful collective outcomes.

11.6
Conclusion

The high number of deaths and injuries caused by accidents in the home presents us with one of the biggest public health challenges of this century. The response of government, health services and the professionals to home safety has been sporadic, low key and preoccupied with largely facile safety education initiatives which has put the responsibility for safety firmly on consumers, carers and accident victims. Prevention through design, accident monitoring, investigation and enforcement has been virtually ignored in home safety policies. What is needed is an institutional framework, perhaps similar to what exists for occupational safety, in which home safety strategies can be applied and enforced. For this to happen the issue needs to be put firmly on the political agenda and backed up by central leadership, guidance and support.

Home safety cannot, and should not, operate in total isolation from other service delivery agencies and the community it is supposed to serve. Effective collaboration is the only practical way forward, particularly between the legislature and government departments, local authority and health authorities and voluntary bodies or organizations. One possible way of improving intersectoral collaboration would be through a national accident prevention committee or council with representation from the appropriate government departments and the various professional and voluntary bodies. This committee would be responsible for taking broad policy decisions and it conceivably could be given some executive powers in order to initiate action. In this way, a national policy and plan could be developed and implemented through local agencies.

Local authorities, as democratically accountable institutions close to the community they serve, are in a unique position to promote health and safety in the home – not just as major public landlords, but also as guardians of the public health. Directors of public health also have an important role in ensuring that health authorities are fully involved in local home safety prevention programmes and may also be able to take on an accident monitoring role.

On an encouraging note, many disciplines have accepted some responsibility for safety within their everyday work and often have made important contributions to local multidisciplinary accident prevention groups.

It is argued that such programmes should not just incorporate educational initiatives, but also engineering and enforcement approaches. Existing housing and building legislation needs to be strengthened to give local authorities statutory powers to deal specifically with unsafe housing. In this respect, there has so far not been the same interest in providing legislative standards relating to home safety design and architectural features *within the home and home environment* as has been given to consumer products and health and safety at work. Nevertheless, the extant legislation could be used more effectively, so that the abysmal progress made so far in reducing home accidents can be reversed.

Without a strong commitment to making home safety a reality, the WHO's Health for All targets, aimed at reducing the number of home accidents by 25% by the year 2000, will not be achieved. The alternative is to subject this and future generations to a self-sustaining legacy of avoidable deaths, pain, injuries and disabilities. A major threat to public health which home accidents represent must not go unchallenged.

Bibliography

Backett, E. M. (1965). *Domestic Accidents*, WHO Public Health Papers No. 26, WHO, Geneva.

Barrow, M. R. (1987). Statistically, home is where the harm is. Paper presented at London Home Safety Council Study Day, London, 11 May 1987.

Brown, G. W. and Davidson, S. (1978). Social class, psychiatric disorder of mother and accidents to children. *Lancet*.

Chandler, S. E. (1960). *Residential Fires in London Related to Housing Conditions and Social Factors*, Building Research Establishment, Garston.

Child Accident Prevention Trust (CAPT) (1966). *Child Safety and Housing: Practical Design Guidances for Commissioning Agencies, Architects, Designers and Builders*, CAPT, London.

CAPT (1989). *Basic Principles of Child Accident Prevention: A Guide to Action*, CAPT, London.

CAPT (1991a). *Safe as Houses: Guidelines for the Safety of Children in Temporary Accommodation*, CAPT, London.

CAPT (1991b). *Local Approaches towards Child Accident Prevention*, CAPT, London.

Constantinides, P. *et al.* (1986). *Child Accidents and Inequality in a London Borough*. Research Report to the North East Thames Regional Health Authority, Locally Organized Research Scheme, NETRHA, London.

Department of the Environment (DoE) (1971). *Safety in the Home* (metric edn), HMSO, London.

Department of the Environment (DoE) (1989). *Home and Leisure Accident Research: Home Accident Surveillance System, Eleventh Annual Report, 1987 data*, Consumer Safety Unit, London.

Department of Trade and Industry (DTI) (1991). *Home and Leisure Accident Research: Home Accident Surveillance System, Twelfth Annual Report, 1988 data*, DTI Consumer Safety Unit, London.

Drennan, V. *et al.* (1986). Health visitors and homeless families. *Health Visitor J.*, 59, 340–2.

Haddon, W. (1973). Energy damage and the ten counter strategies. *J. Trauma*, 13 (4), 321–31.

Home Office (1989). *Fire Statistics: United Kingdom*, Home Office, London.

Jackson, R. H. (1983). A review of the problem of accidents in

Europe. Paper presented at Symposium on Accidents in Europe, WHO (EURO), Copenhagen.

Langley, J. Silvap and Williams, S. (1980). Motor co-ordination and childhood accidents. *J. Safety Res.*, 12, 175–8.

Marcus, I. M., Wilson, W., Kraft, I., Swander, D., Southerland, F. and Schulhofer, E. (1964). An interdisciplinary approach to accident patterns in children. In: Haddon, W., Jr, Suchnau, E. A. and Klein, D. (eds) *Accident Research: Methods and Approaches*, pp. 313–26, Harper and Row, New York.

Martin, G. I. (1971). Perception of hazards by young children. *Dissertation Abstracts 1971*, 31 (7–13), 4367.

Minogue, A. (1989). *Health Survey: Homeless Families and Rehoused Families*, Manchester City Council.

Poyner, B. (1980). *Personal Factors in Domestic Accident Prevention through Products and Environmental Design*, Consumer Safety Unit, London.

Ranson, R. P. (1988). *Healthy Housing Guidelines. Environmental Health in Europe*, Series No. 31, WHO (EURO), Copenhagen.

Ranson, R. P. (1991). *Healthy Housing: A Guide to Action*, Chapman and Hall, London.

Sinnot, R. (1987). The safety of glazing in dwellings. Paper presented at IEHO/ROSPA Seminar on Home Safety and the Environment, London, 14 July 1987.

Thomas, A. and Niner, P. (1989). *Living in Temporary Accommodation, a Survey of Homeless People*, HMSO, London.

Tomalin, N. (1985). *Analysis of Architectural Glass Accidents*, HASS, Consumer Safety Unit, London.

Wedge, P. and Prosser, H. (1973). *Born to Fail*, Arrow Books, London.

World Health Organization (WHO) (1961). Preamble to WHO Constitution. In: *WHO Basic Documents* (12th edn), WHO, Geneva.

WHO (1972). *Development of Environmental Criteria for Urban Planning*, Report of a WHO Scientific Group, WHO, Geneva.

WHO (1984). *Evaluation of the Strategy for Health for All by the Year 2000*, Seventh Report of the World Health Organization, WHO, Geneva.

WHO (1986a). *Health for All by the Year 2000, Regional Targets for Europe*, WHO (EURO), Copenhagen.

WHO (1986b). *The prevention of accidents in the home. Report on a Symposium*, WHO (EURO), Copenhagen.

Appendix: Appraisal checklist for home safety

Home safety requirements

- Are any occupants disabled or chronically sick (*state details*)?
- Do any occupants receive regular medication (*state details*)?
- Are any occupants known alcoholics, heavy drinkers, drug addicts or senile?
- Are all members of family mobile?
- Have there been any previous accidents in home (*state sources*)?
- Have children been screened for lead?
- Are small children regularly left unsupervised?
- Are telephones or other methods of communication easily available? If so, do people most at risk (or in charge) know how to use them?
- Do any of occupants understand first aid and resuscitation?
- Is there an established fire-drill?
- Are all members of family covered by insurance for all accident risks, medical care and income compensation?
- Are medical care facilities and first aid services available (*state location*)?
- Do occupants know location of medical care facilities?

Protection of the neighbourhood against the hazards of vehicular traffic

- Does layout separate pedestrian and vehicle traffic adequately?
- Is parking and traffic turning space adequate?
- Are 'sleeping policemen' or other engineering methods used to restrict traffic speed?

Avoidance of unsafe conditions in the housing environment, in outbuildings and surroundings of the home

(a) Environment

- Is the house subject to periodic flooding, earthquakes or landslip?
- Are there any obvious dangers near to house (*state source*)?
- Is the property adequately fenced to adjacent dangers?
- Are all wells, ditches, drains and pits properly covered or otherwise guarded?
- Are overhead electricity supply lines accessible to children?
- Are there any large dead or dying trees likely to fall?
- Are there any dangerous or poisonous animals or insects in area?
- Are any ponds or swimming-pools fenced off or suitably guarded?
- Are water tanks properly covered?
- Are external paved surfaces, steps and ramps non-slippery when wet?
- Is drainage provided to paved areas?
- Are paths even and properly lighted at night?

- Are there any safety rings set into high walls and chimneys for outside working and ladders?
- Are snow barriers provided at eaves to steep pitched roofs?
- Are balcony areas unclimbable and bulky enough to give reassurance (min. 2.1 m high)?
- Are balcony balustrades spaced at correct intervals (max. 90 mm spacing)?
- Are thresholds to main access doors designed to form the nosing of steps?

- Are dimensions of external steps so designed to give easy going?
- Are there single external steps or unexpected ramps? If so, are they provided with a handrail and marked by a change of colour?
- Are fences and gates so designed that young children cannot climb over or open them?
- Are very low fences clearly visible?
- Is the route to the clothes line and rubbish bins direct and free from unnecessary changes of level?

(b) Outbuildings

- Are power tools and appliances adequately earthed and guarded?
- Are tools, chemicals and other objects accessible to children?
- Is gasoline stored adequately?
- Is lighting satisfactory?
- Is ventilation adequate?

- Can car engine be run easily when garage doors are closed?
- Is the floor level?
- Is room adequately protected against fire?
- Are electric rotor motors provided with automatic circuit breakers?

Protection against the risks and effects of falls

(a) Staircase

- Are floor coverings non-slip?
- Is there a mat well at entrance door?
- Are the stairs too steep (exceeding 37°)?
- Are they regular, straight and of uniform height?
- Are there any shallow steps less than 73 mm height?
- Do tapered steps provide too small a going?
- Are there any winders or tapered treads?
- Do top and bottom steps encroach onto circulation areas?
- Are there any open risers?
- Are the balustrades less than 90 mm apart?

- Are there firm suitable handrails on both sides of stairs unobstructed by handrail fittings?
- Does design of handrail provide good grip for elderly and infirm persons?
- Is the stair carpet pinned securely to the floor at the top and bottom of staircase?
- Do any doors open onto stairs or landings?
- Are the stairs well lit?
- Are windows and light fittings within normal reach?
- Are there two-way light switches at top and bottom of stairs?
- Does artificial lighting shine towards stairs?

- Are there any open stairwells? If so, are they unclimbable?
- Does staircase provide protection against fire?
- Are there any inflammable or dangerous chemicals stored under stairs?

- Are safety gates provided at top/bottom of stairs?
- Are there fixing positions for stair gates?
- Are there any radiators at base of stairs? If so, are they protected?

(b) Halls, landings and circulation areas

- Are light switches between bedroom and WC so placed that way ahead can be lit from either direction?
- Are there any single steps or unexpected changes of level? If so, are they differentiated by change of colour?
- Are thresholds to internal doors so detailed as to minimize tripping?

- Is lighting adequate?
- Are illuminated switches provided in circulation areas?
- Is access to roof spaces by fixed ladder?
- Does roof space have a boarded floor or cat walk and otherwise safe?
- Is roof space properly lit?

(c) Living-rooms

- Is the floor polished?
- Are non-slip floor coverings provided?

- Are edges of floor coverings securely fixed?
- Are ceiling and door heights sufficient?

(d) Kitchen

- Is lighting adequate for room and work surfaces?
- Are floor surfaces slippery?
- Are doors to kitchen so placed as to minimize through traffic?
- Are there high-level storage cupboards? If so, how are they reached?
- Are swings to doors and cupboard doors so planned as to avoid collisions and not situated over cookers?
- Is the external temperature of cooker satisfactory?
- Are electrical plugs safely sited and away from kitchen sink?
- Are open flames from cooking

stoves and heating appliances less than 1 mm from ground?
- Can electric kettles not be pulled over easily and are flexes adequate?
- Are all cooking utensils broad at base with suitable handles?
- Is cooker situated immediately next to a window or door?
- Is there a min. 300 mm width of work surface on either side of cooker?
- Are any hobs in peninsular or 'island' units?
- Are work surfaces flush with level of cooker hob?
- Do worktop fronts have square edges?

- Is the kitchen sufficiently large so that no route through kitchen impinges on the sink/fridge/cooker work triangle?

- Is there at least 12 mm between the fronts of fitments to allow passing?

(e) Bathrooms/WC compartments

- Are floor coverings adequate and non-slip?
- Are handrails installed?
- Does shower tray have a slip-resistant finish?
- Does wash basin overhang the end of the bath?
- Does wash basin have secure bolt fittings?
- Does bath have safety grab handles and a slip-resistant moulded surface?

- Is toilet reached by going up and down stairs?
- Are locks capable of being opened from outside?
- Are pull switches low enough for a child to reach?
- Are locks on bathroom/WC doors openable from outside in an emergency?
- Is there a bell or could a call be heard in an emergency?

(f) Windows

- Are windows above third storey at least 1100 mm above floor level?
- Are windows above third storey capable of being cleaned and re-glazed from inside?
- Are all hand-operated window controls less than 2000 mm from floor?
- Do windows allow continual control of movement?
- Do windows have independent fastenings far beyond a child's reach (where applicable)?

- Do windows below 1350 mm from floor have an automatic device to restrict aperture to 100 mm?
- Are high-level bolts or child-proof locks used on windows above ground floor?
- Do windows which reverse for cleaning have devices to lock them in the fully reversed position?
- Are window sills in children's room not easily climbable and not too wide so that a child cannot sit on them?

(g) Doors

- Do doors not encroach space where a child may be playing?
- Are sliding/folding doors used where space is restricted?
- Is door furniture at sufficient height to enable children to open internal doors safely?

- Are high-level bolts used to prevent the opening of doors leading to unsafe areas (cellars, outbuildings, garages, etc.)?

Provision of adequate facilities for enabling means of escape in case of fire and control and removal of conditions likely to cause or promote fire

(a) Single or two-storey dwellings

- Are roadways, gateways and space around buildings adequate to allow access by fire brigade?
- Are fire hydrants or other water supplies reasonably near buildings?
- Are suitable non-combustible materials used in building construction?
- Is there a suitable fire-break between adjoining dwellings?
- Is there suitable means of escape to outside (including alternative exits)?
- Are doors and stairs to upper storeys protected against fire?
- Do windows to upper storeys allow easy exit?
- Are suitable fire extinguishers (e.g. in kitchen) and hoses available?
- Are smoke alarms installed?
- Are highly inflammable materials used in furnishings, etc.?
- Are wiring, fuses and connections to electrical appliances satisfactory in use?
- Are there any dangerous oil heaters or outdated electric heaters in use?
- Are storage arrangements for inflammable substances satisfactory?

(b) Multiple dwellings (additional precautions)

- Is secondary means of escape provided?
- Are at least two escape routes leading in opposite directions provided to access ways?
- Is there emergency access to adjoining premises (e.g. to roof)?
- Do stairs between dwellings provide at least 30 min fire resistance in event of fire?
- Are all access ways to exits free from obstruction and inflammable materials?
- Are all entrance and cupboard doors of halls and landings self-closing and adequately protected against fire?
- Are windows and emergency exits unlocked, easily openable and large enough for access?
- Is emergency exit lighting provided?
- Are electric switch rooms properly fire-proofed?
- In tall buildings are firemen's lifts and ventilated lobbies provided?
- Are smoke/fire alarms installed?
- Are smoke outlets provided to basements and automatic roof vents to tall buildings?
- Are any other smoke dispersal methods provided?
- Are dry and set rising mains on each storey provided?
- Is there means of communication by telephone for firemen between ground level and higher storeys?

(c) Miscellaneous

- Is a ceiling airer situated over the cooker?
- Is there a fire blanket or extinguisher next to cooker hob?
- Are there ceiling-mounted cupboards directly over a cooker or boiler?
- If Kerosene is used, is it stored safely?

- Are there any oil or gas heaters in passages?
- Is clothing of young children and others non-flammable?
- Are ashtrays of the bowl type and totally enclosed?
- Does the furniture pass current fire safety standards?

Protection against burns and scalds

- Is domestic water delivered at under 54°C?
- Do showers have thermostatically controlled mixer valves?
- Is there an open fire?

- Are heaters and fires adequately guarded?
- Is bath easily accessible to children?
- Is surface temperature of convector radiators effectively controlled?

Protection against asphyxiation or gas poisoning from faulty heating and cooking appliances and services

(a) General

- Are gas appliances checked for leaks and regularly maintained?
- If utility gas is used, is there adequate ventilation?
- If utility gas is used, are pipes, taps and fittings functioning correctly?
- Are gas appliances vented to the outside?

- Do ovens have double doors and an inside light?
- Are open fires well ventilated?
- Are ventilation and safety devices to gas heaters operating satisfactorily?

(b) Liquefied petroleum gas installations

- Are cylinders stored in a safe, accessible, well-ventilated area outside?
- Are cylinders, connectors, pipes, valves, gas regulators and cut-out devices in good condition?
- Are there any signs of leaks?

- Are LPG appliances inspected and regularly maintained?
- Are the appliances properly flued to outside air (where applicable)?
- Is adequate ventilation provided to rooms containing appliances?

Protection against electrical shocks from defective appliances and services

- Are electrical appliances safe and up to approved standards?
- Are any electrical points accessible to young children?
- Are shock stops provided on all unused electrical outlets?
- Are there any electrical contacts between source of current, water supply and individuals?
- Are all electrical points fitted with correct fuse?
- Are any socket outlets situated near to sink?
- Are sufficient sockets provided, i.e. are any overloaded?

- Are there residual circuit breakers on mains supply?
- Are all sources of electricity suitably earthed, insulated and safe?
- Is there an old, poorly serviced electric blanket in use?
- Are any electric heaters used? If so, are they safe and properly guarded?
- Can any electric point or switch be reached while in contact with water?
- Are any light fittings situated over the bath?

Protection against bodily injuries from lacerations and similar injuries

- Is glass weight sufficient for size and position of windows?
- Are all large sheets of plate glass easily visible?
- Do windows project over path and circulation areas?
- Is safety glazing used to doors, especially lower panes, patio doors and windows within 800 mm of the floor?
- Are windows above ground-floor level at least 800 mm from floor or otherwise adequately protected?
- Are all high-speed cutting devices properly guarded?
- Do can openers not leave raw-metal edges?

- Are kitchen knives and other dangerous implements out of reach of children?
- Do powered washers and driers switch off automatically when opened?
- Are appliances regularly checked for safety and properly maintained?
- Are glass doors easily seen?
- Are off-centre pivot doors or closers detailed to avoid trapping of fingers?
- Is safety glazing provided to shower or bath screens?
- Are there mirrors or mantel-shelves fixed above open fireplaces?

Protection against poisoning from dangerous drugs, medicines and household cleaners

- Is a small, lockable, high-level medicine cupboard provided?
- Are shampoos, cosmetics, bleach and cleaning materials out of reach of children?

- Are household cleaners and chemicals stored safely?

Protection against poisoning from plants

- Are there any poisonous berries or fruits in the area? If so, what steps have been taken to eradicate them?

- Are residents aware of what fruits and berries are edible?

Protection against poisoning from soil

- Has garden soil been tested for heavy metals and other toxic chemicals? If so, are results satisfactory?

- Can measures be taken to remove toxic top soil or concrete over contaminated areas?

12

THE EFFECTS ON HUMAN HEALTH OF PEST INFESTATION IN HOUSES

MICHAEL HOWARD

12.1

Introduction

A large number of animal species have become successful through their association with man. This association may provide them with food or harbourage, or both. Houses and the controlled environment which they create have contributed significantly to the usefulness of humans to these species. Indeed only very few animals are truly cosmopolitan and the majority of these have achieved their distribution through exploiting man and human dwellings.

Some of these species are pests, that is they are harmful to people in some way. This harm may take the form of direct damage to health (e.g. blood parasites), indirect health effects (e.g. disease vectors) or damage other than to people's health (e.g. stored product pests or fabric pests). It is those species which cause direct or indirect damage to human health and are associated with houses which are considered here.

The control of disease vectors, such as the malaria mosquitoes, is well developed in terms of technology strategies. Agricultural pest control is also very well understood and thoroughly researched. The control of household pests, however, lags some way behind in terms of control philosophy. Although many of the important household pests which cause problems today are the same or very similar to those which lived in houses in the Middle Ages, the approach to control has developed only slowly compared to that for controlling agricultural pests or outdoor disease vectors.

It has only recently been realized that properly thought-out control strategies are necessary for the control of urban pests. These strategies must be based upon a thorough knowledge of the physiology, ecology and behaviour of the pest species and on informed judgements about the nature and degree of the damage caused by the pest. It is no longer sufficient to simply apply pesticide liberally as it was in the past. Insecticide resistance has been shown to be a significant problem in urban pest control and an increasingly environment-conscious public is concerned more than ever about pesticide residues.

The following section describes the more common species which occur in houses and can cause damage to human health. It provides the basic information on the biology of each group, upon which decisions concerning control should be based. It will often be necessary to call in expert advice from local authorities or private pest control companies. However, the occupiers or managers of houses should, where possible, be in a position to take part in the decision-making process when control strategies are chosen. For this they need a basic understanding of the pest involved and the problems which it presents.

12.2
Insect pests
(a) Blood parasites

A limited number of insect pests attack man directly by feeding on the blood. These parasites often cause local allergic reactions which show as red marks on the skin. The local reactions vary with the susceptibility of the victim but, in some cases, they may be severe. Irritation caused by local inflammation may lead to scratching and injury allowing secondary infections of the skin to occur. The common blood-sucking insect parasites of man are distinct from one another in their anatomy, behaviour and feeding habits, so each group is considered separately, below.

Lice: The human clothing (body) louse, *Pediculus humanus* (*corporis*) (Figure 12.1), the human head louse *Pediculus humanus capitis*

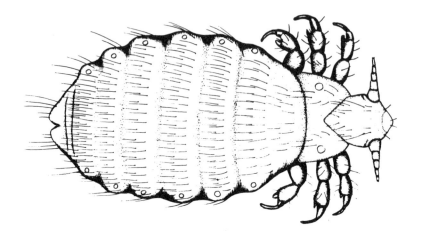

Figure 12.1 The human louse (*Pediculus humanus*) (actual size, 2–4 mm).

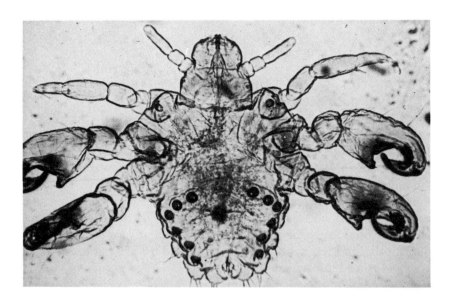

Figure 12.2 The pubic or crab louse (*Phthirus pubis*).

and the pubic or crab louse, *Pthirus pubis* (Figure 12.2), are specific to their hosts and generally human lice will not feed on other species.

Lice can act as vectors for diseases such as exanthematic typhus, trench fever and relapsing fever. The diseases are not endemic in the UK, but still cause deaths in underdeveloped countries. They have, however, the potential to return, even to developed countries, in times of war and natural disasters where people are crowded together for long periods.

Lice live permanently on or close to the body of the host and are probably usually transmitted by direct contact between individuals. They can also be passed on by clothing or other materials, but when away from the host they soon die, so transmission by this route must be rapid to be successful.

Because lice are mostly found on the host, the major method of control is to treat the patient with insecticidal shampoos or lotions. Infected clothing and bedding must also be destroyed or disinfested. Lice are also killed by high temperature and hot washing or steam can be used to disinfest clothing. Lice are not, as is often thought, associated with dirtiness. They may therefore infest people who have high standards of personal hygiene.

Bedbugs: The bedbug, *Cimex lectularius* (Figure 12.3), also feeds on human blood but this species is not specific to man and will feed on some other mammals and birds. It is also different to lice, in that it does not remain on the host all of the time, but only climbs on to the victim's body to feed. The time between feeds depends upon temperature as this determines speed of digestion. Bedbugs can, however, survive for over a year without feeding if conditions are favourable.

There is little evidence for bedbugs as disease vectors, particularly in the developed world. In addition to reactions to the bites themselves, however, people in bedbug-infested houses do seem to suffer significant psychological damage. The bugs and their association with poor hygiene can be very disturbing to residents.

In addition to allergic reactions which some people will suffer from bedbug bites, these insects are also capable of delivering a venomous defence bite. This bite is not often used but can be very painful, so the species should not be handled.

While not feeding, bedbugs live in voids and crevices around the houses of their hosts. The insect's body is greatly dorso-ventrally

Figure 12.3 Bedbugs (*Cimex lectularius*) on human skin (actual size, 4–5 mm).

compressed, so bedbugs can live in very fine crevices between skirting or architraves and plaster, or in cracks in woodwork or behind wallpaper. In this way, the fabric of the house is an important harbourage for bedbugs. For this reason, the treatment of these insects involves the application of high residual insecticide to all cracks and crevices of the rooms where bedbugs may be harboured.

Fleas: Like bedbugs, fleas (Figure 12.4) come on to the body of the host to feed and many species spend a large amount of time in the bedding or around the residence of the host. The larvae, unlike those of bedbugs, do not take blood from the host, but instead feed on the partly digested blood which forms the faeces of the adult fleas. Flea larvae therefore do not come on to the host to feed. Fleas undergo a complete metamorphosis during their life-cycle, so unlike bedbugs and lice, the immature stages are very unlike the adult. The larva is maggot-like and the pupa is ovoid and sticky, so it becomes covered with small particles of debris. Fleas are not totally host-specific, this explains why man is often bitten by fleas whose preferred host is some other species.

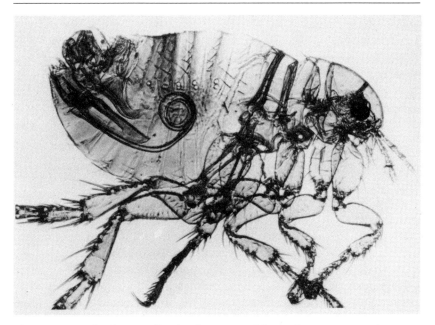

Figure 12.4 The human flea (*Pulex irritans*) (actual size, 2–5 mm).

Pulex irritans, the human flea, is now fairly rare in the developed world, but people are often bitten by cat fleas, *Ctenocephalides felis*, or less commonly dog fleas, *Ctenocephalides canis*. Although infestations of these species are centred on pet cats and dogs, as mentioned earlier, fleas will often bite species other than their preferred host. A number of bird and rodent fleas will occasionally bite man if they are brought into houses by their respective hosts.

Fleas are vectors of plague and murine typhus. Both of these diseases are transmitted by rat fleas. The great plagues of the 14th and 17th centuries in England have been attributed to the black rat, *Rattus rattus*, and the tropical rat flea, *Xenopsylla cheopis*. Both of these species are very restricted in distribution in Britain today, but they may have been more common in earlier centuries. The European rat flea *Nosopsyllus fasciatus*, is common but very rarely feeds on man, so presents little or no health risk. Fleas may also act as vectors for a number of tapeworms of other small species but these parasites are now relatively uncommon.

The control of fleas involves treatment of carpets, bedding and furniture where fleas and their larvae may be living with pesticide dust or spray. The infestation usually centres on pet dogs or cats, so these animals must also be treated with proper veterinary preparations. In Britain cats regularly become infested with fleas, so infestations in houses and bites to people are fairly common. Like lice, fleas are sensitive to high temperature, so hot laundering of clothes and bedding will destroy larvae and adult insects.

The three parasitic groups described above use the fabric of houses and materials in houses for harbourage or transmission. They also exploit housing as a location where people are gathered closely together facilitating transmission and access.

Biting flies: A large number of biting flies may attack man and some of these will enter houses to do so. These are not really pests of housing but some disease vectors, such as the malaria transmitting *Anopheles* mosquitoes, will often rest in homes or shelters. This means that in parts of the world where malaria is endemic, mosquitoes can be an important health risk associated with housing. In these areas, windows and doors are screened to prevent mosquito access and walls are often treated with residual insecticides. These treatments are only successful if combined with proper programmes of larval control in ponds and other still-water environments.

(b) Stinging insects

Several wasp and bee species may cause stings and, as biting flies above, they may enter houses to do so. Problems are more likely to arise when these insects build nests inside the structure of houses. This increases the chances of contact between the insects and man and consequently increases the chances of stings. The sting itself is the only risk associated with these insects. Multiple stings can, of course, be dangerous and some individuals show severe allergic reactions to the sting. Fortunately, wasp and bee nests are easily destroyed and removed from houses.

(c) Other parasites and direct disease vectors

All insect species are limited in distribution by environmental conditions. Some are also limited by their inability to reach certain areas, but those species associated with humans do not suffer this because of man's worldwide distribution. An association with man, and more particularly his dwellings, has enabled many species to achieve an immense distribution which they would not normally have enjoyed. These tend to be species which live in close association with people inside dwellings exploiting the controlled environment that houses provide.

Those species which simply enter houses for shelter or foraging will be determined in their distribution by outside conditions. Because of this, many species which enter houses, and consequently many parasites and disease vectors, are limited in their distribution by local environmental conditions. These species are very numerous and are peculiar to each particular geographical area, so are not dealt with individually here.

(d) Hygiene pests

A number of invertebrates, chiefly insects, are attracted to human food. This behaviour provides potential for the transfer of food poisoning or other disease causing micro-organisms on to the food. Some of these species are also attracted to sewage and this, naturally, greatly increases the potential for disease transmission. The factors involved in determining the likelihood that an insect species will carry disease-causing organisms on to food relate to the behaviour of the species concerned. Attraction to food and to sewage or other waste material, coupled with a high mobility and an ability to live in close proximity to human dwellings are the principal requirements in this respect. Below a number of the more important hygiene pests are considered.

Cockroaches: A number of cockroach species live in close association with man and are only rarely found living away from human habitation. The most common are the German cockroach, *Blattella germanica* (Figures 12.5 and 12.6), the Oriental cockroach, *Blatta orientalis* (Figure 12.7), and the American cockroach, *Periplaneta americana* (Figure 12.8). There are also a number which live around buildings and enter in search for food, and these may be pests in various parts of the world; examples of these peridomestic species are *Supella longipalpa*, *Periplaneta australasiae*, *Periplaneta brunnea* and *Periplaneta fuliginosa*. Cockroaches therefore live in close association with man. Their mobility and omnivorous habits pro-

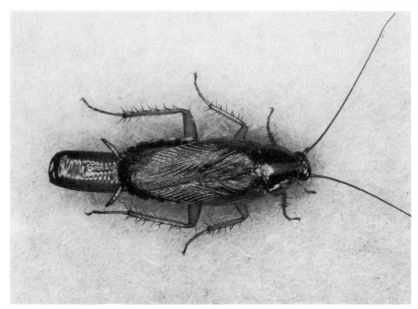

Figure 12.5 A female German cockroach (*Blattella germanica*) carrying an egg case (ootheca). This is retained by the female until just before egg hatch and may contain 30 or more young (actual adult size, 10–15 mm).

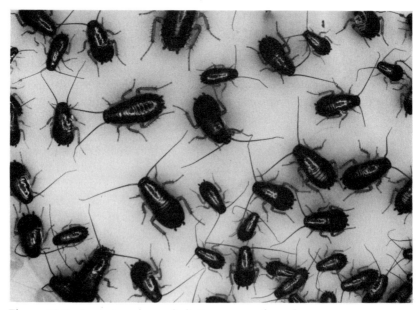

Figure 12.6 Immature (nymphal) German cockroaches.

Figure 12.7 The Oriental cockroach (*Blatta orientalis*) on dried pasta (actual adult size, 20–25 mm).

Figure 12.8 The American cockroach (*Periplaneta americana*) (actual adult size, 30–45 mm).

vide potential for disease transmission as they are attracted to waste materials and to human food. The habit which some species have of living in drains and sewers clearly increases this potential.

It has been shown that cockroaches can transfer pathogenic bacteria from cultures onto food by their normal foraging behaviour. Brenner, Koehler and Patterson (1987) recently compiled a list of 29 bacterial pathogens isolated by various workers from cockroaches in domestic and peridomestic environments. The organisms concerned were the causative agents for conditions such as food poisoning, wound infections and gas gangrene, typhoid, dysentery, pneumonia and leprosy. They also found published reports of pathogenic viruses, fungi, protozoans and helminth parasites in or on cockroaches from domestic and peridomestic environments.

These organisms may not always be present on or in the bodies of cockroaches. Bitter and Williams (1949) found populations of American cockroaches which were largely free of pathogenic bacteria. Animals captured near sewer manholes, however, were often found to carry *Proteus* and *Salmonella* bacteria, indicating that pathogens are picked up during foraging. Alcamo and Frishman (1980), however, found over 89% of the cockroaches they examined in an extensive study of 41 sites, including houses, restaurants, hospitals and prisons in New York City, carried at least three pathogenic bacteria. Morrell (1911) isolated the pathogenic bacterium *Enterobacter aerogenes* from the faeces of 41% of German cockroaches he collected, showing that viable organisms may pass through the gut and out of the insect. In a case investigated by Antonelli (1930), cockroaches collected from open latrines in an area where a typhoid outbreak was occurring were shown to have the causative organism *Salmonella typhi* on their feet and bodies. Food contaminated with the faeces of the cockroaches was also shown to contain *S. typhi*.

There are also other examples of pathogenic organisms being detected on cockroaches in areas close to where they have been responsible for epidemics. German cockroaches have been shown to carry *S. dysenteriae* close to where the organism had caused dysentery. *Salmonella bovis-morbificans* has also been isolated from cockroaches trapped in a hospital ward where the organism had been found to be responsible for an outbreak of gastroenteritis.

A good piece of epidemiological evidence for cockroaches as vectors of disease was provided by the research of Tarshis (1962). In this study, the incidence of infectious hepatitis on a southern Californian housing project was significantly reduced when cockroach populations were controlled with pesticides. After one year, cockroach control was discontinued because residents found the insecticide offensive. The population of cockroaches and the incidence of infectious hepatitis then increased. For the next two years, less offensive insecticides were applied and the population of cockroaches and incidence of infectious hepatitis decreased again, while remaining high on nearby housing projects which were not treated.

The above examples do not, of course, provide conclusive evidence that cockroaches act as vectors of disease agents. Rather they demonstrate the considerable potential for the transmission of pathogens which cockroaches, because of their feeding behaviour, possess. In addition, the epidemiological evidence, although circumstantial, demonstrates that disease epidemics are probably at least augmented by cockroaches in some cases.

Cockroach allergy

It has been known for some time that people, such as laboratory technicians, who are regularly subjected to contact with cockroach tissue and fras (excrement) often suffer from allergic reactions, varying from mild hay-fever symptoms to anaphylactic shock. More recently, sensitivity to cockroaches has been extensively demonstrated in people living in cockroach-infested houses. Kang and Chang (1985) showed that a high proportion of asthmatic and atopic human populations showed intense reactions to cockroach extracts when compared to non-atopic groups. They found that sensitivity to cockroaches could be as high as 79% in children living in dwellings visibly infested with German cockroaches.

Kang et al. (1987) also found that random sampling of bronchial asthmatics revealed that 76% lived in crowded multi-family housing infested with German cockroaches. It has also been reported by Kang and Chang that the incidence of cockroach hypersensitivity was inversely related to socio-economic status. Cockroach allergy appears to be triggered by allergens in the bodies and cuticle of the cockroach rather than the fras, so cast skins will be active in inducing allergy. This is important as a cockroach may not only be inducing allergy by its own movements, but also by the presence of its nymphal skins which it discarded during moults as it developed.

Cockroach infestations

The probability of cockroaches acting as vectors for disease agents or inducing allergic reactions depends, among other things, upon the size of the cockroach infestation. Domestic cockroach species require high temperatures and humidities, although relatively low humidities may be tolerated if free water is available. Buildings tend to provide this warm, moist environment and free water is often to be found leaking from waterpipes, drains or radiators or condensing inside ducts or dead spaces.

For a dwelling to be infested every part of the space does not need to be at temperatures or humidities which are suitable for the long-term maintenance of cockroach populations. The insects can live in small crevices where the micro-climate is suitable and venture out into less suitable environments only to feed. The crevices in which the insects live may be very small. For *Blattella germanica* adults may find harbourage in crevices as small as 2 mm across and nymphs in crevices as small as 0.5 mm.

Cockroaches may infest a wide variety of building types. Older brick terraces which are not damp-proofed provide suitable warm, moist habitats and are often infested. Similarly, modern, centrally heated flats which contain many dead spaces may suffer substantial cockroach infestations if, as we have already mentioned, some free water is available. In warmer areas of the world cockroach infestations may become immense. Koehler, Patterson and Brenner (1987) found, in a survey of 1022 low-income apartments in Florida, USA, that half of them harboured more than 1300 cockroaches. More cockroaches were trapped in the kitchen than in other areas, indicating that the majority of cockroach movement occurred in areas where food was available.

A major factor in determining whether a building will become infested is the degree to which food is available to the insects. Good waste disposal systems are therefore important in limiting cockroach numbers. The association of cockroaches with food, and their greasy surface and unpleasant odour, contribute to the strong aesthetic objections which many people feel towards cockroaches. A survey by Wood *et al.* (1981) taken in two US cities showed that householders in public housing spent 0.4% to 1% of their annual income on pesticide to supplement the pest control service provided by the pest control company employed by the housing authority.

Figure 12.9   The house fly (*Musca domestica*) (actual size, 6–9 mm).

This clearly demonstrates the concern which these residents felt about cockroaches.

Houseflies: The housefly, *Musca domestica* (Figure 12.9), has been shown to have been responsible for the transmission of human diseases during epidemics. These epidemics are now less common, but as this species will carry large numbers of disease-causing organisms in its faeces, a significant risk of disease transmission remains.

M. domestica lives in many parts of the world and is particularly successful in association with man. It feeds and lays its eggs in all kinds of waste and decaying material, including faeces, and is highly mobile. This mobility enables it to seek out human food readily and its potential for disease transmission is considerable. It may transmit pathogenic organisms mechanically on its body or from its gut when regurgitating food during feeding.

The control of houseflies involves good refuse storage and disposal, good hygiene and protecting food from flies during storage and preparation. The removal of refuse and materials suitable for the larvae is the most effective means of control.

Lesser house flies: The lesser house fly, *Fannia canicularis*, is similar to the house fly, *Musca domestica*, in appearance but can be distinguished anatomically by its wing veination (Busvine, 1980). Behaviourally, however, the two species are rather different. *F. canicularis* is more common in agricultural areas, particularly around poultry houses, and comes into contact with human food less than *M. domestica*. It is therefore less likely to transmit disease-causing organisms to food and has not commonly been implicated in epidemics in the way that *M. domestica* has. This species may often enter houses, particularly in agricultural areas and cause significant nuisance.

Blowflies: The bluebottle, *Calliphora vomitoria*, and the flesh fly, *Sarcophaga carnaria*, lay their eggs, when possible, in decaying animal tissue. This means that their larvae are found in rotting meat, fish, etc. The adults may therefore transmit disease-causing organisms to food but they are less attracted to sewage than *M. domestica*, so probably present less of a health risk.

(e) Food, fabric and woodboring pests

Houses contain a wide variety of insect and mite species, not included here. These species may cause allergy in susceptible individuals if they are present in sufficient numbers and in suitable proximity to man. Although household pests, these species are not, in most cases, the direct cause of damage to human health, so are not dealt with here.

12.3
Arachnids

The vast majority of arachnids are not harmful to man and indeed many are beneficial. A few species, however, will act as parasites or may cause allergy through a close association with human dwellings.

The parasitic arachnids come from the group known as the acari, the mites and ticks. Ticks will feed on man, particularly if their preferred host is absent, but these animals are found outdoors and not in houses, so are not considered here. The mites, however, are commonly the cause of disease conditions in man and some of the more important species are described below.

The scabies mite, *Sarcoptes Scabiei*, is a skin parasite of man and a number of other mammal species. The mite seems to occur as a number of varieties each specialized to a particular host but able to parasitise others. Scabies is less common now in the developed world, partly because effective treatment exists. It is still present, however, and may lead to severe secondary bacterial infections in badly infested patients.

The scabies mite appears to be transmitted mainly by direct contact between individuals and consequent transmission of egg-carrying females. It is possible for the mites to be harboured in clothing or bedding, but because of the poor ability of the species to survive for any length of time away from the host, this is probably not a major means of transmission. Experimental work had confirmed that this is the case. For this reason, scabies mites can be considered pests of housing only in a minor sense and are probably better considered as a directly transmissible disease agent.

A number of other parasitic mites may attack man. For example, the follicle mite, *Demodex folliculorum*, and a number of animal mange mite species may occasionally cause problems. Similarly, a number of blood-sucking ticks may attack man. These usually occur when people are working in close association with animals, often poultry, but may be a problem when birds nest in houses and their parasitic mites move on to human hosts.

Mites have been known for some time as an important cause of allergy. House dust mites of the genus *Dermatophagoides* cause asthma in susceptible individuals and in a few may present a significant health risk. In the same way, a number of mites, usually pests of stored food products, have been shown to cause irritation or allergy in those coming into regular contact with them. In the case of both house dust mites and those mites which cause dermatitis, the solution lies in removing the mites by clearing or destruction of infested materials. Mites, in common with many terrestrial invertebrates, are very susceptible to desiccation. They benefit therefore from humid environments and poor housing, conditions such as dampness may aggravate mite problems.

12.4

Vertebrate pests

(a) Rats

Of the many vertebrate pests which may infest buildings, rats are the best known and probably the most important. Rats are fabric pests and will bite if approached but the most significant problem presented by rats is the direct transmission of disease. Rats will act as vectors of a number of potentially fatal human diseases and the degree of danger each disease presents to man depends largely upon the degree of contact between rats and people. This is sometimes complicated by the presence of other vector species which transmit the disease organism from the rat to man – e.g. *Xenopsylla*, the tropical rat flea, transmits plague from rats to humans in its bite.

Rats in rural areas are common, and in many parts of the world they are associated with farming activities; the rats are provided with a plentiful food source and usually good harbourage. The food may be a crop plant or animal feed to which the rats gain access. In rural situations therefore rats may be present in large numbers and people may suffer significant occupational exposure to rats. These rats may well, however, not infest houses if access is difficult and the need to do so is reduced by a plentiful food source outside.

In urban areas the relationship between rats and man is quite different. In this case, there is no abundant natural food source like that provided by farming and the rats must obtain human food. This immediately increases their chances of contact with people. The human food which rats obtain may be stored food; food undergoing preparation; or waste food. All of these will bring rats into, or close to, buildings and thus into contact with people. Stored food, or food which is being prepared, can be protected from rats by proofing of buildings or using properly sealed containers. Waste food must also be properly protected and bins with tight-fitting lids must be used to prevent access for rats. This latter point cannot be too heavily stressed. Poor facilities for, and bad practice in, waste food disposal are major causes of rat infestation in buildings.

Urban rats which are not living inside houses themselves are likely to be living in drainage systems. These may be either single drains to individual houses or large public sewer systems. The drains and sewers provide an available system of prepared burrows for *Rattus norvegicus*, the brown rat, which is the most common rat to infest urban areas and is in the wild a burrowing animal. The drains and sewers need not necessarily be in use. Disused drains, even though stopped up or partly destroyed, will provide useful harbourages for urban rats.

In houses which become infested dead spaces in walls and behind panelling provide harbourage and nesting sites. They also provide covered runs and tunnels between harbourage and food sources, thus houses themselves can provide an ideal habitat for rats.

A large number of diseases and parasitic infections can be transmitted by rats. Rats are well known as transmitters of plague and commonly carry roundworm and tapeworm parasites of man, particularly in Third World countries. In urban areas rats may also act as disease vectors. Populations of urban rats in the UK which appear to be increasing, give cause for concern over the transmittance of leptospirosis or Weil's disease. This disease appears to be most often caught by those involved in outdoor activities in rat-infested areas but is transmitted in the urine of infected rats, so the potential for it to be caught from rats in houses is significant.

In addition to being vectors of specific diseases, rats have considerable potential for transmitting disease-causing organisms on their bodies; their habit of living in drains and sewers and moving into houses in search of food make them ideal carriers of food poisoning and other disease-causing organisms.

It is often possible to proof buildings against entry by rats and food sources can usually be removed or protected. If these measures are not successful alone, rodenticides may be applied and these usually give good control.

(b) Mice

Mice commonly infest houses and are usually regarded mainly as fabric pests. They may, however, carry diseases including a form of leptospirosis, so do present some health risk. Again, the source of food should be removed and poisoning provides a good degree of control.

(c) **Birds**

A number of birds use houses for roosting or nesting and may often carry disease-causing organisms such as *Salmonella*. Here, again, the proximity of the birds to human activity dictates the degree of risk to health. Birds such as pigeons, starlings and sparrows which are attracted to homes to feed, nest and roost are the most likely to cause problems. Pigeon populations may be reduced by reducing feeding in urban areas. Apart from this, control can only be achieved by screening and other deterrent methods and by appropriate building designs to reduce the attractiveness of the building to birds.

(d) **Foxes**

Foxes are not a pest of houses themselves, but have become common in some suburban gardens. Foxes have been suspected of the transmission of *Toxocara canis*, but although they often harbour this parasite, the risk to man appears low compared to that from dogs.

12.5
The control of pests in houses: integrated pest management

Broadly speaking, integrated pest management (IPM) consists of the careful selection of an optimal strategy for pest control rather than simply applying pesticide in a random manner. This optimal strategy involves a number of considerations, these are explained below.

(i) **Damage**

It is important in designing a control strategy to decide exactly how the pest causes damage. A direct disease vector which carries a serious human disease may need to be totally eradicated at least from the areas where it may come into contact with people. On the other hand, a pest which may transmit, for example, food poisoning organisms may need only to be excluded from areas where food is kept if the population is kept low in other areas. An animal which causes only mild annoyance may simply need to be kept down to some acceptable population level. It is clear that an assessment of the damage caused by the pest must be used in making decisions about targets for the size and location of pest populations after control.

(ii) Pesticide specificity

Pesticides should as far as possible be specific to the pest species that they are intended to control. A major concern is, of course, that the pesticide has as little toxicity as possible to man. Specificity is important to the safety of the person applying the pesticide and to people living in the house where the pesticide is applied. It is also important so that other non-target species are not damaged and harm is not caused to the environment generally.

Unfortunately, the vast majority of pesticides are not specific to a single pest species. At best, their maximum toxicity is restricted to a few species or a few groups of species. Other species will still suffer toxicity to some extent. This means that most pesticides are dangerous to non-target organisms and to man, although their toxicity to these is usually considerably lower than to the target pest.

(iii) Pesticide resistance

Resistance occurs in a population because the proportion of naturally resistant individuals increases due to susceptible individuals being killed. It is recognized when a higher dose of pesticide is required to kill any particular proportion of a population than was previously needed. Resistance develops therefore because of the application of pesticides and may occur through a variety of mechanisms.

It follows from the above that the more pesticide that is applied, the more resistance will result. It is therefore essential that as little pesticide as possible is used in pest control, so that as little pesticide resistance as possible is induced. This demonstrates the trade-off which needs to be made between increasing pesticide application to control the pest and reducing pesticide application to minimize resistance.

Insecticide resistance has long been a problem in agriculture. It has now been shown to affect the control of household pests. Reierson *et al.* (1988) identified resistance as causing problems in cockroach control.

(iv) **Pesticide persistence**

Very persistent pesticides have to be applied less often with a consequent reduction in costs. They are more likely, however, to leach out into the environment in a harmful form, and because they are present for longer, more likely to induce resistance in the pest population. In terms of pesticide choice, persistence necessitates another trade-off decision. Pesticides must be persistent enough to be cost-effective but break down quickly so as to not damage the environment or contribute to resistance.

(v) **The choice of a strategy for control**

Good hygiene and secure food storage, food preparation and waste disposal methods are essential to reduce pest populations in houses. These should be sufficient to keep down the numbers of most hygiene pests such as houseflies and cockroaches. In some cases, however, pesticides must be applied, and in these the selectivity, resistance potential and persistence of the available pesticides must be considered. The pesticide must be applied only when necessary in as low a concentration as possible to reduce the induction of resistance. It is also important to see that pesticide is applied where it will be most effective rather than liberally dispersed.

Insect hormone analogues have been developed which interfere with the pest's development. These are chemicals which are similar to the insects' natural hormones, and if applied in excess or at the wrong time in the animals' life, will disrupt the bio-chemistry of the body. They are specific to insects and tend to induce resistance only slowly. These chemicals have been used with some success to control cockroaches and a number of other nest insects. The use of baits can reduce the need to cover the whole of an area if the baits can attract the pest to the pesticide. These also reduce the amount of pesticide which needs to be used.

Biological control methods have been useful in agriculture in reducing pesticide application. Thoms and Robinson (1987) achieved some level of cockroach control using a cockroach egg case (ootheca) parasite but biological control has not generally proved particularly useful for household pests. Ultrasound devices are marketed in many countries, these are intended to deter pests and keep them away from areas where they are harmful. Research has shown that these devices do nothing to deter the insects which it is claimed they affect. The non-pesticide treatments, outlined above, are of course limited in their usefulness. They should be borne in mind, however, in choosing strategies, as these do not induce resistance and are more environmentally acceptable.

A number of attempts have been made to devise integrated pest management strategies for dwellings. These have usually been strategies for persistent hygiene pests such as cockroaches. In assessing damage, Zungoli and Robinson (1984) attempted to define what they called an 'aesthetic injury level' at which action should be taken. They found that as cockroach populations declined, expectations increased and the aesthetic injury level itself moved downwards. Attempts have been made to limit cockroach harbourage by caulking up cracks and crevices into which pesticides often do not penetrate. Unfortunately, this work did not result in more successful insecticide treatments. In later experiments, Thoms and Robinson (1987) carried out extensive structural modifications to buildings, including the blocking of vents and exclusion of dead spaces. They found, however, that the structural modifications were very labour-intensive but resulted in no greater success for chemical treatments.

An extensive IPM programme was devised by Robinson and Zungoli (1985) to control cockroaches in Norfolk, Virginia, USA. This included pest monitoring, a pest resistance profile, tenant education, management training, specific pesticide recommendations and an evaluation procedure. The programme resulted in efficient pest control and a more satisfied customer. It is clear that sophisticated pest management programmes can be developed to reduce pest populations to acceptable levels. The design of buildings is, however, of paramount importance in discouraging pests. It has already been explained that correcting design shortcomings by structural modifications once the building is constructed is very difficult to do effectively. It is therefore of extreme importance that the possibility of infestations be considered when houses are designed. There follows a brief discussion of some important design considerations drawn from the Hulme district of Manchester.

12.6
Building design and infestations: The example of Hulme, Manchester

The Hulme district of Manchester was redeveloped during the early 1960s after the demolition of small terraced houses which formerly occupied the site. These terraces regularly suffered severe infestations of oriental cockroach encouraged by high water availability in the undamp-proofed houses. The area also suffered from substantial rat populations which lived in the decaying Victorian drainage systems.

The whole of Hulme, housing for some 10 000 people, was redeveloped in system-built flats and maisonettes. The majority of the housing was deck access. The basic design of deck access maisonettes and flats, however, was varied through the estate by using different materials, heating systems, refuse disposal systems, etc. This variation provided several different pest habitats and has resulted in several different pest problems.

In one area, the Moss Side Centre, district heating was installed to provide heat and hot water to approx. 200 maisonettes, a sports centre, a shopping centre and an indoor market. Hot water from a central boilerhouse is carried to each maisonette and to all the other facilities in multi-service ducts which also contain soil pipes, cold water pipes, electrical services and telephone cables. The ducts, heated by the hot water pipes, became warm, moist environments, often contaminated with sewage, as soil pipes began to develop leaks. These conditions of high temperature and humidity are ideal for cockroach development, reproduction and movement and soon immense populations of German cockroach built up. To complicate the problem, service ducts ran between the kitchens and bathrooms of each maisonette. In this way, cockroach infestations could move easily from kitchen to kitchen around the estate.

The local authority was eventually forced to carry out whole-block saturation pesticide application in which not only every duct was treated, but also every dead space in every maisonette was drilled and pumped with pesticide. This was (and continues to be) very expensive and could have been avoided if the services were not placed in open ducts and each dwelling was isolated from infestations in other dwellings. Treatment would have been easier if so many dead spaces had not been created by the construction methods used.

When considering the health effects of this cockroach infestation, the total effect of the insects, inconvenience suffered by the households and the toxic effects of pesticides should be considered. Certainly the tenants suffered the risk of pathogens carried on to food by the cockroaches. They also suffered the possibility of cockroach allergy which was increased as the insects moved during treatment with repellent pesticides, and this danger persists as the bodies of killed cockroaches remain in treated dead spaces. The tenants also suffered considerable stress and inconvenience and will have been subjected to pesticide exposure, the dangers of which are difficult to assess. Thus a cockroach infestation which is now merely controlled, eradication not being possible, has caused, and will continue to cause, danger to the health of occupants.

In another area of Hulme, known as Hulme V (five), a different set of infestation problems exist. These maisonettes are not district heated, each has its own electric storage heater system. There are no common ducts and sporadic cockroach infestations in individual dwellings are largely contained and confined to that dwelling. Cockroach infestations have tended to be relatively small in Hulme V as the expensive electric heating results in the maisonettes often being cold. Hulme V does, however, suffer other pest problems. In this area, the old drainage systems were not properly destroyed, so they harbour a substantial rat population which regularly surfaces, as drains rupture, to infest the houses.

Another problem in Hulme V is pigeons. The maisonettes are arranged in regular crescent shapes, some with external and others with internal balconies. While the external balconies seem relatively unattractive to pigeons, the internal ones become obstructed with up to 30 cm of pigeon excrement and nesting material. Tenants soon give up using the balconies as they are impossible to clean and the problem becomes worse as the balcony becomes more and more regularly used by pigeons.

Clearly the residents of Hulme V, while avoiding the health risks of heavy cockroach infestations, suffer risks to their health from rats and pigeons. This contrast in pest problems in the two areas, and consequent health risks, is caused by different design and construction faults. It is not a consequence of geography or tenant type as the two areas are close to one another and contain tenants of similar social status.

In other areas of Hulme, for example, Hulme III and Hulme IV, large cockroach infestations cannot be properly dealt with because the extensive use of asbestos in the construction of the buildings precludes drilling into dead spaces for pesticide application. In these cases, the health risks of cockroach infestations must be weighed against the risks of disturbing asbestos materials.

12.7
Conclusion

Much has been written on the dangers to human health from pests, particularly insects. There is also a great deal of literature which deals with infestations in houses and damage due to food and fabric pests. This chapter has attempted to select those common pest groups which regularly infest houses and present a significant risk to the health of people in those houses.

These pest groups range from direct parasites and disease vectors, through hygiene pests to those species which cause damage solely due to allergy. It is emphasized that recommendations for the treatment of each pest situation will be different and must be based upon a thorough understanding of the physiology and ecology of the pest concerned. A strategy for control must be devised which involves decisions about the nature and degree of damage caused by the pest, the characteristics of the available pesticides other than their absolute efficacy and the physical nature of the building concerned. Pest control therefore consists of a complex series of interdependent decisions rather than simply the application of the most toxic chemical available.

Urban pest problems share with agricultural pest problems one fundamental characteristic. This is that the pest problem is caused by the environment created by human activity. This environment, whether a wheat field or a terrace of houses, is essential to man and cannot itself be removed. The nature of the environment can, however, be altered to the detriment of the pest. In existing houses, good food and waste storage facilities and practices and good hygiene can reduce the attractiveness and usefulness of houses to pest animals. Similarly, new housing can be provided in structures where pest problems are minimized by good design.

These preventive measures can and must be used to reduce the potential for pest infestations and consequent risk to human health from damage by pests in housing.

In many cases, infestations in houses will require chemical treatments. These should be provided as part of a carefully devised pest management strategy. The advice of the local Environmental Health Department and private pest control companies should be sought in this matter.

Bibliography

Alcamo, I. E. and Frishman, A. M. (1980) The microbial flora of field collected cockroaches and other arthropods. *J. Environ. Health*, 42, 263–6.

Antonelli, G. (1930) La blatta nella igiene domestica. *Riv. Soc. Ital. Igiene* (Milan), 52, 132–42.

Bitter, R. S. and Williams, O. B. (1949) Enteric organisms from the American cockroach. *J. Infect. Dis.*, 85, 87–90.

Brenner, R. J., Koehler, P. G and Patterson, R. S. (1987) Health implications of cockroach infestations. *Infections in medicine: infectious disease in medical and family practice*, 4(8), October, 349–55, 358, 359, 393.

Burgess, N. R. H. (1990) *Public Health Pests: A Guide to Identification, Biology and Control*, Chapman and Hall, London.

Busvine, J. R. (1980) *Insects and Hygiene*, Methuen, New York.

Chinery, M. (1976) *A Field Guide to the Insects of Britain and Northern Europe*, Collins, London.

Grundy, J. H. (1981) *John Hall Grundy's Arthropods of Medical Importance* (ed. N. R. H. Burgess), Noble Books, New York.

Kang, B. and Chang, J. L. (1985) Allergenic impact of inhaled arthropod material. *Clin. Rev. Allergy*, 3, 363–75.

Kang, B., Johnson, J., Jones, G. S. *et al.* (1987) Analysis of indoor environment and asthmatic characteristics of urban bronchial asthma. Paper presented at Forty-third Annual Meeting of the Academy of Allergy and Clinical Immunology. Washington, DC.

Koehler, P. G., Patterson, R. S. and Brenner, R. J. (1987) German cockroach (*Orthoptera: Blattellidae*) infestations in low income apartments. *J. Econ. Entomol.*, 80, 446–50.

Morrell, C. C. (1911) The bacteriology of the cockroach. *B. Med. J.*, 2, 1531–2.

Mourier, H. and Winding, O. (1975) *Wildlife in House and Home*, Collins, London.

Reierson, D. A., Rust, M. K., Slater, A. J. and Slater, T. A. M. (1988) Insecticide resistance affects cockroach control. *Int. Pest Control*, November–December, 150–2.

Service, M. W. (1980) *A Guide to Medical Entomology*, Macmillan, London.

Robinson, W. H. and Zungoli, P. A. (1985) Integrated control program for German cockroaches (Dictyoptera: Blattellidae) in multiple unit dwellings. *J. Econ. Entomol.*, 78, 595–8.

Tarshis, I. B. (1962) The cockroach: a new suspect in the spread of infectious hepatitis. *Am. J. Trop. Med. Hyg.*, 11, 705–11.

Thoms, E. M. and Robinson, W. H. (1987) Insecticide and structural modification strategies for management of oriental cockroach (Orthoptera: Blattidae) populations. *J. Econ. Entomol.*, 80, 131–135.

Thoms, E. M. and Robinson, W. H. (1987) Potential of the cockroach oothecal parasite *Prosevania punctata* (Hymenoptera Evaniidae) as a biological control agent for the Oriental Cockroach (Orthoptera Blattidae). *J. Environ. Entomol.*, 16, 938–44.

Van Emden, H. F. (1974) *Pest Control* (2nd edn), Edward Arnold, London.

Wood, F. E., Robinson, W. H., Kraft, S. K. and Zungoli, P. A. (1981) Survey of attitudes and knowledge of public housing residents towards cockroaches. *Bull. Entomol. Soc. Am.*, 27(1), 9–13.

Zungoli, P. A. and Robinson, W. H. (1984) Feasibility of establishing an aesthetic injury level for German cockroach pest management programs. *Environ. Entomol.*, 13, 1453–8.

13

ILL-HEALTH AND HOMELESSNESS: THE EFFECTS OF LIVING IN BED-AND-BREAKFAST ACCOMMODATION

JEAN CONWAY

13.1

Introduction

Homelessness in Britain is increasing rapidly. In 1989 over 125 000 households were accepted as homeless by the local authorities in England – over twice as many as in 1979 (Department of the Environment, 1989). Most are rehoused by the local authority or are nominated to a local housing association. However, some need to be initially placed in temporary accommodation – while inquiries are completed, before being referred to another area, or where the local authority only has a duty to provide temporary housing because they have been deemed 'intentionally homeless'.

The use of temporary accommodation by local authorities fluctuated up to the early 1980s but then increased rapidly, from about 5000 in 1982 to over 36 000 in 1989: 'A critical point seems to have been reached in 1982 at which the number of permanent lettings available to authorities was no longer adequate for the number of homeless households' (Audit Commission, 1989).

While many forms of temporary accommodation are used, the number of households placed in bed-and-breakfast hotels has risen especially sharply from around 2000 in 1982 to at least 11 880 in

September 1989 (Department of the Environment, 1989). However, these figures are an underestimate as several local authorities do not supply figures; these figures thus represent over 35 000 people. In addition, there are an unknown number of households who are not accepted as homeless by local authorities, but resort to bed-and-breakfast as the only kind of housing they can find.

There is little prospect of the number living in hotels falling in the foreseeable future. It could be argued that bed-and-breakfast hotels have now become firmly established as a form of housing. It has been shown that nearly half of those living in hotels are there for over six months, including nearly a quarter living there for over a year (Niner and Thomas, 1989). However, bed-and-breakfast residents receive scant attention from service-providing agencies such as social services, education and health authorities.

As the numbers living in hotels have increased, so has concern that this form of housing presents particular health risks; there are three main reasons for this:

1. Conditions in hotels are often very poor. Facilities for storing, preparing or cooking food are frequently limited or non-existent; washing facilities are unsatisfactory and there is extreme overcrowding. General maintenance is poor, resulting in hazards, especially for young children, and fire precautions are often inadequate. Lack of play space and overcrowding also contribute to the high risk of accidents for children.
2. Living in a hotel is stressful and depressing, making residents more prone to poor health.
3. Those who live in hotels tend to be people who cannot afford any better kind of housing such as the unemployed, those on low wages, large families and those experiencing language or cultural barriers. Even in normal circumstances, such people are vulnerable to health risks.

Housing acts as a crucial link between poverty and health because, as shown by successive house condition surveys, poor people tend to live in the worst housing (Department of the Environment, 1981, 1986). Those who have failed to secure any form of permanent housing, the homeless, are in the worst position of all and are among the poorest and most vulnerable in society.

13.2
The research

A number of studies have documented the problems of those who live in hotels (Department of the Environment, 1981, 1986). This chapter focuses on a study which was specifically designed to examine the needs of homeless hotel residents in relation to health (*ibid*).

In 1988, 65% of those accepted as homeless by local authorities were families with children, and a further 14% included a pregnant woman. About half of those with children or pregnant were one-parent families. This research therefore focused on mothers and children under 5 years old, who form the majority of hotel residents and are thought to be particularly at risk. The study, carried out in 1986 and 1987, had four main elements:

1. an interview survey of 57 women who were pregnant or had children under 5 years who had been living in bed-and-breakfast hotels for several months;
2. a detailed analysis of the diet and eating patterns of the women interviewed;
3. interviews with a range of professionals who have contact with women and children living in hotels, including health visitors, GPs, midwives, paediatricians and Environmental Health Officers;
4. examination of health records for pregnant women and children; data for hotel residents were compared with two control groups of families not living in hotels (from similar socio-economic and ethnic backgrounds in London, and the general population in Manchester).

The findings therefore combine qualitative and quantitative information on the health problems of those living in hotels and highlight the provision of services.

The work was carried out in three areas: London, Manchester and Southend. London has the greatest concentration of families living in hotels. Manchester was included because attempts had been made there to bring together the health and housing services for hotel residents in the city. Southend illustrates another area outside London with a concentration of hotel residents.

Interview sample

Of the 52 women interviewed who had children, 30 had just one child, while there were 11 large families with six or more people. Three of these women were pregnant, and a further five women were interviewed who were pregnant with no children. The families included 110 children, of all ages, with 71 of these under 5 years; 23 of the women had no partner.

Ethnic origin

The ethnic profile of the sample reflects the high proportion of all homeless families from ethnic minority groups, as follows:

Afro-Caribbean	7
African	3
Asian	10
Vietnamese	2
Irish	6
Other British/European	25
Others	4
Total	57

Conditions in hotels

Visits to hotels spread across the three towns provide a catalogue of the conditions in which many homeless families have to live. In general, the standards and conditions found were appalling: most households in the survey had to share the WC and the bath or shower; 11 out of the 57 shared with ten or more people; and for a quarter of the households the WC was on another floor of the hotel, and similarly for a quarter the bath or shower was on another floor. In a hotel where there is little privacy, and where it is not safe to leave young children alone in the bedroom, then the room may have to be locked every time it is left. There may well be queues for the WC or bathroom – having no facilities on the same floor is extremely inconvenient.

The women were very anxious about cleanliness in the hotels. Dirt, smells, fleas and cockroaches were often mentioned. In some hotels the management did not even clean the common areas and the residents had to buy materials and clean the WCs, halls etc., themselves.

People in bed-and-breakfast hotels generally have financial as well as housing problems. Hotel life is expensive, most of those living in them are unemployed, and those who have jobs tend to have low wages. Yet living in a hotel itself makes it more difficult to get work, and some people in the survey found themselves in an 'unemployment trap' where they would not have been able to live in the hotel if they had taken work. The disposable incomes of those in the study were extremely low and people were having to go without basic necessities. Nearly a third of the women were sometimes going without food. The lack of money is likely to affect the health of hotel residents, both by increasing their worries and by restricting their diet.

Overcrowding

While conditions in hotels vary greatly, most would not be comfortable to stay in even for a short period of time. For families with young children who must live there for many months or even years, the most striking problem in this survey was the lack of space. Based on interviewer estimates, over a third of the rooms were thought to be under 110 square feet – the equivalent of a room 10 feet by 11 feet. These were mostly occupied by two people (either a couple or mother and child), but there were five families in the survey where three people had to live in a room of this size. Larger families did tend to have larger rooms and some of the very large families had two rooms. However, one family with two adults and four children were living in a dark basement room approx. 10 feet by 17 feet; with the two double beds pushed together, the sink, wardrobe and chest of drawers, there was little space left for the possessions of a family of six.

An attempt was made to relate the situation of those in the survey to the statutory definition of overcrowding. Of the 42 households where details were obtained, nearly half were statutorily overcrowded.

Of the 110 children of all ages in these families, at least 33 were sharing their bed with another child and 13 had to share with an adult. Some rooms were too small even for a baby's cot. One child had just a mattress on the floor, while another had a fold-up bed which, when open, fitted across the doorway.

The high level of overcrowding experienced by many bed-and-breakfast families is exacerbated by the lack of safety and security many feel in the hotel. There are real fears for young children playing both in halls and stairways and in cramped rooms with kettles and cooking equipment. Open fuse boxes, multiple adaptors and trailing wires were not uncommon. One family had resorted to putting a wardrobe in front of their insecure fourth-floor window to prevent the children from falling out; the small room was in darkness all day. Few women had faith in the fire alarms, where one existed at all. Many also feared the lack of privacy and the fact that strangers had access to the halls and corridors.

The survey included only those who had lived in a hotel for at least four months; time spent in hotels so far was as follows:

4–5 months	15
6–11 months	24
1–2 years	14
Over 2 years	4
Total	57

Nearly a third had already been living in hotels for over a year. All the problems with hotel life are made more acute by the length of time people are there, and this is exacerbated by the fact that they usually don't know when they may be rehoused. The women's general sense of having been dumped in a hotel and forgotten made it harder to cope with the conditions they were having to live in, and it is likely to have increased their stress and anxiety.

Food and cooking

The storage, preparation and cooking of food are all likely to play an important part in determining what kind of foods can be eaten. Food storage was a major problem for most of the women in the survey. Some hotels did not allow residents to keep any food at all in their rooms, and nearly half the women did not have a refrigerator in their room or elsewhere. Six said they could keep no food at all, including two with babies, who felt unable to wean them because of this. The lack of space to prepare food was also a problem, and there was particular concern about using knives in the cramped bedrooms where young children could hurt themselves.

Access to kitchens and cooking facilities is crucially important. The London boroughs' Code of Practice for kitchens suggests that one full set of kitchen facilities should be available for every five people and should not be more than one floor away; facilities include an oven, burners, grill, sink, fridge and storage (London Boroughs Association and Association of London Authorities, 1986). Kitchen facilities available were found to be as follows:

No kitchen	22
Share kitchen with 3–4 other families	5
Share kitchen with 6–7 other families	4
Share kitchen with 11–19 other families	5
Share kitchen with 20 or more families	6
Share kitchen with unknown number	10
Exclusive use of kitchen	5
Total	57

Twenty-two of the 57 women in this survey had no kitchen which they could use at all. This included six who had no means of preparing even a hot drink as there was also no kettle in the bedroom. Only five had exclusive use of a kitchen. The rest shared a kitchen with at least three other families and many shared with large numbers: in six cases over 20 families had to share the kitchen. In one case, there were only six rings for over 20 families; while in another, there were just four rings for over 40 families to use.

The shared kitchens were often a long way from the bedrooms; two-thirds were two or more floors away. Many of the women were concerned about having to carry hot food, pots and pans up and down the stairs, often with young children in tow. Where there were kettles and cooking facilities in the rooms, these were perceived as dangerous.

The survey found that most hotels do not cater for people providing meals for themselves. Many residents are forced to rely on takeaways and cafés for the time they live there. Apart from being very expensive, this has a marked effect on the quality of their diet, as shown below.

Diet

The importance of nutrition to long-term and short-term health has been well known for some time. As part of the interviews with women in hotels, they were asked what they had to eat and drink the day before; if this was not typical, they were asked what was. They were also asked how many times a week they ate 30 different designated foods. The dietician involved in the research was able to assess the diets of 48 of the women: 20 were eating a 'poor' diet, 24 had 'average' diets, while only four had 'good' diets. Well over a third had diets which were very high in fat and sugar and low in dietary fibre.

Seven of the women were living primarily on snacks, only occasionally supplemented with a hot meal. In spite of hotel accommodation being generally referred to as 'bed-and-breakfast', well over half the women never had a hotel breakfast either because none was provided or because it was inconvenient, unsuitable or 'inedible'. There was heavy reliance on take-aways, cafés, snacks and pre-packaged convenience foods. Over a third never prepared a cooked meal for their families, or did so less than once a week.

The overall quality of the women's diets was affected to a great extent by the availability and cleanliness of a kitchen and food preparation facilities (Table 13.1). Those with access to a decent kitchen were much more likely to be eating a better diet than those without.

The lack of money was also an important restriction on diet. Nearly a quarter of the women were going without food from time to time because they could not afford it, and one in ten said their children sometimes went without food. Money constraints were found to play an even greater part in poor diets in this study than in a comparable study of people with low incomes in the general population, suggesting that living in a hotel accentuates financial problems (London Boroughs Associations and Association of London Authorities, 1986).

The women expressed grave concerns about the poor quality of

Table 13.1   Overall quality of diet

	Good	Average	Poor
Use of kitchen	4	12	7
Don't use/have kitchen	0	11	13

their diets and the expense. The less able they were to cater for themselves, the more they worried. They were particularly anxious about the fact that they could not give their children the kind of food they knew they should have.

These concerns were reflected by the health visitors. One health visitor in Manchester felt that the diet 'almost amounts to malnutrition standards in some cases'. Since this research was carried out, there have been changes to the benefit system which leave families in hotels with even less money to spend on food – in some cases, as little as £1 per person a day. It is reasonable to assume that their already inadequate diets are now even poorer.

The women's health

Sheila and her 14-month old daughter live in a room approx. seven feet by 15 feet. The small window is at least six feet high up on the wall and gives very little light. As there is no room for a cot, the daughter shares Sheila's bed and disturbs her through the night. The hotel has no kitchen and food is not allowed in the rooms. Sheila does not even have a kettle to make a hot drink. She is often hungry, but worries more about her daughter who is often ill and does not seem to be growing.

Given situations like that above, found in the survey, it is not surprising that one of the most striking findings was the degree of stress experienced by the women. Tension manifested itself in a number of ways: two women felt that they were very close to battering their children, two had started to drink heavily and one was losing weight rapidly, despite the fact that she was still breast-feeding her baby. Many experienced severe depression and some had started to take pills to help.

Boredom, isolation and loneliness were important factors. Nearly half the women in the survey, especially those with larger families, said they normally spent a least eight hours during the day in their bedroom, often not going out of the room at all except to the WC or bathroom. Many, especially those in London, were also isolated because they had been placed in hotels far from their own area.

In response to questions about health problems, the most commonly mentioned ailments were severe headaches or migraines, which 34 women said they had regularly; 20 women had had diarrhoea, usually with vomiting; and 16 had suffered some kind of chest infection. Other problems often mentioned were bladder and kidney infections and anaemia. Two women said their asthma had got much worse since living in a hotel. Many said they generally felt run down and tired and were more susceptible to coughs and colds. Those normally confined in their rooms for eight or more hours during the day were much more likely to have been ill than those who were normally out more.

GPs and health visitors were extremely concerned about both the physical and mental health of women in hotels. One London GP saw the main problem as 'a pervasive sense of hopelessness, depression and despair. What you see are subtle changes in their health – more chest infections, more headaches and more anxiety.'

Pregnant women

The research looked, in particular, at pregnant women living in hotels (Table 13.2). Nineteen of the women in the survey had had babies while living in bed-and-breakfast and eight were pregnant at the time of the interview. Half said they had had problems during the pregnancy. These included high blood pressure which the doctor

Table 13.2 Number of women with problems recorded in pregnancy and labour (Manchester sample only)

Problems in pregnancy and labour	Homeless in pregnancy	Homeless after birth
Hospital admission	6	2
Bleeding in pregnancy	4	3
Anaemia	4	1
Foetal distress in labour	2	3
Postpartum haemorrhage	3	2
Weight loss/failure to grow	2	2
Caesarean section	3	1
Infection	3	0
Premature labour	1	0
Anorexia	0	1
Total number with problems recorded	13	5
Number with no problems recorded	8	16
Number of women in the sample	21	21

attributed to the stress of living in a hotel, and weight loss in one woman who had been unable to get proper meals. Another woman, finding it hard to walk in the later stages of her pregnancy, often couldn't get to the kitchen which was two floors away from her bedroom. For one, smoking had been a major problem, because she had been too stressed to give up, in spite of having given up smoking during two previous pregnancies when she had not been living in a hotel.

Analysis of obstetric records in Manchester showed that far more problems were recorded in pregnancy and labour for women who had been living in hotels during their pregnancy than for those who had only moved into bed-and-breakfast after the birth. For example, those living in hotels during their pregnancy were more likely to have been admitted to hospital during the pregnancy, had a higher incidence of anaemia and more infections.

The midwives interviewed for the study were extremely concerned about pregnant women in hotels and their babies. These women were often late booking into hospitals and have poor attendance at antenatal classes. Those who have booked into a hospital in their local area often don't change to another hospital near the hotel because they do not know how long they will be living there or where they will move to next.

A good diet is crucially important for a pregnant woman, yet hotel life often makes it very difficult to achieve an adequate diet. The story of one of the pregnant women in the survey highlights the problem. She was seven and a half months pregnant at the time of the interview. She attended college and had to leave in the morning before the time when the hotel breakfast was served. Lunch was usually her first food of the day and she could only afford to buy snack food such as chips or a sandwich. The hotel provided no cooking facilities of any kind for the residents. There was nowhere for storing food and milk could not be kept overnight in the heat of the bedroom. As a vegetarian, she had a very limited choice from the local take-aways, so her evening meal during the week normally consisted of chips and a milk shake with an occasional pizza. Sometimes she just had biscuits and bread in the evenings. She did not even have a kettle in her room. She only had hot meals at weekends when she returned to her family in another part of London. This woman was desperately worried about her unborn baby because the doctors had told her that the baby's health was affected by her bad diet. She said, 'I don't mind if I die, but if my baby dies what will I do?' While hotel life jeopardizes the health of all residents, pregnant women and their babies are especially at risk.

Health of newborn babies in hotels

Birthweight is probably the single most important indicator of a baby's future health. Analysis of the health records for this study shows that, although the number of cases is small, about a quarter of the babies born in bed-and-breakfast hotels have a low birthweight. This is considerably higher than the national average of 7% with a low birthweight. Those born in hotels include a high proportion of Bangladeshi, Indian and Pakistani surnames; yet the incidence of low birthweight in hotel babies is still significantly higher than those for these groups in the general population.

Five out of the 19 babies in the interview survey born while their mothers were living in a hotel were premature, including two with a low birthweight. Altogether five of these 19 babies had not been healthy at birth, and two had stayed in hospital for over ten days. Health professionals, aware of the poor conditions in many hotels, often try to keep newborn babies in hospital longer when the mother lives in a hotel. Nevertheless, the mother must eventually cope with the physical and mental stresses of introducing a tiny baby to a cramped room, often several flights upstairs, in a noisy hotel.

Children's health and diet

There were 71 children under 5 years old in the survey of homeless women, as well as 39 older children. Nearly half of the under–5s had suffered from diarrhoea and sickness since living in a hotel, and over a third had been getting chest infections – a higher incidence than would normally be expected. Infections seemed to pass quickly from one child to another and many women said that coughs and colds were almost constant among the children. Five mothers said their children had developed skin problems since moving to a hotel and several felt that their health problems resulted from their poor diet. One woman, who had no access to a kitchen, no kettle and was not supposed to keep any food in the room, secretly kept some cereal for her 18-month-old daughter and mixed it with hot water from the basin tap to feed her child.

Not only did the hotel children's physical health seem to suffer, but both the mothers and the health professionals identified behaviour problems and slow development. Several children had become regular bedwetters (in one case, the child shared the bed with her mother), and over half were felt by their mothers to have become very bad sleepers for their age. Some had become unusually aggressive or active; one would always scream for long periods when returning to the hotel after a trip out.

The health professionals also saw a direct link between the accommodation and the slow development of many of the hotel children. They blamed late walking, late talking, late potty training and speech delays on the restrictions of hotel life.

These restrictions are often imposed because of the dangers present in the hotel, with kettles and cooking equipment in bedrooms, and often no safe place for knives, razors, disinfectant, etc. During the interviews, it emerged that 22 children had had some kind of accident. These included falling downstairs while playing, burns and drinking disinfectant. One health visitor described how a 1-year-old had received extensive third-degree burns when her mother spilt a pot of hot water over her while carrying the child and the pot up from the basement kitchen to the bedroom. Children either have to spend long periods of time confined to the cramped bedroom or play in the halls and corridors which are not safe or suitable. Some babies are left in their cots or strapped into high chairs or push chairs for long periods to keep them from danger.

Mothers were especially concerned about their children's diet and were distressed that they could not give their children the food they wanted them to have. However, the poor diet of the mothers themselves often forces them to give up breastfeeding and rely on bottles for young babies which, in a hotel, carries a grave risk of infection.

Access to health care

In spite of being a high-risk group, the survey found that many hotel residents have difficulty getting primary health care and few are getting the extra level of support which may be needed.

Looking at developmental tests for young children, the examination of health records shows that, of those babies who moved into bed-and-breakfast soon after being born, over half missed the six-week test which is crucial for identifying any early problems or handicap. A higher proportion (12%) of those whose mothers had been living in a hotel before the birth had had this test, (this is close to the proportion in the control group in London of families from a similar background, but much lower than for the general population in Manchester). However, both groups of hotel children tended to miss subsequent developmental checks more often than those not living in hotels. In general, more children in hotels also missed immunizations and vaccinations than children not living in hotels.

The study also highlighted serious difficulties with access to GPs. Of the 57 women in the survey, 23 were still with the doctor they had prior to moving to a hotel, 13 had permanently registered with a doctor nearer the hotel and 19 were temporarily registered locally; two had no GP at all. Half the children under 5 years were only temporarily registered. Some women preferred to stay with their original doctor, although they were currently living some distance away. However, 14 of the 39 women in London had tried to register with a GP nearer the hotel and had found difficulty in doing so; three of the 18 women in Manchester and Southend had also had problems. In one case, a woman had tried five different GPs before finding one who would take her. Several health visitors in the study felt that there was a lack of concern shown by some GPs.

The Bangladeshi women in the survey seemed to have particular problems finding a local doctor because they had been placed in a hotel far away from their own community and could not find a Bengali-speaking doctor near the hotel.

Because of the poor and crowded conditions in most hotels, the need for health visitors is especially acute. Yet only 14 of the 46 children under 3 years old in the survey had a health visitor who came to see them regularly; 22 had a visit only sometimes or just once; and eight had never had a visit at all.

13.3

The response of health services

Some attempts are being made by the health services to bring a better service to homeless families. In Bayswater, west London, the

Family Practitioner Committee (FPC) will allocate a GP to see a homeless person where there have been difficulties in registering. Manchester City Council has appointed a specialist in community medicine who contacts the FPC where there are problems. In Finsbury Park, north London one GP has been designated as having 'special interest in homelessness' and has been able to promote better access to services. The Health Visitors' Association and the British Medical Association are now working together to improve health care for hotel families, developing practical ideas to improve primary services.

The problem of poor antenatal care has been recognized by one Manchester hospital which allows pregnant women to book into the clinic even if they have no letter from a GP, which is usually required.

Health visitors are often in a unique position to identify the health problems arising from hotel life. In areas with high concentrations of bed-and-breakfast hotels, health visitors often work exclusively with homeless families. However, their caseloads are enormous; in London, Southend and Manchester health visitors often have 120–150 homeless families each. Some can only deal with those who have been placed in hotels by the local authority and are not able to work with other families in hotels.

Health visitors and midwives often do not receive adequate information about homeless families placed in hotels in their area. In many places, particularly in London, families are often placed in hotels outside the area of the local authority which has accepted them as homeless and there is no contact between the local and health authorities in the receiving area. The Association of London Authorities/London Boroughs Association Code of Practice on the use of hotels includes procedures for notification, yet the health visitors found the system did not work.

In Finsbury Park a 'health mobile' van has been introduced. It visits the area where hotels are concentrated and is staffed by a Bangladeshi health worker, two health visitors and a GP. In Bayswater the idea of providing such a basic form of primary care has been rejected, but attempts have been made by the health service to link into other support networks including the playgroup which caters for the homeless.

There are mixed feelings about the provision of specialist services for the homeless. It ensures that the services are geared to those in need and the workers have a good understanding of the issues. On the other hand, working with the homeless is extremely stressful. It is argued that the existence of separate specialist services marginalizes the homeless and the general service may then ignore their needs. There is also the danger that specialist services become second-class services.

13.4
The response of housing services

The Association of London Authorities and London Boroughs Association have developed a Code of Practice on the use of hotels and the Bed and Breakfast Information Exchange has been set up in London to co-ordinate the actions of the boroughs. The success of these initiatives has been restricted by the huge scale of the problem.

The most significant development over the past few years has been the increased use of other forms of temporary accommodation for the homeless, particularly private sector leasing schemes whereby local authorities lease empty private properties to let on a temporary basis to those accepted as homeless. In March 1990 there were nearly 12 000 households placed in private leased homes in London, compared with just under 8000 in bed-and-breakfast hotels (figures from Bed and Breakfast Exchange).

Standards in the privately leased homes are generally far higher than in hotels, and residents normally have exclusive use of facilities including kitchens (London Research Centre, 1989). However, some of the health problems associated with being homeless remain. The use of these schemes is fragmented and notification to other services, such as health visitors and midwives, is even more difficult than where hotels are used. While many authorities have been able to place an increasing proportion of the homeless in hotels in the local area, leased homes are more scattered and many have to move long distances, thus severing their local ties. This means losing support networks and changing GP. Some problems have also arisen concerning who is responsible for controlling the scheme and dealing with conditions in the properties.

The most serious concern is that current housing subsidy arrangements effectively spell the end of private leasing schemes within the next few years; leases cannot be renewed after two periods of three years, and there will no longer be any subsidy on the rent paid for privately leased properties renewed after 1992/93. This means that within the next few years very large numbers of homeless families will once again need to be found some kind of short-term accommodation.

13.5
Conclusion

This study shows that the health of pregnant women, mothers and young children who live in hotels is badly affected. This is partly because the conditions in hotels are so poor and totally unsuitable for families. It is also the result of the stress of being homeless and not knowing when they are likely to be rehoused, or where. The fact that many homeless families are placed in hotels far from their original area adds to their vulnerability. Both housing and health authorities are providing a totally inadequate level of support to meet their needs.

A lot of effort has recently been made to secure other types of temporary accommodation for the homeless which provides considerably better conditions. However, there are still major problems and the families' health is still at risk.

Authorities have not responded to the fact that large amounts of temporary accommodation have been used for many years and have become a long-term feature of the housing system. While the ultimate solution is, obviously, for there to be more permanent housing, authorities should now pay serious attention to the needs of the thousands of families who will continue to live in inadequate accommodation for the foreseeable future.

Bibliography

Audit Commission (1989) *Housing the Homeless: The Local Authority Role*, Audit Commission, London.

Conway, J. (ed.) (1988) *Prescription for Poor Health: The Crisis for Homeless Families*, SHAC, London.

Department of the Environment (1981, 1986) *English House Condition Survey*, HMSO, London.

Department of the Environment (1989) Quarterly Homelessness Statistics – Third Quarter.

Lang, T. *et al.* (1984) *Jam Tomorrow?* Food Policy Unit, Manchester Polytechnic, Manchester.

London Boroughs Association and Association of London Authorities (1986) *Joint London Boroughs Code of Practice. The Use of Hotel/Hostel Accommodation for the Placement of Homeless Families*, LBA/ALA, London.

London Research Centre (1989) Private Sector Leasing in London.

Murie, A. and Jeffers, S. (eds) (1987) *Living in Bed and Breakfast: The Experience of Homelessness in London*, Working Paper No. 71, Bristol School for Advanced Urban Studies.

Niner, P. and Thomas, A. (1989) *Living in Temporary Accommodation: A Survey of Homeless People*, HMSO, London.

Randall, G., Francis, D. and Brougham, C. (1981) *A Place for the Family*, SHAC, London.

Part Three

Remedies and Reforms

14

FUNDAMENTALS OF HEALTHFUL HOUSING: THEIR APPLICATION IN THE 21ST CENTURY

ERIC W. MOOD

14.1

Introduction

In almost all of the more developed countries, recognition has been given to the relationship of the quality of housing to the health of the occupants. While in some cases it is difficult to show a conclusive relationship between the two because of the concomitance of other factors adversely affecting health, such as inadequate medical care, ignorance, poverty, etc., there is a considerable wealth of knowledge that identify the conditions of housing that should be provided in order that a dwelling may be considered to be *healthful*. In this context, 'healthful' is defined as 'serving to promote health of body or mind'.

In the post Second World War era, emphasis in many nations was placed primarily on providing a sufficient number of housing units, particularly in western Europe where there was a great need to replace the houses destroyed during the war. While there is still a great need for additional housing units, the present focus is, or should be, changing to the development of dwelling units which will provide for the health and well-being of the occupants.

The First Report of the Expert Committee on the Public Health Aspects of Housing, convened in Geneva, Switzerland, in June 1961 promulgated a definition for a healthful residential environment

(World Health Organization, 1961). This definition identified two major elements of the residential environment, namely the dwelling unit and the neighbourhood or the setting of the residential structure. This definition established some broad, general health criteria which should be provided for health reasons.

In the recent past, much attention has been given to the health problems of human settlements. Of particular importance is the United Nations Conference on Human Settlements (HABITAT), held in Vancouver in 1976. Other meetings have been convened at which various environmental factors that may adversely affect the health of people in communities have been discussed and minimum conditions have been proposed.

The purposes of defining specific fundamentals of housing that are necessary for the health and well-being of the occupants are manifold. One of the purposes is the identification of those conditions associated with housing that have been identified by various research studies as being of primary importance in providing for the health and well-being of the occupants in the following ways:

1. Those conditions which must be provided to fulfil the requirements mandated by the limitations of the physiology of humans.
2. The environmental conditions of housing needed to prevent or limit the transmission of pathogenic agents.
3. Measures which should be undertaken to prevent injuries incurred by accidents.
4. Facilities which should be provided to obtain optimum mental health and well-being.

As an outgrowth of the work of the Housing Commission of the Health Committee of the League of Nations, the Committee on the Hygiene of Housing, American Public Health Association, functioning as the national committee for hygiene of housing in the USA developed a set of basic principles of healthful housing which address themselves to the above-cited conditions (Committee on the Hygiene of Housing, 1939). Subsequently many of these principles were incorporated into statutes, regulations and public health codes as minimum legal requirements for occupied housing.

14.2

Housing and health for all

In 1981 the Thirty-fourth World Health Assembly adopted a resolution for the health of people by the year 2000. This resolution placed new emphasis upon the need for healthful housing as supporting documents identified safe, sanitary and decent housing as being one of the requisites for healthy people. Various national and international organizations have promulgated criteria and goals that would assist in the attainment of the fundamental objective of health for all by the year 2000. The Regional Committee for Europe (WHO) identified 38 specific targets for achieving the basic objection (World Health Organization Regional Office for Europe, 1985); Target 24 is as follows:

By the year 2000, all people of the Region should have a better opportunity of living in houses and settlements which provide a healthy and safe environment. The achievement of this target will require the acceleration of programmes of housing construction and improvement; the development of international health criteria for housing, space, heating, lighting, disposal of wastes, noise control and safety, while taking into account young families, the elderly and the disabled; legislative, administrative and technical measures to comply with such criteria; the improvement of community planning in order to enhance health and well-being by improving traffic safety, providing open spaces and recreational areas, and facilitating human interaction, etc.; and the equipment of all dwellings with proper sanitation facilities and the provision of sewers and an adequate public cleansing and wastes collection and disposal system in all human settlements of sufficient size.

This goal statement placed new emphasis upon the development and maintenance of healthful housing,

In 1989 the ministers of environment and of health of the member states of the European Region of WHO met for the first time in Frankfurt-am-Main on 7 and 8 December 1989, and developed a European Charter on Environment and Health (World Health Organization Regional Office for Europe, 1990). In the statement of principles for public policy, it is noted that 'substantial geographical differences in the incidence of disease clearly coincide with different housing standards'. The Charter calls for appropriate control measures to reduce the risks to health and well-being. Specifically, appropriate regulations which are enforceable and enforced are called for. Further, it is suggested that standards should be set on the basis of the best available scientific knowledge. Clearly epidemiological studies have identified many of the characteristics of healthful housing. A summary of these studies is set out below.

14.3
Specific characteristics of healthful housing

Prevention of enteric diseases

General concepts

Studies of enteric diseases of occupants of housing have identified seven basic conditions of housing which must be fulfilled as preventive measures as follows:

1. a safe, adequate, potable and palatable water supply which is available to each dwelling unit under pressure;
2. sanitary methods for the collection and disposal of excreta and the prevention of faecal pollution of ground- and surface-water supplies;
3. sanitary collection, storage and disposal of garbage and other solid wastes;
4. prevention of access into dwelling units of insect vectors of human disease;
5. adequate space within each dwelling unit to avoid excessive crowding;
6. freedom within the dwelling unit from rodents, vermin and animals other than domestic pets; and
7. sanitary provision for the proper storage of milk and other foodstuffs.

Most enteric diseases are transmitted by the faecal-oral route. Some enteric disturbances may be caused also by toxic substances (e.g. lead, copper and other heavy metals). Acute lead poisoning may be caused by the corrosive action of acidic water (i.e. water with a pH <7.0), while chronic lead poisoning may be the result of young children chewing on surfaces which have been coated with lead-based paint.

Diarrhoea is the most common symptom of enteric diseases, and when it occurs in children under 5 years of age, may cause death, usually from dehydration. Diarrhoea has been defined as a 'disturbance of intestinal motility and absorption which, once and by means initiated, may become self-perpetuating as a disease through the production of dehydration and profound disturbances, which in turn favour the continuing passage of liquid stools' (Ordway, 1960, p. 73).

Water supply and enteric disease

There is much epidemiological evidence which denotes that safe and sanitary water supply is necessary for the prevention of enteric diseases. Epidemiological studies conducted in migratory labour camps in California showed that the infection rate of *Shigella* in children of 10 years of age and under who live in dwellings with no inside water supply was approximately twice the rate which was observed in children of the same age whose home had an inside water supply and which was provided under pressure (Hollister *et al.*, 1955). In another series of studies conducted in Georgia, *Shigella* infections were about one and a half times more frequent among those persons who resided in dwellings which did not have a source of drinking water on the same premises as the dwelling, compared with persons who resided in dwellings without an inside pipe water supply but who had a source of water on the premises (Stewart *et al.*, 1955). In a third epidemiologic study, the prevalence rate for *Shigella*, the incidence of *Ascaris* infections, and morbidity from diarrhoeal diseases were associated in an inverse manner with the availability of water (League of Nations, Health Organization, 1931; Schliessman *et al.*, 1958; Schliessman, 1959). The lowest rates were found among persons who resided in dwellings which had a water supply piped inside the dwelling and the highest rates were among those whose source of water was off the premises.

Studies conducted by WHO Diarrhoeal Disease Team in Venezuela demonstrated that the further the water source is from the premises, the greater the number of cases of diarrhoeal disease (Wolff, van Zijl and Roy, 1969). Studies conducted in Fresno County, California, revealed that the availability of water for hand washing was an important factor in reducing the incidence of *Shigella* infections (Watt *et al.*, 1953).

The provision of an abundant, readily available supply of clean, pure water for drinking, culinary purposes and hand washing should not be underestimated as a basic means for the prevention of enteric infections.

Disposal of excreta and enteric disease

The relationship between means available for the disposal of human excreta and the prevalence of enteric diseases has been acknowledged as being an important public health measure for almost a hundred years. One of the earliest studies which demonstrated a significant association between the types of toilets serving an urban population and cases of typhoid fever was made by Dr P. Boobbyer, Medical Officer of Health in Nottingham. In 1897, Dr Boobbyer reported his findings of an exhaustive study of the epidemiology of typhoid fever in Nottingham over the ten-year period, 1887–96 (Sykes, 1901). He observed that the case incidence ratio of persons residing in dwellings served by a privy was one in 37, while the case incidence ratio of persons residing in dwellings with indoor flush water closets was only one in 558.

Data collected in 1935 and 1936 during the National Health and Survey in the USA showed an excessive incidence of typhoid and paratyphoid fevers, diarrhoea, enteritis and colitis among persons living in housing lacking private inside flush toilets, as compared with families having a private inside flush toilet (Britten, 1942). In another study which was published in 1935, it was demonstrated that the prevalence of typhoid fever (and infant mortality) was significantly higher in those neighbourhoods in Memphis, Tennessee, in which there were a preponderance of houses lacking indoor flush toilets (Graves and Fletcher, 1935).

In the studies conducted by the US Public Health Service of enteric diseases among residents of several eastern Kentucky mining towns, it was observed that persons living in dwellings which utilized privies as the means of excreta disposal experienced approximately twice as many cases of diarrhoeal diseases as persons residing in houses with inside flush toilets (Beck, Munoz and Scrimshaw, 1951).

The studies of diarrhoeal disease in Guatemala during the 1950s disclosed that the prevalence of *Shigella* infections was approximately three times greater among families living in areas where inside toilets were available in less than half the dwellings than among those families living in areas where more than half the houses had such facilities (McCabe and Haines, 1957).

In a demonstration study conducted in Georgia, USA, where there was a community programme involving the installation of bored-hole privies, there were significant reductions in *Shigella* infections in children under 10 years of age and in rates of morbidity from diarrhoeal disease (*ibid.*)

Basic to the prevention of enteric disease and morbidity from diarrhoeal disease is the provision in all dwellings of a safe, sanitary means for the disposal of human excreta. Indoor, private flush toilets with sanitary means for the disposal of the sewage seems to be by far the best measure.

House flies and enteric disease

Many studies have been conducted in various areas of the world to determine the relationship between flies and enteric disease. In the USA studies conducted in Texas and Georgia showed significant association (Watt and Lindsay, 1948; Lindsay, Stewart and Watt, 1953). The Texas study demonstrated that effective fly control activities in those communities which initially had a high fly population reduced the prevalence of *Shigella* infections and diarrhoeal diseases. The Georgia studies confirmed the results of the Texas studies.

A comparative study of mortality rates for 1949 and 1950 in several villages in Egypt showed that effective fly control was a factor in reducing the number of deaths from enteric diseases (Weir *et al.*, 1953). The studies conducted in Georgia, USA., involving the installation of bored-hole privies, proved an insight into fly control measures as a preventive means of enteric diseases (McCabe and Haines, 1957). This study noted that the curtailing of breeding of house flies in and around privies through the construction of sanitary privies did not reduce significantly the total population of house flies in the communities studies, but did exclude flies from faecal material and hence broke the chain of transmission.

The WHO team studying diarrhoeal diseases in Venezuela noted a direct relationship between house flies and enteric diseases – i.e. those communities with a large population of house flies had high rates of diarrhoeal diseases, while those communities with less house flies had lower rates of the same diseases (Wolff, van Zijl and Roy, 1969).

The above-cited studies show clearly the role of house flies in the transmission of enteric disease agents in and around dwellings. Two important factors of housing hygiene are demonstrated, namely the need to prevent access of flies to human faeces, and the need for screen doors and windows to keep flies out of dwellings and other structures where they may contaminate food.

General sanitation of dwellings and enteric disease

Several epidemiological studies have investigated the relationship between the general sanitation level of dwellings and enteric diseases. A very interesting finding was made in a study in Singapore of the effect on the prevalence of helminthic infestations in Chinese families who were rehoused from urban slums or squatter housing into dwellings with modern sanitation facilities – e.g. piped running water, private indoor flush toilets, etc. (Kleevens, 1966). The results of this study show a reduced prevalence of infections by soil-transmitted helminths such as *Ascaris* and *Trichuris* in children of 12 years of age and younger. This finding seems to be the result of improved sanitary facilities and diminished chances of infection.

In 1967 a US study of an area of Dallas, Texas, was made to evaluate certain epidemiologic, bacteriologic and social factors of 50 households in which a person resided who had a *Shigella* infection (Nelson, Kusmicz and Haltalin, 1967). The findings of this study noted that while no common source of infection was apparent, these families represented the lowest stratum of society in which poor interpersonal hygiene, crowded living conditions, less than optimal diet and ignorance were fundamental characteristics.

The prevalence of infant diarrhoea among American Indian children residing in a Hopi village was studied to determine the effect, if any, of improved sanitation facilities (*ibid.*). The findings of this research observed that children living in sanitary and decent housing tended to contract diarrhoeal diseases less frequently than children living in dwellings lacking in sanitary facilities, even though both groups of children were of similar social and economic backgrounds.

In general, epidemiological studies have revealed that higher morbidity and mortality rates for enteric diseases are found in areas in which housing lacks some of the basic sanitary facilities and where community sanitation is poor. In many studies, difficulty was encountered in isolating and demonstrating the effect of a single environment factor, largely due to the fact that enteric diseases may be transmitted by several pathways involving various sanitation elements.

Prevention of enteric diseases through hygiene of housing

Due to the multiplicity of aetiological agents and differences in the mode of spread of enteric diseases, the prevention of such diseases is dependent upon the provision of sanitary housing and community sanitation such as to prevent direct and indirect transmission of infections agents and to preclude faecal contamination of water and food. The factors of housing which should be controlled to prevent enteric diseases include the following: water supply, excreta and sewage disposal, garbage and other solid waste disposal, fly control, and sanitation of food and milk products.

Prevention of airborne infections

General concepts

Airborne infections, due to a variety of micro-organisms, are common diseases of humans. They are usually spread by close contact and are therefore often associated with overcrowding of dwelling spaces. The mechanisms of transmissions of the infectious agents may be by droplet nuclei which harbour micro-organisms, as well as by direct contact.

Tuberculosis

Much has been written about tuberculosis in connection with housing. One of the early reform leaders for better housing conditions as a preventive against tuberculosis was Mrs Albion Fellows Bacon, who identified tuberculosis as a 'house disease' (Bacon, 1916). She appealed for studies to shed more light upon the relationship between poor housing and tuberculosis. Walker, in his US study in Detroit, Michigan, observed that poor housing conditions and a high death rate from tuberculosis were concomitant (Walker, 1923), and Herman concluded that room-crowding was significantly associated with tuberculosis deaths (Herman, 1929).

Mackintosh (1952) summarized reports from the UK and showed significant relationships of housing and tuberculosis cases and deaths. One of the more detailed studies conducted in the UK during the decade of the 1930s attempted to clarify the role of housing in determining the incidence of and mortality due to respiratory tuberculosis. Stein (1950) analysed the morbidity and mortality rates of this disease for the ten-year period 1930–9 and concluded that there is 'very strong evidence of association between rates of respiratory tuberculosis and conditions of housing'. She felt that overcrowding of dwellings was particularly contributory to the incidence of this disease.

The National Health Survey conducted in the USA in the 1930s included data on tuberculosis (Britten, Brown and Altman, 1940; Britten and Altman, 1941). It was revealed that there was a considerable increase in the frequency of tuberculosis with an increase in crowding of persons within a dwelling unit, particularly among children of the lower economic groups.

In the USA in 1942 and 1943 an intensive study was conducted in Newark, New Jersey, to evaluate the benefit of public housing and to test the hypothesis that rehousing families from slums to decent dwellings would improve the status of their health (Housing Authority of the City of Newark, 1944). Tuberculosis was one of the health factors used; in order to present the data as accurately as possible, only new cases of tuberculosis among persons of 15–40 years were computed. These data indicated that a lower rate of tuberculosis infection occurred among families rehoused in public housing than for those families living in slum housing for both white and black populations.

Schmitt studied housing and health conditions on Oahu, one of the Hawaiian Islands, and in 1955 reported his findings. His data showed that the dilapidation of housing and the overcrowding of dwellings were associated closely with the rate of tuberculosis infection.

Pneumonia

One of the early studies which showed that housing conditions were associated with respiratory illness was a report in 1923 by Walker, who analysed housing conditions and pneumonia deaths in Detroit, Michigan, for 1920 and 1921. He observed a significant relationship between poor housing and deaths due to pneumonia. In 1928, in the same city, Herman observed a similar relationship but pinpointed the specific housing defect responsible for pneumonia deaths to be room-crowding (Herman, 1929). Herman did not find any correlation between room-crowding and scarlet fever, whooping cough or measles.

Benjamin and others studied the incidence of pneumococcal pneumonia with respect to overcrowding of dwellings in Cincinnati,

Ohio, and concluded that in spite of the limitations of the study, the data supported the theory that overcrowding contributes to the spread of pneumonia and was an important factor in the high incidence of this disease (Benjamin, Ruegsegger and Senior, 1940).

Meningococcal meningitis

The relationship of housing to the incidence of meningococcal meningitis has been recorded in two studies. Dauer observed an association between cases of this disease and poor housing conditions during the outbreak of 1935 and 1936 in Washington, DC (Dauer, 1939). An exhaustive study was made from 1944 to 1946 of cases of meningococcus disease occurring in Oak Ridge, Tennessee (Blum and Elkin, 1949). With all other factors being equal, the case rate among white persons living in 'slum' housing conditions was observed to be significantly higher than among white persons living in 'standard' housing conditions. The results of this study are particularly important because the economic status of the 'slum' dwellers was the same as for those living in 'standard' dwellings and was of a high level. The important variables influencing the incidence of this disease were those associated with housing conditions and the residential environment.

14.4
The role of housing in home accidents
General concepts

In the USA approx. 92 500 persons are killed each year by accidents, and about 9 000 000 receive disabling injuries (National Safety Council, 1986). While more people are killed in vehicle accidents than in home accidents, approx. 3 100 000 persons per year receive disabling injuries in home accidents, almost twice the number of persons who receive disabling injuries involving motor vehicles. Falls in and around dwellings are the causes of approx. 40% of deaths due to home accidents and almost 25% of the deaths are due to fires. Home accidents are leading causes of deaths for children under the age of 5 years and for elderly persons. Senior citizens are often involved in falls from stairs, on the floor and in bathrooms and toilets, while young children are injured usually in falls from stairs and out of windows, by lacerations from glass in doors and windows, by getting their hand jammed in doors and by being burned by flames, stoves and hot radiators and similar objects.

Many epidemiologists have studied accidental injuries occurring in housing and have noted that more persons, both males and females, are injured inside the dwelling than outside; the ratio being about 6 to 5. However, males are injured more frequently in a home accident which occurs outside of the dwelling than inside the dwelling. Chapter 11 looks at accidents in the home in more detail.

Factors affecting home accidents

Home accidents, like other types of accidents, result from multiple causes and affects individuals in various ways. A home accident is not usually due to a single event, but is the result of a sequence of related events.

Basic factors in home accidents include environmental, human and agent associated characteristics. Environmental hazards associated with home accidents are numerous, but many of them are related to faulty design and poor maintenance of the dwelling, careless housekeeping and the use of defective or improperly installed house equipment and appliances.

The design of a dwelling may be of critical importance to its inherent safety. Houses should be constructed with safe, durable materials, and in accordance with building codes and similar legislation. Adequate and safe storage space should be provided and located adjacent to areas where needed or used. Doors and windows should be easily accessible, and stairs and steps should be uniform in construction, provided with handrails and properly lighted.

Appliances and equipment intended to be used in the home should be checked periodically to ensure that they are operating properly. It is very important that installed equipment be set up by properly qualified or licensed individuals and used in compliance with operating instructions. Furniture and furnishings should be purchased with consideration of safety, as well as of style and comfort.

The exterior of the dwelling should be kept clear of hazards and obstructions, with special attention paid to walkways and steps. Walks should be level, and fences should be placed wherever there may be particular hazards. Although environmental hazards around dwellings cannot always be eliminated, the danger associated with them can be minimized considerably by common sense and ingenuity.

Less easy to understand and correct are accident factors associated or caused by human traits, such as those related to mental, emotional and physical characteristics. There are definite relationships between accidents and fear, worry, elation, grief, fatigue, poor judgement, insufficient knowledge of the task at hand, inability to appreciate hazards and the generalized condition called 'accident proneness'.

Physical traits include, among others, visual defects, auditory and olfactory abnormalities, instability of extremities due to age, illness, medication or allergic manifestations; and acute conditions such as fainting.

Home accidents involving children

Home injuries may account for as much as 90% of all injuries which occur to children under the age of 6 years (Tokuhata *et al.*, 1974). Several epidemiological studies have examined home accidents and their relation to the design of housing (Neutra and McFarland, 1972). However, very few comprehensive attempts have been made to reduce the number of falls, burns and poisons that occur within the home (Dershewitz and Williamson, 1977; Spiegel and Lindman, 1977). Programmes aimed at reducing home injuries should consider concepts of 'active' and 'passive' intervention strategies, as outlined by Haddon and Baker (Haddon, 1980; Baker, 1981). It is important to acknowledge that no single approach should be expected to reduce significantly the magnitude of childhood injuries that are the results of home accidents; rather several approaches should be used, one in concert with the others.

The high home accident rate of children stems, in large measure, from their lack of experience and knowledge, and their inability to recognize danger. Often, adequate adult supervision is lacking also. To prevent accidents to children the homemaker should remove hazards from the environment of children to the extent possible and practicable. This includes providing adequate and safe storage of all poisonous substances – e.g. household cleaners and medicines, and for such items as matches, firearms and sharp instruments.

Adequate play areas should be provided for children in space removed from the kitchen, laundry and heating rooms. Barriers, safety gates and screens should be installed where needed and kept in good repair. The gap between the floor and lower edge of the barrier or gate should be not more than 2 in (50 mm); otherwise an infant could get stuck under one. Metal guards or screens should be placed around gas or electric heaters, open fires and wood or oil burning stoves. No part of the guard should be closer than 8 in (200 mm) to the heat source. If it is too close, the guard itself could become dangerously hot.

Tap-water burns in the bathroom represent about 25% of hot liquid burns of known etiology, and 50% of these burns occur in young children under the age of 5 years (McLoughlin and Crawford, 1985). Burns from hot water are also a major problem of the elderly. Most persons will suffer a third-degree burn if exposed to 150°F (66°C) water for only 2 s. Burns will occur also with an exposure to a water temperature of 140°F (60°C) for 6 s, or to a water temperature of 130°F (54°C) for 30 s.

To prevent tap-water burns the discharge temperature from any faucet should not be greater than 120°F (49°C) (Baptiste and Feck, 1980). If it is not possible or practicable to limit the temperature of hot water as delivered to outlets, the use of thermostatically controlled mixing valves set at 120°F (49°C) will eliminate the hazards associated with scalding.

Another cause of burns to children are the gratings of a floor furnace; 97% of burns caused by floor furnaces occur to children aged 0–4 years (Berger, 1983). The gratings of these furnaces are usually constructed of metal and are located in the floor, often in a central area. Crawling infants and other children walking around in bare feet may come into contact with these grates and suffer severe burns. The temperature of these grates have been observed to be between 180°F (82°C) and 375°F (191°C), with an average equilibrium temperature of 294°F (146°C).

Sites and related conditions associated with home accidents

Halls, stairs and landings

Many home accidents which result in injuries are the result of falls in hallways, on stairs and on landings. The possibility of a serious fall is greatly reduced by one-level homes which have non-skid floors and non-trip floor coverings. Since it is not practicable to consider only one-level housing in a discussion of housing safety, design considerations which make steps and stairs in housing more safe are necessary.

Small changes in floor levels in dwellings are usually hazardous and therefore single steps, both inside and outside the house, should be avoided. Preferably, stairs should consist of at least three risers. Single risers may be acceptable at the outside entrance to a dwelling unit. Landings for exterior steps should be on approximately the same level as the inside floor. Where small changes of elevation are required, ramps should be considered. If the ramp is to be made to accommodate wheelchairs, the desirable maximum slope of a ramp is approx. 1.25 units of rise in 10 units of horizontal distance. The maximum allowable slope is a rise of 1.5 units of rise in 10 units of horizontal travel.

If a dwelling is to have a basement or to have more than one floor, precautions should be taken in designing and constructing stairways in order to reduce the number and seriousness of falls; the following are some design criteria for stairways:

1. Stairways – both long and short – should have handrails on both sides for all steps. The handling of furniture up or down stairs indicates that the minimum clear width between handrails be at least 3ft 3in (1.0 m). The optimum height of a handrail is 2ft 9in (0.84 m) to 3ft 3in (1.0 m). However, for small children a level of 2ft (0.61 m) to 2ft 6in (0.76 m) is preferred. In such cases, dual handrails may be desirable. In order that the handrail may be easily grasped by both children and the elderly, the maximum cross section should not exceed 2½ in (6.4 cm).

2. Short flights of stairs with landings are preferable to a single straight flight. As a guide, no straight flight should have more than 16 risers.

3. Stairways with winders (steps of non-uniform width) are dangerous, due to the change in width of tread, and therefore are not recommended.

4. Stairways should not be too steep. *Risers should be uniform in height: treads should be uniform in width.* For interior steps, the desirable height of risers is 7 in (17.5 cm). If the dwelling unit is to be used by elderly or handicapped persons, a riser

height of not more than 6 in (15 cm) preferred. For exterior steps, the riser height should be inlimited to 5–6 in (13–15 cm).

For maximum safety, wall-to-wall carpeting is recommended. Partial floor coverings, as with area rugs, are apt to be hazardous since persons may trip or slip on them. If small rugs are used, they should have non-slip pads.

All carpets and rugs should lie smoothly, particularly at the edges where people may start to cross them. If necessary, rugs may be tacked down to minimize tripping hazards.

Kitchens

Many accidents occur in kitchens affecting individuals of all age-groups; particularly susceptible to accidental injury in kitchens are children, especially those of 4 years and younger, and the elderly. The principal mechanisms of these injuries involving scalds from hot water, ingestion of cleaning compounds, kettle/teapot/pan accidents, and burns from stoves. Many of the elderly are injured with lacerations or the result of a slip or fall.

Proper planning and design of kitchens should reduce or modify hazards in this room. Studies of kitchens which have been the sites of injuries have been identified as having one or more of the following basic design flaws:

1. insufficient storage space, particularly in base cabinets;
2. too little counter space provided;
3. the assembly of equipment poorly arranged; and
4. the rooms themselves were not well planned.

In most kitchens, there will be two major appliances and one installed facility, namely a stove, a refrigerator and a sink. These may be considered as the corners of a work triangle. For efficiency and effectiveness, the distances between these units in single-family dwellings measured from the centre fronts of these appliances should be approximately as follows:

- Between refrigeration and sink: 4–7 ft (1.25–2.15 m).
- Between sink and stove: 4–6 ft (1.25–1.85 m).
- Between stove and refrigerator: 4–9 ft (1.25–2.75 m).

In addition, the sum of these three distances should not exceed 22 ft (20 m). Also there should be a clearance in front of each appliance of at least 4 ft (1.25 m). Other factors to be considered include the swing of doors, which should not interfere with the space in front of cooking units and ovens, and no line of traffic should cross any leg of the triangle.

In providing counter space the following are considered as minimum for a family of four to six persons:

- 5 in (0.40 m) beside the refrigerator for setting out articles taken from it.
- 36 in (0.90 m) at the right of the sink bowl for stacking dishes before washing.
- 30 in (0.80 m) at the left of the sink bowl for draining and drying dishes.
- 24 in (0.60 m) beside the stove for setting out dishes, pans or plates.
- 36 in (0.90 m) at some point in the assembly for mixing and for food preparation.

Other safety features of kitchens include the following:

- Stoves should not be placed in front of windows or close enough to windows as would permit curtains to be blown near the stove.
- A low-level kitchen cabinet with a child-resistant lock, or a high-level cabinet or shelf which is at least 4ft 6in (1.40 m) above the floor should be provided for the storage of household cleaning compounds.
- Doors on kitchen cabinets and cupboards should be able to open through a 180° turn, and when open, should be flat against the adjacent cabinet or cupboard.

Bathrooms

Slips, falls and scalds from excessively hot water are the most common causes of injuries occurring in bathrooms. Electric shock and electrocution injure and kill a significant number of persons in this area of the dwelling also.

Many elderly persons are injured in bathrooms as the result of a slip. Therefore it is important that the floor of the bathroom and the bottom of bathtubs and shower stalls be provided with non-slip surfaces. Non-breakable and firmly attached grab-bars should be installed by the bathtub and in shower stalls. Many persons, particularly the elderly, use towel rods as grab-bars. Most towel rods are made of glass, ceramic or brittle plastic which are easily broken leading to an accidental injury.

All electrical outlets in bathrooms should be connected to a ground-fault interrupter (earth) to minimize the danger of electric shock and electrocution.

Room arrangements

To reduce the hazards which may result in accidental injuries attention should be given to design and space arrangements of the dwelling. Efficient arrangement reduces disorder, fatigue and the likelihood of falls. Some of the characteristics of good house design and room arrangements are as follows:

1. Related activity areas should be placed on the same level and close together (e.g. a coat closet should be near the front entrance).
2. Short, simple traffic routes should be provided that are adequately wide for their purpose:
   - general passage halls should be at least 3ft 3in (1.0 m) wide;
   - the passageway in the kitchen in front of any appliance should be at least 4ft 0in (1.2 m) wide;
   - interior doorways should have a free opening of 2ft 6in (0.75 m) to provide clearance for movement of furniture and also for wheelchairs; this means that hinged doors should be at least 2ft 8in (0.80 m) wide, and doorways with sliding doors at least 2ft 6in (0.75 m).
3. Ample storage space should be provided in each room where the stored goods may be used.
4. All rooms should be provided with an ample amount of non-glare light, both natural and artificial.
5. There should be no unnecessary changes in floor levels, and no sharp corners or projections, such as those on some mantels.

Storage areas

Many falls may be averted by providing plenty of well-designed storage spaces and by training members of the household to put objects in their assigned places when not in use. Objects left on the floors and on steps, and the use of makeshift ladders to reach stored objects are major causes of falls.

Storage space should be easily accessible and conveniently located; it is desirable to store objects close to their area of use and within easy reach. Some of the following criteria should be observed in locating, designing and providing storage:

1. No shelf should be higher than 70 in (1.75 m) from the floor. Shelves which are adjustable in height are recommended.
2. Shelves of storage units should be constructed such that they will support the weight of the objects being stored without tipping or collapsing. Glass shelving, when used for such purposes as in medicine cabinets, should be shatterproof.
3. Closets and storage units having full-front and full-height access provide more efficient and less hazardous storage than those having an ordinary door which is narrower and shorter than the closet front.
4. Storage space should be well-lighted. Closets more than approx. 3 ft (1 m) deep should have an electric light, preferably one that automatically turns on and off as the door is opened and closed. To avoid a fire hazard, the light should be located such that no flammable material can come into contact with the bulb.

Windows, doors and glazing

Improperly designed or located windows are associated with a considerable number of home injuries. Windows should be located so as to provide natural lighting to the room during daytime hours. Also they should be located in such a way that they may be cleaned easily by elderly persons, as well as by younger adults. The top of the window should not be higher than 6 ft 10 in (2.08 m) in order that the window may be washed without the use of a step-stool or similar device. For windows located above the first floor, the window sill should be at least 2 ft 6 in (0.76 m) from the floor, except where the window opens into a balcony.

To minimize the possibility of an accident, windows should not be made easy to open by children. If a window is located within 4ft 6in (1.37 m) of the floor, some device should be used which would limit the opening of the window to approx. 4 in (100 cm) as a means to prevent children from falling out. If such a device is used, it should be easy for an adult to override the device in the event of a fire or other emergency.

All windows which cannot be reached from the ground, porch or balcony should be of a type which may be washed from the inside. Windows which may be reversed for cleaning should have reliable bolts or other devices, preferably automatic, which lock them in the fully reversed position.

Permanent-type, combination storm windows and screens that can be removed and cleaned from the inside are recommended. Roll-up or tension window screens used with windows of double-sealed glass (thermo-pane) are very convenient. All openable windows should be provided with screens.

To permit easy exit in case of fire consideration should be given to the provision of either an openable door to the outside or at least one window with a 24in x 36in (0.60 m x 0.90 m) or larger opening in all major rooms, including basement recreation rooms. The sill height of this window should not be higher than 36 in (0.90 m) above the finished floor in all rooms above ground level and 54in (1.35in) in basements. These openings should not be blocked by plants, window air conditioning units or other similar items.

Particular care should be given in the placement of windows at landings of stairs. It is recommended that the minimum height of the window sill of such windows be at least 4 in (10 cm) above the finished floor level. If windows are provided below this height, safety glass should be used. This recommendation applies to all windows and sills which are less than 4 in (10 cm) above the finished floor level. This is a particularly important feature of windows located at stair landings.

Large glazed areas, particularly at an entrance, and glazed panels located near a staircase may be extremely dangerous. These hazards may be almost entirely eliminated by the use of safety, tempered or laminated glass. Similarly, patio doors should be made of safety, tempered or laminated glass or of one of the transparent plastics. All large glass or plastic panels should have decals or similar markings placed on them at eye level as an aid to prevent people walking into the panel.

The hazard of bumping into doors may be materially reduced if hinged doors swing into rooms. An outward swing of a door is allowable only if the door does not open into a line of traffic. Doors should never swing into a downward flight of stairs.

The installation of sliding or folding doors is another means of reducing accidents. These doors are especially recommended for closet fronts since they conserve space.

Cylinder-type lock sets are recommended for all exterior doors because they permit the door to be opened from the inside without the use of a key, as may be necessary in an emergency. Since many bathroom and bedroom doors are equipped with locks from the inside only, it is necessary to have a key or other unlocking device for opening the door from the outside in an emergency. Such key or device should be labelled and placed such that it is readily available when needed.

Shallow closets with full-front access do not usually permit persons to walk into them, hence they lessen the possibility of a person, particularly a child, being trapped when the door is closed. All closets need a device on the inside of the doors such that they may be opened from the inside.

Clothes hooks on doors should be placed above adult eye level.

Glass and china door-knobs represent a breakage hazard and hence are not recommended. Round door-knobs may be difficult for some elderly person to operate: a lever-type door handle is preferred.

14.5

Fundamental psychological requirements

General concepts

Research studies conducted to date indicate that there is no simple relationship between mental health and the kind and quality of housing which people live in (see Chapters 8 and 9). However, there are several fundamental psychological needs that healthful housing should provide. The quality of housing controls, to a high degree, the intimate environment in which an individual lives; it is the setting of family life and, to a great extent, influences a person's behaviour. There is no doubt that some mental illnesses are symptomatic of many types of pathology and that many of these are related to poor housing (Lemkau, 1965). Unfortunately, housing rarely is the sole objective feature of the environment which may affect health. Poor housing is concomitant with poverty, poor nutrition, lack of adequate medical care, noise, stress, etc. Poor housing usually is indicative of poor neighbourhood conditions, a lack of community facilities, crowding, etc. The neighbourhood is also frequently deficient in social organization.

Many characteristics of substandard housing may create added stress and fatigue. Structural and appliance inconvenience, difficulty in cleaning and keeping the premises clean and other similar conditions may present nagging annoyances which probably influence mood negatively and/or cause frustration and exhaustion of the will to resist apparently insurmountable difficulties. Conversely, comfortable, pleasant surroundings and adequate space are conducive to a good feeling and satisfaction and may facilitate the maintenance of friendly interpersonal relationships. The absence of presence of a sense of well-being is of importance in itself and is, to a large extent, a manifestation of the difference between personal expectations and disappointments.

Privacy, aesthetics and comfort

A basic psychological need of occupants of dwellings in our urbanized societies is the provision of adequate privacy of the individual (Committee on the Hygiene of Housing, 1939). There is a need for refuge from the noise and tension of the street and from the stress of everyday life. The same principle applies within the dwelling unit itself. If a housing unit is crowded and lacking in adequate space, the frequent personal contacts may be cause for nervous irritation and may be detrimental to good mental health. Privacy applies to sleeping and dressing rooms and to toilets, in particular.

The lack of privacy may interfere with the proper development of children. In a crowded household a child of school age may have no place to study uninterruptedly, so that it is very easy for him or her to give up the effort and hence the child may soon be in arrears in schooling. Also crowded housing may make it impossible for a parent to control the activities of children and may result in giving up the effort (Lemkau, 1970).

There has been a great deal of discussion on issues of sleeping arrangements as determinants in the psychosexual development of children. Children should not sleep in the same room as their parents. This exposure, when they are at a critical age, confuses them in regard to parental interrelationships. In like manner, mothers sleeping with sons and fathers sleeping with daughters beyond the years of infancy appears to affect personality development through the appearance of distorted parent-child relationships. Brothers and sisters sleeping in the same bed or the same room beyond the earliest years is said to lead to harmful sexual stimulation and experimentation.

Another reason for the provision of adequate privacy stems from the belief of most authorities that people have needs both to be sociable and needs to withdraw from groups from time to time. Crowded living space makes the latter impossible. In a longitudinal study of the effects of housing on morbidity and mental health, one of the observations was a trend toward less leaving home by husbands after resettlement in improved housing with adequate space (Wilner *et al.*, 1962). The act of leaving the home when the family was housed in crowded, substandard conditions was interpreted as a need for anonymity in a crowd – a separateness not possible in the house.

Another fundamental psychological need is the provision of possibilities of aesthetic satisfaction in the home and its surroundings (Committee on the Hygiene of Housing, 1939). It is difficult to quantify this need, but in most people there is a basic, innate desire for beauty and a need to express themselves in an aesthetic manner. The exterior of dwellings should be harmonious with the setting and the interior should provide for a degree of freedom in aesthetic self-expression. This is contrary to the institutional use of a single colour for all interior walls of some residential housing. Some studies of hospitals and schools have shown the effect of colour on attitude and behaviour of people.

The provision of opportunities for a normal family life is another fundamental psychological need of healthful housing (Committee on the Hygiene of Housing, 1939). To meet this need, healthful housing should provide a living-room which can accommodate at one time all of the members of the family, plus reasonable space elsewhere for withdrawal when desired. In some homes the living-room may be combined with the eating area and/or the kitchen. The provisions in the living-room should include those needed for a variety of activities such as reading, listening to music, playing games and entertaining friends and visitors.

If juvenile delinquency is considered a form or syndrome of psychological maladjustment, several studies have noted an association between rates of juvenile delinquency and substandard housing (Faris, 1951; Federal Emergency Administration of Public Works, Housing Division, 1936). One of the factors cited in some of these studies was that teenage children and young adults who had no place within a dwelling unit to spend their leisure time as they wished sought companionship on the street corners and eventually became involved in delinquent acts.

14.6
Fundamental physiological requirements

General concepts

A healthful house should not only provide an environment which affords protection against infections and accidental injuries, but also fulfils basic physiological requirements of the human body. The Committee on the Hygiene of Housing, American Public Health Association (1939), has identified eight basic physiological requirements which should be met in a healthful dwelling as follows:

1. a thermal environment which will avoid undue heat loss from the human body;
2. a thermal environment which will permit adequate heat loss from the human body;
3. provision of an atmosphere of reasonable chemical purity;
4. adequate daylight illumination without glare;
5. adequate artificial illumination without glare;
6. provision for the admission of direct sunlight into one or more rooms of each dwelling unit;
7. protection against excessive noise; and
8. adequate space for exercise and for the play of children.

In essence, these basic physiological requirements pertain largely to heating, ventilation, lighting and noise control.

Heating

Of the many important aspects of healthful housing, probably none is more important in the temperate climate zone than the need to provide and maintain a thermal microclimate within a dwelling unit that not only fulfils all of the basic physiological requirements of the occupants, but also provides for thermal comfort, especially for the elderly, the very young and those persons who may be handicapped or ill (see Chapter 6).

Heat may be exchanged between the occupants of a dwelling and the housing environment by four physical processes as follows:

1. conduction;
2. convection;

3. radiation;
4. liquid-vapour transformation.

These four processes are quantified by the following parameters:

1. the ambient air temperature;
2. the temperature of the floor, walls, ceilings and the furnishings of the dwelling (radiant temperature);
3. the moisture content of the air (relative humidity); and
4. the movement and exchange of air within the dwelling unit.

Much research has been conducted that deals with human physiological responses to variations of the above factors. The effects of heat, cold, clothing and shelter upon humans also have been researched (Lee, 1964). The American Society of Heating, Refrigerating and Air-Conditioning Engineers (ASHRAE) has developed ranges of operative temperatures and relative humidities for persons clothed in typical summer and winter clothing and involved in sedentary activity (American Society of Heating, Refrigerating and Air-Conditioning Engineers, 1981). For all practicable purposes, the operative temperature is the mean of the ambient temperature and the radiant temperature. In general, thermal comfort is enjoyed by most occupants involved in sedentary activity as follows:

	Winter	*Summer*
Operative Temperature	69–75°F(20.5–24°C)	73–79°F(22.5–26°C)
Relative humidity	30%–70%	30%–60%

The 'summer comfort zone' may be extended to an operative temperature of 82°F if there is an air movement of about 30 inches per second.

Under winter conditions, in order to obtain the required operative temperatures without having excessively high ambient temperatures, the exterior walls, floors and ceilings need to be well insulated, windows need to be tight-fitting or to be glazed with thermopane glass, and all exterior doors need to have efficient storm doors.

Health effects of low indoor temperature

The adverse influence of low indoor temperatures of the health of occupants of dwellings may be observed and measured in all age-groups; however, those at greatest risk are infants, the disabled, the sick and the elderly (World Health Organization Regional Office for Europe, 1987). Epidemiological studies have shown a significant correlation between the incidence of acute respiratory illnesses among the elderly (60 years or more of age) and the average indoor temperature. The effects of the indoor climate upon the health of occupiers is described in detail in Chapter 6.

Ventilation

The term 'ventilation' has two different meanings when used in conjunction with indoor air quality. The double meaning may cause some misunderstanding. One meaning of the word concerns the provision of fresh outdoor air to occupied areas of a building, and the other meaning pertains to the circulation of air within a dwelling but does not necessarily include the addition of any fresh air. The ventilation of a healthful dwelling should include the provision of fresh outdoor air, as well as the movement of air within the structure.

In almost every building, there is some ventilation which occurs by infiltration of outdoor air through the building shell – e.g. around doors and windows and through cracks and crevices. The rate of infiltration is dependent upon several factors, including the velocity and direction of the wind, and the temperature differential between the air interior of the building and the outdoor air. In general, energy conservation moves have tended to reduce infiltration. Therefore ventilation by other means has taken on increased importance as pertains to the health and comfort of the occupants.

In order to replenish the oxygen utilized by the occupants of dwellings, to prevent an accumulation of carbon dioxide and other common air pollutants and to remove odours, a considerable number of standards have been promulgated by various agencies and organizations. In general there should be at least 0.5 an air change per hour. If this is not accomplished by infiltration, mechanical means should be used. The American Society of Heating, Refrigerating and Air-Conditioning Engineers (1981a) recommends the following minimum ventilation rates expressed as cubic feet per minute per room:

Residential area	Minimum ventilation rate
General living areas	10
Bedrooms	10
Kitchens	100
Bathrooms	50
All other rooms	10

As a general ventilation plan, it is often recommended that the flow of air should be from bedrooms through dining-rooms, halls, etc. to kitchens and bath and toilet rooms from which the air should be exhausted to the outdoors.

Lighting

A healthful house is one in which the occupants are provided with the possibility of obtaining maximum benefit from both natural and artificial lighting without excess glare, to the extent which they desire or need to perform various household and leisure activities. During the day, dwellings or at least the principal rooms of dwellings, should be illuminated by daylighting. Proper fenestration of a house should permit the admission, control and distribution of daylight into various rooms each day.

The penetration of direct sunlight into dwellings produces favourable psycho-physiologic effects on both thermal comfort and biological activity of humans. Direct sunlight, because of the presence of ultraviolet rays, has some bactericidal effect. Also, since direct sunlight will contain some infra-red rays, there is usually a warming or heating effect which, depending upon other climatological factors, may be highly desirable or undesirable.

Quality of light

The goal of a plan of lighting of a dwelling is to provide sufficient light for the optimal performance of the various tasks that are usually performed in a dwelling. Many factors should be considered such as avoidance of fatigue, economics, possible impairment of vision and health, and the cultural or emotional effects of light. In considering the quantity of daylight to be provided to dwellings located in warm climates, special considerations should be given to the thermal discomfort which may accompany daylight.

Land use regulations (zoning standards) which stipulate set-backs of buildings from property boundaries and other specifications are usually necessary to ensure that some daylight will be available to every dwelling unit. Where possible, it is usually reasonable to require that the sky angle at the lowest window sill of a dwelling be not greater than 45°, which implies that the width of the street, or the courtyard, or the distance to the adjacent buildings is at least equal to the height of those buildings.

At least one window should be provided in all kitchens, living-rooms and bedrooms. It is also desirable that these windows be openable for ventilation. These rooms, plus bathrooms, toilets, hallways and stairways, should be provided with electric light fixtures sufficient to provide the following levels of general illumination without glare:

Area of room	Footcandles of light
Hall and circulation areas	10
Dining areas	10
Living rooms	10
Kitchen	30
Bathrooms	30

Additional supplemental or task lighting should be provided to approximately 50 footcandles for some areas.

Noise control

In many areas, particularly urban areas, there has been a growing concern about the occurrence of loud and/or unwanted sounds, commonly called noise, and their possible adverse health effects upon humans. Many problems are associated with noise in and around dwellings, including interference with conversation and communication, with leisure activities and with sleep. Loud sounds and noise may create stress in some individuals. Unwanted sound, or noise, is one of the more insidious problems facing an industrialized and mechanized society.

In dealing with some aspects of unwanted sound, there is no unanimity of opinion since a sound which is regarded as an intolerable nuisance by one person may be enjoyable to another person. Problems involving noise in dwellings and the residential environment may arise in a wide variety of situations. Therefore many approaches and many factors must be considered in trying to develop a quieter residence and a more healthful acoustical environment.

Effects of noise on humans

At least six specific effects of noise on humans have been identified as follows (World Health Organization, 1980):

1. interference with communication;
2. hearing loss (temporary and permanent);
3. disturbance of sleep;
4. stress;
5. annoyance; and
6. effects on performance.

Various researchers have identified and quantified the above effects.

Controlling noise and quieting dwellings

It is important to realize that noise control is not noise reduction, although many noises in dwellings may be reduced to acceptable levels by a reduction in the sound pressure level at the receiver or receptor end. The common approach to noise control in housing is to reduce the sound pressure level within dwellings at either the source or on the transmission pathway.

Once noise has been created, usually it is difficult to stop its transmission. While noise can be attenuated along the transmission pathway, there is usually still some noise and it may be heard but to a lesser degree. If a noise can be eliminated at the source, there is no transmission pathway and there is no receiver or receptor.

In multi-family dwelling units, a very common source of noise is the activities of the other tenants. Almost any building structure, wall, ceiling, floor, door or window whether made of wood, brick, concrete, steel, etc. when subjected to some disturbance, such as sound pressure waves, will vibrate. Also it will vibrate more readily at certain frequencies, the lowest of which is known as the 'natural frequency' of the structural element. The 'natural frequency' of a party wall in a multi-family dwelling will be influenced by many factors. Usually light-weight panels are more easily set into vibration by sound pressure waves than heavier panel walls, e.g. those made of brick. Architects, engineers and builders should select materials and construction methods which will minimize the transmission of sound from one dwelling unit to another.

In multi-family dwellings it is also desirable to reduce impact noise. To reduce impact sound from being transmitted through the floor of one dwelling unit into another, it may be necessary to provide resilient floor covering (e.g. rubber, cork tiles or carpet).

Sound transmission from one room of a dwelling to another may be the result of airborne sound transmission. In multi-family dwellings sound and noise may be readily transmitted throughout the building by conduits and ducts. For example, in a building with a circulating air heating and/or cooling system to prevent conductive noise, the fan should be isolated on sound absorbing mountings and the intake and outlet ducts should also be isolated. Between the fan and ducting, canvas is an effective and inexpensive method of isolation of sound waves. In such cases, experience has shown that the length of canvas connector should never be less than 12 in (30 cm), and the edges should be firmly and securely fixed.

Some plumbing noises are inevitable and the location of pipes in the walls of kitchens and bathrooms should be given consideration in the planning design of dwelling units. The noise of water running through pipes under pressure may be amplified by some walls, particularly those of light construction. It is preferable not to locate walls that contain plumbing such that they are common with living-rooms, bedrooms and other areas where quiet is desired.

Central heating facilities in multi-family dwellings are a common source of noise, particularly of conductive noises which may be transmitted throughout a structure. The use of sound-absorbing joints and insulation may reduce these noises to acceptable levels.

The sources of many disturbing noises in dwellings are outside the structures and penetrate into the buildings (e.g. traffic areas); this is increasing in intensity and will do so into the foreseeable future. Another source of some noises in some buildings is mechanized industry located near residential areas. Much street and industrial noises are airborne and enter the dwelling through doors and windows. The effect of windows on noise transmission from external sources is as follows:

Window arrangement	Sound level difference dB(A)
Window slightly open	10
Single-paned window – shut	12
Double-paned window or non-openable window	12

Acceptable noise in dwellings

Various studies have resulted in the establishment of recommended permissible maximum sound levels in dwellings. In general, these recommended levels are dependent upon the primary uses of rooms within the dwelling. Often somewhat higher values are permitted if the residential structure is situated in a relatively noisy district.

The following represents a consensus of permissible maximum sound levels in a room in a dwelling according to activity:

Activity in room	Sound pressure level in dB(A)
Sleeping	30
Daytime rest	35
Intellectual work	40
Domestic activities	45

14.7
Creating healthful housing

The creation of healthful housing in the 1990s will be a major task. One of the immediate needs for many countries will be the establishment by legislation of minimum requirements for occupied housing and for the construction of new housing which will reduce overcrowding; ensure the provision of healthful heating, lighting and ventilating of dwellings; reduce injury due to accidents; and provide for the hygienic disposal of wastes. Some national and municipal governments would benefit by the enactment of housing codes similar to the one developed by the American Public Health Association (1986) which is extensively used in the USA.

A special effort should be made to require that some housing units be designed and constructed to meet the special needs of the disabled and the elderly.

Concomitant with the efforts to develop healthful minimum

requirements for the occupancy of existing dwellings and the construction of new housing units is the need for effective and enlightened community planning which would have a major impact on creating healthful residential environments. The need for community water supply, adequate collection and sanitary disposal of solid and liquid wastes, the provision of hygienic recreational areas and of traffic safety are important community measures that will contribute to healthful housing.

Consistent with the goal of the World Health Organization of Health for All by the Year 2000 there should be a concerted effort by governments, agencies and organizations to achieve by the year 2000 opportunities for all persons to live in healthful houses and settlements which provide a healthy and safe environment.

Bibliography

American Public Health Association (1986) *APHA-CDC Recommended Minimum Housing Standards*, APHA, Washington, DC.

American Society of Heating, Refrigerating, and Air-Conditioning Engineers (1981a) *Standards for Ventilation Required for Minimum Acceptable Indoor Air Quality*, ASHRAE Standard ANSI/ASHRAE 62-1981, Atlanta, Ga.

American Society of Heating, Refrigerating, and Air-Conditioning Engineers (1981b) *Thermal Environmental Conditions for Human Occupancy*, ASHRAE Standard ANSI/ASHRAE 55-1981, Atlanta, Ga.

Bacon, A. F. (1916) Tuberculosis and bad housing. *J. Outdoor Life*, 13, 65–9.

Baker, S. (1981) Childhood injuries. *J. Pub. Health Policy*, 5, 235–46.

Baptiste, M. S. and Feck, G. (1980). Preventing tap water burns. *Am. J. Pub. Health*, 70, 727–9.

Beck, M. D., Munoz, J. A. and Scrimshaw, N. S. (1951) Diarrhoeal disease control studies. The relationship of certain environmental factors to the prevalence of Shigella infection. *Am. J. Trop. Med. Hyg.*, 4, 718.

Benjamin, J. E., Ruegsegger, J. W. and Senior, F. A. (1940) The influence of overcrowding on the incidence of pneumonia. *Ohio St. Med. J.*, 36, 1275–81.

Berger, L. R. and Kalishman, S. (1983) Floor furnace burns to children. *Pediatrics*, 71, 97–99.

Blum, B. and Elkin, W. F. (1949) The relationship of housing to the incidence of meningococcus disease in an outbreak in Oak Ridge, Tenn. *Am. J. Pub. Health*, 39, 1571–7.

Britten, R. H. (1942) New light on the relation of housing to health. *Am. J. Pub. Health*, 32, 193–9.

Britten, R. H. and Altman I. (1941) Illness and accidents among persons living under different housing conditions. *Pub. Health Rep.* (Wash), 56, 609–39.

Britten, R. H., Brown, J. E. and Altman, I. (1940) Certain characteristics of urban housing and their relation to illness and accidents. *Millbank Mem. Found. Qrtly*, 18, 91–113.

Committee on the Hygiene of Housing, American Public Health Association (1939) *Basic Principles of Healthful Housing*, APHA, New York.

Dauer, C. C. (1939) Meningococcus meningitis in the district of Columbia. *Amer. J. Pub. Health*, 29, 1140–6.

Dershewitz, R. and Williamson, J. (1977) Prevention of childhood injuries. *Am. J. Pub. Health*, 67, 1143–7.

Faris, R. L., cited in Chapin, F. (1951) Some housing factors related to mental hygiene. *Am. J. Public Health*, 41, 841.

Federal Emergency Administration of Public Works, Housing Division (1936) *The Relationship between Housing and Delinquency*, Research Bulletin No. 1, FEAPW, Washington, DC.

Graves, L. M. and Fletcher, A. H. (1935) Housing problems in a southern city. *Am. J. Pub. Health*, 25, 21–6.

Haddon, W., Jr (1980) Advances in the epidemiology of injuries as a basis for public policy. *Pub. Health Repts*, 95, 411–21.

Herman, S. J. (1929) Congestion and its relation to important social and health problems. *City Health* (Bulletin of Detroit Department of Health), 13, 5–26.

Hollister, A. C., Beck, M. D., Gittelsohn, A. M. and Hemphill, E. C. (1955) Influence of water availability on Shigella prevalence in children of farm labour families. *Am. J. Pub. Health*, 45, 354–62.

Kleevens, J. W. L. (1966) Re-housing and infections by soil transmitted herminths in Singapore. *Singapore Med. J.*, 7, 12–29.

League of Nations Health Organization (1931) *European Conference on Rural Hygiene*, Geneva, Vols I and II.

Lee, D. H. K. (1964) *Heat and Cold Effects and their Control*, Public Health Monograph No. 72, Public Health Service Publication No. 1984, US Government Printing Office, Washington, DC.

Lemkau, P. V. (1965) Prevention in psychiatry. *Am. J. Pub. Health*, 55, 554–60.

Lemkau, P. V. (1970) Position paper on mental health and housing, American Public Health Association, Washington, DC, Mineo.

Lindsay, D. R., Stewart, W. H. and Watt, J. (1953) Diarrhoeal disease control studies, III: effect of fly control on diarrhoeal diseases in an area of moderate morbidity. *Pub. Health Repts*, 68, 361–7.

McCabe, L. J. and Haines, T. W. (1957) Diarrhoeal disease control by improved human excreta disposal. *Pub. Health Rpts*, 72, 921.

McLoughlin, E. and Crawford, F., Jr (1985) Burns. *Pediatric Clinics of North America*, 32.

Mackintosh, J. M. (1952) *Housing and Family Life*, Cassell, London.

National Safety Council (1986) *Accident Facts*, NSC, Chicago, I.

Nelson, J. D., Kusmicz, H. T. and Haltalin, K. C. (1967) Endemic Shigellosis: a study on fifty households. *Am. J. Epidem.*, 86, 683–9.

Neutra, R. and McFarland, R. A. (1972). Accident epidemiology and the design of residential environment. *Human Factors*, 14, 405–20.

Ordway, N. K. (1960) Diarrhoeal disease and its control, *Bull. WHO*, **23**, 73–101.

Rubenstein, A., Boyle, J., Odoroff, C. L. and Kunitz, S. J. (1969) Effect of improved sanitary facilities on infant diarrhoea in a Hopi village. *Pub. Health Rpts*, 84, 1093–7.

Schliessman, D. J., Atchley, F. O., Wilcomb, M. J. and Welch, S. F. (1958) Relation of Environmental Factors to the Occurrence of Enteric Disease in Areas of Eastern Kentucky. *Public Health Monograph No. 54*, US Government, Printing Office, Washington, DC.

Schliessman, D. J. (1959) Diarrhoeal disease and the environment, *Bull. WHO*, 21, 381–6.

Schmitt, R. D. (1955) Housing and Health on Oahu. *Am. J. Pub. Health*, 45, 1538–40.

Spiegel, C. and Lindaman, F. (1977) Children can't fly. *Am. J. Pub. Health*, 67, 1143–7.

Stein, L. (1950) A study of respiratory tuberculosis in relation to housing conditions in Edinburgh; the pre-war period. *B. J. Soc. Med*, 4, 143–69.

Stewart, W. H., McCabe, L. J., Hemphill, E. C. and Decapito, T. (1955) Diarrhoeal disease control studies. IV The relationship of certain environmental factors to the prevalence of Shigella infection. *Am. J. Trop. Med. Hyg.*, 4, 718–24.

Sykes, J. F. J. (1901) *Public Health and Housing*, P. S. King, London.

Thirty-fourth World Health Assembly (1981) Resolution WHA 34.36, Geneva.

The Social Effects of Public Housing, Newark (1944) Housing Authority of the City of Newark.

Tokuhata, G. K. *et al.*, (1974) *Childhood Injuries Associated with Consumer Products*, Academic Press, New York.

United Nations Conference on Human Settlements (1976) Report of HABITAT, Vancouver, 31 May – 11 June 1976 (A/CONF70/15).

Walker, W. F. (1923) Some relation between our health and our environment. *Am. J. Pub. Health*, 13, 897–914.

Watt, J., Hollister, A. C., Beck, M. D. and Hemphill, E. C. (1953) Diarrheal diseases in Fresno County. *Cal. Am. J. Pub. Health*, 43, 728–41.

Watt, J. and Lindsay, D. R. (1948) Diarrhoeal disease control studies. Effect of fly control in a high morbidity area. Pub. Health Rpts., 63, 1319–34.

Weir, J. M., Wasif, I. M., Hassan, F. R., Attia, S. M. and Kadar, M. A. (1953) An evaluation of health and sanitation in Egyptian villages. *J. Egypt Pub. Health Assoc.*, 27, 56.

Wilner, D. M., Walkley, R. P., Pinkerton, T. C. and Tayback, M. (1962) *The Housing Environment and Family Life*, Johns Hopkins University Press, Baltimore, Md.

Wolff, H. L., van Zijl, W. J. and Roy, M. (1969) Houseflies, the availability of water, and diarrheal disease. *Bull. WHO*, 41, 951–9.

World Health Organization (WHO) (1961) *Expert Committee on the Public Health Aspects of Housing: First Report*, World Health Organization Technical Report series No. 225, Geneva.

WHO (1980) *Noise*, Environmental Health Criteria No. 12, WHO, Geneva.

WHO Regional Office for Europe (1985) *Targets For Health For All*, Copenhagen.

WHO Regional Office for Europe (1987) *Health Impact of Low Indoor Temperatures, A report on a WHO meeting*, Environmental Health series No. 16, Copenhagen.

WHO Regional Office for Europe (1990) *Environment and Health: The European Charter and Commentary*, Copenhagen.

15

AN ECOLOGICAL BLUEPRINT FOR HEALTHY HOUSING

RODERICK J. LAWRENCE

15.1

Introduction

Although it is commonly stated that there is a relationship between housing conditions and the health and well-being of residents, there is still no widely shared consensus about the nature of that relationship. None the less, there are some pathological conditions that can be attributed to the quality of dwelling units and their surroundings. For example, it is generally recognized that adequate housing provides protection against exposure to agents and vectors of communicable diseases by ensuring a supply of non-polluted potable water, the disposal of sanitary and solid wastes, adequate drainage of surface water, protection against diseases transmitted from the building structure, non-polluted indoor and outdoor air and facilities for maintaining personal and domestic hygiene, including safe food preparation. In these respects, the performance of built environments in general, and of domestic environments in particular, can be evaluated by examining these kinds of indicators in relation to the health and well-being of the occupants.

Nevertheless, it has become increasingly clear that it is not a simple matter to extract and isolate material housing conditions from other non-physical factors which form an integral part of the life style of the inhabitants, and have an influence on their health and well-being. Inadequate nutrition, for example, and limited access to health services and medical care, have an important role to play. Yet can inadequate nutrition only be considered in terms of socio-economic factors, notably household poverty, or should seasonal variations in the supply of food, and the lack of sanitary facilities for the storage and preparation of food, also be examined? Clearly there are many questions that medical practitioners, social scientists and professional designers can ask about the relationship between human health and well-being, and the design of residential environments.

Despite the contribution of a wide range of studies by Environmental Health Officers, doctors, psychologists, physiologists and housing researchers, recent surveys of the literature on housing and health indicate that little attention has been given to the definition and measurement of housing indicators in order to assess their impacts on human health and well-being. In principle, specific sets of housing and health indicators need to be identified in order to examine the nature of the interrelations between them. Although this complex task is still to be achieved, contemporary research (on the effects of high-rise housing, density, and privacy, for example) shows that it is rare that only one indicator will determine the health and well-being of the inhabitants. Therefore it is inappropriate to isolate these indicators from each other and from the *contextual conditions* in which they occur. None the less, empirical studies of the relationships between housing and health have commonly adopted this kind of approach by examining how one quantifiable indicator of housing conditions in a precise situation (such as the presence of dampness in the building structure, indoor air quality or the floor level above the ground) affects the health and well-being of the inhabitants (Kasl and Harburg, 1975; Jacobs and Stevenson, 1981).

Alternatively, quantifiable measures of the morbidity of resident populations (such as psychological strain) are related to one aspect of the residential environment (such as floor level above the ground in high-rise housing) (e.g. Mitchell 1971). Irrespective of the simplifications inherent in these kinds of approach, the findings of many studies have rarely been replicated in the same or different residential environments, as Churchman and Ginsberg (1984) and Gabe and Williams (1986) have noted. Moreover, recurrent approaches commonly examine the relationship between these isolated variables at only one point in time. Yet there is sufficient evidence to suggest that the aspirations and preferences of people for housing change during the course of the life-cycle (Stokols, 1982); that the health and well-being of people also change; and that the condition of the housing stock varies during the occupation of dwelling units (Hole, 1965).

Beyond the above-mentioned limitations, it is important to challenge those common interpretations of housing and health that examine either the qualitative characteristics of the indoor domestic environment or those characteristics of the outdoor environment, whereas the interrelations between both remain largely unstudied. Yet these interrelations are omnipresent: the nature of their relationship is partly regulated by the performance of the functions of buildings (to be discussed below), as well as the activities of the community and the life style of households. In this respect, comparative research in countries of eastern and western Europe, as well as North and South America, shows that more than half of all non-sleep activities of people between 18 and 64 years of age who are employed occur inside dwellings (Szalai, 1972). Children, the aged and housewives spend even more time indoors. Therefore any shortcomings in the indoor domestic environment may have heavy implications on human health and well-being. None the less, any domestic realm cannot be isolated from the environmental conditions of its site and surroundings. Consequently, housing indicators ought to address both sets of indoor and outdoor indicators across a range of geographical scales.

This introduction has implied that a reorientation and a diversification of studies of housing and health is required. Both theoretical and methodological developments are necessary to formulate and apply a more comprehensive approach. The following paragraphs discuss some theoretical and methodological principles based on a human ecology perspective that can enable this goal to be achieved. We shall then discuss and illustrate how the identification and assessment of housing and health indicators involves the examination of a wide range of quantitative and qualitative factors. Given that this author has no medical training (but professional experience in housing), this contribution will be limited to the development of a checklist of material and non-material housing indicators. This multi-dimensional checklist can be used as a reference source in order to identify those housing indicators related to health and well-being in specific residential environments. The consequences of high-rise housing are examined in order to illustrate how the approach advocated in this chapter can be applied.

15.2
Theoretical principles

During the past three decades, research by social scientists, architectural theorists and building scientists collectively shows that buildings in general, and housing in particular, serve five sets of functions or purposes, which can be considered collectively as a model of building performance (Lawrence, 1987). These functions can be summarized as follows.

First, any building defines and delimits space to shelter human activities by demarcating a private domain from the rest of the world. In this respect, the choice of the location of a building (e.g. overlooking a nature reserve, aligning a busy road or near a power station) ought to account for the quality of outdoor environmental conditions surrounding the building.

Secondly, the building envelope will act as a filter between the interior spaces and the external surroundings. An efficient filter will sustain acoustic, illumination and thermal conditions within prescribed 'ranges of human comfort' that vary between cultures, diverse age-groups in society and have evolved over the course of time. In this respect, indoor climate ought to be explicitly related to the external environmental conditions and the inherent capacity of the building walls, floor and roof to act as an efficient filter, as well as the nature of human activities that occur around and inside the building.

Thirdly, buildings are endowed with meanings. They are symbolic artefacts, not merely with respect to the intentions of the designer and the client, but also in terms of how the public interpret them. From this perspective, the design, the meaning and the use of housing are very different when viewed from the 'bottom up' and from the 'top down' (Abrams, 1964; Turner, 1976). This means that communication between different groups of people is necessary: it may serve as the catalyst for change from imposed solutions that are often inappropriate to processes that incorporate the experience and value of laypeople in meaningful ways.

Fourthly, buildings have environmental and economic implications in terms of the initial use and cost of raw (sometimes non-renewable and polluting) materials, labour and energy, as well as the use of these sets of resources during the whole period of occupation of buildings. From this perspective, adverse indoor thermal environments, for example, should not only be considered by improving the thermal insulation of walls, floors and roofing, but also by assessing the affordability of diverse fuels and equipment for indoor heating and cooling in conjunction with internal human activities.

Finally, buildings have an ecological impact on the biological environment. Plot coverage, building and room densities, and building height and volume, are aspects that influence microclimate; the consumption of resources, and the accumulation of wastes have effects on the health and well-being of people both inside and outdoors.

This multi-functional model of building performance underlines the fundamental principle that housing is a multi-sectorial set of human intentions and processes that can generate a range of built environments having both intended and unintended consequences. In this respect, dwelling units are not just physical shelters, but also the formal means of providing security, of generating employment and household income, as well as the consumption of natural resources and the creation of diverse kinds of waste products.

15.3
Methodological principles

Housing evokes a range of images and concepts commonly related to the material and physical nature of one or more kinds of dwelling unit. None the less, the meaning of 'housing', like the meaning of 'home', varies from person to person, between social groups and across cultures. Houses are commonly accorded an economic value, an exchange value, an aesthetic value and a use value, whereas in addition to these a home is usually given a sentimental and a symbolic value. All these values, as well as domestic roles, routines and rituals, are not simply expressed by individuals; they are acquired, nurtured, transmitted, reinforced or modified by interpersonal communication (for instance, between parents and children, or between members of the same social or professional group).

From this perspective, the interrelations between housing and health are very different when viewed from the legislator's, the public administrator's and the resident's point of view. Trying to understand these viewpoints requires an approach that may be in conflict with arbitrarily defined solutions drawn up and applied by national governments or by international agencies. During this century, the practice of prescribing minimum standards for the quality of a wide range of environmental entities – air, water supply and building materials, for instance – has led to a significant improvement in site planning, building construction and housing design, both in industrialized and developing countries. Yet when these standards are examined in terms of their rationale and objectives, it becomes clear that they have commonly been drawn up with economic, technological and political priorities in mind, whereas the life style, domestic economy, values and well-being of local populations have been largely undervalued or else ignored. A human ecology perspective can correct this practice because it enables the formulation and application of an alternative approach.

Some 2600 years ago, Hippocrates, a Greek physician who taught at a medical school on the island of Cos, maintained that human health and well-being are associated with a desirable state of equilibrium between the human organism and its environmental surroundings. He illustrated this view by describing the living conditions of some populations in Asia and Europe. In order to better understand the health and lifestyles of specific populations, Hippocrates refuted the commonly held beliefs in divine affliction and providence, and instead proposed an ecological perspective. He called for an examination of the impact of microclimatic factors, biological organisms (both animals and plants) and inorganic entities (namely air, soil, sun and water) on human health and well-being. Furthermore, he examined different cultural and societal settings, especially in relation to food, leisure and work in order to explain why people in various regions of the globe have different patterns of disease, health and well-being. In other words, Hippocrates maintained that it was not only the health of individuals or their immediate surroundings that needed to be considered, but also a thorough understanding of their daily circumstances.

Hippocrates' approach is appropriate for an understanding of the interrelations between housing and health. Moreover, it can be complemented and enriched if the architect, the housing administrator or the Public Health Officer ceases to control environmental conditions by formulating standards and imposing regulations and assumes the active role of an 'enabler' who, in contrast to an 'expert', is willing to integrate his or her explicit professional knowledge with the tacit know-how and experiences of lay-people. If this principle is accepted, then public participation is possible.

Public participation in the definition and management of housing and public health is important for at least two reasons. First, only by involving the community is it possible to establish a real understanding of the customs and values of people in their domestic setting. Where participation has been adopted, it often happens that certain basic institutional assumptions about housing and health have been proven incorrect (Turner, 1976; Phillips, 1987). Secondly, public participation can be a useful form of public health education by increasing the awareness of lay-people about the complex range of social, economic and political factors that are involved if we want to improve unhealthy housing and reduce homelessness.

The preceding discussion and examples illustrate that the meaning and use of the housing environment are not intrinsic to a set of physical characteristics, nor the nomenclature applied to rooms and their facilities. This principle, coupled with the preceding discussion, indicates that there are no absolute, static standards that can be translated into optimal indoor and outdoor environmental conditions for human health and well-being. In particular, indoor domestic environments ought to be *responsive* to group and individual differences, as well as to annual, seasonal and diurnal rhythms that not only influence acoustic, illumination and thermal characteristics, but also the physiological condition of the human organism. This perspective challenges the commonly practised normative approach embodied in environmental legislation while underlining the principle of *autonomous environmental control* as a means to adjust or regulate the indoor environment to accommodate specific requirements, such as increasing cross-ventilation in rooms during the summer season, while eliminating drafts during the winter season. The principle of autonomous environmental control acknowledges variability in environmental requirements; it encourages personal or household aspirations and initiatives to be accommodated not only enabling constancy and change in environmental conditions, but also affordability in the use of resources and possible energy savings.

15.4

From principles to policies and implementation

If housing and the built environment are considered too narrowly, then the interrelations between housing, health and well-being may not seem important. In this chapter it has been suggested that an ecological perspective can provide a broad framework for comprehending the range of housing and health indicators that ought to be identified. In this respect, there is little doubt that the physical condition of dwelling units should be examined with respect to forms of housing tenure, household composition and income, the availability and cost of building materials, infrastructure and services, the levels of education and the employment status of residents. In turn, these dimensions of housing environments, domesticity and the health of residents cannot be isolated from their diet, life style, type of employment and the availability of health care.

It is noteworthy that contemporary authorities commonly aim to provide and maintain a healthy environment by the installation or improvement of infrastructure, and by controlling environmental conditions through the enactment and administration of regulations. While there can be little doubt about the pertinence of supplying infrastructure for piped water, sewerage, drainage electricity, and so on, the limitations of prescriptive regulations and absolute standards have been discussed above. In general, a reorientation of contemporary policy formulation and practice is required. A broad outline will now be given.

Contemporary environmental, housing and health regulations are usually *prescriptive principles*. They specify what ought to be achieved. This approach means they decrease the capacity of *autonomous environmental control* that each party can exercise. In contrast, earlier sections of this chapter have stated that environmental control by individuals or households ought to be increased. In order to achieve this goal it is suggested that *proscriptive principles* replace prescriptive ones. Proscriptive principles state what not to achieve or do; they imply that what is not forbidden is permitted, and may engender a wide range of solutions to housing requirements, as many studies of vernacular and self-help housing have shown. These solutions reflect the initiative of the residents and illustrate how environmental control can be implemented, evaluated, modified and improved during the course of time.

In contrast to absolute, environmental standards that prescribe optimal housing conditions, the World Health Organization (1990) has defined the health implications of certain kinds of environmental conditions in terms of three levels of housing environment indicators, the intensity and duration of exposure to these three levels and the vulnerability of particular groups (e.g. children, house-wives, the aged); these three levels are:

1. *'desirable levels* of environmental conditions which promote human health and well-being.'
2. *'permissible levels* of environmental conditions which are not ideal but which are broadly neutral in their impact on health and well-being.'
3. *'incompatible levels* with, if maintained, would adversely affect health and well-being.'

By establishing these levels of housing environment indicators, the task of redefining and reorientating policies and practice is only partially achieved. Other hurdles remain and ought to be overcome.

As Turner (1976) has argued for several years, one major hurdle to overcome in order to implement a reorientation of contemporary policies and practices concerns the perception of decision-makers – legislators and public administrators, in particular. These persons not only have a limited rather than a broad intersectorial interpretation of housing, health and well-being, but they also perceive a healthy environment as one that is controlled by them. Clearly this is not necessarily the case, as the example of high-rise housing presented later confirms.

Bearing in mind this obstacle, and given the premise that more equitable policies and practices are sought, it is suggested that the ecological perspective presented herein provides important cues for the definition of public health policies and programs founded on fundamental principles of:

1. *Preventive medical practice* that helps to overcome recognizable health risks owing to inadequate employment, leisure and residential environments, adverse life style and a lack of health education.
2. *Affordable housing policies* that help to overcome recognizable health risks owing to homelessness, adverse indoor and outdoor environmental conditions in cities and towns, as well as the lack of household and personal control of these conditions.
3. *Ecological environmental policies* that help to identify and overcome the unforeseen and unacceptable consequences of urban and rural development, from the localized scale of harmful substances and conditions on or near specific sites to the impact of

non-sustainable energy policies on global atmospheric conditions.

According to the theoretical and methodological principles outlined above, these three sets of policies ought to be interrelated across traditional academic boundaries and between professional fields of operation. Both the principles and policies have been used in a complementary way to formulate a checklist of housing indicators that can serve as a reference model for applied research on specific residential environments. The checklist will be presented in the following section, and its pertinence will then be illustrated by a critical review of studies of the consequences of high-rise housing.

Checklist of housing indicators

The aim of formulating an analytical checklist of housing indicators is primarily to aid scholars to address the complexity of this subject by using the contributions of diverse interpretations in a complementary way. This multi-dimensional checklist enables scholars to account for all the material and non-material indicators and to explain why some indicators may need to be stressed or put aside with respect to others. From this perspective, researchers and practitioners can situate their approach, forcibly partial rather than inclusive, in terms of this reference model. None the less, an important prerequisite for considering any example as a whole is the definition and comprehension of the component parts, and the reciprocal relations between them. To our knowledge, this conceptual model has not been presented beforehand.

The checklist presented in Table 15.1 not only endeavours to account for all those indicators related to residential environments, but also the reciprocal relations between them. The model comprises eight classes of indicators and their subcomponents. These components have been illustrated in different studies of housing, and by studies of the relationships between housing and health in particular. However, it was noted that few authors considered all classes of indicators simultaneously and none examined the reciprocal relations between them. It is important to note that this checklist is presented as a conceptual reference model for future studies.

Table 15.1 Checklist

(1) Architecture and urban design

Dwelling unit	Type of dwelling (e.g. house or flat); area and volume of dwelling units; potential household density; organization of internal spaces; polyvalence of uses; thermal and acoustic insulation; internal air quality; ventilation; degree of humidity in building structure; sanitary facilities; hygienic storage of food
Residential building	Type of building; number of dwellings; kinds of construction materials and finishes; aesthetics; transmission of internal and external noise; thermal insulation and ventilation; building density; site location; site characteristics concerning drainage, air quality and noise; indoor–outdoor relations
Neighbourhood characteristics	Access to public and private services and facilities; sanitary and solid waste disposal; site drainage; safe water supply; air pollution; noise; neighbourhood density

(2) Housing administration

Housing allocations policy	Choice of building types, house types and tenure; contributions of private and public housing markets; government housing subsidies
Housing maintenance	Ease of maintaining the building and external spaces; efficiency of housing management; efficiency of maintenance works
Building costs	Initial construction costs; maintenance costs; running costs including energy consumption; renovation costs
Financing of housing	Private ownership; private rental; cooperative ownership; public ownership and rental; housing subsidies

(3) Societal factors

	Historical social values and contemporary social values related to housing; evolution of comforts and conveniences; development of domestic technology and social customs related to household life; aspirations and needs of specific groups (e.g. children); leisure activities; delinquency and vandalism

Table 15.1 Continued

(4) Household demography

Composition of population; birth and mortality rates; structure, size and composition of households; male and female domestic roles; parent and child domestic roles

(5) External and internal environmental conditions

External air pollution; noise; sunlight; ventilation; internal pollution due to human activities, construction materials and finishes; stress and illness due to design of residential buildings (e.g. height, lack of sunlight) and use of dwelling units (e.g. overcrowding)

(6) Ergonomics and safety

Hygienic services; food storage and preparation facilities; design of domestic fittings and equipment; domestic accidents, and special needs of residents (e.g. aged, handicapped and others)

(7) Individual human factors

Perception and appraisal of residential environment	Type, size and composition of individual buildings, specific dwelling units and specific rooms
Security	Sense of security inside and around the dwelling units; sense of isolation from neighbours; accessibility and visibility of dwelling unit from street. Incidence of natural disasters (e.g. flooding, earthquakes)
Privacy	Visual and aural privacy from street, between adjacent households and between members of each household; definition of personal space
Personal characteristics of residents	State of life-cycle; residential biography; aspirations and goals of each person; well-being, degree of satisfaction with employment, state of health and family relationships

(8) Residential mobility and well-being

Housing choice; vacancies in housing stock within household budget and easy access to employment; varied composition of housing stock corresponding to varied size and composition of households

An analysis of 200 publications, in English and French, enables us to identify eight classes of indicators which are pertinent to an analysis of the relationships between health and housing. Each of these classes includes one or more indicators and their subcomponents as these are elaborated in Table 15.1; these classes of indicators concern:

1. Architecture and urban design.
2. Housing administration.
3. Societal factors.
4. Household demography.
5. External and internal environmental conditions.
6. Ergonomics and safety.
7. Individual human factors.
8. Residential mobility and choice.

Although there are many studies from diverse conventional academic disciplines or sectorial professional practice that examine one or more of these classes of indicators, it has not been commonplace to apply a multidisciplinary and an intersectorial approach founded on a holistic and an integrative perspective (Lawrence, 1987). Yet the complexity of the subject on the one hand and the non-replication of the results of many studies on the other hand, suggests that both theoretical and methodological development of this kind is necessary. This stance can be illustrated by a critique of studies of the effects of high-rise housing on the health and well-being of residents.

15.5
The consequences of high-rise housing

From 1945 land use and housing policies were enacted in many countries around the world to enable urban renewal, especially the new construction and postwar reconstruction of very great numbers of public and private dwelling units, including a large proportion of high-rise housing. The history of the policies and practices related to high-rise residential buildings, as well as their consequences, have been examined in recent years. In general, although architects, town planners, politicians and members of the construction industry heralded the creation of 'model environments' including 'model homes' (Ravetz, 1974, 1980), recent studies suggest that the distinctive form of high-rise housing estates has provoked several unintended consequences which are at odds with the rationale for promoting urban renewal, housing standards and traditional applications of cost-benefit analysis. In turn, these consequences reflect the widening gap between housing ideals and the reality of domestic life. In sum, there is a growing amount of evidence which confirms that the policy of constructing high-rise housing was counterproductive for a number of reasons, which can briefly be illustrated with respect to national housing policies and practice in Britain:

1. Although urban renewal was justified in terms of new housing, slum-dwellers were commonly rehoused in similar kinds of accommodation or high-rise flats in urban locations rather than congenial suburban housing estates.
2. High-rise housing is a more costly form of residential accommodation than dwelling units in buildings of less than five storeys.
3. From 1956 the national government's housing subsidy was tied to storey height, providing a strong incentive to construct residential buildings above six storeys, so much so that during the following decade high-rise housing was concentrated in the most dense urban areas of Britain.
4. The development of high-rise housing cannot be divorced from an architectural ideology which upheld that this kind of accommodation was appropriate for a modern technological era, and that it was socially responsible and just.
5. The technology for building high-rise housing existed prior to the proliferation of this kind of housing, so that advances in construction technology cannot be interpreted as determining or strongly influencing the adoption of this building form.
6. High-rise housing was predominantly built by a limited number of large (national) construction companies, rather than smaller (local) firms, and constituted a higher proportion of industrialized building techniques than other kinds of public housing.

These findings are founded on research and case studies by Andrews (1979), Darke (1984a, 1984b, 1984c), Dunleavy (1981), Ravetz (1974, 1980) and others, which have examined the merits and limitations of high-rise housing in relation to the discourse of politicians, design professionals, members of the construction industry and a very limited number of community pressure groups. Collectively, these case studies show that local debate about housing issues was rare, and that the adoption of high-rise residential buildings in different cities and regions of Britain followed national trends and housing policies rather than local democratic decision-making. Indeed, Dunleavy's (1981) research underlines that, in each of the three localities he studied, there was no systematic analysis of housing demand, no survey of the existing housing stock or land available for new development, and no formal participatory framework for community involvement in decision-making. Dunleavy suggests that postwar housing policies envisaged high-rise housing as 'a technological short cut to social change': faced with a shortage of dwelling units, 'high-rise and mass housing solutions [were] introduced and promoted as technological shortcuts. They appeared to provide the means of cutting the Gordian knot of . . . conflicting social and institutional pressures confining the public housing programme in a vicious circle of solutions and problem intensification' (p. 102).

The euphoria related to the ability of high-rise housing to meet acute housing shortages as quickly as possible, by using a minimal acreage of land and yield-cost benefits, was eroded by the mid-1960s. The shift of national government housing subsidies in 1967 was a direct result of this change. Although the plausibility of high-rise housing as 'a technological shortcut to social change' has been invalidated, Dunleavy suggests that the full implications of postwar housing policy are far more harmful. Although high-rise housing has not been built by local authorities during the past decade, the aftermath suggests that this kind of housing is omnipresent; there are continual management and maintenance problems related to this kind of housing; the defects of this housing are used as an argument against municipal housing programmes *per se*, and in favour of government policies which encourage home ownership. Last, but not least, the consequences of this kind of housing are counterproductive if these are examined in terms of the confluence of effects on the health and well-being of the residents.

High-rise housing, health and well-being

There are several studies of the design and use of high-rise housing, and the attitudes, behaviour and well-being of the residents: Adams and Conway (1975); Andrews (1979); Churchman and Ginsberg (1984); Fanning (1967); Francescata *et al.* (1979); Gillis (1977); Hope

(1986); Jacobs and Stevenson (1981); Jephcott (1971); Michelson (1977) and Mitchell (1971). These studies have commonly focused on the influence of specific features of the residential environment (such as floor level above the ground in residential buildings) on psychological strain (due to enforced interaction with neighbours, or isolation from them, for example). Studies including those by Fanning (1967) and Mitchell (1971) found that physical ailments and psychological problems are related to housing type (that is, detached houses compared with flatted dwellings), and that psychological strain among residents varies directly with the floor level on which the dwelling unit is located. It is noteworthy that this research has been completed in different countries which have diverse housing standards and no shared domestic culture. Moreover, the studies examined only one or two indicators of the housing conditions of the inhabitants, while the majority of the classes of variables presented above are not included, as Jacobs and Stevenson (1981) have underlined. Bearing in mind these limitations, this chapter requests and outlines a more comprehensive approach. It is suggested that the formulation and application of this approach can be founded on the human ecology perspective summarized earlier if it is applied to examine the interrelations between housing and health indicators in precise situations.

Towards a comprehensive approach

In their studies of high-rise housing in Israel, Churchman and Ginsberg (1984) compare the images and experience of residents in buildings of different heights (ranging between 4, 8, 12, and 16 storeys), with the findings of a limited number of similar studies completed in other countries.

Churchman and Ginsberg examined the following sets of variables:

1. The personal characteristics of the respondents (including demographic and socio- economic variables and their residential biography), which are incorporated in classes 4, 7and 8 of the checklist presented above.
2. The physical features of a sample of extant residential environments and respondents' appraisal of the maintenance and cleanli-

ness of collective areas, which are incorporated in classes 1, 2 and 6 of the checklist.
3. The resident's perception or images of the residential environment, which are incorporated in classes 5 and 7 of the checklist.
4. The appraisal of the residential environment by the occupants.
5. Their degree of satisfaction with that environment, and the reported (rather than the observed) behaviour of the respondents, which are incorporated in classes 2, 3 and 6 of the checklist.

Following the analysis of structured interviews with 344 women, Churchman and Ginsberg (1984) conclude that 'the image shared by the residents of high-rise housing is influenced by their own experience'. Furthermore, although there are apparently no important differences between the images of the occupants of buildings of different heights, 'it is likely that the residents' image is related to the height at which they themselves live rather than to the height of buildings'.

The findings of the study by Churchman and Ginsberg underline that:

1. There is a general consensus among the respondents living in high-rise housing about only two of those disadvantages of building height that have been tabled by several authors; these are a dependency on elevators and fear of children falling from windows. Both these disadvantages are related to the design of high-rise housing, but the second will vary with the demographic structure of households.
2. Concurrently, additional advantages to those listed by other authors were noted, including the view from upper storeys and the possibility of avoiding contact with others. These results not only illustrate a positive correlation between respondents living on the higher floors and the advantages of building height, but they also 'reflect a pattern of relationship between experience and image', which relate to the design and use of this kind of residential environment.

The disadvantages of anonymity and crowding in collective areas, which have been mentioned in several studies were examined by Churchman and Ginsberg (1984), who found that as the residential building increases in height it is more likely that the respondents encounter people, *per se*, and strangers, in particular. However, there is no direct relationship between these variables. Furthermore, there is no variation with respect to age, education or the employment status of women outside the home, whereas there is an important relationship with length of residence and the age of children. Apparently, as the length of tenure increases, the likelihood of encounters with strangers decreases, and respondents with children under 12 years of age are less likely than those with adolescents to encounter strangers. These findings contrast with the number and kind of relations with neighbours, which appear to be independent of building height, length of residence or the employed status of the respondents.

Previous studies in several countries indicate that problems associated with high-rise housing concern the welfare of young children and their opportunity for outdoor recreation: Department of the Environment (1972); Jephcott (1971); Stevenson, Martin and O'Neill (1967). The study of Churchman and Ginsberg (1984) illustrates that the clearest differences between the respondents relates to their status as parents of children under 6 years of age. Problems related to outdoor play and fear of falling out of windows were expressed more frequently by respondents with young children. Although the authors found that nearly all children over 6 years of age are permitted to play outdoors unaccompanied by a parent, the nature of this liberty and its progression with age is not related to the distance above the ground on which they live, but it does have some bearing on the presence of older children in the family.

At a more general level, Churchman and Ginsberg found that the residents' satisfaction with their housing was not directly related to building height, although the respondents living in low-rise buildings had a stronger preference for their extant residence than those respondents living in high-rise buildings. The satisfaction of the residents can be related to feelings of crowding and neighbour relations. This finding suggests that the number of households per elevator – a precise design feature of this type of housing – is a variable that ought to be examined systematically in the future. Moreover, the stage in the life-cycle was an important variable: those respondents with young children who lived in high-rise apartments had a relatively strong preference for lower residential buildings and had stronger intentions to move than those respondents living in low-rise buildings. These results illustrate the relevance of a temporal perspective for the study of the classes of housing indicators tabled earlier in this chapter.

The differences between the generalized results of many studies

of the benefits and problems of high-rise housing and those presented by Churchman and Ginsberg (1984) are significant. A comparison of these studies reveals the pertinence of a wide range
of housing indicators that are contextually defined. Therefore, as
Churchman and Ginsberg note:

> one critical question which should be systematically addressed is
> whether the problems identified are due to the unique attributes of
> high-rise buildings or to attributes and factors such as self-selection,
> social class, stage in the life-cycle, building scale and the particular
> design solution, or to the interaction among some or all of these
> attributes . . . [Moreover] it is important to examine whether problems
> (or advantages) of high-rise housing are cross-cultural, or are related to
> the specific physical, social and cultural context of the countries stud-
> ied. (p. 28)

15.6
Conclusion

The studies of high-rise housing published by Churchman and
Ginsberg (1984) illustrate the need for a comprehensive approach
which explores the reciprocal relations between a range of physical
and non-material indicators that define, and are defined by, the
residential environment in which they occur. If this kind of
approach is to be explicitly concerned with the interrelations
between housing and health (which was not the objective of Churchman and Ginsberg), then their approach ought to be enlarged to
identify and monitor the various costs and benefits of specific types
of housing in relation to the health and well-being of various groups
of residents. For example, high-rise housing is not only distinctive
in terms of building height, but also with respect to an increase in
surface area, in general, and in relation to the depth of dwelling
units between building façades with fenestration. This trend in
housing construction has meant that an increasing proportion of
the habitable spaces in high-rise housing is further removed from
daylight and natural ventilation when compared with traditional
types of housing. Furthermore, a large proportion of dwelling units
constructed since 1945 in multi-storey buildings include toxic building materials (e.g. asbestos-based materials, formaldehyde
adhesives, lead-based paints and radon emissions). Moreover,there
is inadequate acoustic insulation between dwellings in the same

building, as well as between the interior and the exterior. Last, but not least, external walls commonly have inadequate thermal insulation, so that dwelling units are not only hard to heat with an economic supply of energy, but the development of condensation and dampness is encouraged owing to the lack of adequate cross-ventilation.

Given this legacy of contemporary high-rise housing, is it any wonder that respiratory illnesses and allergies have become a primary cause of morbidity and mortality in some European countries? Furthermore, now (or formerly unknown) diseases such as Legionnaires' disease have been identified. Room humidifiers, air ventilation systems and cooling towers, as well as hot and cold water supply ducts, have been found to nurture *legionellae* bacteria and transmit them through the indoor environment, or discharge them into the immediate vicinity of the building. An ecological perspective raises some fundamental issues. We could begin by asking why the water supply has become prone to bacteria; or ask whether it is necessary to install mechanical ventilation and air conditioning systems in high-rise housing when it might be simpler to avoid constructing internal rooms that are devoid of both daylight and natural ventilation. Are there not alternative principles and practices for building construction and housing design, even when high density housing is unavoidable? Clearly a reorientation of policies and practices is required.

All land uses, including housing construction of diverse kinds, generate costs and benefits which ought to be identified in relation to qualitative and quantitative criteria over short and long periods of time. The studies of high-rise housing presented above indicate that the calculation and monitoring of costs and benefits related to housing, health and well-being is a fundamental, controversial task that should be assumed by communities, including their governments, rather than one or more groups of professionals. None the less, Environmental Health Officers, medical practitioners, architects and community groups can make an important contribution to the accounting and monitoring of costs and benefits. Subsequently, alternative policies and practices for housing can be formulated and applied using the principles and policies outlined earlier. Then, and only then, can informed decisions be taken democratically, costs and benefits assigned, and negative impacts reduced. Unfortunately, the majority of housing built during this century, and especially since the Second World War, did not benefit from this kind of approach, and the legacy for current and future generations is a grim one.

Housing and health are complex subjects of inquiry. There is little doubt that the formulation and evaluation of a comprehensive list of housing and health indicators is not a simple task, and that studies of the interrelations between these indicators ought to adopt a holistic conceptual framework and an integrative research method. This contribution has argued that a human ecology perspective can provide the necessary cues for the formulation of this kind of framework and the application of this kind of approach. None the less, academic and professional advances alone are not sufficient. This chapter has argued that public participation in the definition and management of housing and public health is necessary for at least two reasons. First, only by involving the community is it possible to establish a real understanding of the customs and values of people in their domestic setting. Where participation has been adopted, it often happens that certain basic institutional assumptions about housing and health have been proven incorrect. Secondly, public participation can be a useful form of public health education by increasing the awareness of lay-people about the complex range of social, economic and political factors that are involved in order to improve unhealthy housing and reduce homelessness. Last, but not least, although housing policies and public health programmes rarely figure in the manifestos of contemporary governments or political parties, greater public awareness of the issues at stake can lead to a change of priorities. Until then, it is not surprising that there are many indications (including new human illnesses, increasing homelessness and a declining quality of housing and human settlements in many countries) that a fundamental change in human values and behaviour is necessary. This change can be promoted by a much better dissemination of knowledge, know-how and experience between professionals and lay-people, and between the formal and informal sectors. The current worsening situation in many cities of both industrialized and developing countries must be seen as a challenge to Environmental Health Officers, planners and politicians because housing and health are fundamental anthropological concepts, as well as basic human rights.

Bibliography

Abrams, C. (1964) *Man's Struggle for Shelter in an Urbanizing World*, MIT Press, Cambridge, Mass.

Adams, B. and Conway, J. (1975) *The Social Effects of Living off the Ground*, Department of the Environment, London.

Andrews, C. (1979) *Tenants and Town Hall*, HMSO, London.

Churchman, A. and Ginsberg, Y. (1984) The image and experience of high-rise housing in Israel. *J. Environ. Psychol.*, 4, 27–41.

Darke, J. (1984a) Architects and user requirements in public sector housing, 1: architects' assumptions about the user. *Environment and Planning B*, 11, 389–404.

Darke, J. (1984b) Architects and user requirements in public sector housing, 2: the sources of architects' assumptions. *Environment and Planning B*, 11, 405–16.

Darke, J. (1984c) Architects and user requirements in public sector housing, 3: towards an adequate understanding of user requirements in housing. *Environment and Planning B*, 11, 417–33.

Department of the Environment (DoE) (1972) *The Estate Outside the Dwelling*, HMSO, London.

Dunleavy, P. (1981) *The Politics of Mass Housing in Britain, 1945–1975*, Clarendon Press, Oxford.

Fanning, D. (1967) Families in flats. *BMJ*, 18, 382–6.

Francescata, G., Weidemann, S., Anderson, J. and Chenoweth, R. (1979) *Residents' Satisfaction in HUD Assisted Housing Design and Management Factors*, US Department of Housing, Washington, DC.

Gabe, J. and Williams, P. (1986) Is space bad for health? The relationship between crowding in the home and emotional distress in women. *Soc. Health Illness*, 8, 351–71.

Gillis, A. (1977) High-rise housing and psychological strain. *J. Health Social Behaviour*, 18, 418–31.

Hole, V. (1965) Housing standards and social trends. *Urban Studies*, 2, 137–46.

Hope, T. (1986) Crime, community and environment. *J. Environ. Psychol.*, 6, 65–78.

Jacobs, M. and Stevenson, G. (1981) Health and housing: a historical examination of alternative perspectives. *Int. J. Health Services*, 1, 105–22.

Jephcott, P. (1971) *Home in High Flats*, Oliver and Boyd, Edinburgh.

Kasl, S. and Harburg, E. (1975) Mental health and urban environment: some doubts and second thoughts. *J. Health Soc. Behav.*, 16, 268–82.

Lawrence, R. (1987) *Housing, Dwellings and Homes: Design Theory, Research and Practice*, Wiley, Chichester.

Michelson, W. (1977) *Environmental Choice, Human Behavior and Residential Satisfaction*, Oxford University Press, New York.

Mitchell, R. (1971) Some social implications of high density housing. *Am. Sociol. Rev.*, 36, 18–29.

Phillips, S. (1987) Urban health – on the agenda at last? *Planner*, 73, November, 15–18.

Ravetz, A. (1974) *Model Estate: Planned Housing at Quarry Hill, Leeds*, Croom Helm, London.

Ravetz, A. (1980) *Remaking Cities: Contradictions of the Recent Urban Environment*, Croom Helm, London.

Stevenson, A., Martin, E. and O'Neill, J. (1967) *High Living: A Study of Life in Flats*, Melbourne University Press, Melbourne.

Stokols, D. (1982) Environmental psychology: a coming of age, in: Kraut, A. (ed) *The G. Stanley Hall Lecture Series*, American Psychological Association, Washington, DC, Vol. 2, pp. 155–205.

Szalai, A. (1972) *The Uses of Time*, Mouton, The Hague.

Turner, J. (1976) *Housing by People: Towards Autonomy in Building Environments*, Marion Boyars, London.

World Health Organization (WHO) (1990) *Indoor Environment: Health Aspects of Air Quality, Thermal Environment, Light and Noise*, WHO/EHE/RUD/90.2, WHO, Geneva.

16

THE ENVIRONMENTAL ASSESSMENT OF NEW HOUSES

GARY J. RAW AND

JOSEPHINE J. PRIOR

16.1

Introduction

The words 'unhealthy housing' tend to provoke an image of old, ill-maintained homes, but there are important issues to be addressed in relation to new homes. New homes, like any new buildings, have an impact on the global environment, the local environment, use of natural resources and the indoor environment. This has health implications not only for the future (e.g. the possible effects of depletion of the ozone layer), but also for the more immediate present and relating to the environment in which we now live. This chapter describes an assessment method developed by the Building Research Establishment to promote the design of new homes which are more 'environmentally friendly', and concentrates on those issues which have the greatest immediate implications for health.

16.2

Buildings and environmental issues

Environmental issues are becoming increasingly important, and there is an associated increase in public awareness. There is generally less awareness of the contribution that good building design can make to reducing pollution and improving the environment. The environmental issues in relation to buildings can be classed as:

1. *Impact of buildings on global atmospheric pollution:* through, for example, the 'greenhouse effect'; the use of energy for buildings is responsible for half the UK's annual production of 'greenhouse gases', two-thirds of this from housing (Shorrock and Henderson, 1990).
2. *Impact of buildings on the local outdoor environment and depletion of resources:* for example, aspects of local ecology such as the variety or rarity of wildlife and the use of limited natural resources for building.
3. *Influence of buildings on the health, comfort and safety of occupants:* through the effects of, for example, indoor pollution; since the highest concentrations of most airborne pollutants are found in indoor environments and the adult population of Europe and America spends 90% of its time indoors (Moschandreas, 1981) indoor pollutants have great potential to affect health.

In addition to the effects of buildings on the environment, there is the possibility of changes in the environment having an impact on buildings, for example: greater demands for domestic air conditioning if average temperatures rise sufficiently; increased erosion of porous stone due to acid rain; increased risk arising from higher wind speeds, such as wind-driven rain penetrating walls or inadequate building details and, with sufficient increases in temperature, the possibility of an increase in the threat posed by public hygiene pests such as malaria-carrying mosquitoes and verminous rats, and structural pests such as termites and house longhorn beetle.

16.3

The basis of BREEAM for new homes

The Building Research Establishment Environmental Assessment Method (BREEAM) seeks to minimize the adverse effects of new buildings on the global and local environment while promoting a healthy indoor environment; its approach is to:

1. raise awareness of the very important role buildings play in

global warming through the greenhouse effect, in the production of acid rain and the depletion of the ozone layer;

2. set targets and standards, independently assessed, so that false claims of environmental friendliness can be avoided;

3. provide a means for builders to design, and home buyers to recognize, environmentally better buildings, and so stimulate the market for them.

There are several versions of BREEAM in existence or in preparation. The version described here (Prior *et al.*, 1991) is for assessing designs of new single-household dwellings, including sheltered accommodation which has limited communal facilities.

Buildings have a long life which runs into decades and sometimes centuries, so decisions made at the design stage will have long-term effects on the environment. Furthermore, it is easier, less expensive and less likely to create waste if improvements to buildings are made at the design stage rather than after construction; BREEAM/New Homes therefore applies to homes at the design stage. It is based on a review to determine which environmental issues should be addressed, how buildings affect these issues and how building location, design and construction can be altered to reduce adverse environmental effects.

The assessment takes into account building materials, products and processes in which regulated use or control will benefit the environment. The issues currently addressed by BREEAM/New Homes are described in the following sections; in summary they are:

- CO_2 emissions resulting from energy use in the home;
- CFC (chlorofluorocarbons) and HCFC (hydrochlorofluorocarbon) emissions;
- use of natural resources and recycled materials;
- storage of recyclable materials;
- water economy;
- the ecological value of the site;
- ventilation;
- volatile organic pollutants and wood preservatives;
- man-made mineral fibres, asbestos and lead;
- lighting;
- smoke alarms;
- storage of hazardous substances.

There are many issues which are relevant to buildings and the environment which have not been included in the current version of BREEAM/New Homes. The three main reasons for their exclusion are that no clear improvement on current regulations could be defined, or there was insufficient evidence that a problem exists or there was no satisfactory means of assessment at the design stage. The issues included in BREEAM/New Homes are intended to be periodically updated as new information becomes available, and it is likely that the issues currently included could be addressed more rigorously in the future.

It is not rational to assess all the issues on a common scale. The costs to the environment and health of occupants could in theory be assessed in, for example, monetary terms, and it would be possible to devise a weighting scheme. However, such a scheme would be largely arbitrary because of the difficulty in assigning an economic cost to environmental effects as diverse as the health of individuals, ozone depletion and climate change due to the greenhouse effect.

Consequently, each issue is assessed individually for each dwelling design. Credit will be given where satisfactory attention is granted to each of a list of items, as described below. Credit will only be given if the building design has qualities over and above those required by the Building Regulations or other legal or normally accepted standards. Items are included only where there is authoritative evidence that a real risk is involved. Attention is paid to those things which are at the forefront of current knowledge but have yet to become standard aspects of dwelling design.

Assessments will be carried out by independent assessors appointed by BREEAM. The assessor will obtain the necessary information from the builder, calculate the carbon dioxide emission, assess the design against the other issues and award credits where applicable. A provisional report will list the credits achieved and make suggestions for improvement. After further consideration by the designers and re-submission to the assessors, a final certificate will be issued. Builders will make a commitment to achieving in practice the design features for which credit has been awarded, and construction will be subject to the possibility of random inspection.

16.4

Global atmospheric pollution

This heading covers the effects that buildings have on the atmosphere beyond the local region: global warming, ozone depletion and acid rain.

The provision and use of buildings probably has a greater impact on the global environment than any other activity. Environmental damage arises as a result of, for example, energy used during building construction, energy used for heating, cooling and lighting, and the chemicals present in materials used in building services and components. In particular, measures should be taken to maximize energy efficiency and to conserve fuel because:

1. burning any fossil fuel leads to the production of carbon dioxide (CO_2) and so contributes to global warming through the greenhouse effect;
2. sulphur dioxide, nitric oxide and nitrogen dioxide are emitted when fossil fuels (particularly coal and oil) are burnt, thus contributing to acid rain and the problem of damage to the natural environment;
3. burning fossil fuels represents the depletion of a valuable natural resource;
4. an energy-efficient home should be easier to keep warm.

Carbon dioxide production due to energy consumption

Reducing the release of CO_2 into the atmosphere will reduce the rate of global warming. Related benefits will be to reduce acid rain and depletion of fossil fuels. Credit will be given, on a six-point scale, to dwellings which are responsible for the production of less CO_2 per square metre of floor area than would necessarily be achieved by complying with the Building Regulations (DoE/Welsh Office, 1989a).

No credits are given if CO_2 production is greater than 105 kg m^{-2} per year. One credit would be obtained by, for example, a house built to Building Regulations insulation requirements, with space heating supplied by a modern well-controlled gas boiler. Six credits would be awarded for CO_2 production less than 36 kg m^{-2} per year, which could be achieved by a super-insulated house with heating by a gas condensing boiler, a high efficiency heat exchanger for hot water heating, a low temperature heat distribution system and energy efficient lighting.

The energy consumption of a proposed design is calculated using BREDEM, the BRE Domestic Energy Model (Anderson *et al.*, 1985) initially using the National Home Energy Rating Scheme. The energy consumption figures are converted to CO_2 production using the fuel multiplication factors shown in Table 16.1. If the program shows a warning of interstitial condensation (BRE, 1989), the builder's attention will be drawn to which building element is responsible.

Table 16.1 The relationship between primary fuel use and CO_2 emission in the UK (BRE figures: Shorrock and Henderson, 1990, updated to 1991)

Fuel	CO_2 emission (kg per kWh delivered)
Electricity	0.75
Coal	0.31
Fuel Oil	0.28
Gas	0.21

Since BREEAM focuses on the environment, it is appropriate to concentrate on the reduction of the CO_2 production rather than the consumption of delivered energy. Delivered energy does not directly reflect CO_2 production, because CO_2 production per unit of energy delivered depends on the fuel used; CO_2 production is related to the amount and type of fuel consumed. The amount of fuel consumed is, in turn, related to the level of insulation and efficiency of appliances. Homes receiving the highest credit for CO_2 production will have improved insulation, efficient appliances and gas as the predominant fuel.

CFC and HCFC emissions

Reducing the release of chlorofluorcarbon (CFCs) and hydrochlorofluorocarbons (HCFCs) into the atmosphere will reduce the rate of depletion of the ozone layer and of global warming. One credit is given for specifying insulation materials for the structure and the services (e.g. pipes and water tanks) which do not require blowing agents such as CFCs or HCFCs, which have a measurable potential to destroy ozone.

In 1986 buildings accounted for some 7.5% of the annual use in the UK of CFCs (Butler, 1989), mainly as refrigerants in air conditioning systems and as blowing agents for the foamed insulants used in the building fabric. Air conditioning is rarely used in UK homes at present, but may be used more if the predicted consequences of the greenhouse effect are realized. Even then the need for air conditioning could be avoided by appropriate design, for example, the use of thermal mass or external continental-style shutters to control solar gain.

The foamed insulation materials blown with CFCs include rigid polyurethane, extruded expanded polystyrene and phenolic foams; CFCs are used because they contribute to the thermal properties of the product, are non-flammable, stable, cost-effective, have a low toxicity and can result in closed cell structures which are resistant to water penetration. Currently, in many applications in which CFCs and HCFCs have been used, they are being replaced by blowing agents which do not damage the ozone layer. There are also many alternative insulation materials which do not require a blowing agent (e.g. mineral fibres), or which already use a non-CFC, non-HCFC agent as a matter of normal practice.

16.5
Local issues and use of resources

This heading covers those issues which affect the immediate surroundings of a building such as the use of a green-field site for building and of natural resources during construction and after occupation.

Buildings require a great variety of material resources such as wood, brick and stone; in many cases, there is potential for re-using these materials or for obtaining them in other ways which are also less damaging to the environment. Buildings can also be designed in such a way that, when they are occupied, day-to-day consumables such as paper and glass can more easily be recycled and important resources such as water used more carefully.

Beyond the building itself, it is possible to develop a site in such a way that effects on local wildlife and scenery are less damaging (or even enhancing). This can be achieved directly through site selection and layout, but also through consideration of transport requirements.

Natural resources and recycled materials

It is valuable in environmental terms to maximize the use of renewable resources, and to maximize the utility of non-renewable resources for use in the building structure and in fixed furnishings provided by the builder. Five credits are therefore available for specifying materials as follows:

1. timber and timber products for use as an integral part of the building (e.g. structural wood, window frames, architraves) which are entirely either from well-managed, regulated sources or suitable reused timber;
2. timber and timber products for use other than as an integral part of the building (e.g. decorative work or fixed furnishings such as wardrobes and fitted kitchens) which are entirely either from well-managed, regulated sources or suitable reused timber;
3. the majority of material in roof covering to be recycled or reused ('roof covering' means the tiles or slates, not the supporting elements or insulation);
4. the majority of masonry material (e.g. brick, concrete block and stone) in walls to be recycled or reused;
5. suitable uncontaminated demolition materials wherever appropriate in fill and hardcore.

Acceptable material may consist of reused items (e.g. bricks) which make up the majority of the element specified, or items which are composed of a mixture of new and recycled material (the majority recycled). For example, cements, mortars, tiles and aerated concrete blocks can incorporate fly ash or blast-furnace slag. All materials must be fit for their purpose, for example, they must have sufficient strength and frost resistance.

16.6

Storage of recyclable materials

Encouraging recycling of domestic waste on a larger scale will increase the utility of non-renewable resources. One credit is given for providing a set of four containers for household waste, space for them and appropriate access for removal to a collecting point. The size and type of bin would have to vary with the types of collection offered locally, therefore only the number of bins (four) and total capacity (minimum 240 litres) are specified, together with the size and arrangement of the storage space.

Water economy

The purpose of this credit is to reduce wastage of water, which is a valuable resource, and to increase awareness of its importance. One credit is given for specifying either all WCs with a maximum flushing capacity of 6 l or a rain water collection butt.

Water is an increasingly scarce resource with an associated increasing degree of financial and environmental cost from the development of new sources. A well-designed WC can operate effectively at a capacity as low as 3.5 l and 6 l should be achievable without significant risk. The traditional rainwater butt has gone out of favour, due partly to accidents involving butts and the difficulties of avoiding the breeding of midges and other insects. Suitable design would remove these problems.

16.7
Ecological value of site

Wherever buildings are constructed, there is always a risk that, however environmentally friendly the building itself may be, it may represent a threat to local ecology or areas of natural beauty. BREEAM/New Homes gives one credit for minimizing damage to the local ecology, either by selecting a site of low ecological value or by developing a site in a way that protects the most important ecological attributes. Construction of homes does not have to reduce the ecological value of a site; it can be used to enhance the value and a second credit is available for doing this. This part of the assessment has been designed in collaboration with the Royal Society for Nature Conservation – The Wildlife Trusts Partnership.

Derelict sites may include contaminated land providing that adequate measures have been taken to ensure the health and safety of the occupants. The use of landfill sites which are releasing gases should be avoided. Requirements for using contaminated land should be dealt with by the normal health, safety and planning procedures; for example:

1. a thorough analysis of possible soil contaminants should be made as materials such as polychlorinated biphenyls (PCBs) and heavy metals could have health implications;
2. if landfill gas is a potential problem, near to landfill sites, membranes used in conjunction with some form of sub-floor ventilation would be appropriate at some sites to prevent explosions at a later date (measures must also be taken to minimize the risk of subsidence);
3. contaminated land can be cleaned or the contaminants dealt with in a variety of ways using both in-situ and ex-situ methods: techniques to achieve this are under development but some, for example, biological techniques, are currently commercially available;
4. contaminated waste can be excavated and replaced with clean fill (this method does not really solve the problem of contamination, it merely transfers it to another area);
5. advice and guidance are available in DoE Circulars (DoE, 1987, 1989), Building Regulations Approved Documents C (DoE/Welsh Office, 1989b) and Guidance Notes produced by the Interdepartmental Committee on the Redevelopment of Contaminated Land. Site investigation procedures are set out in a BSI Draft for Development (BSI, 1988).

16.8
Local public transport

Encouraging the provision and use of public transport will reduce traffic congestion, air pollution from traffic fumes and fuel consumption. No credit will be given in respect of this issue, but the builder will be asked to provide a description of the available local public transport as part of the assessment.

16.9

Indoor issues

Indoor issues include all those aspects of a building design which have an impact on the health, comfort or safety of the occupants such as air quality and hazardous materials.

Many pollutants are found in the indoor environment, for example, formaldehyde, other volatile organic compounds, wood preservatives, living organisms (e.g. bacteria, moulds, dust mites), particulates and fibres (e.g. man-made mineral fibres, asbestos), radon, combustion products (e.g. nitrogen dioxide) and lead. While there are now satisfactory procedures for dealing with many of these, others are increasingly causing concern.

In homes many issues can be dealt with by good provision of ventilation and careful choice of materials and construction practice. There is also scope for improving physical aspects of the environment, and safety in the home, through simple changes in dwelling design.

Controlled ventilation

An improved level and consistency of indoor air quality can be achieved while maintaining energy efficiency through controlled ventilation. One credit is given for the installation of mechanical ventilation (MV) with heat recovery or a passive stack ventilation (PSV) system.

Mechanical ventilation should supply to living rooms, bedrooms and other 'habitable rooms' and extract where moisture and odour are usually produced (e.g. kitchens, utility rooms, bathrooms, WCs) in order to achieve a minimum whole-home air change rate between 0.5 and 1.0 per hour. Good location of supply and extract terminals is specified in BRE Information Papers (Stephen, 1988; Stephen and Uglow, 1989).

PSV in the main kitchen would be needed (above main cooker if possible) and the main bathroom, with passive stack or extract fan in other kitchens, bathrooms, shower rooms, WCs, utility rooms. Design should be according to guidance given by Stephen and Uglow (1989) to achieve an average air flow rate equivalent to 1–2 room air changes per hour.

PSV is driven by the indoor–outdoor temperature difference and by wind effects and therefore does not require additional energy for fans. There is limited user control, but the ventilation rate will increase with increasing temperature of the room being ventilated, for example, during cooking or bathing. It is also possible that continuous ventilation at a lower rate may be more effective than ventilation at an intermittent higher rate. This is because it is likely that a significant proportion of the moisture and other air pollutants are absorbed into the structure and then desorbed over a period of some hours.

The home must satisfy airtightness criteria to ensure that the ventilation devices are effective: 7 air changes per hour (ach) at a test pressure of 50 Pascals for MV and 9 ach for PSV. These standards should be fairly easy to achieve in timber-framed dwellings but less easy at present in brick/block construction. An airtight dwelling would also require trickle vents to provide adequate controlled background ventilation if PSV is used. Chimneys both reduce airtightness and provide some passive ventilation. BREEAM requires appropriate procedures to be followed to preserve airtightness while not endangering health and safety. In the case of a solid fuel fire or chimney with no heating appliance supplied, a well-fitting chimney closure plate must be provided. Other heating appliances fitted with a chimney or flue must be designed so as to be inherently airtight when not in use.

Cooker hood

In order to minimize the spread of moisture, pollutants and odours within the kitchen and from the kitchen to the rest of the dwelling, one credit is given for installing a cooker hood extract fan ducted to the outdoor air (or PSV or MV system extract point and hood above the cooker) rather than having any of these elsewhere in the kitchen.

This would be of particular value for gas cookers, which produce water vapour and oxides of nitrogen, and would in effect reduce energy consumption because an extract fan in kitchens is required by Building Regulations (DoE/Welsh Office, 1989c) and if the extract fan takes the form of a cooker hood the minimum required air flow rate is halved.

Volatile organic pollutants of indoor origin

The level of volatile organic chemicals (VOCs) in the indoor air of new homes at the time of first occupation can be reduced by ventilation prior to occupation; not using urea formaldehyde foamed insulation (UFFI) or using it only in accordance with British Standards (BSI, 1985a, 1985b, 1985c); and not using coal tar products, which can emit naphthalene, or using them only with product quality control accreditation. One credit is given for doing this.

Many building, insulating, decorating and furnishing materials can be sources of VOCs. For example, UFFI and some paints, varnishes, carpeting, wood-based sheet materials and furniture emit small amounts of a variety of VOCs including formaldehyde and other aldehydes. Occupant activities constitute another major source in the indoor environment, but these are not included in the assessment. While the VOC levels produced in new homes are not regarded as hazardous, they can be unpleasant and may cause minor irritation reactions in a relatively small number of sensitive individuals. One way of tackling this issue would be to specify that certain materials should not be used. Various products are available or being developed which would emit VOCs at a lower rate than materials in widespread current use, but there are problems with requiring the specification of these alternatives.

For example, British Standards (BSI, 1989a) set a maximum level of extractable formaldehyde content for particleboards (25 mg per 100 g of board). Medium density fibreboard (MDF) is covered by another British Standard (BSI, 1989b). Board which satisfies these standards would not normally cause any irritation. In fact particleboard is available which is claimed to emit no measurable formaldehyde. Such board uses an isocyanate-based glue; it has good moisture-resistance properties but it is relatively expensive and rarely used indoors. While such advances are to be encouraged, the indoor environment consequences of the changes are not clear at present, and there are probably no substitutes of equivalent performance and economy for particleboards used in construction. It is therefore not advisable to place limits on the use of particleboard at present, but builders should specify boards which comply with British Standards.

Similarly, varnishes with low solvent content, and water-based paints for interior decoration, are available and would emit lower levels of hydrocarbons. Also UFFI can in most cases be avoided by using an alternative insulant. Care must always be taken to ensure that alternative products do not contain other materials of concern and that they have been sufficiently tested for the purpose for which they are used. The scale of any known hazard from materials currently in use is too small to justify specification of alternatives at present.

In the longer term, the European Community is drawing up guidelines for methods of testing VOC emissions from a wide variety of materials. These could be applied via European (CEN) standards to prevent the use of high emitting materials. For the present, specifiers are encouraged to discuss with suppliers the provision of low-emitting materials.

Until there are accepted alternative materials, BREEAM places emphasis on reducing the levels of organics at the time the home is first occupied. In most cases, UFFI would be introduced well before occupation and there should not be any problem with subsequent release of formaldehyde into the dwelling. Similarly, particleboards and MDF would normally be stored for a time before delivery and/or at the building-site, and then put in place some time before occupation. Additional ventilation during the final stages of construction could help to reduce levels of VOCs still further, and would be of greater benefit in relation to decoration and furnishings, the other main sources of VOCs. In the context of VOC levels, there is little point in discouraging builders from decorating and part-furnishing new homes since materials introduced prior to occupation should have a smaller effect on the occupants than the same materials supplied by the occupant.

Reduction of VOCs can be accelerated by means of a 'bake out' before occupation. This entails turning the heating on high for a period, followed immediately by a fresh air flush with extract fans on full. This might, however, cause cracking of plaster and possibly reduce the effectiveness of building sealing. There is currently no adequate guidance on the safe and effective use of bake out in new homes and it is therefore not included in BREEAM.

The reason that naphthalene is mentioned specifically is that there have been instances of this chemical being released from bituminous cold-applied damp proof membranes containing coal tar. These are commonly used in solid floor and, to some extent, in suspended concrete floor (pot and beam) construction. The possible health effects of low levels of naphthalene are not well understood, but the odour is objectionable to most people and can normally be detected at levels above 0.2 mg m^{-3}.

Wood preservatives

The unnecessary use of wood preservatives can be reduced while maintaining essential protection of vulnerable timber, by specifying no use of treated timber where it is not recommended in the relevant Codes and Standards, and all preserved timber to be industrially pre-treated ready for finishing on site.

Wood preservatives are essential to the long-term integrity of some timber components for buildings and other constructions. Indeed wood preservative treatment is widely accepted as the simplest and most economic means of achieving timber durability appropriate to Building Regulations requirements for certain specific components. British Standards (BSI, 1989c, 1989d) and specific Codes of Practice give guidance on building components where preservative treatment should be considered in the interests of satisfactory performance in service.

Wood preservative use in the UK is regulated under the Control of Pesticides Regulations (MAFF/HSE, 1986) under which it is an offence to sell, supply, use, store or advertise wood preservatives which have not been approved for safety and effectiveness. A list of approved products is published annually by the Ministry of Agriculture, Fisheries and Food/Health and Safety Executive (MAFF/HSE). Additions and amendments are published monthly in *The Pesticides Register* (MAFF/HSE). Specifiers with particular local criteria can select from this list those products which conform with their special requirements.

Specification of preserved timber for new building should favour pre-treatment because this is carried out under controlled conditions by trained specialists. This is preferable to on-site techniques, which are often applied by non-specialist personnel. It also reduces the potential for solvent from treated timber being emitted into the building structure following completion. Timber pre-treated in controlled, industrial plants by specialist professionals suppliers is readily available or can be ordered for specific construction purposes.

Use of preservative fluids on site can therefore be limited to essential operations only (e.g. certain protective decorative finishing and application to cut ends in accordance with published Codes and Standards and the instructions of the suppliers of the timber). Contractors should be directed to adhere strictly to the guidance on handling preservative pre-treated wood provided by the treaters or suppliers.

Although wood of suitable natural durability can be specified as an alternative to preservative treatment, with some species there may be cost penalties, engineering consequences and difficulties in obtaining supplies. In particular, should the selection of naturally durable timber lead to an increase in the use of tropical hardwoods, this will present a conflict with environmental concerns for their conservation and more rational use.

Non-gaseous indoor pollutants

To eliminate minor or occasional health risks which are not at present covered by regulations, two credits are available:

1. One credit for either (a) not using man-made material fibre (MMMF) roof insulation or (b) preventing fibres from becoming airborne with the living space (by boarding any loft area or completely enclosing all MMMF loft insulation in polythene) and fine filter vacuum cleaning after building works are completed.
2. One credit for specifying no use of asbestos or of paints which contain lead.

For safety reasons, loft boarding must include provision of a light in the loft space, which can be switched on without entering the loft using a switch with an illuminated off/on indicator. Boarding should also not compress the insulation material.

Man-made mineral fibres are widely used as insulation materials and the finer fibres, if they become airborne, may enter and be deposited in the lungs. They are linked with irritation of the skin, eyes and the upper respiratory tract. Insulation wools and special-purpose fibres are the ones most likely to cause irritation. MMMF in the domestic situation are not believed to constitute a significant health risk, but credit is given for measures to prevent fibres becoming airborne in order to minimize the possibility of minor skin and airway irritation and to reduce dust and dirt in the home.

Asbestos is a proven human carcinogen and exposure to high levels of airborne white asbestos fibres in the workplace (in asbestos manufacturing) can cause lung cancer. The risk of lung cancer from exposure to the very low levels of airborne fibres normally found in buildings is extremely small – estimated to be between one in 100 000 and one in a million (World Health Organization, 1987). The use of blue asbestos (crocodilite), brown asbestos (amosite), and products containing them is now prohibited in the UK. The use of white asbestos (chrysotile) and products containing it is permitted, although restricted. Today most white asbestos is used in asbestos cement products and in friction materials. However, alternative non-asbestos fibre reinforced materials are available (HSE, 1986) and their specification is appropriate for buildings which are designed in response to environmental concerns.

A European Directive (1991), in effect, prohibits the use of lead paints in new homes. However, this has not yet passed into UK law and, in any case, there may be some residual stocks of lead-based paints. BREEAM therefore credits the use of lead-free paint.

Lighting

Three measures are offered to improve the level of visual comfort, security and safety produced by the lighting of the home:

1. One credit for designing the kitchen and all habitable rooms to meet daylighting criteria (CIBSE, 1987; Littlefair, 1988).
2. One credit for specifying high-frequency ballasts with low-energy lighting in the kitchen and all the habitable rooms.
3. One credit for an external light fitted with a compact fluorescent lamp and a remote sensor consisting of an infra-red source and photocell.

Maximizing the use of daylight, which most people prefer to artificial light, will reduce electricity consumption for lighting. In order to avoid increasing heating energy consumption, double glazing may be necessary. There are two main criteria for achieving good daylighting indoors:

1. The average daylight factor in a room (min. 2% for kitchens, 1.5% for living-rooms and 1% for bedrooms).
2. No significant areas (20% or more) of each room, or any fixed work surfaces or tables, from which the sky cannot be seen from table top height (0.85 m).

In offices, headaches and eye-strain have successfully been reduced when high-frequency ballasts are substituted for conventional ballasts used in fluorescent lights (Wilkins *et al.*, 1989). No corresponding study has been undertaken in homes, but it is unlikely that a similar effect would be obtained.

Smoke alarms

To reduce injury, death and property damage or loss due to fires, there is one credit for installing mains-operated smoke alarms, with battery back-up, at appropriate locations. A secondary benefit will be to reduce the probability of excessive smoke from cooking spreading around the home.

British Standards describe suitable mains-powered alarms (BSI, 1990) and appropriate locations for them in homes (BSI, 1989e). The guidance on locations is also given in a free leaflet (Home Office, 1990) available from fire stations. Where a dwelling covers more than one floor, the system should be linked such that smoke detected on one floor sets off the alarms on the other floor(s).

Storage of hazardous substances and medicines

To help prevent accidental harm due to contact with hazardous substances and medicines kept in the home, there is one credit for specifying two secure cupboards, one for the storage of hazardous substances and one for the storage of medicines. It is recommended that the cupboard for hazardous substances should be located under the kitchen sink. The medicine cabinet should be located out of the reach of children. Both should have a lock and key.

Hazardous chemicals are kept in the majority of homes, for example, corrosive agents (e.g. paint stripper); irritant chemicals (e.g. white spirit); toxic chemicals (e.g. paraquat in weed killer) and flammable substances such as methylated spirits. Specific categories of hazardous material are defined by law and any product containing them must name them on the label and carry an appropriate warning. However, there are instances each year of children suffering injury or death because hazardous substances were stored within their reach. Similarly, medicines are introduced into most homes at some time and the measures specified by BREEAM/New Homes would help prevent accidental ingestion of medicines which could be hazardous in excess.

16.10
Conclusion

There is considerable scope for reducing the adverse impact that buildings can have on the global, local and indoor environments, thus creating short-term benefits indoors and locally and, in the longer term, a contribution to the health of the world and its people. BREEAM makes a start in this work; it will be continuously extended and improved and is already stimulating the development of similar schemes around the world.

Bibliography

Anderson, B. R., Clark, A. J., Baldwin, R. and Milbank, N. O. (1985) The BRE Domestic Energy Model – background philosophy and description. *BRE Information Paper IP 16/85.* Garston, BRE.

BSI (1985a) Guide to suitability of external cavity walls for filling with thermal insulants. *British Standard BS 820: Part 1:* London, BSI.

BSI (1985b) Code of practice for thermal insulation of cavity walls (with masonry or concrete inner leaf and outer leaves) by filling with UFFI systems. *British Standard BS 5618:* London, BSI.

BSI (1985c) Specification for UFFI systems suitable for thermal insulation of cavity walls with masonry or concrete inner and outer leaves. *British Standard BS 5617:* London, BSI.

BSI (1988) Code of Practice for the identification of potentially contaminated land and its investigation. *Draft for Development DD 175/88.*

BSI (1989b) Particleboard. *British Standard BS 5669: Parts 1–5:* London, BSI.

BSI (1989c) Specification for fibre building boards, Part 3. *British Standard BS 1142:* London, BSI.

BSI (1989d) Code of practice for preservation of timber. *British Standard BS 5589:* London, BSI.

BSI (1989d) Preservative treatment for structural timber. *British Standard BS 5268:* Part 5: London, BSI.

BSI (1989e) Code of practice for installation of smoke detectors. *British Standard BS 5839: Part 1*: London, BSI.

BSI (1990) Smoke detectors for residential application. *British Standard BS 5446: Part 1*: London, BSI.

Building Research Establishment (1989) Thermal insulation: avoiding risks. *BRE Report 143*, Garston, BRE.

Butler, D. J. G. (1989) CFCS and the building industry. *BRE Information Paper IP 23/89*. Garston, BRE.

The Chartered Institution of Building Services Engineers (1987) *Applications manual: window design*. London, CIBSE.

Department of the Environment and The Welsh Office (1989a) Conservation of fuel and power. *The Building Regulations (1985) Approved Documents L (1990 edition)* HMSO, London.

Department of the Environment and The Welsh Office, (1989b) Site preparation and resistance to moisture. *The Building Regulations (1985) Approved Documents C (1990 edition)* HMSO, London.

Department of the Environment and The Welsh Office (1989c) Means of ventilation. *The Building Regulations (1985) Approved Documents F (1990 edition)* HMSO, London.

Department of the Environment Circular 21/87 (1987) *Development of contaminated land*. London, HMSO.

Department of the Environment Circular 17/89 (1989) *Landfill sites*. London, HMSO.

European Commission (1991) *European Directive on marketing and use of dangerous substances (EC 76/769)*. 8th Amendment.

Health and Safety Executive (1986) *Alternatives to asbestos products: a review*. HMSO, London.

Home Office (1990) *Wake up, get a smoke alarm*. Reference FB2. The Home Office, December.

Littlefair, P. (1988) Average daylight factor: a simple basis for daylight design. *BRE Information Paper IP 15/88*, Garston, BRE.

Ministry of Agriculture, Fisheries and Food and The Health & Safety Executive (1986) The Control of Pesticides Regulations 1986. *Statutory Instrument 1986 No 1510*, HMSO, London.

Ministry of Agriculture, Fisheries and Food and The Health & Safety Executive. (Annual Publications). Pesticides approved under the Control of Pesticides Regulations 1986. *Reference book 500*. Part B, Section 1, HMSO, London.

Ministry of Agriculture, Fisheries and Food and The Health & Safety Executive. (Monthly update to previous reference). *The pesticides register*. HMSO, London.

Moschandreas, D. J. (1981) Exposure to pollutants and daily time budgets of people. *Bulletin of the New York Academy of Medicine* **57** (10), 845–50.

Prior, J. J., Raw, G. J. and Charlesworth, J. L. (1991) BREEAM/ New Homes: an environmental assessment for new homes. *BRE Report BR208*. Garston, BRE.

Shorrock, L. D., and Henderson, G. (1990) Energy use in buildings and carbon dioxide emissions. *BRE Report BR170*. Garston, BRE.

Stephen, R. K. (1988) Domestic mechanical ventilation: guidelines for designers for installers. *BRE Information Paper IP 18/88*. Garston, BRE.

Stephen, R. K. and Uglow, C. E. (1989) Passive stack ventilation in dwellings. *BRE Information Paper IP 21/89*. Garston, BRE.

Wilkins, A. J., Nimmo-Smith, I., Slater, A. I., and Bedocs, L. (1989) Fluorescent lighting, headaches and eyestrain. *Lighting Research and Technology* **21**(1), 11–18.

World Health Organization (1987) Air quality guidelines for Europe. *European Series No. 23*, Chapter 18. Copenhagen, WHO, Regional Office for Europe.

17

PROSPECTS FOR AFFORDABLE WARMTH
BRENDA BOARDMAN

17.1
Introduction

Adequate warmth in the home is necessary for the health and comfort of the occupants and to ensure that condensation and mould growth do not occur. Yet there is no requirement in building or environmental health standards that a home even contains a heating system. This is one reason why British homes are difficult and expensive to heat and the likelihood of having adequate, 'affordable' warmth is a distant chimera for many households. As a result, thousands of people will continue to suffer from discomfort in their own homes and from cold-related illness and death.

17.2
The health problem

Since 1970 in the UK, there have been 30 000–60 000 extra deaths each winter, above the average level for the rest of the year. Many of these cold-related deaths are avoidable. Both Collins and Markus have provided evidence, but it is worth confirming a few points:

1. these deaths occur in all age-groups, though rarely in the 5–24 age-band (Curwen, 1981, p. 18);
2. a bad winter does not bring forward deaths which would otherwise have occurred shortly after the period of high risk (Curwen and Devis, 1988, p. 18);
3. there is a marked social gradient in excess winter mortality,

Table 17.1 Seasonal mortality and external temperatures: international comparisons

	Mean external temperature in January	Seasonal mortality (coefficient of variation)	
	°C	1978	1984
Ireland	5.0	0.15	0.13
Northern Ireland	4.5	0.12	0.14
England and Wales	4.1	0.13	0.10
Scotland	3.7	0.12	0.11
France	3.3	0.07	0.06
Denmark	0	0.07	0.06
Norway	−1.1	0.05	0.04
Austria	−2.7	0.11	0.05
Sweden	−2.7	0.07	0.05
Finland	−3.0	0.05	0.04
Canada	−7.8	0.07	0.06

Note:
A coefficient of variation of 0.10 is twice as great as a coefficient of 0.05.
Sources:
Column 1: based on Kendrew (1961, pp. 378–83, 458), average temperatures do not vary significantly. Columns 2 and 3: derived from UN Demographic Yearbooks 1980 and 1985, table 30.

with the percentage of EWD being almost exactly twice as great in social class V as in social class I (Curwen, 1981, p. 18);

4. Britain has a particularly bad record on excess winter deaths with a rate that is greater than in countries with similar or colder climates (Table 17.1). With the exception of Northern Ireland, all the countries in the table have shown a drop in seasonal mortality between the two years given.

The danger of using mortality rates in one or two specific years is that the weather may have been abnormal. This risk is reduced by plotting the mortality rate against the coldness of the month, as measured in degree days. Figure 17.1 shows this relationship for the winter months of December–February for England and Wales, and Figure 17.2 for Scotland. In both cases, the data show that there is a correlation between the two datasets, at the 1% confidence level. The correlation is stronger in England and Wales than in Scotland,

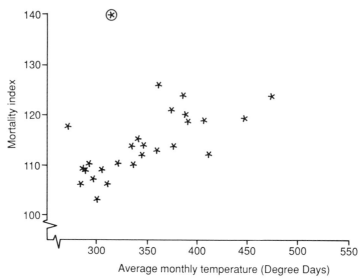

Figure 17.1   Winter mortality in England and Wales in comparison with
the coldness of the weather: 1976–84. Sources: Henwood
(1991); meteorological office data.

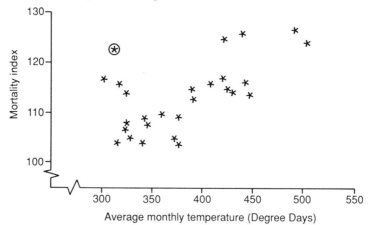

Figure 17.2   Winter mortality in Scotland in comparison with coldness
of weather: 1976–84. Sources: Henwood (1991);
meteorological office.

Winter mortality is expressed as an index, so that 110 is
10% higher than the average for a month of that number
of days in that year. Degree days measure both the depth
and the extent of cold weather in relationship to a base
temperature of 15.5°C: there are more degree days in cold
weather.

⊛Data for February 1986, when there was an influenza
epidemic.

384

where other (unidentified) factors are also influential. In each figure, one of the outliers is February 1976 (as identified), reflecting an influenza epidemic which 'appears to have been associated with over 20 000 excess winter deaths' in England and Wales alone (Curwen and Devis, 1988, p. 18). It is therefore clear that excess winter deaths in Britain are strongly affected by the coldness of the winter and that this relationship is more marked than in other countries with colder winters.

The number of excess winter deaths is declining slowly – at approx. 500 less deaths each year in England and Wales (Curwen, 1981, p. 16). The underlying vulnerability of the population is the same and has not improved since 1949: there will be an extra 8000 deaths for every 1 degC the winter temperatures are colder than average (Curwen and Devis, 1988, p. 18). For instance, during the severe cold weather in February 1991, there were an additional 2000 deaths in the week ending 15 February (*Guardian*, 27 February 1991, p. 8).

Winter temperatures inside British homes are lower than in most of these other countries (Boardman, 1991, pp. 144, 210). So the most likely explanation for the harsh impact of cold weather is that there is a closer relationship between external and internal temperatures in the UK than in many other countries. By implication, people in Britain are failing to keep healthy because they are not keeping warm indoors. This is not because the British, for some perverse reason, like being cold. Mack and Lansley, in their survey of minimal living standards, found that warmth is a commodity that is highly valued: heating the living areas was ranked first, ahead of an indoor toilet, damp-free home and beds for everyone (Mack and Lansley, 1985, p. 54). These cold families are unable to afford adequate warmth, even though they want it – they suffer from fuel poverty.

Homes that are expensive to keep warm are energy inefficient – they lack thermal insulation, have inefficient heating systems and use expensive fuels. All these factors are examined below, but before looking at energy efficiency levels in more detail, the components of affordable warmth are examined.

17.3

How much warmth?

The relationship between indoor temperatures and ill-health is covered in Chapter 6. The recommended temperatures can be combined with average activity levels to show that most adults, when in the home, require an ambient temperature of 21°C for comfort during the day (Boardman, 1985) and 16°C at night. When the house is unoccupied, or in rarely used rooms, a minimum temperature of 14°C is necessary to prevent condensation (Boyd, Cooper and Oreszczyn, 1988).

For most low-income households, the home is occupied during a large proportion of the day. The unemployed, pensioners, the sick and disabled and mothers with young children are likely to be in the home and awake for about 13 hrs a day (Boardman, 1985); for these households, the dwelling is rarely empty. The hours of occupancy and recommended temperatures can be combined to define the level of warmth necessary for health, comfort and a condensation-free home:

13 hours at 21°C
 3 hours at 14°C
 8 hours, at night, at 16°C

to give a 24-hour mean internal temperature of 18.5°C.

17.4

What is affordable?

About 30% of UK households are dependent upon the state for at least 75% of their income (Boardman, 1991, pp. 44–5) and are defined here as 'poor'. All of these 6.7 million households are in receipt of a means-tested benefit, such as income support, housing benefit, community charge benefit or family credit, or are eligible to claim. The poor usually spend about 10% of their income on fuel (Table 17.2); this is apparently 'affordable'. However, at the moment the poor have cold homes, despite dedicating a large proportion of their income to fuel. The aim is for the poor to obtain adequate warmth and other energy services for 10% of their income.

Table 17.2 Household expenditure on fuel, by income: UK 1989 (£/week)

	30% of households with lowest incomes	70% other	Average
Electricity	4.18	5.74	5.27
Gas	2.83	4.63	4.09
Coal and coke	0.84	0.67	0.72
Other	0.51	0.49	0.50
Total fuel expenditure	£8.36	£11.53	£10.58
All household expenditure	£87.28	£283.05	£224.32
Percentage on fuel	9.6%	4.1%	4.7%

Source:
Based on Department of Employment (1989).

The improvements in living standards would bring a lessening of poverty, although the absolute level of expenditure would stay the same.

To ensure adequate energy services for 10% of the income of the poor is a challenging task. As is shown in Table 17.2, the poor are spending less in absolute terms than the rich: £8.36 rather than £11.53 in 1989. To achieve adequate energy services for a poor family for £8.36 implies a greater level of energy efficiency than exists in richer homes. It can only be attained through positive discrimination if the poor are to obtain affordable warmth.

One further point of clarification: heating is only one of the uses of energy in the home, although it is the major one; thus the aim of affordable warmth is a shorthand for all uses of energy. It is equally important to have enough hot water, good lighting and the ability to keep and cook food safely. If warmth is the only use of energy being discussed, this represents about half of low-income energy expenditure (5% of weekly expenditure). When the discussion is about all uses of energy in the home, 10% of weekly household expenditure in low-income homes is the target.

If both the amount of money for heating is defined and the standard of heating, then the only way that these two fixed parameters can be achieved is through the energy efficiency of the home (Figure 17.3).

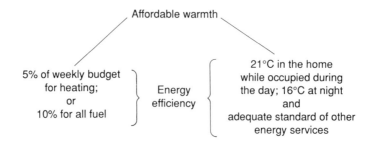

Figure 17.3 The relationship between income, warmth and energy efficiency.

17.5
Measuring energy efficiency

The measurement of the efficiency of the home is vital if there is to be any certainty that a household, on its income, can achieve affordable warmth. This measurement is undertaken with an energy audit, using a computer. Details of the house, the family, life styles and ownership of appliances are combined. In broad terms, the following four factors increase together, particularly for families on benefit:

1. the floor area of the dwelling;
2. total fuel costs to achieve a set standard of energy services;
3. the number of occupants;
4. their total income and thus the amount available for energy expenditure.

The first two factors are combined in the energy audit, and the last two can be used to identify the level of energy efficiency needed. For instance, a couple and two young children, with an income of £90 per week, could be living in a 90m² house. To give them affordable warmth, all heating and other energy services (including standing charges and maintenance) have to be accessible for £9 per week (10% of their income). This is equivalent to 10p/m²/week for all costs or 8p/m²/week for energy consumption, excluding standing charges and maintenance, if gas is used.

With an energy audit, the end-figure is an index (Milton Keynes Energy Cost Indicator or MKECI) or points (with Starpoint) or a rating (with National Home Energy Rating, NHER). The latter is growing in popularity, but whatever the coding system, the approach is similar. All of these auditing methods establish the total fuel expenditure required to achieve a set standard and divide this by the floor area of the dwelling. The final number is therefore a good indicator of energy efficiency as the fuel costs are normalized for the size of the dwelling.

To provide affordable warmth for a low-income family, the home has to be capable of achieving a NHER of 8, or a MKECI of 120. This is a high level of energy efficiency and above the standard of the 1990 Building Regulations. In a home with gas central heating, the level would be achieved in a new building, provided that it also had double glazing.

There are virtually no homes in the UK that provide this level of energy efficiency and are occupied by low-income families – perhaps, at most, 100 000. It is thus possible to state that, with rare exceptions, the poor in this country do not have affordable warmth. As a result, they suffer from fuel poverty and are likely to have, at the most, one warm room for a limited number of hours a day.

Cold weather increases the cost of heating disproportionately in a home that is already expensive to heat. Thus low-income households with little disposable income living in energy inefficient properties are unable to respond to periods of severe cold weather: they cannot afford to spend more on heating, just because it is colder. Hence the increase in winter deaths that occurred in February 1991 and similar periods.

17.6
Heating systems

The relationship between the increased ownership of central heating and declining winter deaths was identified in the USA by Sakamoto-Momiyama (1977, p. 21). Since then, increasing emphasis has been placed on central heating ownership as if it were a crucial parameter in the provision of healthy housing. This focus will only be correct when the resultant indoor temperatures are adequately warm. For instance, in 1979, France and Denmark had similar levels of excess winter deaths (Table 17.1) and indoor winter temperatures of about 18°C (Boardman, 1991, p. 144). However, central heating ownership was 54% and 92% respectively (Nationwide Building

Table 17.3 Calculated temperatures in UK homes: 1970–86 (°C)*

	Centrally heated	Non-centrally heated	Average
1970	14.58	12.08	12.93
1986	16.46	13.96	15.76

Note:
* 24-hour average internal temperature during the six winter months.
Source:
Henderson and Shorrock (1989), p. 23.

Society, 1979, p. 8), so that the level of warmth was dependent on some other factor than central heating ownership. In France, in 1979, even homes with individual fires were warm.

In the UK the reverse is true. The average home is cold, whether or not it has central heating. Centrally heated homes are slightly warmer, but the mere presence of central heating is not sufficient to ensure a warm, healthy home in Britain. Using a constant difference of 2.5 degC between centrally heated and non-centrally heated homes, the Building Research Establishment have calculated that temperatures have risen by just less than 2 degC in each category over the 1970–86 period (Table 17.3). The BRE have validated these calculations against assessments of total energy consumption and average heat loss in the housing stock.

Calculated temperatures have been necessary, because of the shortage of measured data for the whole UK. The only national survey was undertaken in 1978. Subsequently, data were obtained in a wide sample of English homes during the 1986–7 winter, but by March 1991 these had not been published by the Department of the Environment.

The temperatures predicted in non-centrally heated homes are abysmally low and well below those required for both comfort and health (see Chapter 6). In centrally heated homes, usually occupied by better-off families, the level of warmth is still insufficient in comparison to known comfort levels. It is therefore simplistic and incorrect to state for Britain that the wider use of central heating now means that we have warm homes. We do not. Keatinge, Coleshaw and Holmes (1989) made this mistake. They correctly demonstrate the wider ownership of central heating, but then assume, incorrectly, that this means the homes of the vulnerable are warm enough to prevent coronary and cerebrovascular mortalities (p. 76). If the most vulnerable in society now have central heating – and there is little evidence that they do – this still does not mean that

Table 17.4 Central heating ownership by household age: UK 1976–86 (%)

	Pensioner household		Non-pensioner household	
	1976	1986	1976	1986
Central heating				
Electric	15	13	13	9
Oil	4	1	6	4
Solid fuel	6	7	7	8
Gas	12	31	24	52
All types	38	54	50	73
No central heating	62	46	50	27

Sources:
1976, Department of Energy (1978), table 5.2; 1986, Hutton and Hardman (in press), table 6.2.

the poor are able to spend sufficient on heating to keep themselves healthily warm.

As demonstrated, even in the UK a centrally heated house is usually warmer than one with individual fires. There are two reasons for this: the cheapest warmth is provided by central heating, or gas-fired individual fires (Sutherland, 1990). Secondly, because of the large capital cost involved, central heating is most likely to be found in the more affluent homes. It is for these two reasons, together with ease of operation, that centrally heated homes are generally warmer than non-centrally heated ones. Thus central heating does provide cheaper warmth, but it will be found mainly in the homes of better-off families, where higher levels of warmth are also more affordable.

The ownership of central heating has been increasing in the UK, but there are still significant variations between different population groups. For instance, pensioners are lagging about ten years behind non-pensioners in the acquisition of central heating (Table 17.4). In the table, the pensioners are from all income groups, so that in poorer homes the proportion would be lower still. Thus one group that is known to be particularly vulnerable to the cold is less likely to have an energy-efficient heating system than less vulnerable, younger people.

Further proof that many British homes are cold comes from evidence on the effect on temperature levels of improving insulation. When a home has insulation added, it is cheaper to

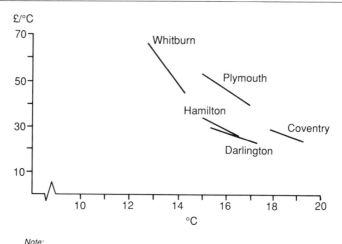

Note:
An energy efficiency improvement results in a lowering of the cost of warmth – each
degree rise in temperature costs less to achieve (y-axis)

Figure17.4 Demand curves for warmth from Better Insulated House
Programme. Source: Boardman (1991), based on Campbell
(1985).

keep warm. The respondents take part of this new benefit as
additional warmth, demonstrating a latent desire for greater comfort
(Figure 17.4).

When energy efficiency improvements are carried out on properties, the occupants will benefit from both increased warmth and
reduced expenditure on energy. Some of the benefit is taken as
additional warmth, even where the original temperature was relatively high. For instance, the houses at Coventry had temperatures
of nearly 18°C before improvements and of 19°C afterwards (Figure
17.4). Low-income homes will have a considerable need for both
more warmth and additional income. The competition between
these demands will mean that even in quite cold homes, when the
cost of warmth is lowered, some of the benefit will be taken as
energy savings. On average, in the 120 homes in the DoE's Better
Insulated House Programme, 40% of the benefit was taken as savings in energy costs and 60% as additional warmth (Boardman,
1991, p. 185). In monitored trials, including owner-occupied proper-

ties, the benefit has always been taken as some combination of money savings and additional comfort.

The most expensive form of heating is on-peak electric and some forms of electric central heating such as underfloor or ceiling heating. Low-income families are at least twice as likely to be all-electric as better-off families, and nearly twice as likely to have electric central heating (based on Hutton and Hardman, in press). In total, 11% of all UK households depend upon electricity for their space heating, of which about half are using the on-peak tariff (Boardman, 1991, p. 97). An additional one million homes depend upon open coal fires, which are expensive, and at least 2 million heating systems in England are inadequate, based on the English House Condition Survey findings (DoE, 1988, pp. 21, 93).

17.7

Thermal insulation standards/energy efficiency levels

The level of thermal insulation of a building depends upon what was constructed and subsequent additions. In Britain, the 1974 Building Regulations were the first ones to require noticeable amounts of insulation and only 15% of the housing stock has been built since then. Of these (slightly) higher standard dwellings, about half a million are occupied by low-income families (Boardman, 1991, p. 64). These properties still do not provide affordable warmth. Thus adequate insulation in low-income homes depends upon rehabilitation and added insulation, even of relatively new buildings.

There is a distinct social class bias in the ownership of insulation, particularly combinations of measures (Table 17.5). The poor are disadvantaged through their low level of ownership of insulation measures and hence the lower level of energy efficiency of their dwellings. The homes of poor families cost more to keep warm.

It is difficult to assess the effect of multiple disadvantages on the energy efficiency of the home, for instance, how many of those with the most expensive heating systems also have no insulation. Energy audits do combine the data, but no national database from measured surveys is available. The following statements come from several sources, so they cannot be combined; for the 6.7 million low-income families (Boardman, 1991, p. 224):

393

Table 17.5 Types of insulation in the home and the presence of central heating, by socio-economic group GB: 1986 (% of households with measure)

	Loft insulation	Full double glazing	Cavity wall insulation	Cavity + loft + double glazing	Any type of CH
AB	87	23	23	17	95
C1	80	17	18	10	76
C2	77	13	15	6	73
D	69	9	9	1	63
E	68	7	9	1	55
Average	76	14	15	7	73

Note:
Socio-economic group E represents about half the poor.
Source:
Mintel (March, 1987), pp. 68, 73.

- 0.5 million live in modern (post-1974) dwellings;
- 2.5 million have some loft insulation or draughtproofing, or both;
- therefore, at least 3.7 million live in older dwellings with little or no added insulation;
- 59 000 homes in England have no visible method of heating;
- 2.8 million households use expensive heating systems:
    - 1.1 million households use general tariff electricity;
    - 0.7 million other households use problematic electric central heating, such as underfloor or ceiling heating;
    - 1 million use open coal fires;
- 2 million households have a heating system that is incapable of heating their home to minimal standards.

There is likely to be a considerable overlap between the ownership of expensive and inadequate heating.

It has been estimated that to bring the 6.6 million low-income homes up to the standard needed to provide affordable warmth it will cost an average of £2500 per house and a total of £16.5 billion (Boardman, 1990). This expenditure should ensure that every home has a standard of about NHER 8 or MKECI 120 – the equivalent of the 1990 Building Regulations with the addition of double glazing and gas central heating. To treat the homes of the fuel poor in a reasonable time period would require 500 000 properties to be improved each year at an annual cost of £1250 million. The programme of work could then be completed in about 13 years.

17.8
Government programmes

Government programmes to grant-aid the installation of loft insulation were introduced in 1978 and for draughtproofing in 1981. Lagging hot water tanks and pipes have been included with these schemes, but there has been no grant-aid beyond basic measures. Local authorities have undertaken work on their own properties, but this has usually included more extensive energy efficiency measures only under special schemes such as Estate Action.

The government has also supported community insulation groups. The latter provide temporary employment and training while utilizing the grants to benefit the poorer members of society. Initially, loft insulation grants were targeted on the more affluent households and only since 1988 have they been means-tested. As a result, of the £550 million spent on energy efficiency improvements since 1978, only about £300 million (56%) has gone to low-income families, including £90 million on employment initiatives (Table 17.6).

This £300 million over 12 years has to be compared with a proposed programme costing £1250 million each year. It is clear that present levels of expenditure are barely sufficient to keep pace with the deteriorating housing stock and are certainly not making a significant impact on fuel poverty.

Of the initiatives listed in Table 17.6, local authority energy conservation programmes have been diminishing annually since the 1979 peak (DoE, 1990, p. 94). By 1989, expenditure in Britain was about £4.5 million, of which about half is going on the homes of the poorest 30% of households.

The other programmes for loft insulation, draughtproofing and community insulation projects have been combined under a new initiative, the Home Energy Efficiency Scheme (HEES). The HEES is national, means-tested and all tenure groups are eligible. It covers the basic provision of loft insulation, draughtproofing, pipe and tank lagging, together with in some circumstances the provision of £10 worth of advice on energy efficiency. Thus, after a period of nar-

Table 17.6 Government-funded capital expenditure on energy efficiency improvements: GB 1978–1979

	Loft insulation grants		Draught- proofing	LA energy conserva- tion	Employ- ment initiatives
	66%	90%			
Totals					
Properties treated	3.7m.	0.6m.	0.7m.	2.4m.	
Expenditure	£190m.	£55m.	£30m.	£184m.	£90m.
Low-income households					
Percentage of total	20%	100%	100%	50%	100%
Properties treated	0.7m.	0.6m.	0.7m.	1.2m.	
Expenditure	£38m.	£55m.	£30m.	£92m.	£90m.

Note:
The allocation of one in five of the 66% loft insulation grant to low-income households is believed to be generous: there are no supportive data. The 50% of local authority energy conservation work going to the poorest homes reflects the proportion of households that are defined as poor in this sector.
Source:
Boardman (1991), p. 70.

rower availability, these insulation measures will again be accessible to all the fuel poor.

The level of HEES funding is about equivalent to the schemes previously operating, at £24 million in 1991/92, with an additional £2 million for the administrative costs of the Energy Action Grants Agency. The government has doubled the target of jobs to be done to 200 000 a year. The HEES is set up under the *Social Security Act 1990*, clause 15, and has the potential to expand into new energy efficiency measures such as cavity wall insulation and replacing heating systems. However, this growth will depend upon the HEES delivering a good standard of service nationally and on the government providing the financial support necessary for the proposed level of activity. The former is a challenging requirement, and the latter politically unlikely.

The government has recently announced the Green House programme, to fund higher levels of insulation in otherwise sound properties belonging to English local authorities. This will be worth £10 million in 1991/92 and £50 million in 1992/93. Although a welcome initiative, it is only a demonstration project and so has, presumably, a limited life. In 1991/92, government expenditure on energy-efficiency investment in low-income homes will be about £2 million through local authorities' own conservation work and a further £5 million (50% of the total) with the Green House programme. Added to the £24 million under HEES, this gives £31 million in comparison with the estimated need to spend £1250 million on the same properties each year. The government does not appear to have recognized the scale of work to be undertaken, nor the expenditure required.

17.9
Recent legislation

The upgrading of the Building Regulations in 1990 (effective in Scotland from 1991) has meant that new homes have an increased level of insulation. They still do not need to include a heating system. The new Fitness Standard has also been improved but, as far as energy efficiency is concerned, to a lesser degree. Thus the range in standards between the best and the worst housing in the UK is increasing, to the detriment of the poor.

The Fitness Standard in England and Wales and the Tolerable Standard in Scotland determine which homes are fit for human habitation. Where a dwelling fails to meet the requirements, the local Environmental Health Officer can insist on the work being done with the aid of a mandatory grant. None of the items that determine fitness and the mandatory grant include thermal insulation, though for the first time in England and Wales the heating system is included. The definition of an adequate heating system is technological and does not involve the running costs, or their affordability:

for heating a main 'living' room, provision for fixed heating capable of efficiently maintaining the room generally at a temperature of 18 deg C or more when the outside temperatures is −1 deg C, and for the other main habitable rooms, provision for heating capable of maintaining an equivalent temperatures of 16 deg C or more. (DoE, Circular 6/90)

This standard is similar to that used in the 1986 English House Condition Survey and which determined that 'approximately 1.7 m dwellings were considered inadequate . . . Nearly nine out of ten of these had no fixed central heating' (DoE, 1988, p. 21). When grossed up to the UK, this is the figure of 2 million already quoted. Local authorities still have discretion in whether to declare a property unfit, so that these additional powers may not result in much improvement for the fuel poor. Part of this discretion applies to the requirement that the heating is 'fixed' as the guidance does also state that a 13 A wall socket could be sufficient. It is hoped that local government officers recognize the high cost of on-peak electricity and ensure that no improved home is still dependent upon the most expensive form of heating.

Local authorities also have discretion in making grants available for minor works. These are means-tested, for private sector tenants and owner occupiers. The minor works assistance can be for a variety of reasons, one of which is thermal insulation. Elderly households can also obtain help with improvements to their heating systems. The minor works grant has only been in operation since 1 April 1990, so it is difficult to assess its likely impact. In the third quarter of 1990, 3362 grant applications for minor works assistance were approved in England (Hansard, February 1991, WA col. 541–2). These cannot be broken down between insulation and other types of grant. This confirms the impression that minimal amounts of money are being earmarked for this discretionary grant by local authorities and thus minor works grants will have a negligible effect on improved energy efficiency in low-income homes.

17.10
Conclusion

The amount of new building, activity by local authorities and government grants are not making a significant impact on the extent of fuel poverty and there are no indications that any programmes of the necessary magnitude are being considered by government. There are 6.6 million households suffering from fuel poverty in the UK in 1991, because of the energy inefficiency of their homes. A programme for affordable warmth would cost about 40 times more per annum than is currently being spent on energy-efficiency programmes, through central and local government. There is therefore no prospect of an alleviation of fuel poverty and many thousands of the poorest people in the UK will continue to die each winter as a result of their inability to keep their homes adequately warm for comfort and for health.

Acknowledgements

Table 1, figure 4 and tables 5 and 6 in Boardman (1991) are reproduced with the kind permission of Belhaven Press.

Bibliography

Boardman, B. (1985) Activity levels within the home. Paper presented at Joint Meeting CIB W17/77, Controlling Internal Environment, Budapest, 18–20 September.

Boardman, B. (1990) *Fuel Poverty and the Greenhouse Effect*, National Right to Fuel Campaign, Neighbourhood Energy Action Heatwise Glasgow, Friends of the Earth.

Boardman, B. (1991) *Fuel Poverty: From Cold Homes to Affordable Warmth*, Belhaven, London.

Boyd, D., Cooper, P. and Oreszczyn, T. (1988) Condensation risk prevention: additions of a condensation model to Bredem. *Building Services Engineering Research and Technology*, 9(3), 117–25.

Campbell, P. M. (1985) *The Better Insulated House Programme*, Reference report for the Department of the Environment, prepared by Databuild Ltd, DoE, London.

Curwen, M. (1981) *Trends in Respiratory Mortality 1951–75, England and Wales*, OPCS DH1 No. 7, HMSO, London.

Curwen, M. and Devis, T. (1988) Winter mortality, temperature and influenza: has the relationship changed in recent years? *Population Trends 54*, OPCS pp. 17–20, HMSO, London.

Department of Employment (1989) *Family Expenditure Survey 1989*, Department of Employment, London.

Department of Energy (1978) *Family Expenditure Survey: Expenditure on Fuels 1976*, Department of Energy, London.

Department of the Environment (1988) *English House Condition Survey 1986*, HMSO, London.

Henderson, G. and Shorrock, L. D. (1989) *Domestic Energy Fact File*, Building Research Establishment, HMSO, London.

Henwood, M. (1991) *Excess Winter Mortality: International Comparisons 1976–1984*, King's Fund Institute, London.

Hutton, S. and Hardman, G. (in press) *Expenditure on Fuels 1986*, Gas Consumers Council, London.

Keatinge, W. R., Coleshaw, S. R. K. and Holmes, J. (1989) Changes in seasonal mortalities with improvement in home heating in

England and Wales from 1964 to 1984. *Int. J. Biometeorol.*, 33, 71–6.

Kendrew, W. G. (1961) *The Climates of the Continents* (5th edn), Clarendon Press, Oxford.

Mack, J. and Lansley, S. (1985) *Poor Britain*, Allen and Unwin, London.

Mintel (1987) Market Intelligence Reports (monthly), Mintel, London.

Nationwide Building Society (1979) *Housing and housing finance in the European Economic Community*, NBS, pp. 1–12.

Sakamoto-Momiyama, M. (1977) *Seasonality in Human Mortality*, University of Tokyo Press, Tokyo.

Sutherland, C. M. J. (1990) *Comparative Domestic Heating Cost Tables*, Sutherland Associates, Banstead.

THE LEGAL ENVIRONMENT OF HOUSING CONDITIONS

ROGER BURRIDGE AND DAVID ORMANDY

18.1

The contours of legal intervention

Earlier chapters have outlined the circumstances in nineteenth-century England surrounding the passing of legislation to control the dangerous practices of Victorian industrialism. This chapter outlines the legal actions that have evolved from the *Nuisance Removal Acts* and the *Artisans and Labourers Dwellings Act 1868*. In outlining the variety of actions that may be invoked today to draw legal attention to hazardous housing conditions, two currents affecting the impact of law are discussed. The impact of law on housing conditions is affected both by a move from public regulation to the award of individual subsidy and the transfer of responsibility for maintenance of housing fabric from the landlord to the owner-occupier. Both currents, it will be argued, flow towards a legal response to unhealthy housing conditions which is individual, private and fragmented. The present response can be contrasted with earlier efforts to ameliorate bad housing conditions which evinced a wider community concern characterized by collective, public and locality-based action. A subsidiary but significant factor affecting the relevance of law to housing defects has been the emergence of modern housing hazards in the public sector housing stock which are beyond the reach of local government enforcement. The chapter argues that in the general retreat from regulatory public intervention, the legal actions that remain to the victim of dangerous housing conditions are complex, expensive and inadequate.

18.2
Public and private legal action

The distinction between public and private legal response emerges between statutory interventions and the efforts of public officials to ameliorate bad housing on the one hand, and the remedies afforded individual occupiers on the other hand, who turn to the courts for redress and compensation from those who have inflicted harmful housing. The following account of the legal environment within which housing conditions in England and Wales maintain or are constrained, reveals a haphazard pattern of judicial pronouncements of individual responsibilities alongside parliamentary declarations of local government duties. The law shifts between concern for the public condition – identifiable in measures to protect community health and the environment, to promote sanitariness, and to prevent disease – and the judicial fixation with individual property rights – manifest in landmark decisions concerning the sanctity of contract and the limitations of personal obligation. The contrast between public health and private illness (see Chapters 3 and 4) is thus replicated in the legal process. The distinction between the general practitioner's focus on the individual patient and the community physician's concern for collective health is reflected in the roles of high street solicitor and the present-day sanitary policeman – the Environmental Health Officer. The latter has historically been entrusted with powers to protect households, streets and even larger collectivities. It is a role which, it will be argued, is increasingly being redirected towards the individual dwelling and is dependent upon the poverty of the occupier.

The changing emphasis between the collective and the individual impact of law is the product of wider economic and social currents, which reflect free market or interventionist ideology. This chapter concludes that while there has not been the espousal of a deregulatory stance and a return to market influences as the determinants of housing conditions, the process of the implementation of public housing standards represents nevertheless a withdrawal from the enforcement model of regulation. The identification of housing hazards in the preceding chapters suggests that there is fresh impetus for a more robust approach to enforcement and increased intervention. The mechanisms by which such intervention can be achieved are explored in the final section.

The rehearsal of the legal controls of housing in England and Wales, while inevitably reflecting the topographical idiosyncrasies of the locality and its climate, is of more than parochial interest. The early onset of industrialization and the urban form, the variety of legal intervention applied and the history of public health are illustrative of the tensions surrounding intervention and the significance of a housing policy that espouses a collective concern.

Public alarm, charitable concern and industrial interest concerning the hazards of housing combined to introduce legislative proscription of the housing conditions identified as most dangerous in the mid-nineteenth century. The passing of the *Public Health Act 1875*, according to Cornish and Clark (1989, p. 163) was acknowledgement that 'public health had come to be seen as too embracing and too complex a question to be left to the vagaries of the market'. Three distinct procedures had been developed. Environmental health dangers (including unhealthy housing conditions) were dealt with by the issue of directive notices to those responsible for health nuisances, issued by local officials and enforced by penal sanction against offenders who failed to comply. Alternative procedures specifically geared to unhealthy dwellings empowered the same local officials to intervene to ensure the closure and, if necessary, demolition of individual unhealthy houses or groups of houses. New buildings were subject to bye-laws specifying minimum space, ventilation and construction standards. The model in all cases was coercive and represented the primacy of public health concerns over private property rights. The intervention was prompted by the acknowledgement that the unfettered market and private law remedies of contract were inadequate to ensure the health of occupiers. The emergent public health movement was carried forward by a succession of public law interventions – regulatory controls of private landlords that were imposed for the sake of community health.

18.3

The limitations of private law

The English judiciary fashioned a legal system founded upon private actions for private wrongs. In the century before Chadwick, Snow and Southwood Smith, the victim of unhealthy housing could find little comfort from the law. Those involved in disputes about interests in land could look only to the property lawyers of Exchequer or Chancery, whose exploits were graphically publicized by Dickens in *Bleak House*, for redress for the infringement of a personal obligation commonly arising from a contractual relationship. Landed property was the historic and enduring form of wealth, and owners dictated the terms upon which its use would be extended to others. Hence contracts for the lease of land were invariably phrased in favour of the lessor and judges were reluctant to construe agreements beyond the plain words of the document. Land scarcity placed both profits and power in the pockets of the landowners.

By the late nineteenth century only 10% of the urban population lived in housing that was their own (Cornish and Clark, 1989, p. 123). Leases for long periods of occupation were primarily the privilege of the middle classes. Agricultural labourers, mill workers and journeymen had been reliant upon their employer for housing or rented from week to week, or the more affluent ones from year to year. Migration into the towns resulted in ever-decreasing partitioning of accommodation space as subtenants further sublet a portion of their housing (Burnett, 1978). Lodgings on a daily or weekly basis could be obtained in larger properties which maximized the income potential of rooms or beds, the forerunners of modern bed-and-breakfast accommodation.

In the 1890s, 90% of all houses were rented from a mixed array of landlords, from the great landed lords of north London to the sparse holdings of a couple of houses in the hands of a rentier class, typified in Birmingham and elsewhere. Relationships between occupier and freeholder were often distanced by a pattern of intervening sublessors.

Against this complex background of legal entitlements and practical preoccupations with keeping a roof over the family's head, the bench were rarely called to intervene. Those who inhabited the rookeries and slums would have been unable to afford a lawyer, even if their lease had promised better conditions than they endured. The house knacker's regular rent demand (Muthesius, 1982) was a powerful disincentive to upset the landlord with counterclaims of his derelictions. The bailiffs and debtors' prisons policed the housing market.

'In the matter of overdue rents, the justices could be trusted to know their duty' (Cornish and Clark, 1989, p 136), and judicial attention was only likely to be drawn to the occupier's plight in a response to the landlord's demand for unpaid rent. The lease generally imposed upon the tenant or lessee responsibility for repairs, and even if it omitted to do so, the judiciary declined to imply into the contract any obligation binding the landlord, even to the extent that the property let was suitable for occupation. Neither, unless the landlord was the builder, was there any liability on behalf of the landlord for dangerous defects.

An exception was made where the house was intended to be for immediate occupation. Thus in 1843, Lady Marrable was absolved from the obligation to pay rent for a house which was infested with bed bugs. She received no compensation for the experience but the court had confirmed a common law obligation upon a landlord of property for immediate occupation to ensure that it was fit for habitation.

Apart from this modest exception, wealthy housing conditions were essentially a private affair, between landlord and tenant. The legal fiction of freely contracting parties and the practical and financial obstacles of legal services ensured that such private injuries were unlikely to be argued in public.

18.4

The shape of statutory intervention

The statutory intervention that was prompted by the inadequacy of private legal remedies was dependent upon the establishment of both a centralized office to generate the policy and local agencies for its implementations (Cornish and Clark, 1989). As early as 1838, the fourth Annual Report of the Poor Law Board had identified a direct relationship between disease and the physical environment. The development of public health and housing reform and its dependence upon the establishment of local government is well documented (Finer, 1952; Burnett, 1978; Moore, 1987; Ormandy and

Burridge, 1989). Progress was piecemeal. Successive administrations adopted differing forms of regulatory control, increasing their scope as the nascent local government structure evolved to enforce an offence-orientated approach. Public health concerns became enmeshed in housing policy; local bye-laws unevenly paved the way for national Acts, themselves to be periodically reorganized in an attempt to codify the unwieldy agglommerations of official powers. The evolution of housing standards in Britain and housing codes in the USA followed similar paths and reflected comparable challenges to their introduction (Mood, 1987; Burridge and Ormandy, 1990). The procedures were directed to the abatement of local environmental hazards, the demolition of insanitary housing which was beyond improvement, and the construction of new houses which avoided dangerous practices and promoted healthier living. Subsequently, intervention was directed towards dwellings which, while fit for habitation, required repairs.

Public nuisances

In England the earliest legislative intervention in 1846 was in the form of the court endorsement of a complaint by two medical officers that the filthy and unwholesome condition of any dwelling house was a 'nuisance likely to promote or increase disease' (*Nuisance Removal and Diseases Prevention Act*). The court was empowered to order the cleansing of any such building. A succession of Public Health Acts gave Sanitary Inspectors and latterly local government Environmental Health Officers wide powers to order the abatement of nuisances where any premises were in such a state as to be 'prejudicial to health or a nuisance'. A slightly reformed procedure has recently been re-enacted in the *Environmental Protection Act 1989*.

Unhealthy premises are only one of a number of environmental health threats that the concept of statutory nuisance embraces; and the enforcement process was seen as being restricted to the temporary abatement of the problem, and thus insufficient to deal with the housing hazards of the emerging industrial cities. A more robust and comprehensive legal intervention was necessary to demolish the slums and make way for new city structures and communications.

Houses fit for habitation

Housing was singled out as a particular source of ill-health in the *Artisans and Labourers Dwelling Act 1868,* which required local authorities to deal with 'any premises . . . in a Condition or State dangerous to Health so as to be unfit for Human Habitation'. In 1954 the requirements of a fit house were statutorily defined and a duty was imposed upon local authorities to deal with any houses in its district which were unfit for human habitation. If any dwelling was 'so far defective in one or more' of a prescribed list of criteria as to be not reasonably suitable for occupation, it was deemed to be unfit. Unfit houses had to be either repaired to a suitable standard, closed or demolished.

The criteria were reminiscent of nineteenth-century housing hazards and the 'sanitary idea':

- repair
- freedom from damp
- natural lighting
- water supply
- facilities for preparing and cooking food and for disposing of waste water
- stability
- internal arrangement (added in 1969)
- ventilation
- drainage and sanitary conveniences

The standard was a broad declaratory norm, susceptible to wide subjective interpretation and reflecting an approach that housing could be uninhabitable for other reasons than its being an immediate hazard to the physical health of the occupier.

The English and Welsh standard was redefined in the *Local Government and Housing Act 1989.* This replaced a broad cumulative assessment with a requirement that a dwelling must fail at least one of the prescribed criteria before it is classified as unfit for habitation. The standard was 'improved' by the addition of requirements that in order to be fit for habitation a dwelling-house should contain adequate provision for heating, a hot water supply and suitably located personal washing and sanitary facilities. Subsequently the health basis of the revised standard was emphasized in new Guidance Notes which elaborated the health hazards if the prescribed conditions are not maintained. The new standard thus reflects a greater concern for occupiers than its predecessor, and more closely relates housing conditions to the available scientific knowledge of housing hazards.

Housing discomfort and disrepair

The recognition that housing decay warranted early intervention to prevent structural deterioration that was expensive to remedy prompted the introduction of a power to impose mandatory repair on properties which were not unfit. Public Health Inspectors, as they were then called, were empowered to take action where substantial disrepair was present in a house (*Housing Act 1957*, section 9(1A) as amended by *Housing Act 1969*). By 1980, it was felt that action should be possible against a landlord in circumstances where there might not be substantial disrepair, but where there was some lesser disrepair which 'interfere(s) materially with the personal comfort of the tenant' (*Housing Act 1957*, section 9 (1B) as amended by *Housing Act 1980*). These provisions have been reaffirmed in the *Housing Act 1985*.

A local authority in the 1990s therefore has wide powers to intervene to obtain the improvement of the local housing stock – powers which include enforced repair, demolition and compulsory purchase; Draconian measures elevating state functionaries above private property interests in the pursuit of public health and national progress. Moreover, state intervention in the landlord-tenant relationship is not restricted to conditions where the health of occupiers is at risk, but is authorized in circumstances where comfort alone is in question. The discussion below explains that these regulatory powers are rarely wielded today.

Construction standards

The emphasis placed in Britain upon disrepair and unfitness is a reflection of the obsolescence of the housing stock and the scarcity of land. In many countries where housing provision lags behind population growth, and land costs are less significant than construction costs, the focus for improving housing conditions will be the codification of standards for the construction of healthy homes.

The Building Regulations in England and Wales until 1985

afforded an example of detailed prescriptive regulation affecting most aspects of construction – i.e. safety, insulation, convenience, sanitation, space, stability. They are illustrative of the potential for a technical/objective approach to regulation that could be deployed in other fields of intervention. The approach to the equivalent of a fitness standard advocated by the American Public Health Association includes detailed prescription of adequate window sizes in existing houses. In 1985 building control became the target for a governmental commitment to deregulation. Alongside the enforcement of the Building Regulations by local public officers, builders were offered the option of employing approved private sector surveyors who would supervise design and construction. The effects of non-compliance would be underwritten by insurance. At the same time, the detailed prescriptive requirements of many of the regulations were replaced by broad duties, accompanied by a Code of Guidance detailing specific performance criteria. This example of the release of the construction industry from public enforcement in favour of self-regulation by the design and surveying professions switches responsibility from public sector finance for the supervision to private sector costs of insurance premiums and market professional fees.

The effects of non-compliance upon the health and safety of occupiers are difficult to evaluate. While any resultant loss or injury may be the subject of a claim for compensation in the future, the experience of actions for negligent design and construction has revealed the expense and difficulty of establishing liability for defects inherent in processes and which may not materialize for a number of years.

18.5

The withdrawal from enforcement

The legal framework established in the nineteenth century remains broadly intact today. Public law intervention in the housing market, however, has altered significantly, and as conditions and legal standards have improved, so has the emphasis shifted from sanction to subsidy.

The improvement of standards

The fitness standard provided the justification for the widespread housing clearances of the 1950s and 1960s. Medical Officers of Health through the Public Health departments invoked it to declare whole localities as unfit for human habitation and fit for demolition. Compulsory purchase of private houses was achieved by relatively generous compensation awards to owners and occupiers.

Reconstruction and planning became the primary concern of housing reformers. The Commissions of the 1950s and 1960s urged the adoption of improved construction standards and national planning strategies. Reports such as *Planning Our New Homes* (Scottish Housing Advisory Committee, 1944), *Homes for Today and Tomorrow* (Scottish Housing Advisory Committee, 1944) and the *Post War Building Studies* (Interdepartmental Committee, 1944) emphasized the creation of a spacious, well-ordered internal environment to replace the Victorian dwellings flattened by bombs and planners.

The need for new housing and a preoccupation with a vision of the healthier environment constructed in new communities were a direct response to the insanitariness and overcrowding of many of the existing conurbations. Public health was now the background against which new concerns of comfort and convenience could be introduced. The plans for the new homes contained progressive standards and culminated in the adoption of generous space provision in public housing developments. The 'Parker Morris' standards were adopted for all new local authority housing in 1971. The mood was exemplified in a Report by the Cullingworth Committee in 1967:

The present 'unfitness' provisions are essentially based on nineteenth-century concepts of public health. By contrast the standards adopted for houses improved with grant aid and for newly built houses are based on considerations of convenience, amenity and socially acceptable conditions. We think that the time has come when the minimum standards should be similarly based. In short we should now look beyond narrow public health concepts to the expected standards of modern living. (Scottish Development Department, 1967, para. 87)

While Cullingworth's Committee did not imply an abandonment of health concern as a rationale for housing control, the embracing of a wider concept of environmental well-being carried the potential of distracting attention from any continuing manifestations of

Victorian housing conditions. It is arguable that it also obscured new emergent health hazards as resources failed to keep pace with the higher aspiration of environmental improvement.

Healthy model housing was thus achieved in the offices of architects and planners. On the building sites cleared by demolition orders, councils set about constructing housing estates conforming to higher standards than those required by the Building Regulations. Government subsidy provided the explanation of the enforcement. The more unfit houses were cleared, the greater was the Exchequer contribution. The building systems and designs adopted allowed for higher standards to be achieved through economies of scale and technological construction advances.

Arguably the period represents the zenith of formal building standards in this country. Public health was implicitly acknowledged in its widest sense of physical and mental well-being. Internal and external space standards, convenient kitchens, green spaces and insulation emphasized comfort as a prerequisite of mental health, rather than a narrow reflection of sanitary decency or the control of contagions. On the other hand, health issues were implicit rather than analysed and avoided. While the early work of researchers into the effects of flats on families was beginning to emerge, the modern form of tower blocks was too convenient and economic a remedy for the suppliers of mass housing to respect the caution in their conclusions.

By the 1970s, the thrust of housing policy changed in the direction of urban renewal. The fitness standard was thenceforward invoked to identify those dwellings to be afforded government improvement grants. Area action continued to be an objective pursued by government, but increasingly individual action became a major activity for local authorities. Grant aid had replaced the compulsory purchase order as the mechanism for improvement.

From sanction to subsidy, 1949–89

First introduced in 1949, improvement grants to owners to improve their properties and install amenities, were initially discretionary. Local authorities, especially in London, were slow to make use of them (Milner Holland, 1965, p. 112). Since 1959, when a mandatory standard grant was introduced to assist in the provision of the five amenities, individual housing subsidy has become the dominant mechanism for dealing with substandard housing.

State investment in the housing stock, as contrasted with policing those who default on their repairs, has much to commend it. The fitness standard was used to evaluate dwellings for the award of mandatory grant, and government efforts were directed towards remedial work on the structure and amenities rather than to the bureaucratic enforcement of landlords' responsibilities. Housing fabric had become the focus of attention rather than obstinate land-lords.

In the process the interfering and officious Sanitary Inspector had become the beneficent and solicitous Environment Health Officer, whose authoritarian powers would only be invoked against stub-born or dilatory landlords. The gradual evolution from the regulat-ory stick to the carrot of subsidy has been explained elsewhere (Daintith, 1989) as the manifestation of the modern state's prefer-ence for exercising power through controlling activity by tax and subsidy ('dominium'), rather than executive directive backed by penal sanction ('imperium').

The enforcement of public law housing standards by the mid-1980s bore little recognition therefore to the local endeavours of the Sanitary Inspectors of the previous century. The statutes still proclaimed the regulatory models of nuisance abatement and enforced improvement, but the daily workload of environmental health officers had become increasingly involved with the adminis-tration of private housing grants and localized urban renewal.

As local government expenditure became increasingly con-strained, area action decreased even more. The pattern of implemen-tation reflected local resources and concentrated upon individual properties. Regional and local distribution of housing subsidy, allo-cated on the basis of local interpretations of the law, was becoming a significant factor in the shaping of urban British geography (Bur-ridge and Stewart, 1989).

The abdication from control of public housing

The failure of the private sector to provide healthy housing for a substantial proportion of the working population led to the public provision of housing in Britain. Ironically, postwar public housing production resulted in a housing form – the concrete multi-storey block and other non-traditional houses – which harboured new health hazards. Condensation dampness, cockroach infestation, asbestos and defects in the construction of systems-built dwellings have become commonplace. Remedy is disproportionately expensive and demolition is a frequent response.

The hazards would be prime targets for remedial intervention by Environmental Health Officers, but in 1983 the High Court decided that local government officials were powerless to serve any notices or other proceedings on their own local authority (*R. v. Cardiff City Council ex parte Cross*, 1982). Regulation of the public sector stock by those officials entrusted with control was thereby rendered impossible, unless the housing authority differed from the enforcement authority. This quirk surrounding the legal status of Environmental Health Officers coincided with the emergence of health problems in industrialized building systems which bore a remarkable similarity to the hazards of the previous century.

18.6
Private law responses

It would be misleading to suggest that in the rise and fall of regulatory control of housing, private law remedies had remained dormant or marginalized. In the intervening years, Parliament had introduced new remedies for the victim of some bad housing conditions. These are inevitably restricted to actions on the contract or claims in tort. They are dependent upon a plaintiff establishing a legal relationship with a defendant of tenant, occupier or neighbour to whom a duty is owed. Decisions to issue proceedings are beset by legal niceties, success is unpredictable, and the Legal Aid system both eliminates those on modest incomes and may consume a substantial proportion of a successful litigant's damages.

Contractual intervention

Statutory recognition of the tenant's weakness in contracting freely with the landlord has resulted in the imposition of covenants implied by law into some residential tenancies. In 1925 a covenant of fitness for habitation, established in Lady Marrable's case, was implied into all leases of 'small houses' (defined by reference to a low rent). The provision has been successively re-enacted and at present exists in the *Landlord and Tenant Act 1985*. It is rendered entirely ineffective, however, by restricting its application to tenancies let at rents which are today rarely, if ever, applicable (e.g. an annual rent in London of £80 or less).

A more effective implied covenant has been the obligation by many landlords to keep the structure and exterior of a dwelling in repair as well as the installations for the supply of water, gas and electricity and for sanitation (*Landlord and Tenant Act 1985*, section 11). The covenant raises difficult legal distinctions between repair and improvement, but it has been frequently invoked by tenants, who have obtained from the courts injunctions against landlords to carry out repairs and damages for the conditions suffered.

Liability for dangerous defects

Periodically, Parliament has addressed the plight of particular categories of victim by extending their common law rights to sue those who have caused them injury or loss. Examples are the *Defective Premises Act 1972*, and the *Housing Defects Act 1984*, although the latter is concerned solely with compensating owners for the structural state of their homes rather than any physical damage.

These measures went some way to providing some occupiers with a legal remedy in circumstances where the public controllers were unable or unwilling to act. Thus local authority tenants suffering disrepair resorted more and more to the implied covenant by a landlord to keep the structure in good repair.

In other respects, the judges have been reluctant to extend the landlord's obligations beyond the narrow contractual basis. As recently as 1988, the Court of Appeal confirmed a view expounded in 1901 (*Cavalier* v. *Pope*) that a landlord owed no liability for dangerous defects in the property at common law to a tenant (*McNerny* v. *Lambeth Borough Council*).

More recently, the courts have retreated even further from a preventive approach to building defects. The possibility that the owner of a dangerous building could recover from a negligent party the economic losses incurred in putting the building to rights has been denied by the House of Lords, who insisted that any remedy only lies when physical damage has occurred (*D. and F. Estates* v. *Church Commissioners*).

Modern hazards otherwise denied an adequate legal redress have attracted the attention of older actions. The early Public Health Acts had included a provision for any person aggrieved to make a complaint of a statutory nuisance direct to the court. The procedure is maintained with some modifications in the *Environmental Protection Act 1990*, and has been widely invoked to deal with condensation dampness and cockroach infestations. Actual physical damage to health need not be established, it being sufficient to satisfy the court that the conditions complained about are 'prejudicial to health'. Its use is a direct consequence of the abdication of responsibility for the health of their own council tenants imposed on Environmental Health Departments by the courts. It is an unwieldly procedure, however, and one for which Legal Aid is not available.

The practical obstacles of private law remedies have already been described. Other factors, in addition to Legal Aid and the historic fragility of the tenant's claim for enforcement of the landlord's obligation, indicate the deficiencies of the private action.

Private law remedies, dependent as they are upon counterposed parties, inevitably represent a litigious approach to housing problems. In focusing upon a compensatory resolution, the private action is most effective when it operates after the event, when harm to health has occurred. Record damages represent record pain, illness, discomfort and even death, whereas the regulatory model is essentially preventive, coercing action before damage occurs. Furthermore, the adversarial court process is costly and the expense of lawyers, legal aid and court services as a procedure for controlling housing standards is not recovered from the parties. The system is arguably less economically efficient than the processes of local government enforcement, especially if account is taken of the savings to health services which the preventive model promises.

The litigious nature of resort to the enforcement of private rights results in a lego-technic approach to housing renovation. To technical arguments concerning the nature of the contract – lease or licence – can be added disputes over the meaning of repair and improvement; the requirement for adequate notice of the defect; the measure of damages; and procedural defects and obstacles such as the limitation of actions. While the cost of disrepair falls upon the private sector, the public purse bears a considerable burden in the process of resolving the dispute.

Public administrative control by way of contrast expends resources more directly upon the administration of improvement; the discretionary framework of enforcement and the broad requirement of public servants to act reasonably and fairly, discourages courtroom challenge. Perhaps most significant, however, is the dependence of public law intervention upon the environmental health profession. In the individual action for damages general practitioners are often at a significant disadvantage reliant as they are upon the medical model of illness. The courts' insistence that in order to succeed in any claim, the breach of any obligation has to be proved to have been a direct cause of an illness, has often led to the failure of a case. The general practitioner's inability to trace a clinical condition to a specific housing condition has resulted in a number of sick occupiers failing to achieve judicial and financial acknowledgement of their plight. In many respects therefore the undoubted expense of regulatory agencies should not overshadow the inefficiency, limitations and impoverishment of private law remedies.

18.7
The legal promotion of community health

The foregoing analysis of the legal response to health and housing reveals considerable scope for reform. The normative influence of the fitness standard and Building Regulations, and the fiscal support of the improvement grant system are the levers of control most susceptible to legislative reform.

The new fitness standard and its accompanying Guidance Notes represent a significant advance in the incorporation of health concerns in the control of housing conditions. The introduction to the Notes is explicit that 'primary concern should lie in safeguarding the health and safety of any occupants'. The separate criteria, such as heating provision, are elaborated by reference to the health hazards that they seek to overcome.

The linkage of the fitness standard to means-testing for mandatory grants, however, amounts to a departure from a health-orientated housing policy. The alleviation of poverty rather than the promotion of health has become the rationale for intervention.

It is true that there is a direct correlation between poverty, social status and the poor health of occupiers (Byrne *et al.*, 1986), but intervention in the decay and obsolescence of housing may be impeded by dependence upon the financial eligibility of the owner. The grants are now susceptible to Exchequer variation of the eligibility criteria. Experience of the take-up of welfare benefits and other grants suggests a large discrepancy between entitlement and claim. Housing action is likely to be predicated upon a means inquiry rather than a survey of the building. If the fitness standard represents the minimum health and safety standard for occupiers, it is difficult to justify non-intervention when such conditions exist but the owner (most probably an owner-occupier) declines to take remedial action. Means-testing is also likely to present an obstacle to area action where neighbouring occupiers have varied incomes.

While the 1989 reform to the fitness standard reasserts the significance of health criteria, there is still scope for improving the standard and promoting better health through housing. Internal arrangement was omitted from the revised standard. The high incidence of accidents in the home can be attributed, in many cases, to design and layout deficiencies which the reintroduction of internal arrangement would reduce (see Chapter 11). The requirement that homes contain a source of heating (the present requirement is only that there be provision for the use of a heating appliance) and a minimum standard of thermal insulation would reduce the incidence of cold-related illness, as is advocated in Chapter 17.

The effectiveness of the public control of housing conditions would be enhanced by reform of the organization of enforcement to relieve the plight of those who occupy council-owned dwellings prone to condensation. In England and Wales such conditions would probably result in a classification of unfitness, but in Scotland condensation dampness is not a criterion of 'sub-tolerability' (the Scottish equivalent of the fitness standard). The lacuna is an obvious target for reform, and underlines the comparatively weaker dissipation of enforcement powers affecting issues of home safety among local councils, in contrast with the centralized power exercised by the Health and Safety Executive over safety at work matters. In other spheres, separation of authority between regulator and regulated is axiomatic, and the isolation of council tenants from the protection afforded other occupiers is a departure from an important regulatory principle.

Reform of the private rights of occupiers to promote healthy housing are less conspicuous because of the reactive approach of private law implicit in post-problem compensation. Nevertheless, the present ineffectiveness of the fitness covenant implied into tenancy agreements by the *Landlord and Tenant Act 1985* renders it an urgent target for updating (Ormandy, 1986).

The Cullingworth Committee recognized that intervention by any prescriptive standard involves two stages: a minimum standard prescribing conditions beneath which houses should not be allowed to fall and hence triggering intervention; and a target standard which substandard housing should be required to attain after intervention. Unless the attainment standard is higher than the intervention standard, any improvement will be short-lived and housing conditions overall would never improve. The notion of an attainment standard recognized that subsidy intervention would be uneconomic unless public investment on a substandard house resulted in an improved property that was likely to remain habitable and not fall below the intervention standard for a number of years. It is within the twin poles represented by the intervention standard and the attainment or target standard that the key to directing healthful housing policies lies: arguably public health concerns should be the justification for an intervention standard, whereas convenience, amenity and social equality may be the objective of the attainment standard. Such a strategy would allow for prescriptive regulatory intervention to protect the health of occupiers, if necessary, by coercive measures, but would be more effectively achieved by the reintroduction of non-means-tested mandatory grants. Such a reform could be accompanied by a discretionary subsidy or tax relief to enable a property to achieve the attainment standard.

The means-testing of grants is a blunt and unimaginative response to the need to control Exchequer expenditure. Mandatory grants to bring dwellings up to the basic fitness standard with means-testing for work that takes a dwelling beyond the standard could be investigated as could schemes for the certification of fitness for habitation of a dwelling upon transfer of ownership, linked perhaps to the award of mortgage interest tax relief. Grants could also be replaced by loans and secured by a charge on the property, recoverable upon sale.

A powerful argument against coercive action by Environmental Health Officers against owner-occupiers has been the inability of many, particularly elderly owners, to finance the necessary repairs. In England and Wales the introduction of means-tested grants has enabled the poorest to qualify for grant aid for the full extent of any works. While this, in theory, should enable those in the greatest need to renovate their unfit house, there will continue to be many who feel unable to afford their calculated contribution, or who remain ignorant of the hazards involved. Arguably their 'choice' to suffer unhealthy housing conditions and their decision to spend their financial resources elsewhere than on a new roof should be mediated by the public in maintaining a healthy housing stock, and reducing the consumption of scarce health care resources on avoidable housing-related illnesses. This argument is the more powerful when the decision not to repair a building affects children or others with no influence over the decision but vulnerable to the unhealthy conditions.

Other mechanisms that would concentrate resources upon those dwellings revealed to be a danger to health and consequently legally considered to be unfit for human habitation are feasible. The cost of housing production and supply in Britain historically has been beyond the wage-earning capabilities of a significant proportion of the workforce and fiscal intervention has been a hallmark of British housing policy.

A return to renovation subsidy directed towards unfit housing regardless of the means of the occupier, for example, could be achieved by treating the grant for the cost of remedial work as a loan to be repaid upon disposal of the dwelling by the occupier. Equity sharing would obviate unpalatable punitive intervention by local government officers in circumstances where occupiers are reluctant or unable to find the expense of the necessary repairs. It runs counter to recent notions of privatization and represents a state investment in the national housing stock. Initially costly, but as improved houses gradually were disposed of, it would eventually become more economic than the present practice of making outright gifts to owner-occupiers for housing renovation. It would conform with the historic objectives of a regulatory approach justified by the preservation of health. Unless the available evidence is that bad housing conditions do not significantly affect the health of those who endure them, health has a strong claim to maintain its significance as a determinant of housing policy.

18.8

Future perspectives

The studies of the potential effects that housing conditions can have on the health of occupiers represented in this book indicate the importance and urgency of reasserting the primacy of health as a justification for housing action. At the same time, the poverty of private law remedies urges a reassessment of the retreat from regulation. There is a continuing need to ensure that the control of house construction affords adequate protection from existing and emerging housing hazards, but it is the eradication of existing unhealthy housing that poses the greater problems for housing administrators in Britain. With its disproportionate stock of older housing and an acute land scarcity, the implementation of the fitness standard in England and Wales and the tolerable standard in Scotland presents the more immediate target for analysis and reform.

The prognosis, however, is not healthy. The *English House Condition Survey 1986* revealed a small reduction in unfit dwellings and no significant change in the proportion of the stock in serious disrepair. Furthermore, the Survey again revealed very large variations in the pattern of substandard accommodation with marked regional disparities, and within regions significant differences between sectors of the population who suffered poor housing conditions. Single-parent families, those with one or two children, long-term residents and those who lived in their home for between five and ten years were most likely to have experienced deterioration in their housing conditions (Department of the Environment, 1989, para. 9.23).

The regional distribution of dwellings in poor condition is compounded by a regional disparity in activity to improve the housing stock. Thus while the north-west, Yorkshire and Humberside, and the West Midlands, had significantly higher numbers of dwellings in poor condition, 40% of local authority activity took place in the south-east, which included less than a quarter of the dwellings identified in this category (Department of the Environment, 1989, para. 217).

The deficiencies in the housing stock will not be remedied by the waving of some legislative wand. At best, legal intervention can provide normative standards for fiscal or coercive action, and a framework for implementation. Deeper solutions lie in the political arena. There is a pressing need for a housing policy which embraces again the perspectives of public health and the maintenance of a healthy national housing stock. As significant is the acceptance that both the internal and external conditions of the home are an environmental matter. Indoor pollutants, home accidents and atmospheric control demand similar attention to the concern that is shown over lead in petrol and road safety. The recognition, for example, that housing is a health promoter, rather than a source of illness, reverses the emphasis and encourages positive intervention.

The acknowledgement that housing and health is an interdisciplinary concern, however, and a perspective based upon collaboration between community physicians, general practitioners, Environmental Health Officers and Housing Managers will begin to make up the ground that has been lost in recent years. It would be misleading to suggest that defective housing could be remedied or replaced by the collaborative efforts of the housing and medical professions alone. The analysis above argues for greater intervention. It is supported by claims such as those by the institution of Environmental Health Officers that at present levels of activity it will take 250 years to eradicate unfit housing (IEHO, 1990). Such intervention requires increased national resources, both for the cost of remedial work and for those entrusted with its implementation. The mechanisms for spreading the costs of improvement and for recouping any subsidy from the equity in a property are feasible and economically viable (Hill, 1991). The prospects for healthier housing need not therefore be lost sight of in an unresolvable confrontation between public sector borrowing requirements and public health.

Acknowledgement

The authors wish to acknowledge the useful comments on an earlier draft of this chapter from Dr John McEldowney of the School of Law, Warwick University.

Bibliography

Arden, A. and Partington, M. (1983) *Housing Law*, Sweet and Maxwell, London.

Baldwin, R. and McCrudden, C. (1987) *Regulation and Public Law*, Weidenfeld and Nicolson, London.

Breyer, S. (1979) Analyzing regulatory failure: mismatches, less restrictive alternatives and reform. *Harvard Law Review*, 92, 547–60;

Burnett, J. (1978) *A Social History of Housing 1815–1970*, Methuen, London.

Burridge, R. and Ormandy, D. (1990) The role of regulation in the control of housing conditions. *J. Socio. Soc. Welfare*, 17(1), 127–42.

Byrne, D. S. *et al.* (1986) *Housing and Health: The Relationship between Housing Conditions and the Health of Council Tenants*, Gower, Aldershot.

Cornish, W. R. and Clark, G. de N. (1989) *Law and Society in England*, Sweet and Maxwell, London.

Cotterrell, R. (1984) *The Sociology of Law: An Introduction*, Butterworths, London.

Daintith, T. (1989) The executive power today: bargaining and economic control, in J. Jowell and D. Oliver (eds) *The Changing Constitution*, Oxford University Press, pp. 193–218.

Department of the Environment (DoE) (1988) *English House Condition Survey 1986*, HMSO, London.

DoE (1990) *Area Renewal, Slum Clearance and Enforcement Action*, Circular 6/90, annex A, HMSO, London.

Finer, M. (1952) *The Life and Times of Sir Edwin Chadwick*, Methuen, London.

Hill, J. (1991) *Unravelling Housing Finance: Subsidies, benefits and taxation*, Clarendon, Oxford.

Hutter, B. M. (1988) *The Reasonable Arm of the Law?*, Oxford University Press, Oxford.

Institution of Environmental Health Officers (1990) *Annual Report*, IEHO, London.

Interdepartmental Committee (1944) *Post War Building Studies*, Reports of the Interdepartmental Committee.

Milner Holland (1965) *Report of the Committee on Housing in Greater London*, Cmnd 265, HMSO, London.

Mitnick, B. M. (1980) *The Political Economy of Regulation*, Columbia University Press, New York.

Mood, E. (1987) Housing and health programmes in the USA. Paper presented at the Unhealthy Housing: Prevention and Remedies Conference, Warwick University,

Moore, R. (1987) The development and role of standards for the older housing stock. Paper presented at the Unhealthy Housing: Prevention and Remedies Conference, Warwick University,

Muth, R. (1976) Housing and land use, in: *The Politics of Planning: A Review and Critique of Centralised Economic Planning*, Institute for Contemporary Studies,

Muthesius, S. (1982) *The English Terraced House*, Yale University Press, New Haven, Conn.

National Audit Office (1991) *The Condition of Scottish Housing*, HMSO, London.

Nuttgens, P. (1989) *The Home Front*, BBC, London.

Ogus, A. I. and Veljanovski, C. G. (1984) *Readings in the Economics of Law and Regulation*, Oxford University Press, London.

Ormandy, D. (1986) Legislation to secure fitness for human habitation of leasehold dwellings. *Journal of Planning and Environment Law*, pp. 164–73.

Ormandy, D. and Burridge, R. (1989) *The Environmental Health Standards in Housing*, Sweet and Maxwell, London.

Parker Morris (1961) *Homes for Today and Tomorrow*, Report of the Parker Morris Committee,

Posner, R. A. (1974) Theories of economic regulation. *Bell Journal of Economics*, 5, 335–51;

Shogren, J. F. (1989) *The Political Economy of Government Regulation*, Kluwer, Scottish Development Department (1967) *Scotland's Older Houses*, HMSO, London.

Scottish Housing Advisory Committee (1944) *Homes for Today and Tomorrow*, SHAC.

Stewart, A. and Burridge, R. (1989) Law and space, in A. Gamble and C. Wells (eds) *Thatcher's Law*, University of Wales.

Worsdall, F. (1991) *The Glasgow Tenement*, Chambers, Edinburgh.

CITIES 2000 PROJECTS: GOLDFISH BOWL

GEOFF GREEN

19.1

Introduction

Goldfish, making love and washing clothes – all part of life below deck on the giant Hulme Estate, Manchester, in the 1970s. And according to Housing Officers of Manchester City Council and other agents for the landlord, this steamy life style voluntarily chosen by tenants was the biggest contributor to damp and dreadful housing conditions. How remarkable the influence claimed for these specks of humanity in the interstices of a megastructure of concrete and glass.

The contrary view owed much to independent academic research; Sean Damer, David Byrne and others on the streets, with tenants, challenging, critical, essentially Marxist, materialist, tracing the causes back to structures – political, economic and determinably physical. Meticulously they charted penetrating damp through broken seals between concrete ceilings and walls, enumerated the insulation values of concrete walls and floors to predict levels of condensation. Then they traced these physical causes back to an earlier set of pressures in the capitalist production process. They described the tenants, in the wrong place at the wrong time, but predictably so for reasons of class and economic marginalization. Such analysis helped make what is now known as the New Public Health.

19.2

Historical background

The old public health had run its long course. For a hundred years the Medical Officers of Health responsible for the health of each British town or city had made the connection between poor housing and poor health. Their research had linked structural failure, over-crowding, lack of daylight and sanitation – in short, squalor – to illness and contagious diseases like typhoid and tuberculosis. Public health was paramount in the legislation which cleared the slums at the turn of the century, in the interwar years and after 1955. But by 1970, the rationale had all but disappeared from Public Health Inspectors reluctantly priming? the legal machinery to clear the last nineteenth-century bye-law terraces. Few tenants of these modest artisan houses believed them to be a health risk and life-threatening contagious diseases had almost disappeared. The old public health links were disappearing fast and Medical Officers of Health failed to establish new ones.

Popular resistance to the bulldozer grew when residents defended the quality of their comfortable terraced homes and rejected the newly constructed alternatives – flats primarily, where you couldn't keep pigeons or dogs, park a bike, hang out the washing or keep warm. Academics helped, creatively, critically, certainly not under contract to the establishment. It was a golden age for community action-research with the new *Community Action* magazine listing scores of confrontations between people and planners in nearly all Britain's industrial cities and towns. Researchers and tenants together defended the old and criticized the new by emphasizing cultural, social, environmental and community qualities, but not health. The public health paradigm was not countered with research evidence denying its link with housing conditions. There was some criticism of the process of slum clearance because of the strain and stress of protracted waiting and uncertainty, but health remained very definitely a province of the National Health Service (NHS). Doctors' notes about poor housing conditions might lift a tenant up the queue for new, but were not used to justify staying and improving.

The link between housing and health resurfaced in the public sector and focused on non-traditional stock; point blocks and mega-structures, the deck access/streets in the sky estates starting with

Parkhill, which still dominates Sheffield's eastern skyline. At first, tenants criticized design. Kelvin, Sheffield's second Parkhill, was Alcatraz from the start, gaunt, prison-like. But when in the 1970s the wear and tear began to show in estates all over the UK, including the infamous Hulme, radical academics, supporting the principle of public sector housing, were willing to concede it could damage your health.

Radical lawyers and Environmental Health Officers (only one in 1000, it has to be said) were prepared to rubbish council houses for individual tenants, using section 99 of the *Public Health Act 1936* against the landlord, painfully accumulating detailed evidence on damp and draughts, winning individual cases and never quite attaining the class action available in the USA. But, of course, there were wider implications and in a silver decade from 1973 these were analysed and described by researchers working primarily with law centres, the community-based Public Health Advisory Group and Shelter. Their discovery of a new set of causal connections, actionable in the public domain, is the genesis of the New Public Health.

In the early 1980s their radical critique of council housing form and condition was incorporated into state policy and programmes, locally and nationally. For a Conservative government, it was another nail in the coffin of council housing as a tenure form, evidence of failure in collective arrangements and a pointer to the market. For local authorities, it justified reinvestment in their ailing stock. The characteristic play of the 1980s was that council housing departments, having largely abandoned new building, would argue the case for government funds to improve their residualized, non-traditionally designed stock. And the Conservative government, intent on diminishing public spending, would consistently deny most of the funds and divert some of the rest to programmes linked to a change of tenure. Health, except implicitly in its very broadest sense of physical, social and mental well-being, did not figure much on either agenda.

Perhaps this was a failure of Environmental Health Departments to assert their institutional strength within most local authorities. Undoubtedly, their power had diminished in the 1970s as the first public health agenda came close to completion and the Medical Officer of Health's responsibilities were largely divested to health authorities, which treated public health as a cinderella. Characteristic of this period are those dreary Annual Reports on activity levels – numbers of silver fish eliminated and rats visited – prefaced or followed with routine reports on contagious diseases at barely perceptible levels by the Medical Officer of Environmental Health, displaying little of the vibrancy, analysis and urgency of the nine-teenth-century reports, when the connections made, meticulously researched, between housing and health were clear for all to see and act upon.

When their renaissance came in the mid-1980s, departments did not focus on housing since the biggest slum landlord was legally beyond their reproach, but instead swept broadly over poverty, class and life style as primary determinants of health inequalities. Green issues and healthy life style caught popular imagination and raised the profile of environmental health. But Environmental Health Departments struggled to link cause and effect without taking on the world and failed to detail the impact of poor housing on illness and health.

19.3
The New Public Health

The New Public Health is a powerful concept, which in the UK is yet to attain the political force of its predecessor. In Europe, the World Health Organization has made it a more dynamic force, with member states signing up to a European Charter on Environment and Health in 1989 after agreeing, in 1984, to 38 *Targets for Health for All*. Environmental reforms (Targets 18–25) by the mid-1990s, including those to human settlements and housing, are a condition of improved health in member states by the year 2000. The many cities and towns in the UK which have adopted or adapted the targets or the ideal of Health for All have implicitly (often vaguely) accepted the link between housing and health, and challenged as far as the intersectoral coalitions of local and health authorities can, any denial by UK central government that such a link exists. It strikes a chord with the gut-feeling of city councillors representing the poor in the poorest houses. They are usually Labour council-lors. The alliance of Labour-controlled cities with Europe on this dimension of social policy is only part of the move by the Labour Party nationally to embrace Europe.

The political climate in the 1990s is favourable to further research on housing and health so long as it leads to action. The government Green Paper, *The Health of the Nation*, may have lost a few home truths in the final drafting, but at least it admits of a link. Labour councillors now have few inhibitions admitting (politically if not legally) that much council house stock is defective and can damage your health. Their administrations in cities and towns would welcome clearer evidence to strengthen the case for more resources or to focus available resources so as to make the most impact. District health authorities (which since the 1990 management reforms in the NHS) have strategic responsibility for mapping the health of their citizens and seeking the most cost-effective interventions and would welcome clarification of the complicated economic and environmental factors which nearly all recognize as the primary determinants of health. And the people themselves could use the evidence collectively, proactively, countering the grand inquisitors of their lives and life styles.

19.4
Problems and weaknesses

However, there is a weakness at the conceptual heart of the linkage. The English, from Chadwick and countless Medical Officers of Health like Dr Duncan, the world's first in Liverpool, have excelled in empirical research to show association, connection, causality. Yet the New Public Health is complex and difficult to handle. The phenomena it describes are often invisible and not as photogenic as rotting slums or smoke-filled air; you cannot often see crap in the River Mersey, but you know it's there. The interactions are difficult to disentangle and isolate, the balance between behaviour and structure difficult to assess, compared with the overwhelming economic and environmental determinants of Victorian city life. Pity, then, the empiricist who must hold all the world constant to isolate the specific elements of housing and health.

The other problem is institutional. Local councils could commission empirical survey and critical research. Academics might do it anyway, to help tenants or provide a public service, or simply to enhance a tradition of independent academic research: it does not work out this way. Councils are marginalized away from the debating frontier. Money for development and innovation is top-sliced away from mainstream housing management. A decade of financial pressure barely leaves enough cash for conferences, let alone funds for commissioned research. Environmental Health

Departments remain subordinate, unable to intervene with council housing, make some impression on the acute but marginal health-related problems of homelessness and bed-and-breakfast accommodation; nevertheless, most cities and towns are light-years away from commissioning substantial research contributions to the New Public Health.

The research community itself is out of condition, starved of funds, pressed to promotion by referred books and articles with fewer readers than would fill a tenants' meeting hall to acclaim the value of their public service. Then there are the restraints of a contract culture. A second measure of academic esteem is the number of contracts awarded to an individual or department. Generally councils and tenants are in no financial position to commission. The Department of the Environment, the Health Education Authority can – from within an ideological strait-jacket and with copyright that buys body and soul.

19.5
Conclusion

Despite all these drawbacks, there is on the margins constructive critical research. The work of Sonja Hunt and others with tenants in Glasgow and Edinburgh was a scientific breakthrough linking damp via microbiology to respiratory disease, and a political breakthrough with councillors in Glasgow. Liverpool Healthy City 2000 commissioned the same research outfit in tandem with Liverpool Polytechnic to go a step further and discover whether the City's massive investment in the Urban Regeneration Strategy of comprehensive housing improvement had a health dividend. The evidence painfully collected and summarized in *Better Housing, Better Health* points in this direction – not just a general proposition, but how specific improvements are linked with mental health and physical well-being. We have clear guidance for future public investment in the housing stock. Our job is to deconstruct it for post-modern academics, unwrap it for tenants, parcel it up and take it to the decision-makers.

If the long winter is over, is there a prospect of a plural and equitable balance of power between central and local government? Coupled with partial eclipse of the contract culture, it could release the talent of a thousand researchers from a corrosive obsession with print to throw intellectual light at least on the grey housing estates of poverty and ill-health, enabling and reforming, in partnership with residents, always on tap, never on top.

Bibliography

Department of Health (1991) *The Health of the Nation: A consultative document*, Cmd. 1523, HMSO, London.

Galen Research and Consultancy (1990) *Better Housing, Better Health*, Liverpool City Council.

World Health Organization (1985) *Targets for Health for All*, WHO Regional Office for Europe, Copenhagen.

World Health Organization (1989) *European Charter on Environment and Health*, WHO Regional Office for Europe, Copenhagen.

INDEX

Absolute humidity 142
Accidents xvi, 223–5, 417
  definition 232–3
  domestic 43
  epidemiology 226–32
  factors affecting 314–15
  high-rise housing 183–4
  hotel residents 295
  relationship with ambient
    temperature 136–7
  role of housing 313–23
  sites 316–23
  see also Safety
Acid rain 365
Acoustic insulation, high-rise
    housing 356–7
Adolescents, high-rise dwelling 173
Aesthetic factors
  high-rise housing 185–6
  housing 325
Affluence, diseases of 47–8
Aggregate health 51–2
AIDS 50, 58, 62
Airborne infections, prevention
    311–13
Air conditioning 135, 357, 367
Aircraft noise 194
Air movement 119, 120, 122,
    147–8, 327
Air pollution 131–2
Air temperature 119
Airtightness 372
Alcohol, secondary hypothermia
    129, 130
Allergy 70, 357
  alveolitis 78
  cockroaches 267, 279
  house dust mites 126
  moulds 110, 111, 122
Ambient temperature 327

American cockroach 263, 266
American Public Health
    Association 409
  Committee on the Hygiene of
    Housing 304, 333
American Society of Heating,
    Refrigeration and Air-
    Conditioning Engineers 327,
    328–9
Amosite 377
Anopheles 262
Animal studies, extrapolation from
    13
Antibodies 78
Appliances, home, safety 314
Arachnids 270–1
Architects 239, 240
Architecture 348, 350
  high-rise buildings 185–6
Area health authorities, xxvii, 62
Areal studies 53, 59–60
Artisans and Labourers Dwelling
    Act 1868 407
Asbestos 13–14, 36, 280, 376–7, 413
Ascaris 307, 310
Aspergillus fumigatus 79
Asthma 43, 97, 126, 267, 271
  children xv, 99–102, 122, 153
  objective measurement 102–5
Atmospheric pollution, global
    365–7
Atomist fallacy 53–5

Babies, *see* Infants
Bacilli 56
Bacteria 78
  transported by cockroaches 266
Bathrooms
  safety 319–20
  sharing 286